"In the decades leading up to the creation-evolution sideshow of the Scopes Trial, a far more sophisticated and important conversation about Darwin's theory occurred at Princeton University. Conservative, inerrantist, and solidly orthodox Princeton theologians responded thoughtfully and often constructively to evolution. Bradley Gundlach's *Process and Providence* brings this important conversation to life in a sure-footed, well-researched, and engaging narrative. I highly recommend this book for its important contribution to understanding the American response to Darwin."

— KARL GIBERSON
author of *Saving Darwin: How to Be
a Christian and Believe in Evolution*

"Writing with the meticulous care of a historian and with a profound knowledge of his subject drawn from years in the archives, Bradley Gundlach has produced a book that will cause us to rethink much of what we know about the relationship between evolution and evangelicalism in American life."

— JOHN FEA
author of *Was America Founded
as a Christian Nation?*

D1595872

Process and Providence

The Evolution Question at Princeton, 1845-1929

Bradley J. Gundlach

WILLIAM B. EERDMANS PUBLISHING COMPANY

GRAND RAPIDS, MICHIGAN / CAMBRIDGE, U.K.

Published 2013 by
Wm. B. Eerdmans Publishing Co.
2140 Oak Industrial Drive N.E., Grand Rapids, Michigan 49505 /
P.O. Box 163, Cambridge CB3 9PU U.K.

Printed in the United States of America

19 18 17 16 15 14 13   7 6 5 4 3 2 1

Library of Congress Cataloging-in-Publication Data

Gundlach, Bradley J., 1958-
Process and providence: the evolution question at Princeton, 1845-1929 /
Bradley J. Gundlach.
pages   cm
Includes bibliographical references and index.
ISBN 978-0-8028-6898-5 (pbk.: alk. paper)
1. Evolution (Biology) — Religious aspects — Christianity —
History of doctrines. 2. Evolution (Biology) 3. Evolution —
Religious aspects — Christianity. 4. Evolution. 5. Theology —
History. 6. Princeton Theological Seminary — History.
7. Princeton University — History.   I. Title.

BT712.G85   2013
231.7'6520974965 — dc23

2013014361

www.eerdmans.com

For Rebecca

Contents

CONTENTS

Preface

I began work on Princeton and evolution in 1979-80, as a senior in the history department at Princeton University. In need of a thesis topic, I was filing subject cards in the Catalog Maintenance division of Firestone Library, where I worked part-time. In the *S's* I came across what was then a brand-new book, Herbert Hovenkamp's *Science and Religion in America, 1800-1860,* which, I soon learned, opened and closed with vignettes of Princeton. This was my first inkling that Princeton was at all important in the development of ideas on science and religion. After a few inquiries with my adviser David Hammack and professor emeritus Arthur S. Link, I had a topic for my thesis, driven in by a long-standing personal interest in fossils and evolution, but also by a more recent, personal commitment to evangelical Christianity — two things that had coexisted for me in my college years largely on the terms of an explicit nonaggression pact. Now I began to open the borders.

And the rest, as they say, is history — except in my case it is history in a very literal sense, for I have pursued questions of science and religion through the discipline of history, off and on, ever since. Historical study of these questions, I might as well admit, offered a way of delving into them while retaining a certain sense of safe detachment. I asked not how to fit science and religion together, but how *others* did it some time ago. Thanks to a pointed comment from John Servos, the second reader of my senior thesis, I strove increasingly to separate the normative from the descriptive in my consideration of these questions. It was good advice; whatever air of safe distance historical study lent me, beneath it lay a close, compelling interest in the questions themselves. Such interest, I believe, drives us to devote energy to historical inquiries, but at the same time it threatens to make our inquiries ahistorical by intruding our categories, our concerns, into the past figures we seek to understand. History offers perspective from thinkers of the past, but what drives us to them may lead us to misconstrue them.

In view of these considerations, I framed further projects in graduate school — an M.A. thesis at Trinity Evangelical Divinity School under John Woodbridge and a Ph.D. dissertation at the University of Rochester under Christopher Lasch and Robert Westbrook — around a question rather than a thesis. I examined "The Evolution Question at Princeton" as something deliberately undefined, intending to leave the posing of questions, like the answering of questions, to the Princetonians themselves. I found that "the" evolution question changed with time and circumstance. Both the landscape of discourse (philosophical commonalities and differences, mutually observed boundaries, professional identities and their relative degrees of public esteem, etc.) and the configuration of allegiances and enmities changed over time, and with them the sense of peace or battle, crisis or relative unconcern.

I also left the subtitle's second term, "Princeton," slightly fuzzy. My chief interest, the intersection of science and religion, suggested a focus on Princeton Seminary, where Charles Hodge, A. A. Hodge, B. B. Warfield, and others set for themselves the task of guarding Calvinist orthodoxy in an increasingly un-Calvinist and unorthodox, if evangelical, century. But after all, it was at the college that Princeton's scientists and philosophers posed and answered the evolution question most immediately in connection with their work, and it was there that James McCosh earned himself the distinction of being the first major religious leader in America to announce publicly his support for evolutionism. Until about 1900 the college and seminary, never officially tied, functioned as a close-knit, mainly Presbyterian club of gentlemen and scholars — who indeed consciously saw themselves that way. After the turn of the century "Princeton" lost its cohesive identity, owing to the complicated process of secularization at the university and to the seminary's involvement in distinctly sectarian politics: the Presbyterian heresy trials and pronouncements on the Bible and the Westminster Confession in the 1890s. This division of the old Princeton legacy forms an important part of the story, culminating in the fundamentalist controversy of the 1920s — where we find the relations of university and seminary contributing much to the intensity of battle, and Princeton's scientists and theologians right in the thick of it.

Preface

The strength of this study lies, I believe, in its sharp institutional focus on a profound and multifaceted issue. At Princeton we find a distinct, self-identified set of men who approached the evolution question from a broad range of disciplines, yet until the second decade of the twentieth century shared a strong sense of solidarity in philosophical and religious commitments. More, these were highly influential men at two highly influential institutions who left a profound and profoundly mixed legacy of national proportions. Their interactions — internal squabbles, united responses to outside challenges, public face-offs and more amicable exchanges of ideas — situate what is basically a study of ideas in time and place. An exploration of the process by which the Princetonians posed and answered the questions involved in evolution is valuable not just for the outcome of the story, but also for the issues raised along the way.

In the years since I completed the doctoral dissertation, it has occurred to me that the Calvinistic doctrine of providence lies at the heart of Princeton's assessment of the many facets of evolutionism, from cosmology to biology to sociology to the history of Christian doctrine. It was confidence in God's sovereign government of the universe through what the Westminster Confession calls "second causes" — mediate rule rather than unmediated fiat — that prompted the Princetonians to find development over time, in all the aforementioned areas, basically congenial to their prior understandings of God, the world, and religion. This book will reveal many areas in which the Princetonians embraced developmentalism. But their doctrine of providence also had particular content, ruling out many varieties of evolutionary thought. Providence grounded and explained process, and the Princetonians, contrary to common misconception, had no problem thinking in terms of change over time — but *how* one thought in terms of change could take many forms, many of them unacceptable to orthodoxy. The Princetonians rejected the antisupernaturalism of twentieth-century evolutionary science and modernist religion. Process was an inherent part of the idea of providence, but providence required certain definite understandings of process.

I might as well admit that I find the Princetonians on the whole a pretty admirable bunch, and offer this study of their explorations of the multifaceted evolution question out of more than antiquarian interest. Historians almost never study the past out of idle curiosity or mere love of what amounts to a kind of travel into another world. I find the

Princetonians to offer a good model, on the whole, of thoughtful engagement between Christian faith and the thought currents of one's time and
place. Many historians have pointed out the Princetonians' mistakes, as
they see them, especially in the areas of methodology and philosophy. I
do not refuse their readings altogether, as the reader will find. But I also
think we have much to learn from the Princetonians — both from their
assessment of the evolution question in all its ramifications, and from
their dedication to relating the evolution question, within a unified field
of knowledge, to their Christian faith.

I AM GLAD to have the opportunity to acknowledge the many people who
helped me prepare this work. First, I am grateful for the financial support
provided by a Rush Rhees Fellowship at the University of Rochester, a
teaching fellowship from the Council of Independent Colleges, and a
Charlotte W. Newcombe Dissertation Fellowship from the Woodrow
Wilson National Fellowship Foundation. These awards provided not
only money but also affirmation of my project, and I am deeply grateful.
A one-semester load reduction at Trinity International University, where
I regularly teach four courses per semester, greatly aided my revision of
the work for publication.

Robert Westbrook, my dissertation adviser at the University of Rochester, provided encouragement and needed structure as well as excellent
advice in writing. A one-on-one course with him in the philosophy of history was probably the most formative experience of my coursework
there. I am astounded by his breadth and depth in historiographical
questions, and have tried to emulate them in my teaching. They recall
my earlier mentor and dissertation adviser, the late Christopher Lasch,
who taught me lessons about writing and thinking that I appreciate
more with each passing year. I hold before me his example of close scholarship, sincere liberality, and inveterate interest in the big questions.

John Woodbridge, of Trinity Evangelical Divinity School, urged me to
continue with Princeton and evolution after my master's work under his
fine direction. I am especially grateful for his perennial encouragement.
It was he who first opened up to me the world of career scholarship, its
joys and its rigors.

Bill Harris, retired archivist of Princeton Seminary, offered me in-
valuable help, loyal friendship, and sincere interest beyond any telling.
The depth of detailed knowledge I garnered in the archives under his
care, only a hint of which appears in this work, owes directly to his hav-

ing thrown open vast resources to me, and often to his initiative in bringing related items to my attention. He supplied me not only with source materials, but also with some of the most stimulating and fruitful discussions I have had about the Princetonians. From him I learned to see the past as people, not just as ideas — a lesson I value tremendously.

My sincere thanks go to Earle Coleman, late archivist of Princeton University, and to Ben Primer, his successor, for their expert and friendly help. I am grateful also to the staff of the department of Rare Books and Manuscripts, Firestone Library, where I spent many pleasant hours in that splendid reading room. I thank as well the staff of the Robert E. Speer and Henry Luce III Libraries at Princeton Theological Seminary, the McGill University Archives, the Library of Congress Manuscripts Division, the Presbyterian Historical Society in Philadelphia, the American Museum of Natural History, the New York City Historical Society, and the New York Public Library. By no means least, I am grateful to the librarians and staff of the Rush Rhees Library at the University of Rochester, the Ambrose Swasey Library at Colgate-Rochester Divinity School, the James Oliver Buswell Library at Wheaton College, and the James E. Rolfing Memorial Library at Trinity International University.

Mark Noll and David Livingstone have encouraged me greatly with kind words, keen collegial interest, and fruitful discussions in person and by correspondence. Mark has faithfully and repeatedly urged me to go forward with the publication of this and other Princetonian projects, sharing his work on them with me. His advice and encouragement have finally brought this project to press. Michael Ruse's unexpected encomiums on the value of my dissertation rekindled my interest in the book manuscript when college teaching and other work had turned my focus elsewhere. Ron Numbers generously shared with me his knowledge of Princeton's twentieth-century connections to antievolutionism, and provided helpful criticisms that pushed me to refine and strengthen the thesis of this book. Jim Moorhead affirmed my project by publishing a version of chapter 4 in the journal *American Presbyterians*.

I am thankful also for Ray Cannata, with whom I enjoyed many heartfelt discussions about the Princeton theologians while he was assisting in the seminary archives; for Scott Brenon Caton, my good friend and colleague in Rochester, whose close insights into the Princetonians repeatedly revived and refreshed me; and for Denis "Dawson" Lamoureux, a fellow seeker in matters of evolution and religion, with whom agreement and disagreement are equally stimulating. The late Rev. Dr.

Allan MacRae, with the assistance of Steve Haig, affably shared his personal memories of the 1920s and allowed me to peruse his vast collection of papers, including those of Robert Dick Wilson. The late Rev. Dr. G. Hall Todd offered his delightful hospitality and a wealth of minute recollections of the old Princetonians. The late Benjamin B. Warfield II graciously devoted three days' attention and energy, despite advanced age and ill health, to a series of interviews about the Warfield family. The Rev. Dr. Donald MacLeod kindly let me use his father's beautifully copied notes of Princeton Seminary classes in the 1920s, now housed in Special Collections at the Princeton Theological Seminary Library. My heartfelt thanks go to all of them.

My colleagues at Trinity International University deserve my gratitude. In his capacity as chair of the history department, Steve Fratt has managed departmental schedules and duties so as to maximize my few opportunities for research, and I am deeply grateful. Steve Pointer and Angelo Rentas involved me in their team-taught honors seminar, "Christianity and Darwinism," and I now have the pleasure of working with Angelo myself since Steve's retirement. Doug Sweeney, in our seminary's church history department, has provided constant encouragement and has modeled scholarship in the service of both church and academe. Hans Madueme updated me on current theological controversies surrounding the question of human evolution. This community of scholars has been a wonderful place to work on the Princetonians.

Chris and Amy Baldwin, Matt and Karen Ristuccia, and Jamie Rankin have hosted me repeatedly on research trips to Princeton. They have proven themselves faithful, supportive friends time and again. So have Chris Loughridge, Paul Bialek, and my fellow perfectionist, John Monson. These friends probably do not realize how much their words of perspective and confidence have meant to me.

My parents, Arthur and Carol Gundlach, have stood by me through the many years of this project. I am ever grateful to them for their love and quiet encouragement. My children, Nathan, Lucie, Anna, and Laura, refresh my soul and keep me grounded in the world that is here and now.

Most of all, I thank my true companion and best friend: my wife Rebecca, to whom I dedicate this book with love.

Introduction

*History in all its details, even the most minute, is but the evolution
of the eternal purposes of God.*

Charles Hodge, 1872[1]

Providential Developmentalism

In the annals of the history of science and religion, Princeton theologian
Charles Hodge rivals England's Bishop Samuel Wilberforce as the most
famous clerical opponent of the theory of evolution. His conclusion in
1874, "What is Darwinism? It is atheism," is probably the most frequently
quoted antievolutionary statement of all time. It may come as some surprise, then, to find him using the term "evolution" in such a positive and
theological sense as appears in the epigraph above. One might expect
such a statement from Hodge's fellow Princetonians James McCosh and
B. B. Warfield — men renowned and often celebrated for their combination of orthodox Calvinism and evolution — but not from the systema-
tizer of the Princeton theology himself. The surprise one feels on discovering Hodge's statement (and in his definitive *Systematic Theology*, no
less) is emblematic of the driving interest of this book. This is a study of
the surprisingly complex and often close relationship of the leading

---

1. Charles Hodge, *Systematic Theology* (New York: Scribners, 1872-73; reprint, Grand
Rapids: Eerdmans, 1993), 1:538.

theological conservatives in America, the Princetonians, with what they often called "the development hypothesis."

Hodge penned the above statement in the course of treating that most Calvinistic of doctrines, God's eternal decree. He was following the doctrinal standard of the Presbyterian churches, the Westminster Confession (1647), in which the distinctively Reformed constructions of creation, providence, sin, salvation, predestination and reprobation, divine sovereignty and human free agency all trace back to the doctrine of the decrees. The Confession puts it thus: "God from all eternity did by the most wise and holy counsel of his own will, freely and unchangeably ordain whatsoever comes to pass; yet so as thereby neither is God the author of sin; nor is violence offered to the will of the creatures, nor is the liberty or contingency of second causes taken away, but rather established."[2] In this seventeenth-century statement — long predating the nineteenth-century controversies over evolution and even the eighteenth-century controversies over deism — we find a robust affirmation of the agency of "second causes." And we find it in the same (long) breath as an equally robust affirmation of God's sovereign foreordination of all events and things. This emphasis on the combination of God's unchangeable purpose with the reality and efficiency of creaturely action, from universal laws like gravity to the minutest choices of individual people, is a distinctive teaching of Calvinist orthodoxy that enabled the Princetonians to embrace evolutionary thinking (carefully construed) not only as compatible with their theology, but even as an expression of it.

I intend this statement to raise eyebrows, for some of the Princetonians are famous for rejecting evolutionism outright, while others are renowned for "making peace" between evangelical religion and evolutionism — that is, for accepting evolutionism only when carefully limited and explained. Mark Noll and David Livingstone describe B. B. Warfield's use of Westminster Calvinism to "set acceptable boundaries" on evolutionary ideas. James R. Moore classifies A. A. Hodge and James McCosh as "Christian Darwinisticists" — men open to Darwinian evolution, but only on the condition of significant modifications to suit their theology.[3]

2. Westminster Confession of Faith, iii.1 (chapter 3, section 1). I quote from *The Constitution of the Presbyterian Church in the United States, Containing the Confession of Faith, the Larger and Shorter Catechisms* ... (Richmond, Va.: Presbyterian Committee of Publication, ca. 1910), pp. 23-24.

3. Mark A. Noll and David N. Livingstone, in Benjamin Breckinridge Warfield, *Evolution, Science, and Scripture: Selected Writings*, ed. Noll and Livingstone (Grand Rapids:

Intentionally or not, these turns of phrase suggest an image of the Princetonians engaging in compromise at a negotiating table to which they came only under duress, or of their building a dike either to reclaim some of the territory that had been taken by the relentless tides of scientific inquiry or to hold back those tides at theology's key points. These are ultimately adversarial images, despite a quite proper notice of Princeton's peacemaking with evolution. The adversarial image has a great deal to commend it — not least its clear use by the Princetonians themselves, as I will argue at some length. But it is not the whole story. By the 1890s the Princetonians not only "accepted" evolution with qualifications, not only "struck a compromise" with the idea, not only "allowed" evolutionary science a limited sphere; in significant ways they *assimilated* evolutionary ideas, *embracing* them as something belonging properly to their confession all along, something to which the rise of evolutionary science simply brought fresh attention.

B. B. Warfield wrote, "No one will doubt that Christians of to-day must state their Christian belief in terms of modern thought. Every age has a language of its own and can speak no other."[4] On this principle, Warfield and his fellow Princetonians had no problem with the notion that modern evolutionary thought would, in God's providence, bring out more fully the developmental aspects of Calvinist orthodoxy. And so we find the Princetonians not only affirming evolutionary biology, geology, and astronomy, but also finding *development* a useful idea for understanding the history of religion, church history, and even the Bible itself — all the while championing the inerrancy of Scripture, resisting the revision of the Westminster Confession, and waging an aggressive war against theological liberalism. Evolutionary thought is well known to have structured and impelled modernism; now, in this book, I find that a certain kind of evolutionary thought, not just *imported into* the Princeton theology but in key ways *evoked from* it by the thought currents of the day, structured and impelled the conservative position taken by these intellectual leaders of evangelical orthodoxy.

Several commentators have described the Princetonian response to

---

Baker, 2000); James R. Moore, *The Post-Darwinian Controversies: A Study of the Protestant Struggle to Come to Terms with Darwin in Great Britain and America, 1870-1900* (Cambridge: Cambridge University Press, 1979), pp. 241-51.

4. Benjamin Breckinridge Warfield, review of *Foundations,* by B. H. Streeter et al., *Princeton Theological Review* 10 (1913): 528.

modernism generally — to evolutionary science, biblical criticism, and theological liberalism — as due fundamentally to a *static* conception of reality. Theological modernists like Shailer Mathews leveled this charge against conservatives routinely. Historians, too, often with far less sympathy for the modernist theological project, have observed in the Princetonians "a tendency . . . to regard theological truth in static categories which were not influenced by historical development." This last quotation comes from no less a scholar than Mark Noll, one of the top evangelical historians today, and himself a Presbyterian and an admirer of the Princeton theologians in significant respects. Mark S. Massa, explaining the contest between B. B. Warfield and C. A. Briggs around 1890, cites as a fundamental difference between the two "the Princeton belief in theology as a static entity unaffected to any appreciable degree by historical development." Inasmuch as evolution, in Presbyterian historian Lefferts Loetscher's phrase, "substituted change for fixity as the law of all things," it would seem that the defenders of the unchanging truths of the Bible and the old-time gospel must have opposed it — or must have accommodated it only at the peril of their cherished beliefs.[5]

But a close look at the course of Princetonian interaction with evolutionary notions reveals a different pattern. Instead of refusing to think in categories of historical change, they came increasingly to see development over time as a very helpful category indeed: helpful not only in providing new insights into sacred and secular history, but also in furnishing the orthodox with potent arguments *against* relativizing the teachings of the Bible or revising the confession of faith. In their hands developmentalism *supported* Calvinist orthodoxy and biblical authority. It all depended on one's brand of evolutionism. While Darwinian evolutionism posited goalless, undirected change, non-Darwinian developmental evolutionisms did not — and it was the non-Darwinian doctrines of neo-Lamarckism and orthogenesis that flourished among Princeton's

5. Shailer Mathews, *The Faith of Modernism* (New York: Macmillan, 1924); Mark A. Noll, ed., *The Princeton Theology, 1812-1921: Scripture, Science, and Theological Method from Archibald Alexander to Benjamin Breckinridge Warfield* (Grand Rapids: Baker, 1983), p. 30; Mark Stephen Massa, *Charles Augustus Briggs and the Crisis of Historical Criticism* (Minneapolis: Fortress, 1990), p. 60; Lefferts A. Loetscher, *The Broadening Church: A Study of Theological Issues in the Presbyterian Church since 1869* (Philadelphia: University of Pennsylvania Press, 1954), pp. 9-10. Loetscher borrowed the idea from John Dewey's *Influence of Darwinism on Philosophy, and Other Essays in Contemporary Thought* (New York: Henry Holt, 1910), pp. 1-2.

scientists in the decades around 1900. These growth-analogy evolutionisms hinged on the idea that the development of the individual recapitulated the development of the life-form — "ontogeny recapitulates phylogeny" — an idea that preserved and furnished stronger evidence that *purpose* is built into the structure and history of life. Thus growth-analogy evolutionisms could actually strengthen the theistic argument from design. Historians have recognized this for some time. What is new is that this non-Darwinian concept of evolution not only preserved teleology, but also provided positive arguments for biblical integrity and confessional Calvinism. In their espousal of providential developmentalism, the Princetonians found a notion that combined an affirmation of both the permanence of truth *and* historical change. Development, the unfolding of built-in potentials over time and in interaction with the environment, was precisely God's usual way of doing things. When understood in the context of God's eternal purposes and continual sovereign control of the universe in all its complexity, under the distinctly Reformed concept of providence that guards the real efficiency of second causes, the idea of development made eminent sense. Thus, while the Princetonians opposed historicism, they embraced developmentalism. *Like* their liberal opponents, they found the category of change over time proper and useful. And they applied this idea to biblical theology, church history, and systematics in a way that clearly echoed currents of evolutionary biology in their day.

This is by no means to say that the Princetonians did not exhibit alarm at scientific antisupernaturalism, or at times stand staunchly against evolutionism in general and Darwinism in particular. The story of the evolution question at Princeton from the 1840s to the 1920s involves something of a rise and fall, from antievolutionism to providential evolutionism to some antievolutionism again, as the fortunes of evolutionary science rose and fell. It also involves a pretty constant expression of concern about the metaphysics of evolutionism and about naturalistic-evolutionary theories of religion, ethics, society, and the Bible. There was much about evolutionism that bothered them — but there was much too that made sense to them as Calvinists and as philosophical empiricists. Two of the occasional barriers to evolutionary thinking — biblical religion and Common-Sense philosophy — turn out also to have been instrumental in the Princetonian *embrace* of evolutionary thinking. Their simultaneous attraction to and repulsion from evolution make the story dramatic and fascinating.

The Princetonians

Princeton was the most important center of conservative Protestant thinking on matters of science and religion in America. The two related institutions in that pleasant borough midway between New York and Philadelphia — the College of New Jersey[6] and the Theological Seminary of the Presbyterian Church in the United States of America — carried on a lively, scholarly, theologically conservative interaction with the intellectual trends of the nineteenth century. Known today as Princeton University and Princeton Theological Seminary, these two institutions exercised an enormous influence, from the conservative side, on the hegemonic culture of nineteenth-century evangelicalism. Conservatives of diverse confessional stripes within that culture — not only Presbyterians but also Methodists, Baptists, Congregationalists, and others, not to mention Calvinists abroad in England, Scotland, Northern Ireland, and as far away as New Zealand — looked to Princeton for sound guidance on the religious import of modern scientific inquiry.[7]

American colleges and seminaries today are less amenable to identification with a "school" of thought than they were in the nineteenth century, thanks to the triumph of the modern university ideal of utterly unfettered inquiry and the postmodern celebration of diversity. Institutions today usually aim at multiplicity of viewpoints and consider a department, let alone a whole school, to suffer from inbreeding if too many of its faculty are alumni of that institution or sharers of the same ideological or philosophical stance. Not so a century and a half ago, when theologies were often identified by their institutional base — the New Haven theology, the Mercersburg theology, the Princeton theology — and diversity *among* institutions was more prevalent than diversity *within* institutions. Since theological fine-points were not the main business of colleges, they tended to be more uniform in promulgating a generic evangelical Protes-

---

6. Not to be confused with the present College of New Jersey, formerly Trenton State College, which took that name about a century after Princeton University abandoned it.

7. In his magisterial study of theological education in America, Glenn T. Miller writes, "In short, the Princeton of 1870 was the compleat American seminary, a symbol of American theological education at its best. Closely related to its church, to a theological tradition, to its social location, and to churches of like faith and order around the world, Princeton set the standard for much of contemporary American theological education." Miller, *Piety and Profession: American Protestant Theological Education, 1870-1970* (Grand Rapids: Eerdmans, 2007), p. 6.

tantism. But in the case of Princeton, college and seminary formed a coherent society at the outset of our story, and remained intertwined (though not always in agreement) right through it, to the 1920s.

It makes real sense, then, to speak of "the Princetonians" as a coherent group, and to approach the evolution question at Princeton as a sort of group odyssey. For nearly fifty years the professors of the two institutions produced a quarterly journal called the *Biblical Repertory and Princeton Review*, which stated on its title page that it was the work of "a club of gentlemen." Their group identity as Princetonians overrode their institutional identities.

Princeton's Orange Key tour guides today routinely tell visitors that the university has always been nonsectarian and institutionally distinct from the Presbyterian seminary a block away down Dickinson Street. While technically true, the statement is profoundly misleading. The college charter, granted in 1746, indeed stipulated that the institution would have no official sectarian identity, but in fact the college was the creation of New Side (prorevival) Presbyterians during the Great Awakening. Its third president — who unfortunately died of a smallpox vaccination after only three months in office — was none other than the great Calvinist theologian and interpreter of the revivals, Jonathan Edwards. To nearly the end of the nineteenth century the college's presidents, trustees, and faculty were overwhelmingly Presbyterian and evangelical, and even in 1896, when the college officially became Princeton University, its president taught regular courses at the seminary. Throughout that period the presidents reported each year to the trustees on the religious state of the college and the prospects for, or blessed news of, evangelical revivals on campus. In these and other respects Princeton College was hardly atypical; as George Marsden has shown in his masterful book, *The Soul of the American University*, the bulk of the nineteenth century represented the triumph of an evangelical ideal of higher education over the Jeffersonian enlightenment ideal that had prevailed in 1800. What was unique about Princeton, though, was its dogged stand for the evangelical ideal even as the nineteenth century came to a close. "If a more traditionalist Protestant intellectual alternative to the emerging definitions of American academia was to survive at any major school," Marsden writes, "Princeton was the foremost candidate."[8]

---

8. George M. Marsden, *The Soul of the American University: From Protestant Establishment to Established Nonbelief* (New York: Oxford University Press, 1994), p. 196.

Historians have sometimes made the mistake of ascribing the strong evangelical identity of Princeton College to its alleged domination by the seminary. It is true that for much of the nineteenth century the seminary was the more powerful of the two institutions in leading the intellectual debates of the times, thanks especially to the identification of Princeton's quarterly journal with the seminary in particular. In an age when clergy shaped the thought world of most Americans, when graduate study centered in the seminaries, and when theological quarterlies were the main venue for academic discussions, the intellectual importance of seminaries was enormous — and Princeton was arguably the most influential of all. Founded in 1812 as the Presbyterian church's first theological seminary, it quickly grew into a bastion of erudition in the service of orthodoxy. Its emphasis on scholarly influence (one of the supporting themes of this book) grew over time, so that by 1929 the seminary had produced 480 college presidents — 320 of them since 1880. Even while non-Calvinistic denominations overtook the Presbyterians and Congregationalists in terms of church membership, Princeton Seminary remained one of the largest centers of theological education in America, and arguably the most powerful. "For much of the nineteenth century," conclude Peter Wallace and Mark Noll, "Princeton was *the* theological seminary of North America." By about 1900 it was attracting significant numbers of international students as well. Only lately, they report, have other seminaries "begun to approach its national and international stature."[9]

Relations between college and seminary were reciprocal and intimate. Until about 1880 the professors of the two institutions met regularly to give papers and discuss topics of intellectual interest in a group they called simply "the Club."[10] There was also a significant overlap of personnel on the boards: Charles Hodge, for example, was senior professor at the seminary and head of the college board of trustees at the same time; James McCosh was simultaneously college president and a member of the seminary board of directors. These men worshiped in the same churches, contributed to and ran the same journal (Hodge's right-hand man in editorial work was college philosophy professor Lyman Atwater),

9. Marsden, *Soul*, p. 79; Peter J. Wallace and Mark A. Noll, "The Students of Princeton Seminary, 1812-1929: A Research Note," *American Presbyterians* 72 (1994): 203-15; cf. Roger Finke and Rodney Stark, *The Churching of America, 1776-1990: Winners and Losers in Our Religious Economy* (New Brunswick, N.J.: Rutgers University Press, 1992).

10. Charles Hodge regularly noted meetings of "the Club" in his memoranda (Hodge MSS, PTS Special Collections).

preached each other's funerals, and married their children to each other. Of course, there were little feuds and mutual differences, but it is appropriate to say that until the end of the century Princeton was in a very real way a single community of thinkers.

This close-knit little society looms large in the annals of the encounter between science and religion in America, and occupies center stage in the religious engagement with evolutionism. John Witherspoon, president of the College of New Jersey (now Princeton University), introduced to America the Common-Sense Realism of his native Scotland in 1768, and for the entire antebellum period, that philosophy framed the discussion of science and religion in this country.[11] In 1845 the *Biblical Repertory and Princeton Review* carried the first American review of Robert Chambers's *Vestiges of the Natural History of Creation,* a pre- and non-Darwinian work that pioneered evolutionism in the English-speaking world. In 1871 James McCosh became the first religious leader in America to embrace evolutionism — even Darwin's doctrine of natural selection — in the name of Christian belief. Charles Cashdollar identifies this Princeton president as the leading figure among the "judicious conservatives" who reshaped mainstream British and American Protestantism in response to the insights and challenges of positivism. Meanwhile, Charles Hodge penned in 1874 his well-known equation of Darwinism with atheism. These two Princetonians, McCosh and Hodge, quickly became icons in the standard triumphalist histories of the "conflict" or "warfare" between science and theology. They remain to this day the most famous pair of religious thinkers for and against evolution.[12]

When Hodge's son and successor, Archibald Alexander Hodge, wrote an introduction for a book called *Theism and Evolution,* the religious public took it as Princeton's imprimatur on the doctrine of descent, properly construed. It was, according to historian James R. Moore, "a

11. Theodore Dwight Bozeman, *Protestants in an Age of Science: The Baconian Ideal and Antebellum American Religious Thought* (Chapel Hill: University of North Carolina Press, 1977), p. 32; Henry F. May, *The Enlightenment in America* (New York: Oxford University Press, 1976), pp. 64, 346-47.

12. Moore, *The Post-Darwinian Controversies,* p. 242; Charles D. Cashdollar, *The Transformation of Theology, 1830-1890: Positivism and Protestant Thought in Britain and America* (Princeton: Princeton University Press, 1989), pp. 350-55. For a recent example of the standard use of McCosh and Hodge, see Edward J. Larson, *Summer for the Gods: The Scopes Trial and America's Continuing Debate over Science and Religion* (Cambridge: Harvard University Press, 1998), pp. 18, 20.

turning point for the acceptance of evolution among American Protestants." Benjamin Breckinridge Warfield, who with the younger Hodge championed the doctrine of biblical inerrancy, welcomed the transmutation of species — in stark contrast to the fundamentalists who lionized his Bible doctrine later in the twentieth century. Thus the most venerable defenders of scriptural authority at Princeton, whose formulations of the doctrines of verbal inspiration and biblical inerrancy are the classic modern statements of those views, allowed and even embraced a qualified doctrine of evolution. Indeed, it was their conservatism on biblical authority that made their proevolutionary statements so very important for concerned evangelicals, then and now.[13]

Princeton — orthodox, Calvinist Princeton — took the lead in the advent of evolutionism in American religion. The Princetonians were proud to maintain strict orthodoxy while pursuing and welcoming modern science, eager to mold opinion in both the religious and scientific realms, and determined to play a leading role in maintaining a peaceable union of the two. Their commitment to academic rigor in tandem with orthodox belief — using "scholarly means to evangelical ends," standing as a bridge "between faith and criticism"[14] — made them the intellectual heroes of much of the evangelical world. That reputation would continue and indeed grow in the years of evangelical resurgence from the late 1940s onward. When fundamentalist radio evangelist Charles Fuller launched the leading neo-evangelical seminary that bears his name, the founding pro-

13. Moore, *The Post-Darwinian Controversies*, p. 245; David N. Livingstone and Mark A. Noll, "B. B. Warfield (1851-1921): A Biblical Inerrantist as Evolutionist," *Isis* 91 (2000): 283-304. For a dissenting view on the extent of Warfield's evolutionism, see Fred G. Zaspel, *The Theology of B. B. Warfield: A Systematic Summary* (Wheaton, Ill.: Crossway, 2010), pp. 369-87.

14. Here I invoke well-turned phrases by Louise L. Stevenson and Mark A. Noll. Stevenson's book, *Scholarly Means to Evangelical Ends: The New Haven Scholars and the Transformation of Higher Learning in America, 1830-1880* (Baltimore: Johns Hopkins University Press, 1986), traces a "creative symbiosis of learning and piety" at mid-nineteenth-century Yale — just the sort of thing Princeton and other schools were engaged in. What makes Princeton unique among elite institutions is that it persisted in this symbiosis well into the twentieth century. Noll's *Between Faith and Criticism: Evangelicals, Scholarship, and the Bible in America* (San Francisco: Harper and Row, 1986) similarly helps us to place the Princetonian ideal of faith and scholarship in wider context, while at the same time calling attention to the uniqueness of Princeton's role as time went on. "In the first decades of the [twentieth] century," Noll writes, "the Presbyterians at Princeton flew the banner of conservative scholarship in the battlefields of the day pretty much by themselves" (p. 51).

fessors all considered their task to be the revival of the old Princetonian ideal — now that Princeton Seminary itself had, after forcible reorganization by the mainline Presbyterian church in 1929, "gone liberal."[15] When in the 1960s and 1980s Fuller Seminary underwent successive controversies about scholarship and biblical authority, Trinity Evangelical Divinity School and Gordon-Conwell Theological Seminary saw themselves as relay athletes, picking up the fallen baton and continuing to run the good Princetonian race. And while these evangelicals outside the confessional Calvinist fold looked to Princeton for a model of faithful scholarship, conservative Presbyterian schools also grew and multiplied: Westminster Theological Seminary (Philadelphia and California) and Redeemer Seminary (Dallas) for the Orthodox Presbyterians, Covenant Theological Seminary and the various campuses of Reformed Theological Seminary (Jackson, Orlando, Charlotte) among the burgeoning membership of the conservative Presbyterian Church in America.

Old Princeton thus has no lack of latter-day admirers; indeed, their numbers continue to swell, even as their particular interests in the Princetonian legacy have diversified. Some laud Princeton's evidentialist apologetics, some its inerrantism, some its stance toward evolutionism, some its fully orbed Westminster Calvinism (versus a stripped-down set of "fundamentals"). And old Princeton receives its share of criticisms from the same heirs, seeking to correct what they see as imbalances in Princetonian performance, even as they hail the overall vision of scholarship in the service of faith. Evidentialism, inerrantism, and confessionalism sometimes become targets for correction, as do Princeton's doctrine of the cessation of charismatic gifts and Princeton's connection with Scottish Common-Sense Realism. Whether in celebration or in warning, then, Princeton continues to loom large in the consciousness of many educated Protestants.[16]

---

15. George M. Marsden, *Reforming Fundamentalism: Fuller Seminary and the New Evangelicalism* (Grand Rapids: Eerdmans, 1987).

16. Admirers of old Princeton include David B. Calhoun, *Princeton Seminary*, 2 vols. (Edinburgh: Banner of Truth Trust, 1994, 1996); Gary L. W. Johnson, ed., *B. B. Warfield: Essays on His Life and Thought* (Phillipsburg, N.J.: P&R, 2007); and Paul Kjoss Helseth, *"Right Reason" and the Princeton Mind: An Unorthodox Proposal* (Phillipsburg, N.J.: P&R, 2010); not to mention numerous leading evangelical theologians such as J. I. Packer. Detractors include John C. Vander Stelt, *Philosophy and Scripture: A Study in Old Princeton and Westminster Theology* (Marlton, N.J.: Mack, 1978); Jon Mark Ruthven, *On the Cessation of the Charismata: The Protestant Polemic on Post-Biblical Miracles* (Sheffield: Sheffield Aca-

While scholars following Donald Dayton's lead warn against over-emphasis of the "Presbyterian paradigm" in American religious history,[17] the fact remains that in intellectual leadership and sheer output of books and articles the Princetonians were chief among the interpreters of modern scholarship for conservative Protestants in America. Even to-day, one can read Mark Noll's provocative *Scandal of the Evangelical Mind* as a call to return to the seriousness about scholarship that character-ized the Princetonians, to whose history and example he has repeatedly guided us.[18] Their consideration of the evolution question — what it en-tailed, what it portended, its legitimacies and illegitimacies — is a sub-ject of both historical and present interest.

Method, Layout, and Themes

Though this study is built upon careful analysis of text and historical sit-uation, in conception and structure it is less an analysis than a story. It has, of course, analytical and synthetic components throughout, but at heart it is a narrative of the ways in which the community of thinkers at Princeton College and Seminary defined and answered the questions posed by evolutionism. I follow the lead of David Livingstone, who urged some years ago "that there needs to be a greater awareness of the spe-cific encounters between advocates of science and religion at particular points in time and in particular geographical settings."[19]

---

demic Press, 1993); and John William Stewart, "The Tethered Theology: Biblical Criticism, Common-Sense Philosophy, and the Princeton Theologians, 1812-1860" (Ph.D. diss., University of Michigan, 1990).

17. Donald W. Dayton, *Discovering an Evangelical Heritage* (New York: Harper and Row, 1976). See also George M. Marsden, "Demythologizing Evangelicalism: A Review of Donald Dayton's *Discovering an Evangelical Heritage*," *Christian Scholar's Review* 7 (1977): 203-11. *Christian Scholar's Review* devoted the entire Fall 1993 issue to this debate, with Dayton, Marsden, and others participating.

18. Mark A. Noll, *The Scandal of the Evangelical Mind* (Grand Rapids: Eerdmans, 1994). While Noll charts attitudes toward scholarship across a wide field, by no means centering on the Princetonians, he makes judicious use of them at key points — notably, for our pur-poses here, concerning the evolution question. B. B. Warfield, Noll writes, stated "'the better way' toward science that evangelicals, to their great loss, largely abandoned in the wake of fundamentalism" (p. 208). Cf. his anthology *The Princeton Theology* and especially his introduction (with David Livingstone) to Warfield, *Evolution, Science, and Scripture*.

19. David N. Livingstone, "Darwinism and Calvinism: The Belfast-Princeton Connec-

The narrative presents a kind of group biography, consciously avoiding organization around either essentialist taxonomies or individual thinkers. In this way it differs radically from important and influential books in the field: James R. Moore's *Post-Darwinian Controversies* and Jon H. Roberts's *Darwinism and the Divine in America* (taxonomies), and Livingstone's earlier book, *Darwin's Forgotten Defenders* (sampler of thinkers).[20] There are of course numerous books narrating the overall history of the relations between evolution and religion, but in its particular group-biographical focus on the Princetonians, this book is unique.[21]

John Hedley Brooke and Geoffrey Cantor have pointed out the fruitfulness of biography as a method for exploring the historical relations of science and religion. Biography emphasizes particularities of experience, allowing subjects to be themselves and not just who we want them to be for our purposes. Biography illustrates the "existential tensions" real people face in real time-space experience and offers a glimpse into the process of the "construction of science-religion relationships." It requires the writer to face "an exacting genre that raises a host of demanding historiographical problems," humbling us in the face of the daunting task of trying to re-create the lives of people long dead. Many possible narratives present themselves, and the writer must choose which is most

---

tion," *Isis* 83 (1992): 428. See also his "Science and Religion: Towards a New Cartography," *Christian Scholar's Review* 26 (1997): 270-92. Livingstone champions what he calls the "historical geography of ideas."

20. Moore, *The Post-Darwinian Controversies;* Jon H. Roberts, *Darwinism and the Divine in America: Protestant Intellectuals and Organic Evolution, 1859-1900* (Madison: University of Wisconsin Press, 1988); David N. Livingstone, *Darwin's Forgotten Defenders: The Encounter between Evangelical Theology and Evolutionary Thought* (Grand Rapids: Eerdmans; Edinburgh: Scottish Academic Press, 1987). Also following the sequence-of-thinkers approach is Deryl Freeman Johnson, "The Attitudes of the Princeton Theologians toward Darwinism and Evolution from 1859-1929" (Ph.D. diss., University of Iowa, 1968). Denis Oswald Lamoureux, "Between 'The Origin of Species' and 'The Fundamentals': Toward a Historiographical Model of the Evangelical Reaction to Darwinism in the First Fifty Years" (Ph.D. diss., Toronto School of Theology, 1991), combines the taxonomic and sequence-of-thinkers approaches.

21. Important large-scale histories of evolution and religion include Ronald L. Numbers, *The Creationists: The Evolution of Scientific Creationism* (Berkeley: University of California Press, 1993); Michael Ruse, *Monad to Man: The Concept of Progress in Evolutionary Biology* (Cambridge: Harvard University Press, 1996); Ruse, *The Evolution Wars: A Guide to the Debates* (New Brunswick, N.J.: Rutgers University Press, 2001); and David N. Livingstone, *Adam's Ancestors: Race, Religion, and the Politics of Human Origins* (Baltimore: Johns Hopkins University Press, 2008).

fitting. In their complexity and particularity, their situational and contextual emphases, biographies "challenge stereotypes to show that the
experience of the individual is often far more complex and interesting
than the stereotype will allow." I have found these observations strikingly
appropriate to the Princetonian consideration of evolutionism.[22]

Close attention to individual lives (and group lives) quickly reveals
the inadequacy of those approaches that seek to place thinkers into
essentialist categories. People move freely from one category to another
as times and circumstances change. They have to negotiate competing
allegiances, competing goals, less-than-perfect terrains of battle. In its
attention to these complicating aspects of intellectual history, biography
allows us to "emphasise the role of human agency working in history and
society." The subject becomes "an active agent who deploys different
strategies creatively."[23]

In so highlighting the creative agency of people in their complex historical circumstances, a biographical approach might seem to threaten
any notion that the positions these people held — say, drawing the line
on human evolution at the evolution of the body, but not the soul — possess any stability, any force, any ultimacy. If it's all construct, does truth
value go out the window? Surely not. We are seeking to see these people
as real people, to penetrate beyond pronouncements to their prior intellectual context as well as to their situations, allegiances, interpersonal
relations. In so doing we can make better use of their precedent. I am not
ashamed to say that I find the Princetonians as a group, and certain individuals especially, very admirable. Their assessment of and answers to
the evolution question can best serve our generation if we look to them
as models of how to approach this and similar issues in our day, duly noting as well their blind spots and missteps.

There is some irony in this purposed avoidance of categorizing, this
narrative, group-biographical approach. The Princetonians were themselves essentialists and deeply enamored of taxonomical approaches.
This is nowhere better illustrated than in Francis Landey Patton's *Fundamental Christianity* (1926). Patton was Princeton Seminary's first professor of the Relations of Science and Philosophy to the Christian Religion,

22. John Hedley Brooke and Geoffrey Cantor, "Is There Value in the Historical Approach?" chapter 1 of their Glasgow Gifford Lectures, *Reconstructing Nature: The Engagement of Science and Religion* (Oxford and New York: Oxford University Press, 1998).
23. Brooke and Cantor, "Is There Value in the Historical Approach?"

and later president in turn of the college and seminary. Anyone who opens his book will find it full to saturation with isms, as if ideas float around quite independent of people to think them. Defining the boundaries of sound and unsound, especially in matters of Christian doctrine and basic metaphysics, was essential to the Princetonians. And such border patrols are not without their legitimate uses. But if we are to understand fully the Princetonians' position, and not just to attempt to cut-and-paste it into a new domain, we need careful, narrative, situated study. That is the purpose of the present book.

MY RESEARCH METHOD is heavily weighted toward primary sources, especially archival materials (lecture notes, correspondence) and periodical literature, where we see the day-to-day and year-to-year development of Princetonian thinking in its institutional, ecclesiastical, and professional aspects within a republic of ideas that was at once transatlantic (witness Warfield's *Presbyterian and Reformed Review*) and provincial (in-house Presbyterian battles, etc.).

The story proceeds through a series of skirmishes with foes outside the camp (Robert Chambers, Charles Darwin, Herbert Spencer, Thomas Huxley, Joseph Le Conte, and many more) and within (controversies involving Charles Woodruff Shields and James Woodrow, the growing religious rift between seminary and university after 1900, the brewing fundamentalist-modernist controversy). My piecing together of the story proceeded on the initially somewhat unconscious assumption that controversies very often serve as moments of definition and decision. The materials I encountered soon confirmed that notion. Whatever appeal a "peaceable" history of the encounter of Christianity and evolution might have,[24] it quickly became apparent to me that the Princetonians were driven by a warfare metaphor to describe their present call, even as they affirmed as guiding background assumption the ultimate unity of truth scientific and religious.

This is then as much a study of *conflict* as of *consensus* within the Princeton school — but conflict driven much more by ideational matters than by class or power or even institutional interest. In the messiness of Gilded Age institutional growth and competition with other schools, church controversies over the origin and authority of Scripture and the

---

24. Cf. Moore's call for "non-violent and humane" histories of the encounter between science and religion. *The Post-Darwinian Controversies,* p. 19.

extent to which confessional statements were binding, and alliance building across denominational lines for purposes of faith and practice (fundamentalism) and sociopolitical action (the antievolution campaign of Bryan), Princetonians considered, defined, refined, and revisited the issues they believed were involved in the evolution question in their generation.

Chapters 1–3 set the stage by describing Princeton's assessment of developmentalism before Darwin, the general relations of science and religion, and the tactics needed to maintain the unity of God's word and works in an enlightened, empirical age. Characteristically, chapter 1 opens with conflict: the Princetonians' consideration of Robert Chambers's *Vestiges of the Natural History of Creation,* the immediate evolutionist forerunner of Darwin's work. As Charles Gillispie and others have shown, the *Vestiges* called forth a strongly antievolutionary response that daunted Darwin and disinclined the scientific and religious communities from welcoming his work. Princeton's quarterly journal gave the first serious American review of the *Vestiges,* and that review articulated the metaphysical and epistemological objections that would remain prominent in Princeton's handling of the evolution question for decades. A telling alternative soon appeared in Princeton in the person of Swiss geologist and geographer Arnold Guyot, whose German idealist developmentalism received hearty welcome at Princeton — revealing Princeton's prime concern for a supernaturalist metaphysic alongside a perhaps surprising willingness to think in terms of change over time. Chapters 2 and 3 find in the pre-Darwinian geological controversies a careful, sometimes alarmed consideration of how the faithful should make use of reason and science to defend the faith. The Princetonians, like many others of their era, made free use of battle imagery to describe and chart out their task. I argue that a frank exploration of the Princetonian use of "the military metaphor," whatever its unsavoriness to current tastes, opens up for us the thought world of that generation on the relations of science and religion. We find the Princetonians laying out a plan for reconnaissance and tactics for engagement that the next generations would carry out with remarkable consistency.

In chapters 4, 5, and 6 the Princetonians encounter the evolution question in the far more forceful form Darwin, Spencer, and Huxley gave to it. Chapter 4 considers the famous antithesis of Charles Hodge and James McCosh, arguing that the common ground between them proved far more important than their differences to the Princeton community then and later. Chapters 5 and 6 witness the Princetonian offensive in the name of science and Christianity, as Charles Woodruff Shields, Charles Augustus Aiken, and Francis Landey Patton are hired into chairs newly created to treat the relations of science and philosophy to religion. From the 1860s through the 1880s the Princetonian community, college and seminary, was still functioning in solidarity, and devoted considerable energy to the structure of apologetics, of systematic theology in relation to other sciences, and of science and religion broadly. Two key controversies — the Shields affair at Princeton College and the Woodrow affair in the Southern Presbyterian Church — together with a prolonged effort at the college to hire a geologist — brought Princeton to a moment of decision in 1880-81, when Patton came to the seminary to promulgate a scientifically updated theism as the foundation for a sound edifice of faith and learning, and Charles Hodge's own grandson, William Berryman Scott, became the first science professor at Princeton College to espouse the transmutation theory in his classes. That same year, tantalizingly enough, also saw the Princetonians A. A. Hodge and B. B. Warfield publish the classic formulation of the doctrine of biblical inerrancy.

Chapters 7 and 8 turn our attention to the relationship at Princeton between progressionism in evolutionary biology and progressionism in orthodox Calvinist theology. In both fields the Princetonians carried forward the project of embracing what they saw as truth in evolutionary thinking, while limiting and explaining it in view of truths they held from religion — especially divine design, human responsibility, and human fallenness. At the very time they were engaged in church battles over biblical inerrancy and the high Calvinism of the Westminster Confession, Princeton's theologians found progressive development a fruitful notion for explicating Bible history and church history. Non-Darwinian evolutionary models not only were acceptable for explanations in biology, but found analogues in Princeton's orthodox theology, in what I call "theological orthogenesis." Still, the Princetonians were wary of the abuses of evolutionary thought, as it easily served as an excuse to do away with supernatural intervention not only in nature, but in religious experience itself. The Princeton theologians embraced a negative evolutionism — a theory of degeneration, which again was a hot topic in the evolutionary biology at the turn of the century — to counter liberal-tending paeans to ever-upward progress. Early in the new century a note of overt complaint entered Princetonian discourse about evolution — complaint against antisupernaturalism masquerading as science, complaint against a world one of Warfield's comrades described as *"evolution-mad."*

In chapter 9 we observe the breaking apart of the old consensus about theism and evolution. The various heirs of McCosh's Princeton reached a point of definite rift, as the scientists at Princeton University and especially Princeton alumnus and former professor Henry Fairfield Osborn (director of the American Museum of Natural History) took leadership in opposition to William Jennings Bryan's antievolution campaign of 1922-25. Meanwhile, university biology professor Edwin Grant Conklin lent his scientific authority to outright manifestos of theological modernism, and some seminary professors entertained public doubts about evolution. As the 1920s drew to a close, Princeton Seminary itself was torn asunder by differences of opinion as to how to deal with theological modernism, premised as it was on evolutionary concepts.

The inner drama of this narrative, and its climax in the 1920s, might suggest that evolutionism and biblical theism form an inherently unstable mixture. I consider the consequences of the story in the conclusion. While my goal is much less to prescribe normative content than to describe historical events and understandings, some clarification of thought and method for our time is not only possible but also desirable at the end of this particular story. The Princetonians do, after all, continue to function as a model, both positive and negative, for many in our day.

CHAPTER ONE

Natural History and the Moral Sphere

Dull atheist, could a giddy dance
Of atoms lawlessly hurl'd
Construct so wonderful, so wise,
So harmonized a world?

Erasmus Darwin[1]

The Horrible Vision

One summer's day in 1845, Albert B. Dod, professor of mathematics at the College of New Jersey, picked up his pen to write a review of Robert Chambers's new book, *Vestiges of the Natural History of Creation.*[2] The article appeared in the October number of the *Biblical Repertory and Princeton Review,* a highly respected theological quarterly under the firm editorial hand of Charles Hodge of Princeton Seminary. Chambers's anonymous book was the first publication to attempt to popularize an evolutionary theory in the English-speaking world. Dod's review was the first significant treatment of evolutionism to emanate from Princeton, and one of the first American reviews of the *Vestiges.*[3]

---

1. Erasmus Darwin, quoted in Charles Coulston Gillispie, *Genesis and Geology: A Study in the Relations of Scientific Thought, Natural Theology, and Social Opinions in Great Britain, 1790-1850* (New York: Harper Torchbooks, 1959; orig. 1951), p. 33.

2. Robert Chambers, *Vestiges of the Natural History of Creation* (London: J. Churchill, 1844).

3. Peter J. Bowler, *The Non-Darwinian Revolution: Reinterpreting a Historical Myth*

However pleasant the weather may have been that day, Dod's mood was by no means sunny. A pious and keen-witted man whom Charles Hodge admired for his gentle spirit and childlike faith,[4] Dod was vexed at the philosophical and religious implications of the book. His review was scathing. "Of what avail is it," he asked, "to give us the idea of a Creator, if He who created does not govern us?" Chambers gave his readers a creation of sorts — creation by a natural process of evolution — but no providence. If God were but a remote First Cause who merely set the universe to turning some vast ages ago, Dod argued, we may as well have no God at all in the here and now. Chambers's theory was a specimen of applied deism, and deism was practical atheism.[5]

The *Vestiges* magnified the reign of natural law, applying to the biological world the analogy of Newtonian physics: just as the wonder of orderliness in the inorganic world had inspired reverence for an intelligent First Cause, Chambers argued, so the discovery of lawfulness in the organic world should redound to the greater glory of God. But Dod pointed out that by Chambers's account God had created of necessity, and all things in the universe, from galactic nebulae to the minutest microbes, were bound together in the inexorable chain of cause and effect. The implication was that "the universe, in all its parts and beings, in all its processes and results, is but a stupendous machine, whirled about by its own inherent tendencies and driving on to we know not what end." The *Vestiges* so distanced God from his works that the individual soul had no solace in its Creator's attentions. Dod pressed the point to its logical entailments: adoration of the divine wisdom and power would be inappro-

---

(Baltimore: Johns Hopkins University Press, 1988), p. 11. Ryan Cameron MacPherson treats Chambers's reception in the United States in "The *Vestiges of Creation* and America's Pre-Darwinian Evolution Debates: Interpreting Theology and the Natural Sciences in Three Academic Communities" (Ph.D. diss., University of Notre Dame, 2003). One of those communities is Princeton. MacPherson emphasizes the Old School Presbyterian doctrine of divine sovereignty as the key to the Princetonian rejection of the *Vestiges*. See also his "Natural and Theological Science at Princeton: 1845-1859; *Vestiges of Creation* Meets the Scientific Sovereignty of God," *Princeton University Library Chronicle* 45 (2004): 184-236.

4. Charles Hodge, "A Brief Account of the Last Hours of Albert B. Dod" (Princeton: John T. Robinson, 1845), pamphlet, PTS Special Collections.

5. Albert Baldwin Dod, "Vestiges of the Natural History of Creation," *Biblical Repertory and Princeton Review* 17 (1845): 533. For a handy chart of the various Princeton quarterlies, see Mark A. Noll, ed., *The Princeton Theology, 1812-1921: Scripture, Science, and Theological Method from Archibald Alexander to Benjamin Breckinridge Warfield* (Grand Rapids: Baker, 1983), p. 24.

priate, for raw intelligence and raw power could serve evil as easily as good — and in a fatalistic system, evil and good had no meaning anyway. Worse, this vast, brute force took no consideration of us as individual persons. Law and order prevailed in the grand scheme of things, but this relentless mechanism left the individual unable to call upon a watchful, caring heavenly Father. Here Dod's rhetoric of moral horror reached its height: "Abandoned to the operation of general laws, that without any discernible purpose or feeling work out their results, — left to take our chance amid the prizes and the blanks, and worse than blanks, distributed by a stern undiscriminating necessity, — we see not that there is any occasion for admiration, reverence, or love towards the Creator. To love Him would be, as Spinosa says, to deny His nature. To pray to Him would be as idle as a dog baying at the moon."[6]

Clearly Dod's condemnation of the book was no cool, dispassionate dismissal. This professor of mathematics waxed eloquent in his ardor, painting a Horrible Vision of the loveless fatalism Chambers's system entailed. He appealed to the heart as well as to the intellect, drawing the reader into a lively sense of the consequences at stake. If the universe really were governed by "stern, undiscriminating necessity," then the practices of devotion and prayer were idle — or worse than idle, a pitiable, empty delusion. To the believing Christian the picture was horrible indeed.

Thus it was not the *Vestiges'* lack of empirical evidence nor its flights of speculation that troubled Dod (though he did take pains to point these out) — nor the doctrine of the transmutation of species (though he rejected that as well) — but rather the book's moral and philosophical entailments, which he viewed not as dry academic points but as matters of extreme urgency to the human heart. Did God indeed notice the fall of every sparrow, and bring forth every lily of the field, and number every hair of our heads? For Dod the vital question was religious: "In what relation then do we stand to the Creator?"[7]

Here, then, at the first appearance of a modern evolutionary theory in the English-speaking world, the point of controversy was not the "how" of origins, nor primarily the question of fit with Genesis chapters 1 and 2, but rather the religious and metaphysical issue of God's relation to his works. Chambers put this religious dimension very much in the fore-

6. Dod, "Vestiges," p. 533.
7. Dod, "Vestiges," pp. 533, 535.

front of the *Vestiges.* He had no interest in isolating the "scientific" question from the "religious" one. But note the *critical eye* that Princeton turned toward science's tribute to God. Not all paeans to divine handiwork were created equal: the philosophical tendencies and spiritual ramifications might be healthy — or they might be disastrous. For Dod, the *Vestiges* tended emphatically in the latter direction.

From Chambers's point of view, however, the *Vestiges* made a most edifying contribution to natural theology, the study of the knowledge of God accessible to all people prior to any supernatural revelation. By revealing a grand design in the origin of species, Chambers meant to bolster the teleological argument for the existence of God — that the evident purposefulness of nature implied a Designer. He intended to confirm and elevate teleology, not to promote atheism.[8] An outsider to the scientific community, he wrote the *Vestiges* to sketch out for the reading public a grand developmental view of the history of the earth and the life upon it — a panoramic spectacle that would show forth the wonderful outworking of a divine plan programmed into nature. Later overshadowed by Charles Darwin's *On the Origin of Species,* the *Vestiges* was in its time a sensation, widely read and discussed by all classes, from working men to Queen Victoria and Abraham Lincoln. According to James Secord, the book reached at least a hundred thousand readers. "Mentioned in thousands of letters and diaries, denounced and praised in pulpits, discussed on railway journeys, and annotated on an Alabama River steamboat," the *Vestiges* went through fourteen editions in Britain and twenty in the United States, creating a controversy that lasted decades. Jonathan Topham adds that it was the *Vestiges,* not Darwin's work, that made "sweeping narratives of evolutionary progress . . . central to British culture" — and that influence crossed the ocean to America.[9]

The *Vestiges* began with an exposition of the "nebular hypothesis" of

---

8. Gillispie, *Genesis and Geology,* p. 153; John M. Lynch, introduction to *"Vestiges" and the Debate before Darwin,* vol. 1, *Selected Periodical Reviews, 1844-1854* (Bristol, U.K.: Thommes Press, 2000), pp. xx-xxii.

9. James A. Secord, *Victorian Sensation: The Extraordinary Publication, Reception, and Secret Authorship of "Vestiges of the Natural History of Creation"* (Chicago: University of Chicago Press, 2001), pp. 23, 37; Jonathan R. Topham, "Science, Religion, and the History of the Book," in *Science and Religion: New Historical Perspectives,* ed. Thomas Dixon, Geoffrey Cantor, and Stephen Pumfrey (New York: Cambridge University Press, 2010), p. 224. Secord's work is widely recognized as the indispensable study of the *Vestiges,* pathbreaking in its methodology and interpretation.

Kant and Laplace, the theory that the solar system had formed out of an original cloud of stardust under the natural operation of Newtonian gravitational forces.[10] This elegant, natural-law explanation of cosmogony cut two ways, religiously speaking, as observers had been quick to point out. Laplace had earned a reputation as a notorious infidel, for when Napoleon asked him where God was in the process, he replied that he had no need of "that hypothesis." But others pointed out that natural law implied a Lawgiver; therefore an emphasis on the regularity of nature, far from banishing divine providence from the world, gave evidence of providential design on a grand scale. This was Chambers's view; he embraced the nebular theory as eminently purposeful, and therefore eminently theistic. Scientific scrutiny of the ways of God in his works became a doxological, or worship-inspiring, endeavor.[11]

Chambers's new contribution to theistic argument lay in his finding a biological parallel to the progressiveness of the physical world portrayed in the nebular theory. Unveiling the process of formation of the solar system had magnified the hand of God; so now unveiling the process of organic evolution, right up to man, would evoke similar praise for the all-wise Creator. As Newton had glorified God by revealing the simple yet grand law of gravitation, now Chambers would glorify God by tracing an equally simple and equally grand law for living things. "It is most interesting to observe into how small a field the whole of the mysteries of nature thus ultimately resolve themselves. The inorganic has one final comprehensive law, GRAVITATION. The organic, the other great department of mundane things, rests in like manner on one law, and that is, — DEVELOPMENT." Perhaps, Chambers suggested, these two overarching laws of physical existence might even resolve into one. He fairly gasped with awe at the prospect of discovering a "unity which man's wit can scarcely separate from Deity itself."[12]

Chambers thus expected his extension of doxological science into the realm of living things to please scientist and religionist alike. His his-

10. See Ronald N. Numbers, *Creation by Natural Law: Laplace's Nebular Hypothesis in American Thought* (Seattle: University of Washington Press, 1977).

11. On the entrenched tradition of "doxological science," see Theodore Dwight Bozeman, *Protestants in an Age of Science: The Baconian Ideal and Antebellum American Religious Thought* (Chapel Hill: University of North Carolina Press, 1977); Herbert Hovenkamp, *Science and Religion in America, 1800-1860* (Philadelphia: University of Pennsylvania Press, 1978); and Gillispie, *Genesis and Geology*.

12. Chambers, *Vestiges*, p. 360.

tory of the creation of life on earth presented a linear, goal-oriented, in-evitable ascent up the chain of being — concepts all welcome in the scientific and religious discourses of his day — but it substituted transmutation for special creation. In this way Chambers tried to reha-bilitate the ancient idea of evolution — a theory dating back to the pa-gan Greeks — baptizing it for the glory of God.[13]

Chambers was drawing upon a new version of teleological argu-ment, one that historian Peter Bowler has called the "idealist version of design." In contrast to William Paley's popular argument in *Natural The-ology* (1802) — that the utilitarian contrivances of specific adaptations, such as the wing for flight, bore testimony to a divine designer — from about 1830 onward proponents of the idealist argument saw more pro-found evidence of intelligence and purpose in the whole *system* of laws governing our world.[14] The idealist argument carried the additional ad-vantage of not seeking exact correspondences between science and Scripture. The scientist was freed up to find the laws behind the pro-cesses without worrying about how they fit with the Bible, for in any case law must imply a Lawgiver.[15]

But a God above nature, to whom the reign of law testified, was not necessarily the Bible's covenant God who heareth prayer. The idealist ar-gument from design could go too far, ending up in deism — or worse. The regularity of nature was one thing; rank fatalistic mechanism was quite another. This, as we have seen, was Dod's chief concern in his re-view. Though he devoted considerable space to refuting Chambers's de-velopment hypothesis, Dod reserved his strongest words for the implica-tions of utter uniformitarianism. His Horrible Vision was a picture not of a man or a woman descended from an ape,[16] but of a universe whirling

13. Bowler, *The Non-Darwinian Revolution,* pp. 59-60.

14. Richard Owen and the *Bridgewater Treatises* had set forth this line of argument in Britain in the 1830s, though it traces ultimately to the German philosophical tradition — hence the appropriateness of the term "idealist." Bowler, *The Non-Darwinian Revolution,* p. 61; David N. Livingstone, *Darwin's Forgotten Defenders: The Encounter between Evangeli-cal Theology and Evolutionary Thought* (Grand Rapids: Eerdmans; Edinburgh: Scottish Ac-ademic Press, 1987), pp. 5-6.

15. Livingstone, *Darwin's Forgotten Defenders,* pp. 4-6, 19-20.

16. The Horrible Vision, as I have called it, was a remarkably common device in philo-sophical argumentation in the early nineteenth century. Gillispie records an "outburst" of Adam Sedgwick, the British catastrophist, upon reading the *Vestiges.* Sedgwick's Horrible Vision used the image of *womankind* to highlight the moral dangers of Chambers's work: "If our glorious maidens and matrons may not soil their fingers with the dirty knife of the

on inexorably without any intervening or even superintending Providence — of mankind orphaned in a cold and fatherless cosmos.

Chambers held no brief for materialism or atheism. Where, then, did this horrible tendency to fatalism come from? Dod's answer is very instructive. The tendency sprang from a surprising source: the scientific method itself, Baconian induction, that icon of enlightenment and key to unlocking the mysteries of God's creation.

Like the many Puritans and later evangelicals who took part in the scientific revolution of the seventeenth and eighteenth centuries, antebellum American Protestants eagerly followed the inductive method Francis Bacon had set forth in his classic *Novum Organum* (1620).[17] Thanks to induction — the careful collection of data from real experience rather than from venerable thinkers such as Aristotle — early modern science had made more progress in a few generations than at any other time in history. Empirical observation and a carefulness not to run ahead of the evidence had unseated ancient misapprehensions of the natural world and dispelled many superstitions — which for Protestants included many doctrines of Roman Catholicism. Protestantism and enlightened science had moved forward arm in arm.[18] No wonder Bacon was such a hero. But at Princeton, at least, devotion to Bacon was not unqualified. In the present case the qualifications are as revealing as the general veneration of inductive method.

Dod argued that the value of induction was restricted by its range. Classical Baconianism limited induction to those phenomena presented to the senses from outside the perceiving mind, and so was incapable of transcending the material realm and its inexorable reign of cause and effect. Pure empiricism led to fatalism because of its limited purview. It provided law, but no freedom, for it dealt only with matter, not with

---

anatomist, neither may they poison the springs of joyous thought and modest feeling, by listening to the seductions of this author; who comes before them with . . . the serpent coils of a false philosophy, and asks them again to stretch out their hands and pluck forbidden fruit — to talk familiarly with him of things without raising a blush upon a modest cheek; — who tells them — that their Bible is a fable when it teaches them that they were made in the image of God — that they are the children of apes and the breeders of monsters" (Gillispie, *Genesis and Geology,* pp. 149-51). Women, after all, made more shocking progeny of apes than men did.

17. Bozeman, *Protestants,* pp. 3-4, 24-30; Hovenkamp, *Science and Religion,* pp. 23-24.

18. For a good introduction to the subject, see Keith Thomas, *Religion and the Decline of Magic* (New York: Scribner, 1971).

mind or spirit or unconditioned will. Dod found Chambers's system wanting because, following Bacon, "it makes the senses the only inlet of ideas, and induction the only instrument for reaching the truth. From this beginning atheism is the necessary conclusion." According to pure inductive empiricism, "we are acquainted with no phenomena but those of matter," and reasoning back from their effects yields only "an original, uncaused, self-existent matter" from which all that we are and all that we see evolved. Here was the age-old theory of the Greeks.[19]

In view of Bacon's materialistic limitations, Dod pressed his readers to consider other facts in the world — moral facts, mental phenomena — facts not external and material, but real nonetheless. What saved Chambers himself from the atheism of his theory, Dod said, was the influence of his "moral feelings." Any scientific (i.e., inductive) inquiry was incomplete if it ignored the facts of consciousness. Just here lay the force of the Horrible Vision. It was not a mere rhetorical flourish, a sentimental appeal for a sentimental age; rather it was the best, most fitting way to call upon the testimony of the moral realm by agitating the moral feelings, pressing their reality upon the reader's awareness. To feel the horror of the vision was proof of a universe higher and deeper than the materialist's universe. That is why Dod and many others painted such a vivid picture of the desolations of materialism, the prospect of a universe without goodness, without truth and nobility — "a giddy dance of atoms lawlessly hurled." The human heart responded in dismay to such a prospect of hopelessness — and this nightmarish feeling was direct, incontrovertible evidence of the reality of moral things. The experience was the proof.

Philosophically speaking, Dod was alerting his readers to the importance of a dualistic metaphysic — the distinction between matter and mind. He objected to the *Vestiges'* monism, its methodological blindness to the spiritual realm. In its metaphysics, Dod argued, the *Vestiges* harked back to the infidel philosophy of Spinoza.[20] Now, to conjure up the image of philosophy's arch-rationalist to indict Chambers for undue empiricism may appear a bit muddled, but Dod knew what he was doing. The link between Chambers and Spinoza was their monism — their metaphysics, not their patently dissimilar epistemologies. They started from radically different premises but arrived at the same bleak conclu-

19. Dod, "Vestiges," p. 532.
20. Dod, "Vestiges," p. 533.

sion. To love the God of the *Vestiges* "would be, as Spinosa says, to deny His nature. To pray to Him would be as idle as a dog baying at the moon." The desolation of Spinoza's rationalism was the same as the desolation of Chambers's empiricism. "It is instructive to observe how a pure materialism, and a pure idealism meet in the same final result, though reaching it by different roads," Dod commented. Both systems were "destitute of all moral purposes and aims," landing us in pure fatalism. This arose from the necessity inherent in the law of cause and effect that governs nature, and the necessity inherent in the laws of rationality. A monism of mind was no better than a monism of matter: in either case no agency existed free from the tyranny of cause and effect. "If we are entirely subject to this law, then we have no philosophy possible, but to etherealize matter and become ideal pantheists, or to make mind only an error in terms and run into materialistic fatalism. These are the only two courses left open to us, and it seems to us a matter of small moment which is taken. We see little to choose between the spectre world of Spinosa, and the sty of Epicurus. When a man has taken away virtue from us we care not what also he takes or leaves."[21]

Here lay a philosophical concern well worth noting. Metaphysical dualism was utterly basic to the Princetonians' understanding of theology, science, and indeed all fields of learning. They made this point time and again, with an insistence that was at times shrill, at times smug. They alternated between sounding an alarm of impending danger and pronouncing an unperturbed confidence in the unassailability of their position. The shrillness of the alarm is explained in part by the function of the Horrible Vision as moral appeal; hyperbole is, after all, a useful and accepted device, and serves well to call forth moral feeling, thus impressing the mind with the reality of its effects. But there was more to it. The Princetonians believed in system building, and systems were built upon foundations. A small error in the basement could produce a large deviation several stories up; so the Princetonians always looked to the foundations to assess the security of the house. A fundamental error was worth squawking about. Systems could present a very impressive aspect to the unsuspecting, as by dint of good logic they built up a large and well-proportioned edifice; but unless the foundations were sound, the building would eventually collapse on its sorry inhabitants. Dod's focus on the philosophical underpinnings of Chambers's evolutionism, more than on

21. Dod, "Vestiges," p. 553.

the evolutionary theory itself, was no deviation from the norm. Attention to foundations characterized the Princetonian approach to all sorts of questions.

The Princeton College mathematician charted a clear course in answer to the philosophical challenge he espied in the *Vestiges*. It was not enough, he said, to take on each particular system of materialism that caught the public eye. It was not enough to expose its "scientific blunders." For, "though we may thus refute one, we leave the way still open for the introduction of another." Symptomatic treatment did not strike at the cause — Dod wanted preventive medicine. In an almost prophetic vision of the Darwinian controversies ahead, Dod admitted that while he had refuted the scientific claims of the *Vestiges*, "we have not shown that some other explorer in the same direction may not be more successful."[22] Chambers failed in the eyes of scientists and theologians alike to revive a viable evolutionary doctrine; but might not some abler proponent make a more convincing case on the same naturalistic grounds? This, of course, Darwin did. He presented such a mass of data, such a broad range of material induction, that his readers could not dismiss his theories for lack of evidence, as they had the *Vestiges*.[23] Fourteen years before the publication of the *Origin*, however, Dod offered an antidote against any naturalistic theory of the universe, whatever empirical, inductive detail the theory might amass. "It is among the facts of consciousness," he declared, "that we must find the evidence which sets aside this, and all other systems of like kind." He explained: "We are undoubtedly subject, in a degree, to the same kind of restraint which governs the physical world. We are placed within the range of the law of cause and effect, and form thus a part of nature. . . . But if besides the world of necessity there exists also a world of freedom, and if these two worlds manifest their interpenetration in man's consciousness, then another philosophy is not only possible but necessary, and materialism and idealism are both discredited as partial and incomplete." The answer was very simple: once our observation is extended beyond the external world so as to include mental phenomena, "consciousness decides the question." All that was

22. Dod, "Vestiges," p. 553.

23. Bowler has argued pointedly against viewing the *Vestiges* as a lesser precursor of the *Origin*, for the two evolutionisms differed enormously in essence and entailments (*The Non-Darwinian Revolution*, pp. 53, 60). That observation notwithstanding, both were naturalistic theories of evolution, and for Princeton their common antisupernaturalism far outweighed their technical differences.

needed to overthrow any and every materialistic view was "the simplest case of perception, the transformation of an external object into an act of thought or will." One act of perception would disprove the monistic claim that all was matter or all was mind, for perception — which involved both subject and object — bridged the two realms.[24]

Dod's response to the *Vestiges* foreshadowed several important aspects of the Princetonian answer to the evolution question after Darwin, and indeed well into the twentieth century. He warned that atheism was a necessary consequence of any system that excluded moral ends, or teleology — and so presaged Charles Hodge's famous conclusion in *What Is Darwinism?* (1874): "It is atheism." He distinguished the man Chambers from the theory he proposed, prefiguring Hodge's separation of Darwin's personal religious beliefs from the logical consequences of his theory.[25] Dod looked to "the facts of consciousness" to overthrow monistic metaphysics, a characteristic argument of the Scottish Common-Sense philosophy of which James McCosh was the last great American exponent. Dod identified materialism and idealism as the monistic extremes between which a dualistic metaphysic and a dualistic epistemology must position themselves, and took notice of the affinities between evolutionism and monism — a point that was to become very important in Princeton's partial turn away from evolutionism in the early twentieth century. And he used the Horrible Vision to impress his readers with the reality of moral things, while warning of the desolations of a godless universe — a warning that echoed in the rhetoric of the fundamentalist controversies after World War I.

An assessment of the philosophical implications of evolutionism thus not only preoccupied the Princetonians from the first, but remained remarkably unchanged in its basic concerns and strategies for many decades to come. Interestingly enough, none of the later Princetonian writers on the evolution question cited Dod at all. His review simply expressed a system of thought and commitments shared among Princetonians even of differing philosophical backgrounds.

24. Dod, "Vestiges," pp. 553-54.
25. Charles Hodge, *What Is Darwinism?* (New York: Scribner, Armstrong, and Co., 1874), pp. 176-77.

Chambers's Evolutionism

Although Princeton rejected Chambers's evolutionary theory because of its philosophical and religious implications, it is instructive to analyze the particulars of the theory as a scientific explanation of the history of life. Certain points at which it differed from Darwin's later theory became, in the post-Darwinian period, the very foundations of Princeton's qualified acceptance of evolutionism. The *Vestiges* was actually more characteristic of the so-called Darwinian revolution than Darwin's *Origin of Species* was. This is Peter Bowler's important insight, and the Princetonians appear to have typified the non-Darwinian revolution Bowler describes.[26]

What, then, were the salient features of Chambers's evolutionism in contrast to Darwin's? Most prominent was what Bowler calls "the growth analogy." The very term "evolution" originally referred to the growth of an embryo, the unfolding of its potentiality into the mature form. Clearly this usage denoted purpose, teleology: the original fertilized egg contained within it the perfections of the adult, but in potential only. It was a "perfect germ" that nevertheless had to undergo a process to instantiate itself fully. Its potential unrolled, or evolved, over time. Evolution under this concept was the unfolding of a plan. It preserved intact the older concept of a fixed pattern or hierarchy of existence, from the mineral to the vegetable to the animal to the spiritual, and added only the dimension of time. Thus, though this idea of evolution emphasized diachronic progress, it preserved a basically static concept of a divine order of existence. Dynamism prevailed in the development from potential to actual, but stasis prevailed in the pattern or plan that came thereby into actuality. The embryological analogy lay at the heart of Chambers's grand developmental vision, captured in his telling phrase, "the universal gestation of nature."[27]

Chambers's view cannot properly be called a growth *analogy,* for in it embryology was of a piece with natural history. The relation was real, not metaphorical. Chambers advocated and was probably largely responsible for popularizing the notion that an embryo's development not

26. Bowler, *The Non-Darwinian Revolution,* pp. 4-5, 48-49, 60.

27. Bowler, *The Non-Darwinian Revolution,* pp. 4-5, 48-49, 60. Bowler quotes Chambers ("the universal gestation of nature") on p. 50. See also Arthur O. Lovejoy, *The Great Chain of Being: A Study in the History of an Idea* (New York: Harper and Row, 1960; orig. 1936).

only paralleled the evolutionary history of its species, but in a very real sense reenacted it.[28] In later years the German biologist Ernst Haeckel gave this view its classic formulation, "ontogeny recapitulates phylogeny." According to Bowler, the embryonic connection was characteristic of the *Vestiges,* but decidedly not of the *Origin.* On the growth analogy, variation from the established type was an *addition to* growth, a step onward toward a predetermined goal, rather than a random *disturbance of* growth, deviating in unforeseen ways from the type.[29] This distinction is difficult, but crucial, involving two related but separable issues. Unpacking them can help clarify the state of the evolution question in the 1840s and the future field of contest when Darwinism came on the scene.

Variation as an addition to growth carried with it, first and rather obviously, the element of direction or purpose. The embryo grew toward a predetermined goal. To thinkers interested in the authority of the Bible, this was a familiar concept. The embryo was like the seed, producing "first the blade, then the ear, after that the full corn in the ear" (Mark 4:28 KJV). Evangelicals welcomed such analogies between the spiritual and earthly realms: here was another way in which nature testified to her God. The idea of development over time came as no sudden shock to them. Such were the ways of God as described parabolically by Jesus himself, with reference to the life and growth of the church. So the growth analogy was, in its organic imagery as well as its teleological entailments, most welcome.

Variation as an addition to growth also meant that the embryological connection was real. As the embryo grew toward its predetermined goal, it advanced through distinct stages, each of which constituted a step up the ladder of being. The individual hopped off the ladder, so to speak, at the level corresponding to its adult form.[30] Thus a fish embryo developed gill slits and a tail, but did not grow limbs and lungs. A

---

28. The idea did not originate with Chambers, however, but with Karl Ernst von Baer and Louis Agassiz. See Michael Ruse, *Monad to Man: The Concept of Progress in Evolutionary Biology* (Cambridge: Harvard University Press, 1996), pp. 111-12.

29. Bowler, *The Non-Darwinian Revolution,* p. 11. Haeckel occupies a prime place in Bowler's story of the non-Darwinian revolution, for as a self-proclaimed Darwinian he propounded a fundamentally non-Darwinian theory (the growth analogy), confusing the issue for generations to come.

30. Chambers, *Vestiges,* p. 212, gives a diagram that conveys this concept exactly. Cf. the "trees" Bowler reproduces (especially from the works of Ernst Haeckel) in *The Non-Darwinian Revolution.*

lizard embryo, by contrast, first developed gill slits and a tail, looking re-markably like a fish embryo, but then grew lungs and limbs. And a hu-man embryo passed through both stages, but went on to lose the tail and develop opposable thumbs, binocular vision, a very large brain, and the other physical attributes of humanity. Thus the embryonic model of evo-lution described not a mere parallelism between ontogeny (the growth of the individual embryo) and phylogeny (the history of the whole species), but a real connection. The individual relived the evolutionary history of the race. The embryonic stages allowed for the development of adult forms and preserved the pattern of past progress, showing where and how additions to growth carried life history up the ladder of being.[31]

It is clear, then, how fundamentally different Chambers's evolution-ism was from Darwin's later theory. The growth analogy at the center of the *Vestiges* preserved "exactly those features of the creationist view of na-ture that Darwin challenged": orderliness and teleology. Darwin posited a process of random variation, a haphazard disturbance of growth patterns that environmental conditions then either favored or disfavored in the struggle for existence — random variation coupled with selection by na-ture rather than by the action of divine will — in stark contrast with Chambers's "preordained unfolding of a rationally ordered plan."[32]

"The evolution question," even when limited to the question of the origin of species, is not a simple matter. The very concept of transmuta-tion is less precise than it appears at a glance. Transmutation by salta-tion is so abrupt and so large a change as to seem quite miraculous — not much distinguishable from fiat creation. And transmutation by tiny gradations, though it may fit better with naturalistic probabilities, is not without its own explanatory problems, such as how variations in an indi-vidual organism can affect an entire population. Add to this that none of these terms was defined in the mid–nineteenth century, and that the sci-ence of genetics was many decades off — and it is easy indeed to see why the evolution question was so fuzzy. Did Chambers's version of evolution really have more in common with Darwinism than it did with creationism? It depends on what aspect of the theory we consider. They were unlike in their relations to teleology — this is Bowler's emphasis. They were alike, however, in their advocacy of transmutation of species, a brute ancestry for man, and an uninterrupted reign of natural law.

31. Bowler, *The Non-Darwinian Revolution*, pp. 10-14, 57-58.
32. Bowler, *The Non-Darwinian Revolution*, pp. 50-51.

Dod and Princeton did not embrace the evolutionism of the *Vestiges,* despite its possible selling points to evangelicals. Its fatalistic and materialistic entailments rendered it profoundly unacceptable, and its scientific merits were scanty anyway. The book also failed to convert the larger reading public to evolutionism. But it did popularize the concept of progressive evolution,[33] and it had established the terms of debate on the evolution question when Darwin appeared on the scene.

In the meantime, the developmental views of another European scientist received a hearty welcome at Princeton. Darwinism did not become a serious intellectual concern in America until after the Civil War, and Chambers's evolutionism made no significant inroads — but in the mid-1850s Princeton hired a Swiss geologist who, like Chambers, embraced the nebular hypothesis and posited a law of development for the organic and inorganic worlds. He brought developmentalism to Princeton in a form far more palatable than Chambers's theory.

The Beatific Vision

Just three years after Dod wrote his review, the revolutions of 1848 in Europe displaced Arnold Henry Guyot from his position on the faculty of the Neuchâtel Academy in Switzerland. In 1855 Guyot became the first professor of geography and geology at the College of New Jersey, and until the 1870s he served as the resident expert on earth science for both the college and the seminary. A close friend of Louis Agassiz, a committed Calvinist,[34] and a highly regarded scientist in his day, Guyot was a pio-

33. Topham, "Science, Religion," p. 224.

34. Guyot's faith was almost legendary. Francis Landey Patton described him as "a man of humble faith in God," and "simple as a child." Patton, in "Exercises at the Unveiling of a Memorial Tablet to Arnold Guyot, Ph.D., LL.D., in Marquand Chapel, Princeton, N.J., Tuesday, June 10th, 1890" (Princeton: C. S. Robinson and Co., 1890), p. 14. Cf. James Dwight Dana, "Biographical Memoir of Prof. Arnold Guyot," from the *Smithsonian Report* for 1886-87 (Washington, D.C.: Smithsonian Institution, 1889), p. 720; Leonard Chester Jones, "Arnold Henry Guyot" (pamphlet reproduced from Union College faculty papers, vol. 23, 1930, PU Archives), p. 7. The preaching of Rev. Samuel Petit-Pierre in 1827 so affected Guyot that he planned to forsake a scientific career, for which he had been preparing at the University of Karlsruhe, and go into the ministry. But in Berlin, where he had begun his theological training, Karl Ritter's integration of evangelical faith and earth science led him to devote his energies to furthering Ritter's "beatific vision" (Livingstone, *Darwin's Forgotten Defenders,* p. 23).

neer in the study of glaciology. His other interests included physical geography, weather forecasting, cartography, and the pedagogy of geography. His extensive meteorological measurements and his work for the U.S. Geological Survey secured a lasting place for him in American science. His revolutionary texts, maps, and charts remained in print decades after his death. His wall maps and atlases won the Medal of Progress at the Vienna Exposition in 1873 and the Gold Medal in Paris in 1888. Still more enduring monuments to his scientific prowess are three Mount Guyots, the Guyot Glacier in Alaska, and even a Guyot Crater on the moon.[35]

Shortly after Guyot's arrival in America, the Lowell Institute in Boston invited him, thanks to Agassiz, to give a series of nightly addresses based on his Swiss lectures. Guyot was so new to this country that he delivered the addresses in his native French; scientific subjects and the latest European ideas were so popular in Boston that the talks appeared in full in the *Boston Traveller* after each session, translated into English by a Harvard professor. Guyot's lectures attracted many of the luminaries of New England, including Longfellow, Hawthorne, and Horace Mann. They were immediately published in book form as *The Earth and Man*. The original edition of 5,000 quickly sold out. Guyot's book attracted so many readers that it was reprinted in America more than thirty times, reaching into the twentieth century. It also went through five British editions and was translated into French, German, and Russian.[36]

In addition to its scientific merits, Guyot's treatment of earth science was both novel and edifying — two excellent qualifications in antebellum America. An advertisement in the front of the book raved that Guyot presented science like a preacher. His lectures were lively and thought provoking, glorifying divine providence in the physical world. Going beyond the conventional doxological glosses so common at the end of Anglophone scientific treatises, Guyot made the idea of purpose a guiding principle in his whole approach to earth science.

35. Alexander Leitch, *A Princeton Companion* (Princeton: Princeton University Press, 1978), pp. 232-33; Jones, "Arnold Henry Guyot," p. 5. Philip K. Wilson is currently at work on a scientific biography of Guyot. In the meantime, see his "Influences of Alexander von Humboldt's 'Kosmos' in Arnold Guyot's 'Earth and Man' (1849)," *Omega: Indian Journal of Science and Religion* 4 (2005): 33-51, and "Arnold Guyot (1807-1884) and the Pestalozzian Approach to Geology Education," *Eclogae Geologicae Helvetiae* 92 (1999): 321-25.

36. Jones, "Arnold Henry Guyot," p. 3; Wilson, "Influences," p. 34; Wilson, "*Guyot* of Guyot Hall" (leaflet for the Department of Geosciences, Princeton University, 2007).

In his introductory address Guyot proclaimed that geography "should not only describe, it should compare, it should interpret, it should rise to the *how* and the *wherefore* of the phenomena it describes."[37] He described the globe in terms of its life, its "physiology," an interplay of vital relations between the physical environment and its living inhabitants. Guyot took an organic view of geography, treating the globe in its relations rather than in the isolation and systematization of its parts. The earth was a pulsating, changing, growing totality that, like an animal's body, lost its most important aspect when dissected and dead. Guyot confessedly derived this organic view of the world from German *Naturphilosophie,* especially as he learned it in Berlin from Alexander von Humboldt and Karl Ritter. As a view of the natural world bound up with the romantic philosophy of Goethe and the post-Kantian idealists, *Naturphilosophie* emphasized the intimate connections between science, religion, ethics, and aesthetics.[38] Science remained truly "natural philosophy." In this way the German school differed significantly from the British empirical tradition, with its characteristic Baconian inductivism. Following the German view, Guyot treated the "wherefore" of his geology as indispensable. He said, "We must elevate ourselves to the moral world to understand the physical world, which has no meaning except by it and for it."[39] The connection between the physical and moral spheres went beyond mere parallelism to an inherent, organic relation. It was a "universal law of all that exists in finite nature, not to have in itself, either the reason or the entire aim of its own existence," but to find that aim instead in the totality of things, "of which the plan and idea go infinitely beyond it." Here clearly was the influence of German idealism. But Guyot's idea was no detached castle in the air; it had concrete, earthly meaning. There was a specific way in which each being found its place in the totality of things, for each served as the basis for the levels of existence above it. The geographic environment existed not only for itself, but also as a home for the plant and the animal. They, in turn, served with it as "the condition of the existence of man," the crown of earthly creation. In man's hands the environment transcended its own nature,

37. Arnold Henry Guyot, *The Earth and Man: Lectures on Comparative Physical Geography, in Its Relation to the History of Mankind,* trans. C. C. Felton (Boston: Gould, Kendall, and Lincoln, 1849), pp. 3-4.

38. On *Naturphilosophie* see A. Gode von Aesch, *Natural Science in German Romanticism* (New York: Columbia University Press, 1941), and Ruse, *Monad to Man,* pp. 64-72.

39. Guyot, *The Earth and Man,* p. 11.

serving as an instrument in his education, performing "in his service functions more exalted and more noble than its own nature" but "for which it was made." The life of the earth, from mineral to man, was thus an intricate network of means and ends, in which each part needed the other to complete its existence, its created purpose. And in like manner the creation itself was not a cosmos unto itself, but found its completion in the Creator. "It is, then, the superior being that solicits, so to speak, the creation of the inferior being, and associates it to his own functions; and it is correct to say that inorganic nature is made for organized nature, and the whole globe for man, as both are made for God, the origin and end of all things."[40] In Guyot's beatific vision of creation, design was not just a gloss on existence, but an integral part of it. It was not something we inferred from being; it inhered in being and connected all being together and to God himself. Science's doxology was the song of creation itself, creation's very heartbeat.[41]

The Earth and Man undertook its lofty task by first describing the physiographic form of the continents and seas, then showing how they interacted with human history. Then, to display "these great organs in their operation," that is, "in life, acting and reacting upon each other," Guyot introduced the fundamental law that undergirded his entire geology, the law of progressive development. All historical progress, according to Guyot — again revealing the idealistic underpinnings of his science — was a *development,* propelled by the interaction of differences or unlike conditions. Guyot's dialectic was not abstract; it proceeded in both the growth of the individual organism and the history of life on the globe. Here was, in other words, a deliberate use of the growth analogy. As an embryo began in a state of homogeneity (as a cluster of undifferentiated cells) and then specialized into various interdependent organs to form a harmonious whole, so the earth and the life upon it developed from simplicity to complex interrelatedness. Individual species, whole continents, and even human societies developed in this common way.[42]

It is striking how much Guyot sounds like Chambers. Both the *Vestiges* and *The Earth and Man* undertook to show forth the Creator's glory in his works. Both posited a grand, universal law of development

40. Guyot, *The Earth and Man,* p. 11.

41. For the roots of Guyot's ideas in his studies at the Friedrich-Wilhelm-Universität Berlin, especially under Humboldt, Ritter, Hegel, Ranke, Steffans, and Neander, see Wilson, "Influences," pp. 35-39.

42. Dana, "Biographical Memoir," p. 705.

to explain the history of life on earth, explicitly appealing to the analogy of embryonic growth. Both conceived of divine design in idealist terms, locating it not in particular creaturely contrivances such as eyes for sight or wings for flight, but in the vast, cosmic plan of existence that progressively came to be. But Guyot, unlike Chambers, received Princeton's unqualified approval. In his first months in the States he made use of a letter of introduction to Charles Hodge, and with the publication of *The Earth and Man* Princeton College considered Guyot such a valuable prospect that the trustees created a chair for him before securing permanent funding, confident that Guyot's eminence would attract donations for the endowment.[43] Hodge soon incorporated Guyot's geological views into his theology lectures. In the 1860s Princeton Seminary invited Guyot to give a perennial series of extra-curricular lectures on the bearing of physical science on theological questions.[44] He was, in short, immediately embraced by the professors at Princeton as one of their own, whereas Chambers's work met with swift condemnation. Evidently certain differences between them were more important than their similarities.

What distinguished Guyot's idealist progressionism from Chambers's version? In the first place, Guyot was a reputable scientist who handled the subject matter of geology with obvious authority. He had an earned doctorate from the renowned University of Berlin, having studied under the greatest luminaries of that time in the fields of geography and geology. He had held the position of Professor of Physical Geography and Universal History at the Academy of Neuchâtel, and had already authored several technical scientific publications. Chambers was a dabbler — a dedicated amateur, but a dabbler nonetheless. He made his living as the editor of an influential weekly periodical in Edinburgh, and with his brother published an amazingly wide array of handy reference books, from biographies to travel guides to religious tracts.[45] Although he took a prolonged leave of absence from Edinburgh to prepare the *Ves-*

---

43. Dana, "Biographical Memoir," p. 705; Thomas Jefferson Wertenbaker, *Princeton, 1746-1896* (Princeton: Princeton University Press, 1946), p. 274.

44. Arnold Henry Guyot, *Creation; or, The Biblical Cosmogony in the Light of Modern Science* (New York: Charles Scribner's Sons, 1884), pp. viii-ix; John O. Means, "The Narrative of the Creation in Genesis," *Bibliotheca Sacra* (1855): 323-38; Charles Hodge, *Systematic Theology* (New York: Scribners, 1872-73; reprint, Grand Rapids: Eerdmans, 1993), 1:573; Leitch, *A Princeton Companion*, pp. 232-33.

45. Gillispie, *Genesis and Geology*, pp. 159-60.

tiges, Chambers simply did not have the command of the material that a career scientist like Guyot did. Chambers also took on too much, seeking impressionistic analogies between scientific disciplines that would show the universality of law and development, but failing to impress his scientific readers.

But the difference was more than a matter of credentials and careful attention to established facts. For one thing, Guyot was a catastrophist, Chambers a uniformitarian. Where Chambers tried to explain the progress of the ages in terms of the uniform operation of natural laws still in operation today, without any breaks or miracles, Guyot interpreted the geologic record as a series of creations and demolitions in which God did indeed work in an orderly way through secondary causes, but not without significant breaks. The world process executed God's decree, but there was still a place in the world process for divine intervention. Guyot's Creator was both a God of the process and a God of the gaps. So where Chambers's view implied deism or pantheism — either an aloof God who set up the process but now does not intervene, or a God so present that he (it?) is identified with nature and natural law — Guyot's view provided room for both natural law (by divine decree) *and* divine intervention. These points were more than mere implications; both writers explicitly owned the religious entailments of their views.

Guyot, like Chambers, embraced the nebular hypothesis as a Newtonian-style explanation of how God made the worlds. But the Swiss geologist infused his Newtonian mechanism with idealist organicism, so that terms of *life* and *relation* were as important as terms of structure and function.[46] He took Newton beyond the machine analogy to a complete growth analogy. Chambers, who with Guyot likened the development of species to the growth of an embryo, still propounded an essentially mechanistic explanation. Guyot's idealism was more complete than was Chambers's, and so, in turn, his growth analogy was truer. Here is the resolution of the irony we observed earlier. Princeton rejected Chambers and yet accepted the growth analogy and idealist design, but Princeton took its growth analogy from Guyot, not Chambers.

And of course, Guyot differed from Chambers on the evolution question per se, the transmutation of species. He sang the praises of development, but maintained all the while that the relation between forms was

---

46. Following Humboldt and Ritter, Guyot stressed the interconnectedness *(Zusammenhang)* of all things in God's creation. Wilson, "Influences," p. 37.

ideal, not genetic.[47] How else could the higher form, coming later in time, "solicit" the appearance of the lower? In the unfolding of the plan of God, time was of the essence; but in the plan itself, the ideal order of things, time was inconsequential — indeed, the order of time was reversed. The last was first — last in time, first in priority. It is no wonder that Bowler regards the growth analogy, which Guyot held in a peculiarly pure form, as inimical to the goallessness of Darwinism.[48]

Guyot lectured for three decades at Princeton on the harmony of Genesis and geology, but did not publish his views until 1884, the last year of his life, when they appeared in a little book called *Creation; or, The Biblical Cosmogony in the Light of Modern Science.* There he explained that he had not set out originally to prove anything concerning the bearing of science on Scripture. As early as 1840 he had dismissed the attempts of others as "entirely inadequate" and resigned himself to wait for "more light" — to follow his scientific studies and leave the question of how they bore on Scripture for a later day when more facts were in. But after preparing a lecture on creation for a public course on physical geography in Neuchâtel, Guyot recalled, "it flashed upon my mind that the outlines I had been tracing, guided by the results of scientific inquiry, then available, were precisely those of the grand history given in the First Chapter of Genesis." In the early 1850s he expanded upon that initial insight and took the opportunity to plumb the depths of philosophical and religious meaning that the light of science revealed in Genesis. The resulting harmony of science and Scripture remained basically unchanged in outline to the end of his career.[49]

Guyot's published understanding of the respective purposes of Scripture and science is worth noting. He believed the Bible to be intended for the benefit of our spiritual life, not for the teaching of science. It was cast in the simple, nontechnical language of plain people, so that however advanced a society might be, the Bible would speak to it meaningfully. He called Genesis 1 a "grand poem," rhythmic, symmetrical, and

---

47. Cf. Ruse, *Monad to Man,* p. 71: "Just as German Progressionism led [the *Naturphilosophen*] to evolutionism, it just as firmly led them away again." He quotes Hegel (p. 72): "Nature is to be regarded as a *system of stages,* one arising necessarily from the other and being the proximate truth of the stage from which it results: but it is not generated *naturally* out of the other but only in the inner Idea which constitutes the ground of Nature."

48. Bowler, *The Non-Darwinian Revolution,* p. 51.

49. Guyot, *Creation,* pp. vi-vii; Numbers, *Creation by Natural Law,* pp. 92-94.

profound, and he cautioned his readers not to "seek from the Bible science which it does not intend to teach." Nevertheless, Guyot did not regard the statements of Scripture as irrelevant to scientific knowledge, or as pertaining to a transcendent order that had nothing whatever to do with the earthly order. The words of the Bible conveyed spiritual truth, but that truth would not contradict the truths of science. And more to the point, biblical revelation uniquely legitimated scientific inquiry. Guyot argued that faith in the doctrine of creation *ex nihilo,* revealed in Genesis 1, provided the only secure basis for science. Apart from a fundamental distinction between the Creator and his creatures, "pantheism and materialism are at the door, with all their internal impossibilities" — here Guyot appealed to rational concerns — "and with all the contradictions they engender in the bosom of a free, moral, spiritual being, in the heart of humanity" — here was a moral appeal not unlike Dod's. But once we "accept, on *trust,* the truth of creation as an ultimate fact, not to be reached by any reasoning process," both the mind and the heart are enlightened with the true knowledge of "the relations of the universe" as well as the religious relations of humankind to God. These fundamental truths — creation out of nothing and a God distinct from nature — Guyot regarded as truths inaccessible to mere reasoned inquiry into the natural world, truths "which without the sanction of God's word were doomed to remain simple hypotheses, incapable of proof."[50]

So Guyot set up scientific and scriptural study as separate domains, yet straddled them with the Anselmian principle of believing in order that we may know. Faith and knowledge were at once distinct and inseparable.

With this understanding Guyot set out to show how natural science could open Genesis 1 to reveal its deep spiritual meaning, while at the same time answering the question of whether the Bible's account was "a sort of parable" or a reliable set of "facts which correspond to those furnished by the results of scientific inquiry."[51]

On the assumption that the Bible's truthfulness was not at issue, but only the question of what the passage at hand *meant,* Guyot identified the most obvious difficulties facing a reconciliation of science with the creation story. The Bible spoke of "days," each with evening and morning, before the appearance of the sun to measure those days; of heaven as a

50. Guyot, *Creation,* p. 32. In this connection Guyot cited Heb. 11.
51. Guyot, *Creation,* pp. 22-23.

firmament or vault somehow separating waters above it from the waters on the earth; of plants growing before there was sunlight to make growth possible. Such difficulties, he noted, had driven some Christians to treat the story as a myth, true in a spiritual sense but not in any physical sense. Guyot found this option extreme, for the text itself certainly seemed to purport to be some kind of veridical report of how the heavens and earth came to be, however untechnical its approach and however dominant the spiritual aspect of its message. There had to be some way to square Genesis with the established facts of geology.[52] Were it not for the sequencing problem centering especially around the creation of the sun, it would be easy to regard the creative "days" as geological ages, and be done with it. Guyot found the "gap" theory, a frequent alternative to the day-age theory, less attractive. According to the gap theory, Genesis 1:1 described the original creation of matter, and the verses from Genesis 1:2 on described a *re*fashioning of the universe after it had been destroyed at the fall of Lucifer. Between the first two verses of the Bible, in other words, was a gap of aeons of time that the record of creation passed over in silence. Proponents of the gap theory reasoned that the geological ages were inconsequential in the divine plan of redemption, and so were left out of the account. To Guyot this seemed a theory of last resort if ever there was one, presumably because it had no textual warrant whatever, but even more so because it rendered all geology and astronomy utterly meaningless to the creation story.[53]

Dissatisfied with the range of options, Guyot had abandoned the question for a time. But he found new insight in an unlikely place: Laplace's "nebular hypothesis." Genesis 2:4, which Guyot regarded as a concluding statement of the account in chapter 1 rather than an introductory statement to the story of chapter 2, gave him his textual warrant: "These are the generations of the heavens and the earth." According to this reading, the creation story concerned the celestial bodies and the earth together. It occurred to Guyot that Laplace, following Newton, had found a unitary process for the formation of stars and planets — the heavens and the earth. And that process of nebular concentration, separation, and cooling also provided the key to unlocking the problem of the sun's

52. Guyot, *Creation*, pp. 24-28.

53. Guyot, *Creation*, p. 49, appears to allude to the gap theory, among others. For an explanation of the theory and a detailed account of its fortunes, see Ronald L. Numbers, *The Creationists: The Evolution of Scientific Creationism* (Berkeley: University of California Press, 1993).

order in the creation story. Guyot put the two together in the following way, which became, according to Ronald Numbers, the most popular harmonization of Genesis and geology in nineteenth-century America.[54]

In the miracle of miracles, creation out of nothing, God called into existence a cloud of gaseous matter that he then fashioned into the heavens and the earth in the developmental process of six creative "days." In the primordial cloud the earth was indeed "without form and void"; it had no shape, no definition. Guyot noted that the Hebrew word for "waters" sometimes referred to vapor — so in truth, "the Spirit of God was brooding upon the waters." Guyot read that verse as a solemn declaration of the distinctness of the Creator from his creation. When on the first day God said, "Let there be light," the nebula became luminous with the onset of movement and chemical action — the first activity of matter. Acting under the force of gravitation, the cloud began to concentrate itself around heavy centers, separating itself into distinct luminous clouds. This was the separation of light from darkness. The space between the nebulae was the biblical "firmament" — Guyot regarded the Vulgate *firmamentum,* indicating a solid vault, as an unfortunate intrusion of Egyptian thought into the classical translation; the Hebrew word was better rendered "expanse." The waters below the expanse constituted the nebula that later became our galaxy; the waters above were the galaxies of deep space.[55] The mass that became the earth spun off from the sun, and as it cooled there developed around the molten core a solid crust, continents and oceans on the surface, and a still luminous atmosphere surrounding it: the "photosphere." During this stage (day three) the first primitive plants appeared, lit not by the sun, which was still invisible to the earth's surface, but by the earth's own photosphere. Thus day four's appearance of the sun, moon, and stars described really the *dis*appearance of the photosphere, so that the light from the celestial sources became visible from the earth, establishing regular patterns of days, seasons, and years.[56]

54. Numbers, *Creation by Natural Law,* chapter 8. Guyot's view was popularized by James Dwight Dana of Yale, since Guyot held off publishing his harmonization until the last years of his life, and fretted over it. See also James Dwight Dana, review of *Creation; or, The Biblical Cosmogony in the Light of Modern Science,* by Arnold Guyot, *Bibliotheca Sacra* 42 (April 1885): 201-24.

55. Guyot cited Ps. 148 for supporting evidence (*Creation,* p. 37).

56. Guyot, *Creation,* pp. 43-93. Guyot was not, by the way, the first at Princeton to embrace the nebular theory. Stephen Alexander, professor of astronomy at the college, had

In the rhythm of six creative days Guyot found a symmetry as meaningful as it was beautiful. He noticed that Moses had divided the week into two sections of three days each of work, preceded by a prologue and followed by a seventh day of rest. The third and sixth days were further divided into two parts each. The Bible's choice of verbs was illuminating: while the text routinely spoke of "forming" or "making" (Hebrew *'āśāh*), only at three points — three very significant points — did it speak of "creating" *(bārā')*. Those points were distributed symmetrically (in the prologue and at the end of days three and six) and philosophically, for they described the introduction of three irreducible domains of reality: matter, life, and spirit.[57] In the prologue God created the original stuff of the cosmos out of nothing; at the end of the third day God created plants, the first and lowest form of life in the chain of being; and at the end of the sixth day God created man in his own image, that is, with a spiritual nature. The history of the cosmos thus comprised two great eras: the era of matter, when the environment for life was prepared, and the era of life, when the living theater for human history was prepared. At the end of each era was a creation that formed a prophecy of the age to come: primitive plants in day three foreshadowed the dawn of the era of life, when the whole range of plants and animals would appear; and the creation of human beings in day six presaged a new realm of activity, the moral realm of human history. The seventh day, in which God rested from his creative labors, had no evening and morning; it had not yet ended. It was the era of human history, in which humans, moral beings, had dominion over the earth and its flora and fauna, using them to subserve higher purposes.[58] As the life principle in plants and animals harnessed lifeless materials for its own purposes, so the human spirit had dominion over the lower creation. One day the present sabbath age would end, and the pure spiritual life of which this worldly existence was but a prophecy would become a glorious actuality.[59] The grand poem of creation displayed a beautiful and elevating divine plan unfolding in time, in the successive progress of created being.

---

already published in the *Mathematical Journal* a complicated set of calculations showing how the nebular theory predicted the actual state of our solar system. Guyot cited him on pp. 67, 71. What Guyot did was to incorporate the nebular theory into a simple day-age harmony, squaring Genesis in broad outline with current scientific discoveries.

57. Guyot, *Creation*, p. 30.

58. Another reason, by the way, for reading the six "days" as ages.

59. Guyot, *Creation*, pp. 131-33.

ERA OF MATTER.

Introduction.

THE BIBLE.	SCIENCE.
In the beginning God created the Heavens and the Earth. And the Earth was desolateness and emptiness; and darkness was upon the face of the deep.	Matter is not self-existent. Primitive state of matter. Gas indefinitely diffused.
First Day. And God said, Let Light be, and Light was. And God separated the light from the darkness.	*First Activity of Matter.* Gravity. Chemical Action. Concentration of diffused matter into one or more nebulæ, appearing as *luminous* spots in the *dark* space of heaven.
Second Day. And God said, Let there be an expanse in the midst of the waters. And God made the expanse, and separated the waters under the expanse from the waters above the expanse.	*Division.* The primitive nebula is divided into smaller nebulous masses. Formation of the visible, lower, starry world.
Third Day. *a.* And God said, Let the water under the Heavens be gathered to one place and let the dry land appear. *b.* And God said, Let the earth bring forth vegetation.	*Concentration.* The nebulous masses concentrate into stars. Our sun becomes a nebulous star. Formation of the mineral mass of the earth by chemical combination of the solid crust, the ocean, and atmosphere. The earth self-luminous; a sun. First appearance of land. Azoic rocks. First infusorial plants and protophytes.

ERA OF LIFE.

Fourth Day. And God said, Let luminaries be in the expanse of the Heavens to separate the day from the night, and they shall be for signs, and for seasons, and for days, and for years.	Chemical actions subside. The earth loses its photosphere; sun and moon become visible. First *succession* of day and night, of seasons and years. Differences of climate begin. Archæan rocks. Protophytes. Protozoans.
Fifth Day. And God created the great stretched out sea monsters and all living creatures that creep, which the waters breed abundantly, and every winged bird.	Plants and animals appear successively in the order of their rank—marine animals, fishes, reptiles, and birds. First great display of land plants. Coal beds. Paleozoic and mesozoic ages.
Sixth Day. a. And God made the beasts of the earth, and the cattle and every creeping thing of the ground after its kind. b. And God created man in his image.	Predominance of mammals; the highest animals. The beasts of the earth, Carnivorous; the cattle, Herbivorous animals. Tertiary age. Creation of man. Quaternary age.
Seventh Day.—Sabbath. And God saw all that he had made, and behold it was *very good*. And God rested on the seventh day.	No material creation. Introduction of the moral world. Age of man.

Day-Age Harmonization from Guyot's *Creation* (1884) (Arnold Guyot, *Creation; or, the Biblical Cosmogony in the Light of Modern Science* [New York: Charles Scribner's Sons, 1884], pp. 137-38)

At the arrival of mankind the word *bārā'* appeared three times: "So God created man in his own image, in the image of God created he him; male and female created he them" (Gen. 1:27 KJV) — emphasizing again and again the distinctness of human life from all other life. Guyot regarded the creations of matter, life, and spirit as three utter miracles, three creations out of nothing; but the third was paramount. There was a radical and ineradicable distinction between man and all brute creation — the entirely new principle of moral choice.[60]

Guyot turned a very neat trick. He tied all of existence together under God's progressive plan, yet maintained a profound break between the moral and physical spheres. Man alone straddled the chasm. Man's inalienable dignity, his uniqueness in the created order, stood secure. Where Chambers's developmentalism slid into materialism and pantheism, Guyot's developmentalism preserved the fundamental duality of matter and spirit. Where Chambers's emphasis on the reign of law left mankind bereft of a caring God who superintends us and intervenes on our behalf, Guyot gave a God of cosmic plans who yet is near to his creatures and attentive to their prayers, whose whole creation points to man's glory in his opportunity to know his God. Guyot's developmentalism not only comported with the Bible, it made the Bible's spiritual message shine forth in its physical incidentals. No wonder Princeton was thrilled.[61]

60. Guyot, *Creation*, p. 122.

61. Guyot's day-age progressionist interpretation lives on in evangelical circles today, with some updating of the science and revision of the scriptural interpretation. See, e.g., Robert C. Newman, "Old-Earth (Progressive) Creation," in *Three Views of Creation and Evolution*, ed. J. P. Moreland and John Mark Reynolds (Grand Rapids: Zondervan, 1999), pp. 107-8. Names for such a position abound. James R. Moore (*The Post-Darwinian Controversies: A Study of the Protestant Struggle to Come to Terms with Darwin in Great Britain and America, 1870-1900* [Cambridge: Cambridge University Press, 1979], pp. 212-13) calls it "discontinuous transcendental progressionism" — this in describing the view of John William Dawson, which was very similar to Guyot's.

CHAPTER TWO

The Battle Cry

When the enemy comes in like a flood, the Spirit of the Lord shall lift up a standard against him. It is a giant with whom we have to wrestle — but a blind giant after all — blind to the intuitions of our nobler and immortal nature, to the soul, God, and immortality: "a Cyclops with one eye, and that in the back of its head," and giving us the "ouran-outang theology of the origin of the human race in place of the Book of Genesis." Let us pierce with the sword of the Spirit, which is the word of God, this Monstrum horrendum, informe, ingens, cui lumen ademptum, *and we need not fear the issue. We shall be more than conquerors through Him that hath loved us.*

Lyman H. Atwater, 1865[1]

Glory, glory, Hallelujah! His truth is marching on.

Julia Ward Howe, 1861

The "Darwinian Revolution"

In 1859 there appeared in England a fat book by Charles Darwin bearing the now legendary title, *On the Origin of Species by Means of Natural Se-*

---

1. Lyman H. Atwater, "Herbert Spencer's Philosophy; Atheism, Pantheism, and Materialism," *Biblical Repertory and Princeton Review* (hereafter *BRPR*) 37 (1865): 270.

lection; or, The Preservation of Favoured Races in the Struggle for Life. It was published in a flurry of activity after two decades of patient investigation, thinking, and rethinking. It is a familiar story — Darwin's unhappy relationship with his father, his early preparation for the ministry, his five-year voyage around the world on the *Beagle,* the Galápagos finches, the insights of Charles Lyell on uniformitarian geology and Thomas Malthus on the pressures of overpopulation, the years of indecision about how to present an evolutionary theory to a scientific world that had summarily rejected the *Vestiges,* the final rush to publish after receiving word from Borneo that Alfred Russel Wallace had lit upon the same basic hypothesis. One is hard pressed to name another book whose background, appearance, reception, and consequences are so thoroughly and so widely known. The literature of the "Darwin industry," as Peter Bowler calls it, is breathtakingly immense.[2]

It is a matter of conventional wisdom, on both the popular and the academic levels, that Darwinism rocked the intellectual world. That evolutionism in some form energized the natural and social sciences and captivated generations of minds is beyond dispute, as is the fact that Darwin's book struck the match that started whole fields of knowledge blazing like wildfire. If ever there was a scientific revolution, surely the Darwinian revolution would seem to be one. The intellectual world was a vastly different place just a few short decades after that momentous year 1859.

Darwin gave his name to the evolution revolution, but careful historians of science and ideas have long realized that the revolution did not originate with him, nor did it ever possess a unitary character even as a limited scientific explanation of the origin of species. James Mark Baldwin believed that Wallace never got his due — we might say with equal justice (though not equal sonority) that "Wallacism" could serve to name the epochal movement.[3] But that is beside the point, for there was

2. Peter J. Bowler, *The Non-Darwinian Revolution: Reinterpreting a Historical Myth* (Baltimore: Johns Hopkins University Press, 1988), p. 14. Among the standard works on Darwin are E. J. Browne, *Charles Darwin: A Biography,* 2 vols. (New York: Knopf, 1995-2002); Gertrude Himmelfarb, *Darwin and the Darwinian Revolution* (Garden City, N.Y.: Doubleday, 1959); Philip Appleman, ed., *Darwin,* 3rd ed., Norton Critical Edition (New York: Norton, 2001); Adrian J. Desmond and James R. Moore, *Darwin: The Life of a Tormented Evolutionist* (New York: Norton, 1991); Bowler, *Charles Darwin: The Man and His Influence* (Oxford: Blackwell, 1990).

3. James Mark Baldwin, *Between Two Wars, 1861-1921: Being Memories, Opinions, and Letters Received by James Mark Baldwin* (Boston: Stratford Co., 1926), 1:71.

never just one evolutionism to be labeled properly with anyone's name, but rather a whole host of evolutionisms that for the sake of convenience, or for lack of intellectual acuity or surfeit of zeal, were promiscuously thrown together under the catchword "Darwinism." Qualifications to the idea of a unitary evolution revolution are legion. Ernst Mayr has shown that the *Origin* itself contained not one but at least five separable theories.[4] The fascination with development that we have seen in Chambers and Guyot antedated Darwin's book and derived largely from German idealism and *Naturphilosophie*. Herbert Spencer, who coined the phrase "survival of the fittest," propounded an independent and far more sweeping evolutionism than Darwin ever dared. Lamarckism, or the inheritance of acquired characteristics, though in retrospect set in opposition to Darwin's mechanism of natural selection, survived as an alternative or supplementary mechanism even in Darwin's own view, and enjoyed a renaissance in the later decades of the century among some of the leading American scientists. In short, "the" evolution revolution as Darwin's brainchild is what the Victorians would have called a "phantasy." While popular scientific literature and dozens of television documentaries perpetuate the Darwin-equals-evolution myth, professional scientists and historians are equally responsible. Even a discriminating book like David Livingstone's *Darwin's Forgotten Defenders,* whose whole point is that there were and are many mediating evolutionisms between fiat creationism and goalless, atheistic, "pure" Darwinism, succumbs to the allure of symbolic value in the name Darwin. Darwinism does not equal evolutionism, and evolutionary ideas permeated academe under a host of theories whose common feature was merely the belief in change by natural modality, a concept clearly not unique to Darwin.[5]

4. Ernst Mayr, *One Long Argument: Charles Darwin and the Genesis of Modern Evolutionary Thought* (Cambridge: Harvard University Press, 1991), pp. 35-37.

5. David N. Livingstone, *Darwin's Forgotten Defenders: The Encounter between Evangelical Theology and Evolutionary Thought* (Grand Rapids: Eerdmans; Edinburgh: Scottish Academic Press, 1987). Recent historians of science have followed John Hedley Brooke's "complexity thesis," finding not only that large, reified ideas like "science" and "religion" mean different things to different people at different times and in different locales, but that particular scientific theories like "Darwinism" resist univocal definition when we look at how people have understood them. John Hedley Brooke, *Science and Religion: Some Historical Perspectives* (Cambridge: Cambridge University Press, 1991); cf. Noah Efron, "Sciences and Religions: What It Means to Take Historical Perspectives Seriously," in *Science and Religion: New Historical Perspectives,* ed. Thomas Dixon, Geoffrey Cantor, and Stephen Pumfrey (New York: Cambridge University Press, 2010), pp. 247-62.

Not only is the unitary character of the evolution revolution in question, but trenchant historical work threatens its very status as a revolution, a sudden shift of scientific paradigms. Bowler's *Non-Darwinian Revolution* shows the persistent progressionism that animated most so-called acceptances of Darwin's theory; a teleological worldview not only survived the putative revolution, it fueled it. If certain thinkers saw and were attracted to the inherent atheism of Darwin's theory, far more overlooked it or misread it, or found a way to convince themselves that natural selection somehow comported with divine purpose. Bowler might have called his book "The Darwinian Non-Revolution," for he locates the real revolution in the 1930s when Mendelian genetics solved the riddles that had plagued the theory all along and, he says, rendered any teleological glosses on Darwin impossible. The Darwin industry, he argues persuasively, conflates a century-long process into a mythical revolutionary moment.[6]

It should come as no surprise, then, that the men of Princeton showed no sudden shock at the appearance of the *Origin*. Its first edition did not earn even so much as a short notice in the *Biblical Repertory and Princeton Review (BRPR)*. Chambers's book, by contrast, had elicited Dod's long and ardent article. Not until about 1870 did Darwinism become a lively concern in America. As Darwin had feared, his theory suffered by association with the *Vestiges*. It suffered also for its status as mere hypothesis. It lacked the authentication good inductive science required, and it lacked support among the most esteemed American scientists, most notably Harvard's Louis Agassiz. A theological journal saw little need to treat an unlikely scientific theory when there were bigger issues to attend to.

What did figure prominently in the *BRPR*'s pages after 1859 was the larger and prior issue of the relations of science and religion — an issue Darwin's book inflamed but certainly did not ignite. The discussion began earlier in the decade, when a host of books on the natural theological ramifications of geology began to appear. While the Princetonians criticized some of those books, they greeted the principle of scientific forays into natural theology with pleasure, and took the occasion to treat the

6. Bowler's work, by the way, is no polemic against Darwinism. When he locates the essence of Darwinism in goallessness, he concurs with Charles Hodge, but to an opposite end. He does not question the utterly naturalistic ateleology he finds lacking in the so-called Darwinian era; indeed, he identifies a "truly historical" worldview with the repudiation of teleology. Bowler, *The Non-Darwinian Revolution*, p. 51.

theoretical and practical relations of science and religion at length. Often they defended the new science from theological detractors, "with the confidence burning in our very bones, that some of the most brilliant achievements in the contested field of the Christian Evidences, are yet to be accomplished."[7]

When around 1859 a note of alarm reentered these discussions, it had a familiar ring. It echoed Dod's review of the *Vestiges.* It sounded not against Darwin and the *Origin,* but against Spencer, Mill, and Huxley and their Chambers-like reduction of reality to the material, their denigration or denial of the mental and moral sphere. It protested the use of science as a front for philosophical materialism. Against that movement Princeton raised a bloody battle cry.

The Military Metaphor

Only reluctantly did the Princetonians describe the relations of science and religion in terms of conflict. After all, their whole apologetical point was that knowledge was no enemy to faith, that the two were neither hostile nor indifferent to each other, but the closest of friends. "Religion and science are twin daughters of heaven," declared Charles Hodge in 1868, choosing yet a closer metaphor of relationship. "There is, or there should be, no conflict between them."[8] Hodge was voicing a decades-old commonplace among evangelical educators, lay and clerical. It was an extension of the distinction between natural and revealed religion, a confirmation of both the right and the expectations of scientific inquiry. Science had until very recently been called "natural philosophy," after all, and the pursuit of knowledge by the light of nature stood in the same relation to the truth claims of Christianity as natural theology did. Each had a right to its domain; each buttressed the knowledge of God that, coupled with trust, could save. Each also could have a nasty tendency to discount the supernatural.

Hodge tellingly described the relations of science and religion with both an indicative and an imperative. There *is* no conflict; or at least

7. Short notice of *The Course of Creation,* by John Anderson, *BRPR* 24 (1852): 151.

8. Charles Hodge, in "Inauguration of James McCosh, D.D., LL.D., as President of the College of New Jersey, Princeton, October 27, 1868" (New York: Robert Carter and Bros., 1868), p. 10.

there *should be* no conflict. By extension from the concept of natural theology, the duality of science and religion presented both a promise of peace and a threat of war. Science and religion were harmonious voices, twin daughters, two books; by whatever metaphor, they were both distinct and alike, both independent and coordinate. They pursued truth by different routes, but their results agreed — or ought to agree. All truth was God's truth; where theology and natural science conflicted, one or both of them had simply erred. Certainly the truth was still there to pursue, and knowledge of it was possible. The trick was in the interpretation, whether of the book of nature or the book of God's Word. Even if agreement was not yet apparent, it must be there.[9]

The difference between the "is" and the "should be" was the difference between the actual and the theoretical, the real and the ideal. Hodge and his fellow Princetonians had every confidence in the unity of truth in God, grounded ultimately in the doctrine of creation. They had high hopes of the human knowledge project attaining to that unified vision by a painstaking and thorough application of the inductive method to the whole of experience, subjective and objective. But it was obvious that human knowledge still had a long way to go. The present state of each discipline was far from perfect — even the older subjects, philosophy and theology, were as yet incomplete.

For the theologians at Princeton, two broad questions were involved in the duality of science and religion. One was theoretical: How did science stand in relation to theology? The other was practical: What to do in the period of progress through imperfection? — and especially, What to do when science's doxology was not orthodox?

The pages of the *BRPR* reveal a deep preoccupation with both of these questions in the years leading up to and including the Civil War. Indeed, by a striking coincidence the national catastrophe paralleled developments in Princeton's understanding of the relations of science and

9. On the widespread imagery of nature as "God's book," see Peter Harrison, "'Science' and 'Religion': Constructing the Boundaries," in *Science and Religion*, ed. Dixon et al., pp. 23-49. Harrison contends that "so inextricably connected were the dual concerns of God and nature that it is misleading to attempt to identify various kinds of relationship between science and religion in the seventeenth and eighteenth centuries." Only in the mid–nineteenth century, he argues, did "science" and "religion" become "independent entities which might bear some positive or negative relation to each other." That may be so — but the concept of the two books of God's Word and God's works traces back centuries, with the implicit task of comparing the two.

religion. A cherished and somewhat tenuously achieved union of sovereign states now threatened to dissolve into open antagonism. Where there had been amicable mutual support through difference, now the questions of future expansion and leadership divided the union into warring factions, the one bent on seceding from the relationship, the other fighting bitterly to secure it, compelled to fight a civil war when it wanted peace and unity.[10]

The War between the States took a heavy toll on Princeton, where about one-third of the college and seminary students were Southerners. Secession brought a sudden drop in enrollment, and with it a serious financial emergency. For Charles Hodge and many of his colleagues, who in political sympathies were perhaps more akin to Southern Whigs than to New England Republicans, the war was bitter indeed, rending their loyalties asunder. Hodge's best friend was a Virginian; his eldest son held a Virginia pastorate.[11] Because the Princetonians were surrounded by the emergencies of a political war and the threat of an intellectual one, it is no wonder that in their treatment of science and religion in the 1860s they turned from the language of concord to the language of conflict. While continuing to affirm their confidence in the ultimate agreement between those "twin daughters of heaven," they repeatedly and characteristically used battle terminology to describe their own troubled relations with science. The goal remained harmony, but their description of the means to achieving that goal, and of the many threats facing them in the attempt, was profoundly military.

10. Geoffrey Cantor suggests that the Civil War helped shape the idea of essential and inevitable conflict between science and religion, pointing out that John William Draper published his *History of the American Civil War* (1867-70) just a few years before his *History of the Conflict of Religion and Science* (1875) — which latter work set the tone of what historians of science call the "conflict thesis." Geoffrey Cantor, "What Shall We Do with the Conflict Thesis?" in *Science and Religion,* ed. Dixon et al., p. 294.

11. Thomas Jefferson Wertenbaker, *Princeton, 1746-1896* (Princeton: Princeton University Press, 1946), pp. 265-71; Addison Atwater, "The Faculty," in *The Princeton Book* (Boston: Houghton, Osgood and Co., 1879), p. 140; Faculty Minutes, 3 February 1860, PTS Special Collections; Charles Hodge to J. R. Backus, 30 January 1860, Hodge Family MSS, PU Library; Raleigh Don Scovel, "Orthodoxy in Princeton: A Social and Intellectual History of Princeton Theological Seminary, 1812-1860" (Ph.D. diss., University of California, 1970), p. 338; A. A. Hodge to Charles Hodge, 4 April 1861, Hodge Family MSS, PU Library. A letter dated 1 January 1866 from J. K. Lyle to Peter Walker, publication manager of the *BRPR,* reveals that the war hurt the journal, too, for it drove up the price of paper and severed ties with a considerable Southern readership. Hodge Family MSS, Charles Hodge letters, box 11.

In recent decades many historians of science and religion have sought to discredit what James R. Moore calls "the military metaphor." By way of introduction to his acclaimed book *The Post-Darwinian Controversies,* Moore spends about a hundred pages tracing the rise of the metaphor, its seductive appeal, and its profoundly misleading consequences in historical interpretation. Historians have erred, he contends, in taking on the view of partisans in the nineteenth-century conflict between science and religion. They have swallowed whole Thomas Huxley's deliberately inflammatory pill of stark alternatives: "Fight or surrender; there are no other options." Huxley insisted the orthodox Christian admit that his religion was fundamentally, irretrievably opposed to natural science, that there was no middle ground. He was an ardent polemicist and a notorious agnostic who utterly polarized science and religion; his language of battle was colorful and rich — and tantalizingly quotable — but it was hardly the language of dispassion and careful nuance that historians should employ. Moore laments three grossly misleading tendencies the military metaphor has fostered. First, it posits a clear polarization between scientific and religious sides. In fact, many Christian thinkers, such as Asa Gray, James Dwight Dana, and James McCosh, maintained a clear evangelical commitment even as they embraced a form of evolutionism. Second, the metaphor of battle suggests two well-organized opponents, but such organization was completely lacking in the nineteenth century. Instead we find deep divisions among scientists and theologians alike. Third, the metaphor suggests open antagonism, while Moore points out the often amiable relations between the supposed antagonists. "So the military metaphor perverts historical understanding," Moore concludes, "by teaching one to think of polarity where there was confusing plurality, to see monolithic solidarity where there was division and uncertainty, to expect hostility where there was conciliation and concord." He urges, "Henceforth interpretations of the post-Darwinian controversies must be non-violent and humane."[12]

Moore's book is a monumental step toward such a "nonviolent" history, amassing evidence of a whole range of options between the two poles symbolized by Huxley and Bishop Wilberforce, whose famous debate over Darwinism in 1860 cast the conflict between science and reli-

---

12. James R. Moore, *The Post-Darwinian Controversies: A Study of the Protestant Struggle to Come to Terms with Darwin in Great Britain and America, 1870-1900* (Cambridge: Cambridge University Press, 1979), pp. 19, 58-65, 99-100.

gion in high relief. Moore even argues that orthodoxy sometimes showed more affinity with Darwinism than heterodoxy did, and calls Darwinism "the legitimate offspring of an orthodox theology of nature."[13] The point, in short, is that there is a significant history of evangelical friendliness toward evolutionism. Thus, Moore suggests, evangelicals today would do well to consider what kind of a mark of orthodoxy antievolutionism ought to be.

This last argument is taken up explicitly by Moore's friend David N. Livingstone in *Darwin's Forgotten Defenders.* Livingstone tells us precisely what he is about: "If my case is sustained, and a considerable number of evangelical evolutionists are rediscovered, then the onus will be on the creationists to satisfy us that theirs is not a thoroughly modern movement cut off from the mainstream of the conservative Christian tradition. My argument may be seen as merely multiplying testimonials. So be it." Joining Moore and Livingstone in their condemnation of the military metaphor are many other writers, notably David Lindberg and Ronald Numbers.[14]

Both the old and the new histories of the religious response to evolutionism assign a very important role to Princeton Seminary and College. The leaders of the two institutions after 1868, Charles Hodge and

13. James R. Moore, *The Post-Darwinian Controversies,* p. 16. Orthodox Calvinism entertained no saccharine illusions of unrelieved sweetness in this world; it faced the problems of evil and sin and suffering squarely, and so was tough-minded enough not to be thrown off balance by a world that achieved its progress through struggle and loss. George Frederick Wright made this point already in 1880: Darwinism, rightly understood, was the "Calvinistic interpretation of nature." Wright, quoted in Denis Oswald Lamoureux, "Between 'The Origin of Species' and 'The Fundamentals': Toward a Historiographical Model of the Evangelical Reaction to Darwinism in the First Fifty Years" (Ph.D. diss., Toronto School of Theology, 1991), p. 236.

14. Livingstone, *Darwin's Forgotten Defenders,* pp. x-xii; Livingstone, "Farewell to Arms: Reflections on the Encounter between Science and Faith" (paper given at the conference "Christian Theology in a Post-Christian World," the Billy Graham Center, Wheaton College, March 22, 1985); Livingstone, "The Idea of Design: The Vicissitudes of a Key Concept in the Princeton Response to Darwin," *Scottish Journal of Theology* 37 (1984): 329-57; David C. Lindberg and Ronald L. Numbers, "Beyond War and Peace: A Reappraisal of the Encounter between Christianity and Science," *Perspectives on Science and Christian Faith* 39 (1987): 140-49. Karl W. Giberson and Donald A. Yerxa, however, point out that "there is a sense in which 'warfare' can serve as a helpful metaphor for understanding the twentieth century's unfolding hostilities between creationism and evolution." Giberson and Yerxa, *Species of Origins: America's Search for a Creation Story* (Lanham, Md.: Rowman and Littlefield, 2002), pp. 8-9.

James McCosh, seem to personify the two possible responses to the evolution question, opposition and conciliation. Hodge found Darwinism unacceptable because it denied divine design in the creation, summing up his argument with the famous words, "What is Darwinism? It is atheism." On the face of it, this would certainly seem a terse declaration of opposition if ever there was one. Opponents of evolutionism agreed with Hodge and cited him routinely. McCosh, on the other hand, became the first major religious leader in America to embrace a form of evolutionism, insisting on the possibility of finding a *modus vivendi* between transmutationism and theism. "Whether there may not be a new species developed out of the old," he stated shortly after his arrival in Princeton, "is a question for science to settle. And, whichever way it is settled, there is room for irreligion — I am sorry to say; but there is room also for religion."[15] McCosh became an icon of mediation, Hodge an icon of opposition, between science and faith in general, and on the evolution question in particular.[16]

This seemingly straightforward duality is in fact quite confusing, for the terms in the couplet are not stable. What two things are being juxtaposed? Evolutionism and antievolutionism? But McCosh was speaking of evolutionism in general, Hodge of Darwinism in particular; and in any case, each term is subject to enormous fluctuations in meaning. Science and faith? Both men agreed that science was the primary guide to natural truth, that the design argument was crucial to reasoned theism, and that the Bible taught truth in natural things, though only incidentally, not directly as science did. In short, the iconographic use of McCosh and Hodge obscures as much as it reveals.

Surprisingly, the very metaphor that produced this obfuscatory polarity also provides a way out of the fog. If instead of shunning the military metaphor we embrace it as the language of discourse during the

15. Charles Hodge, *What Is Darwinism?* (New York: Scribner, Armstrong, and Co., 1874), pp. 176-77; James McCosh, *Christianity and Positivism* (New York: Robert Carter and Bros., 1871), p. 39.

16. See especially Andrew Dickson White, *A History of the Warfare of Science with Theology in Christendom,* 2 vols. (New York: D. Appleton and Co., 1896), 1:80; Joseph E. Illick III, "The Reception of Darwinism at the Theological Seminary and the College at Princeton, New Jersey," *Journal of the Presbyterian Historical Society* 38 (1960): 152-65, 234-43; and Dennis Royal Davis, "Presbyterian Attitudes toward Science and the Coming of Darwinism in America, 1859-1929" (Ph.D. diss., University of Illinois/Urbana-Champaign, 1980).

evolution controversies — if we turn from the role of advocate to the role of explorer — we find in the imagery of battle some fairly clear outlines of how the Princetonians assessed the issue and how they proposed to answer it. We can discern where they agreed and where they differed — and we can thereby erase some of the anachronistic errors the old iconographic polarity (a thing common to both progressive liberals and fundamentalists) has produced.

As Davis Young has observed, the myth still persists today that modern geology set out to overthrow the Bible and Christianity — or more generally, that science is necessarily dangerous to faith. Young, Livingstone, and others urge their readers, many of whom are evangelicals interested in scholarship, to "recapture that cooperative spirit" some leading nineteenth-century evangelical thinkers had. Certain of the Princetonians (Guyot, James McCosh, A. A. Hodge, B. B. Warfield) serve as their prime examples.[17] Refusing to grant Huxley's stark polarization of science and faith, they held fast their religion while affirming the value of natural science and even evolution.

But in praising the cooperative and welcoming attitude such men held toward scientific progress, the "nonviolent" histories tend to perpetuate an important tenet of the militaristic histories they despise. They portray the "conciliators" or "mediators" by contrasting them to a group of oppositionists. The good guys shine in comparison to the bad guys. This was the basic tactic of Andrew Dickson White's *History of the Warfare of Science with Theology in Christendom,* one of the most egregiously militarized interpretations ever put forward. His was a tale of liberation, of free inquiry fighting a long and painful battle against clerical oppression — a triumphalist tale of progress from darkness to light as grand as any Enlightenment dream. To achieve his purpose, White freely assigned white hats and black hats to his characters according to their positions for or against a particular scientific truth at issue. There were those for science and free inquiry, and those against it; the agents of progress and the agents of suppression.[18] This kind of history assumes a unitary and obvious path of scientific progress that at the very best is discernible only by Whiggish hindsight, to the exclusion of any appreciation of the complexity of discourse at the time. More to the

17. Davis A. Young, "Theology and Natural Science," *Reformed Journal* 38 (May 1988): 12-13.

18. White, *A History of the Warfare of Science with Theology in Christendom.*

present point, it tends to do an injustice to the people in black hats, whose own complexities the authors pass over in their haste to provide a foil for the people in white. Even the "nonviolent" histories, while they eschew White's simplistic categories, tend to preserve a certain opposition. There are still good guys and bad guys. The good guys pursue a peaceable coexistence of religion and science; the bad guys set science and religion against each other. Once again interpretive polarization threatens to dismiss important points of agreement.

To pick up Moore's terms, the "violent" histories of science and religion perpetuate the metaphor of battle to the detriment of the ideal of unity; they see a war, but not a civil war, a war to save a union. The "nonviolent" histories so emphasize mediation that they miss the nuances of meaning in the militant language of the time. There is no getting around the prevalence of battle imagery on all sides starting in the 1860s. The pertinent literature of the day is striking for its constant, even insistent, use of terms of war. In this Princeton was no exception. Through the military metaphor the Princetonians conceived of their practical relations with true science and with science "falsely so called," and through the military metaphor they articulated a remarkably clear plan to do battle with their foe. In *reconnaissance* and *tactics* — two very martial themes — a hearty collaboration becomes apparent between college and seminary in the years of alleged internal conflict over the evolution question.[19]

The Union Forever: Science and Theology

For the theologians at Princeton, and for Baconians in general, the term "science" rightfully belonged to any disciplined approach to knowledge, from physics and biology to metaphysics and theology. To distinguish theology from science was as impertinent as to distinguish geology from science. What characterized science were method and system: careful attention to the full range of facts and careful assembly of those well-

---

19. My work so far joins the camp of "contextualist" historians advocating a "complexity thesis," as nicely described by Cantor: "They are good listeners and seek to understand the arguments and motivations of historical actors in their own terms" (Cantor, "What Shall We Do?" p. 286). However, in so doing I find plenty of evidence *for* the imagery of conflict. To Cantor's query, "Have we over-reacted to the very notion of conflict?" (p. 287), I answer: *Yes*.

ascertained facts into a coherent, self-consistent whole. Science stood opposed not to religion per se, but to dogma and speculation — to knowledge claims exempted from or unsupported by any a posteriori validation. Science paid unswerving attention to empirical fact; it let the facts suggest a theory, and not the reverse. The system of belief contained in the Westminster Confession and elaborated in the theologies of Turretin and Hodge commended itself to people's minds; its explanations and its proofs were a matter of public record, open for all to judge for themselves. As a set of truth claims, the Princeton theology was proud to call itself a science.[20]

As a field of study, theology in Europe and America was experiencing a kind of puberty, a transforming growth spurt under the new categories of "theological encyclopedia" Friedrich Schleiermacher had introduced. Its rapid expansion and diversification in the nineteenth century, at least in terms of personnel and organization, paralleled the growth of the natural sciences. For structural reasons as well as philosophical ones, many theologians began to claim scientific status for their field.[21]

Science, to proceed at all, required the assumption of a unified field of inquiry, but it divided that one field into many subfields according to the nature of the object of study and the evidence appropriate to it. The two grand principles of this view of science may be called the *unity of truth* and the *division of labor*. Creation ultimately grounded the unity of truth; the inductive method grounded the division of labor. That method was the same in all fields, just as the truth was one and consistent; a well-read layman in any field could survey the whole sweep of scientific truth and form valid judgments. Here were the beauty and the appeal of the inductive method. It was so simple, so straightforward, yet it so mightily swept away the old authoritarian systems. It encouraged a highly democratic view of science. No qualitative line separated the layman from the expert save how one earned one's living. Until midcentury,

20. Charles Hodge, *Systematic Theology* (New York: Scribners, 1872-73; reprint, Grand Rapids: Eerdmans, 1993), 1:1, 10-16; cf. Theodore Dwight Bozeman, *Protestants in an Age of Science: The Baconian Ideal and Antebellum American Religious Thought* (Chapel Hill: University of North Carolina Press, 1977).

21. "The church is willing to meet men of science on equal terms," announced the writer of "The Testimony of Modern Science to the Unity of Mankind," reviewing J. L. Cabell's book of that title. *BRPR* 31 (1859): 106. Half a century later Henry Collin Minton echoed this theme in his Stone Lectures at PTS. "All we ask for is a mutual recognition of status." Minton, *The Cosmos and the Logos* (Philadelphia: Westminster, 1902), p. 115.

in fact, many of the key contributions to science were made by amateurs, especially in geology.[22]

Unlike other disciplines, though, theology had an established accrediting system. Theologians were ordained clergymen. Their status as scientists was therefore inherently unequal. Only later in the century did professional organizations arise in secular fields and rival (or overtake) the status claims of the clergy. The Presbyterian church was representative rather than hierarchical in structure, but its polity militated against the democracy of science and compromised its theologians' claims to simply scientific status.

Induction's division of labor by object of study enhanced this structural inequality. As the knowledge of God and our relations to him were the highest field of study, so the sisterhood of sciences preserved a ranking, theology being the eldest sister. Hodge's talk of "twin daughters of heaven" obscured this point somewhat. A more telling image was the classical metaphor of theology as "queen of the sciences," a metaphor whose use became more explicit in the later decades of the century, along with Princeton's preoccupation with natural theology.[23] But before and during the Civil War years the Princeton theologians did couch their discussions of science and religion in terms that betrayed what we may call — not pejoratively, but merely descriptively — an "imperial" view of theology. This view coexisted with the "twin daughters" view, but only

22. Mary Anning (discoverer of *Ichthyosaurus*) and Hugh Miller (popular Scottish geologist and author) are prime examples.

23. B. B. Warfield best expressed this imperial view of theological science toward the end of the century in his inaugural to the chair of the Hodges: "Theology, formally speaking, is . . . the apex of the pyramid of the sciences by which the structure is perfected. . . . All other sciences are subsidiary to it, and it builds its fabric out of material supplied by them. . . . The several sciences deal each with its own material in an independent spirit and supply a multitude of results not immediately useful to theology. But so far as their results stand related to questions with which theology deals, they exist only to serve her." Warfield, "The Idea of Systematic Theology," in *The Works of Benjamin B. Warfield*, ed. Ethelbert D. Warfield et al., vol. 9 (New York: Oxford University Press, 1932; Grand Rapids: Baker, 1991), pp. 71-72. Though it was Warfield who stated this imperial view of theology most explicitly, it was no new development at Princeton. For example, more than forty years earlier the *BRPR* urged that the "new, brilliant, and fascinating science" of comparative physiology stood in need of baptism "into its legitimate discipleship to Christianity, to compel it, in common with the countless living forms whose mysteries it seeks to penetrate and reveal, to bring its tribute of worship to the great Creator." Short notice of *The Indications of the Creator; or, The Natural Evidences of Final Cause*, by George Taylor, *BRPR* 24 (1852): 145.

tenuously, for the two views were in uncomfortable contradiction on the point of priority.

As queen of the sciences, theology rode high on the shoulders of all other disciplines. As the study of God and his relations to his creatures, theology had a vital interest in the study of the natural world. Each new branch of science not only presented new opportunities to sing the praises of God in his works and to magnify his wisdom and beneficence, but also provided new insights to illumine obscure passages of Scripture. Guyot's idealistic interpretation of Genesis 1 by the light of geology was a prime example of this. The fact that the ancients knew nothing of nebulae and geological succession only magnified the supernatural character of the biblical record, for it now became apparent that its authors wrote better than they knew. Natural knowledge not only aided biblical interpretation, it exalted biblical inspiration.[24]

But even *within* the imperial view of theology there inhered a tension. The queen of the sciences, lifted up on the shoulders of other sciences, depended upon them for support. They informed her; to that extent she had to submit herself in practice to their dictates. The Princetonians were fond of repeating that the Bible was not a scientific textbook; insofar as it touched on matters of science and history, it was true when rightly understood, but the church had erred many times in seeking to answer secular questions with appeals to Scripture. The well-established facts of science served a legitimate purpose in biblical interpretation, but the trick was knowing when a theory became sufficiently attested to serve that interpretive function.

A favorite case in point for contributors to the *Princeton Review* was the notorious seventeenth-century condemnation of Galileo. Here a potential embarrassment to the nineteenth-century church provided an occasion to laud science and to demonstrate its positive interpretive value. Galileo's story presented a morality play about the dark dogmatism of Rome, in contrast to which the Protestant emphasis on open inquiry into the meaning of Scripture shone brightly.[25] It demonstrated the

24. See, for example, "The Testimony of Modern Science to the Unity of Mankind," *BRPR* 31 (1859): 106.

25. One article admitted that earlier Protestant divines were not immune to the same charges of dogmatism — even the Swiss theologian Francis Turretin, whose systematic theology was the standard text at Princeton Seminary until the 1870s. The contributor hastened to add, however, that they "did exactly what the philosophers demand. They interpreted Scripture according to the science popular in their day and country.... The mis-

difference between the Scripture itself and a given interpretation of Scripture. The persecuted man with a telescope symbolized the importance of answering scientific questions with empirical evidence.

On the other hand, the Galileo affair revealed that the use of science as an interpretive aid posed some difficulties for the Protestant doctrine of scriptural perspicuity. One writer likened the dispute over the age of the earth to the dispute over geocentrism, asserting that in each case the "most natural" interpretation was contradicted by the light of science. "We should be glad therefore if the results of science would leave us in quiet possession of our old methods of understanding the first chapter of Genesis. But we have no idea of giving up the Bible for the sake of that interpretation."[26] Scientific knowledge did shake things up a bit; there was no denying that the original audience had not understood the mundane entailments of scriptural teaching in the same way moderns did with the aid of science.

Still, the Princetonians wanted "nothing but the wide-awake truth."[27] They preferred a bracing empirical slap to cozy dogmatic slumbers. Their belief in *sola Scriptura* did not deny the necessity of scholarship. Science was a far more welcome interpreter of Scripture than any authoritative magisterium, for science lay open to all who would undertake its rigors. So the perspicuity of Scripture stood fast: if the Bible was not utterly pellucid to all, its meaning was still accessible to all by diligent inquiry.[28]

---

take of those great divines consisted in their permitting science to stamp its interpretation on the Bible" when it was not warranted by empirical evidence. James R. Eckard, "The Logical Relations of Religion and Natural Science," *BRPR* 32 (1860): 580-81. Some years later Charles Hodge discussed explicitly the question of adjusting biblical interpretation to authenticated facts, using the Copernican revolution as a classic example. Hodge, *Systematic Theology*, 1:57.

26. Short notice of *Geognosy, or the Facts and Principles of Geology against Theories*, by David N. Lord, *BRPR* 28 (1856): 163.

27. Henry J. Van Dyke, "The Charge," in "Addresses at the Inauguration of the Rev. Francis L. Patton, D.D., LL.D., as Stuart Professor of the Relations of Philosophy and Science to the Christian Religion . . ." (Philadelphia: Sherman and Co., 1881), pp. 16-17.

28. There was good Calvinistic precedent for placing a positive valuation on the difficulty of scriptural interpretation, even if it did seem to contradict the principle of perspicuity. For example, John Lightfoot, the seventeenth-century Westminster divine, wrote: "The Holy Ghost hath purposely penned the Scriptures so as to challenge all serious study of them. . . . He could have penned all so plain, that he that runneth, might have read them; but he hath penned them in such a style, that he that will read them, must not run and read, but sit down and study." Lightfoot, "A Sermon, Preached upon II Sam. xix.29," in *The Whole Works of the Rev. John Lightfoot*, ed. John Rogers Pitman, 13 vols. (London: J. F. Dove, 1822-25), 7:208.

The Inquisition's insistence on Ptolemaic cosmology provided a powerful negative object lesson about the care the church should exercise when seeking to understand the Bible by the light of science. It was all too easy to mistake a scientific theory, however venerable, for fact — to run ahead of the evidence when interpreting Scripture by science. Science was an indispensable aid to biblical understanding, but the Galileo affair warned the church against endorsing a scientific theory simply on account of its prevalence. Theology could afford to be patient, to wait calmly until scientific truth claims had been fully established. Let empirical fact guide biblical interpretation, but let the church be exceedingly cautious in authenticating empirical fact.[29]

The call for patience was characteristic of the *Princeton Review*'s treatment of science and religion. The "is" and the "should be" of that relation were sometimes far apart; only after decades of careful fact-gathering would the apparent conflicts between Christian theism and natural science vanish. In the meantime, *both* sides should suspend judgment: the church should allow science to proceed unmolested, and scientists should refrain from hasty pronouncements against cherished Christian doctrines. Let religion assume the best of science, but let science also assume the best of religion. Let both sides support the union. Let neither declare independence from the other. With patience, the Princetonians believed, the union would stand.

From Concord to Conflict

In the 1850s the *Princeton Review* had maintained an air of happy indifference to what some people were calling scientific threats to religion. No note of alarm nearly as urgent as Dod's review of the *Vestiges* had sounded there in some time. The Princetonians maintained their self-definition as defenders of the faith and kept watch against any irreligious tendencies in scientific or philosophical developments (especially post-Kantian subjectivism in Germany), but on the whole in those years they welcomed the progress of natural science in the English-speaking world.

29. Very illuminating is Charles Hodge's discussion in *Systematic Theology*, 1:57. He argues that whereas reason may only judge the *credibility* of a revelation (i.e., whether the claimed revelation be *not impossible*), reason must verify claimed scientific facts *beyond the possibility of doubt* — otherwise theologians would be adjusting doctrine to every wind of speculation, against the apostle Paul's warning.

Geology in particular, one of the youngest and most exciting sciences, yielded thrilling new evidences of the wondrous workings of the creative mind. With Arnold Guyot in residence at Princeton and the presses turning out books in Britain like Hugh Miller's *Footprints of the Creator* and James McCosh's *Method of the Divine Government*, and at home George Taylor's *Indications of the Creator; or, The Natural Evidences of Final Cause* and Edward Hitchcock's *Religion of Geology*, the Princetonians could, together with most scholarly evangelicals, assure any literal-minded folks that the new science did not threaten the Scripture, but rather magnified the work of God in both the minutiae of special creaturely contrivances and the grand scheme of divine government by natural law. New vistas of divine design more than compensated for any exegetical adjustments required.[30] A short notice in 1856 assured friends of the Bible that the long ages of geology need not trouble them. Should the geologic timetable be proved true, "then we will with the utmost alacrity believe that the days of the creation were periods of indefinite duration." There was no cause for alarm. "We give ourselves no concern about the matter. We know the Bible is of God and we therefore know that it will prove itself in harmony with all truth."[31]

Princeton took special delight in the works of the popular and highly respected geologist Hugh Miller, an eloquent self-made man who, like Guyot, hailed the wonders of the Almighty in the vastness of geologic time and in the ideal progress of creation in the fossil record, yet rejected transmutation. A leader in the evangelical Disruption of the Scottish Kirk in the 1840s, Miller personified the ideal of an inductive doxological scientist. Without benefit of formal training he roamed the highland quarries and painstakingly pieced together the first organic history of Scottish Devonian sandstone fossils, glorifying along the way the Cre-

30. Reviews of James McCosh's *Method of the Divine Government* and George Taylor's *Indications of the Creator* discussed the promising prospect of what Bowler has called "idealist versions" of the design argument (*BRPR* 23 [1851]: 598-624; 24 [1852]: 141-46). The latter article explicitly argued that Paleyan arguments from specific adaptations were outdated (p. 145). On Paleyan versus Owenian (idealist) concepts, see Livingstone, "The Idea of Design."

31. Short notice of *Geognosy*, p. 163. Similarly, a short notice concerning the nebular hypothesis advised patience and confidence: "it is as well to stand aloof from the controversy, until it approaches its termination. . . . We have not the slightest fears of the judgment of modern science determining permanently to a wrong verdict." Short notice of *The Indications of the Creator*, p. 144.

ator's ideal plan in nature. The "twin daughters of heaven" proceeded arm in arm in Miller's books. In 1849 Miller penned *Footprints of the Creator,* a direct rebuttal to the evolutionism of Chambers's *Vestiges,* and Princeton cheered. "A more complete demolition we have never seen on any subject," a reviewer glowed in 1851. "The record of creation graven on the rocks in unmistakable symbols, by the Creator himself, thus flatly and firmly contradicts the development hypothesis." The Princetonians felt assured that impartial natural science demolished evolutionism, even without recourse to the kind of moral arguments Dod had put forth.[32] Science supported Christian theism.

For several decades, then, Princeton defended the prerogatives of natural science against hasty theological assertions of the "plain teaching of Scripture," as when in 1856 a reviewer scolded an overzealous young-earth proponent: "We deny his right to embark the whole hopes of Christianity in one boat, and [to] make the salvation of men through Jesus Christ, depend on the success of his argument against geologists."[33] Princeton insisted that scientific claims should be judged on their scientific merits, exhorting theologians against the kind of wrongheaded "defenses" of the faith that pitted theological claims against scientific evidence and made it look as though all religion would fall with a given interpretation of the Bible's meaning. Princeton's voice was one of calm assurance and patience, of mutual friendship with science. Indeed, it tended to side with natural scientists rather than theologians when the latter raised objections to the new discoveries.

By 1859, however, the *BRPR's* attitude toward science began to shift from easy confidence to uncertain complaint. Scientists, it appeared, were not returning theology's favor.

32. Livingstone, *Darwin's Forgotten Defenders,* pp. 9-13; short notice of *Footprints of the Creator,* by Hugh Miller, *BRPR* 23 (1851): 172-73. Cf. short notice of *The Course of Creation,* p. 149. Livingstone lists Miller's impressive array of distinctions to demonstrate the insufficiency of the categories inspired by the military metaphor: "For literary style he was commended by Dickens and Ruskin; in science he was highly rated by Huxley, Lyell, Agassiz, Murchison, Owen, and Darwin; as a moralist he was admired by Thomas Carlyle.... Miller was a romantic Scottish nationalist who thoroughly approved of the union with England, a highly skilled laborer who penned sentimental verse, a fierce Presbyterian stalwart who favored Catholic emancipation, a devout evangelical who defended secular education. Perhaps the case of Hugh Miller, more than anyone else in the era, served to smash those categories of interpretation by which historical complexity is so often reduced to stereotyped heroes and villains" (p. 9).

33. Short notice of *Geognosy,* p. 162.

... while the church, in the consciousness of her fallibility in the interpretation of the infallible word of God, is willing to bow her judgment as to its meaning before the well-ascertained revelations of God in nature, she has a right to demand of men of science, first, that they shall be cautious in announcing facts even apparently hostile to the generally received sense of Scripture. Instead of pouncing on such facts, and parading them as if in triumph, . . . they should be slow to admit them and withhold their sanction until the evidence admits of no contradiction or doubt. The interests at stake demand this of every right-thinking man.[34]

If theology must yield to the truths of natural science, so natural science must not despise "the facts of religion." The Princetonians conceived of a unified project under the rubric of inductive science. Theology, to the extent that it involved truth claims about this-worldly reality, was part of that project, and to that extent it was analogous to any other science. Each involved interpretation, each should freely admit it, and each should refrain from making premature pronouncements of fact — especially when those pronouncements contradicted the well-attested truths of another discipline. If theology must be slow to denounce scientific theories, how much more ought science to be slow to denigrate cardinal religious beliefs. If theology must acknowledge the provisional character of any mere interpretation, so ought science to acknowledge the provisional character of its theories — and all the more so when those theories contradicted established views in religion and moral philosophy, views considered by their advocates to be properly matters of scientific (though not naturalistic or material) *fact.*

These views of science and fact are very easily misunderstood, so it bears repeating that the unspoken equation of science with natural science — an equation now so thoroughly entrenched that we assume it — was precisely the bone of contention in these discussions in the 1850s. The Princetonians did not grant that equation. And because they regarded theology as a science, they appear to have been guilty of inserting into religion the very Enlightenment rationalism they were pledged to oppose. Clearly the Princeton theology borrowed heavily (and indeed consciously) from the Enlightenment; but the Princetonians were careful to

34. "Testimony of Modern Science," pp. 106-7. See also Eckard, "The Logical Relations," p. 602. This complaint was directed, by the way, not at Darwin but at polygenism, the claim that mankind comprised several separate species.

distinguish theology from religion. Theology was a study, a science; religion was, as Charles Hodge said in the title of his most popular book, *The Way of Life*.[35] It involved knowledge, but it was more than knowledge.

As for the phrase "facts of religion," here again the terminology is misleading to present-day readers. Facts to the Princetonians were not items of indubitability. According to the Common-Sense Realist philosophy that structured (but arguably did not determine) much American thought at the time, *all* claims of truth or fact involved an exercise of the moral faculty in forming a *judgment.* All assertions of fact were characterized by a degree of probability, not by ineluctable certainty, and thus all claims of truth involved a degree of responsibility, of moral action, on the knower's part.[36] With this understanding such phrases as "theological science" and "the facts of religion" did not appear as oxymorons. Studies of Common-Sense Realism have focused on the realist claim (contra Kant) that there were no mediating ideas between the knowing subject and the cognized object — that the object itself, not an idea of it in the knower's head, was known. This position is sometimes called "naïve realism," and historians have been rather free in attributing naïveté to any adherent of this brand of epistemological monism, including the Princetonians.[37] But Common-Sense Realist understandings of

35. Charles Hodge, *The Way of Life* (Philadelphia: American Sunday School Union, 1841).

36. S. A. Grave, *The Scottish Philosophy of Common Sense* (Oxford: Clarendon, 1960), pp. 111-12; Charles Augustus Aiken, "Valiant for the Truth," in *Princeton Sermons* (New York: Fleming H. Revell Co., 1893), pp. 52-53, 62; Aiken, "Christian Apologetics: The Lectures Constituting the Course in Ethics and Apologetics, for the Middle and Senior Classes, Princeton Theological Seminary" (Princeton: Press Printing Establishment, 1879; pamphlet in PTS Special Collections), pp. 52-53. According to Richard Olson, the Scottish school divided on this point, Thomas Brown and Dugald Stewart departing from Thomas Reid by emphasizing the scientist's creative and interpretive role. See Olson, *Scottish Philosophy and British Physics, 1750-1880: A Study in the Foundations of the Victorian Scientific Style* (Princeton: Princeton University Press, 1975), pp. 97-98. I am grateful to the late Thomas Torrance for bringing this thought-provoking book to my attention.

37. William Pepperell Montague, *The Ways of Knowing; or, The Methods of Philosophy* (1925; reprint, New York: Humanities Press, 1978), pp. 237, 240-42. John C. Vander Stelt, *Philosophy and Scripture: A Study in Old Princeton and Westminster Theology* (Marlton, N.J.: Mack, 1978), and John William Stewart, "The Tethered Theology: Biblical Criticism, Common-Sense Philosophy, and the Princeton Theologians, 1812-1860" (Ph.D. diss., University of Michigan, 1990), exemplify the argument that philosophical naïveté underlay the Princeton theology. Cf. Mark A. Noll, "Common-Sense Traditions and American Evangelical Thought," *American Quarterly* 37 (1985): 216-38.

"moral argument" and of the probability of knowledge reveal another dimension to the philosophy — one explicitly taught at Princeton.

In their calls for mutual scientific fairness, the kinds of religious facts the Princetonians had in mind were usually not matters of biblical chronology or history, but matters of doctrine like the solidarity of the human race in Adam's fall, or matters of religious experience like the personal sense of assurance a believer felt in the gospel. While there were coherent philosophical reasons for grouping together such disparate categories under the one rubric of "fact," this nomenclature did tend to obscure metaphysical distinctions under a unitary epistemic umbrella. Calling things "facts" made them susceptible to the inductive method and thereby to scientific study, and few people would question the validity of trying to make sense of doctrinal commitments or of the phenomena of religious experience. But it gave the appearance of saying that such widely diverse objects of study as fossil trilobites, the covenant of works, and the joy of the Holy Ghost fit somehow in the same epistemic category. Not that the Princetonians or their fellow inductivists claimed this. On the contrary, they frequently insisted that disparate fields of study demanded due recognition of the peculiar character of their objects, and that the immateriality of psychological phenomena, for example, did not render them impenetrable or unreal, but demanded a peculiar application of the inductive method. It was one of the leading motifs of the Common-Sense philosophy that inductive scrutiny could open up a science of man (that is, of our mental and moral attributes) as substantial as the science of material things.[38] This certainly was a recurrent theme in Princetonian discourse.

But the men of Princeton seemed unsure where to locate theology among the sciences, as the competing images of twin daughter and queen suggest. Often the Princetonians spoke of theology as one of the fields of study, on equal terms with, say, geology. At other times, though, they reverted to the older imperial image. Charles Hodge defined theology as the knowledge of God and of his relation to his works, a definition that ended up placing everything under theology's purview.[39] Benja-

---

38. Grave, *Scottish Philosophy,* pp. 140-41; Olson, *Scottish Philosophy,* pp. 11-15.

39. On the other hand, Charles Hodge distinguished theology from philosophy, stating that theology "does not assume to discover truth, or to reconcile what it teaches as true with all other truths. Its province is simply to state what God has revealed in his word, and to vindicate those statements as far as possible from misconceptions and objections." Theology held a "limited and humble office." *Systematic Theology,* 1:535.

min B. Warfield called theology the *scientia scientarum,* the science of sciences, the pinnacle of knowledge. While his view drew on the medieval notion of a hierarchy of knowledge culminating in divine wisdom (which includes much more than mere knowledge), in its nineteenth-century context it made theology virtually equivalent to the culmination of induction, Science with a capital *S.* Conceiving of theology both as *a* science and as *queen* of the sciences poised it ambiguously as one realm on the map and as the map itself.

This imagery of realms, borders, and sovereignties became common in Princetonian discussions of science and religion after 1859.[40] It was an explicit application of the military metaphor. Sometimes the Princetonians asked for a mutual respect for the sovereignty of each field, as though natural scientists in theological territory, like the Wicked Witch of the West in Munchkinland, had "no power here." But induction united the fields — the deceptively plain terminology of "fact" hid, for some unnuanced contributors, metaphysical and epistemic distinctions between kinds of experiential data — and the very expectation that science bring its garlands to adorn the temple of God amounted to an invitation for science to cross the border. Perhaps not inconsistently with the metaphor of realms, boundaries, and battles, the Princetonians were willing to accept a friendly border crossing, but quick to cry "Invasion!" when the crossing was hostile.

It was about 1859 that the *Princeton Review*'s accustomed confidence in science as an ally began to give way to complaints against it as an invader. The military metaphor was never wholly absent from the polemical articles Princeton routinely issued in fulfillment of its founding mandate to defend the doctrines of Calvinism, but it now became prominent in articles on the scientific evidences of religion. What occasioned this shift was not Darwinism, however tantalizing that year, 1859, may be. What troubled Princeton in the late fifties was another theory altogether, one that evolutionism actually ended up putting to rest. That theory was polygenism, the belief that the human race constituted not one but several separate species. In the controversy over polygenism a scientific claim came into direct conflict with both the Bible and the Reformed system of doctrine. Louis Agassiz of Harvard, Guyot's close friend, advocated the polygenist theory and lent it considerable scien-

40. The most succinct and systematic example is Archibald Alexander Hodge, *Outlines of Theology,* 2nd ed. (New York: Robert Carter and Bros., 1878), pp. 247-49.

tific prestige, but he did not originate it. In 1839 an American physician named Samuel Morton published *Crania Americana,* a book that presented such striking differences between the skulls of various human races as to argue against classifying them all in the same species. A successor volume, *Crania Aegyptiaca* (1844), compared newly discovered skulls from the tombs of ancient Egypt to modern skulls, concluding that the differences between the races had persisted virtually unchanged for four thousand years. If humankind constituted one species, then the various races must have come about long before the biblical Adamic chronology allowed; otherwise the human races must form separate species. Either way, scriptural anthropology was threatened, especially its entailments for Christ's work of redemption as the "second Adam" based on the solidarity of the race.[41] Doctrinal consequences notwithstanding, the polygenist view served to legitimate Negro slavery, and enjoyed a heyday in the mid-1850s that peaked with the publication of the collaborative work of two of Morton's followers, Josiah Noll and George Gliddon: *Types of Mankind* (1855) and *Indigenous Races of the Earth* (1857).[42]

In the wake of the polygenist debate the *BRPR* carried two articles, appearing in 1859 and 1860, that marked a new wariness toward natural science. The first, "The Testimony of Modern Science to the Unity of Mankind," addressed polygenism directly. It also took that occasion to lodge a complaint, noted earlier, against the glee with which certain polygenists had waved their theory in the face of the orthodox. Churchly scholars had been exercising self-restraint and good faith toward science; why did these scientists not return the favor? The writer proceeded to suggest some very illuminating answers to that question, answers the second article, "The Logical Relations of Religion and Natural Science," discussed in considerable detail.

41. Reformed theologians called this the doctrine of federal headship. It was based on Rom. 5:12-21. Verse 19 reads, "For as by one man's disobedience [— Adam's —] many were made sinners, so by the obedience of one [— Christ —] shall many be made righteous" (KJV). In the poetry of Handel's Messiah, "For as in Adam all die, even so in Christ shall all be made alive." This typology of two Adams standing as representatives for all humanity before God underlay the whole covenantal system of Calvinistic theology. The human race was condemned in Adam's breaking of the covenant of works; it was offered salvation in the new covenant in Christ, the covenant of grace. Thus polygenism not only contradicts the Bible, argued the *BRPR,* but "it subverts the great doctrines of the common apostasy and redemption of the race." "Testimony of Modern Science," p. 107.

42. Charles F. O'Brien, *Sir William Dawson: A Life in Science and Religion* (Philadelphia: American Philosophical Society, 1971), pp. 32-33.

The articles suggested two possible reasons why some natural scientists treated theological science unfairly. On the one hand, it might be raw wickedness, a desire to get out from under the authority of God by denigrating Holy Writ. This suggestion — that a scientific theory might be advocated out of proportion to its empirical merits because it served as a rationalization for spiritual rebellion — was highly unusual in the pages of the *BRPR,* and continued so in its successor publications into the twentieth century. Assuredly there *were* people who used science as a platform to rail against religion, but Princeton usually played the gentleman and assumed the good faith of its adversaries. On this particular occasion the *BRPR* did suggest a suspicion, but in the form of an admonition, without mentioning any names. "There is in every community a large class of men eager after an excuse for unbelief," the article stated. "Men of science should not become panders to this depraved appetite."[43]

On the other hand, however, and at much greater length, the *Review* offered another explanation — a rather trenchant one based on the nature of scientific investigation itself. "Physical science, at the present day, investigates phenomena simply as they are in themselves. This, if not positively atheistic, must be of a dangerous tendency. Whatever deliberately omits God from the universe, is closely allied to that which denies him."[44] This was the opening statement to "The Logical Relations of Religion and Natural Science." In a day of unguarded paeans to empiricism, here was a note of warning that the very pursuit of science might backfire against religion. Inquiries into nature necessarily entailed questions about the source of all things, the writer argued, and those questions could be answered in any of three ways: the inquirer could acknowledge God openly, or profess atheism openly — or he could pursue a kind of *methodological atheism* by simply leaving God out of the picture. In this

43. "Testimony of Modern Science," p. 107. The author of "The Logical Relations" was more explicit: "In every community there are many who dislike religious restraint and the authority of God. The more ambitious amongst these wish to be gods themselves in their own small way; and they hope by means of science to gratify this desire. If nothing more is gained, they may at least escape from the Bible. It is easy to find plausible hypotheses concerning strata, fossil remains, Egyptian hieroglyphics, or the races of mankind, which are utterly at variance with the Scriptures. With little or no investigation, views are adopted which free the soul from all unpleasant belief in the Book which tells of the strait gate, the narrow way, and camels passing through a needle's eye." Eckard, "The Logical Relations," p. 579.

44. Eckard, "The Logical Relations," p. 577.

last option, "a resort to that concealed atheism which quietly sets God aside without directly denying his existence," lay a threat far worse than any particular theory.[45]

These two themes — a wariness against the abuse of natural science as a rationalization for irreligious motives, and a dawning suspicion that the method of natural science itself might prejudice its outcome in religious matters — began after 1859 to qualify the antebellum confidence in science Princeton had shared with most of Anglophone academia. These themes clashed with the accustomed hymns of praise to scientific progress. To understand the dissonance, and to devise a strategy to resolve it, the Princetonians turned to the metaphor of war.[46] There were several important theoretical tensions to work out in the relations of science and theology, but there was also a defensive battle to plan and to fight.

It was Lyman Atwater who raised the battle cry. The *BRPR* had for several years carried sporadic complaints against scientific impetuosity. Now the professor of mental and moral science at Princeton College, serving also as Charles Hodge's right-hand man on the *Review*, issued a veritable call to arms. He espied "a positive and semi-positive school . . . assailing the fundamental, moral, and religious convictions of men from the scientific side, with weapons claimed to be forged in the laboratories of physical science." Together with Romanism and idealism — despite their mutual antagonisms — they formed a "combined and fearful host arrayed against the faith once delivered to the saints, the truth as it is in Jesus." He continued, "The signs are manifold that this thing is not done in a corner, but that the assault upon the fundamentals of faith will be

45. Eckard, "The Logical Relations," p. 577. In this observation was an early predecessor to the presuppositionalism that historians have associated with the Dutch Calvinists Herman Bavinck and Abraham Kuyper, and emphatically *not* with Princeton. It suggested that science was not entirely objective, that religious (or irreligious) precommitments colored the inquiry and its results. On underplayed Princetonian affinities with the Kuyperians, see Peter J. Wallace, "The Foundations of Reformed Biblical Theology: The Development of Old Testament Theology at Old Princeton, 1812-1932," *Westminster Theological Journal* 59 (1997): 44, 46; Paul Kjoss Helseth, *"Right Reason" and the Princeton Mind: An Unorthodox Proposal* (Phillipsburg, N.J.: P&R, 2010), p. 95; and Helseth's two essays in Gary L. W. Johnson, ed., *B. B. Warfield: Essays on His Life and Thought* (Phillipsburg, N.J.: P&R, 2007).

46. This appears to be an instance of what Colin Russell calls the "methodological" version of the conflict thesis. Russell breaks the conflict thesis into four distinct types in his "Conflict of Science with Religion," in *The History of Science and Religion in the Western Tradition: An Encyclopedia*, ed. Gary B. Ferguson et al. (New York: Garland, 2010), pp. 12-16.

transferred from the old world to the new, and rage from within as well as without the pale of the church. Those set for the defence of the gospel must therefore gird on their armor. They must watch, detect, expose, confront, and overpower their foe."[47] The year was 1865. The Civil War was just ending, but a new war was beginning.

47. Lyman H. Atwater, "Herbert Spencer's Philosophy," p. 289. A portly and dignified man, Atwater cut a memorable figure on the Princeton College campus. See John Moore, "Recollections of the Faculty and of the Course of Study," in *Fifty Years of Princeton '77: A Fifty-Four-Year Record of the Class of 1877 of Princeton College and University,* ed. Henry Fairfield Osborn (Princeton: Princeton University Press, 1927), pp. 54-55.

CHAPTER THREE

Seize and Master

A contest against iron-clad ships can be sustained successfully only by iron-clad ships, or something better.

Joseph Clark, 1863[1]

Atwater's battle cry in 1865 was military allusion at its most conscious. He painted a vivid, ominous picture of gathering armies intent upon the destruction of Christianity at its foundations. "A combined and fearful host arrayed against the faith" would wage its unholy war on unwonted soil: in virtuous America as well as corrupt Europe, within the church as well as without. It was a heinous prospect, an infiltration onto hallowed ground. One heard the deep rumble of impending invasion — a war undesired but unavoidable. A battle was brewing. "Those set for the defence of the gospel must therefore gird on their armor," he cried. How would the defenders of the faith respond?

Atwater issued more than a call to arms; he provided concrete suggestions for conducting the defense. His call to "watch, detect, expose, confront, and overpower [the] foe" conveyed more than mere zeal — it presented a thoughtful, deliberate summation of strategy for meeting the perceived attack. In those few words Atwater gave the outlines of a battle plan of *reconnaissance* and *tactics* that two generations of Princetonians then put into practice. It was a most remarkable instance of strategizing

1. Joseph Clark, "The Scepticism of Science," *Biblical Repertory and Princeton Review* (hereafter *BRPR*) 35 (1863): 65.

and implementation. The plan persisted at Princeton College into the 1890s; at the seminary it lasted even longer, into the 1920s.

By no means was Lyman Atwater the solitary mastermind of the operation, though he gave the strategy its most concise formulation. No particular reference to his call to arms survives in either printed literature or private correspondence; rather, his statement encapsulated a wide and ongoing discussion in the *Princeton Review* of the 1860s as to how religious leaders (especially Presbyterian ones)[2] should respond to the challenge of natural science. Numerous articles and book notices[3] articulated the battle plan in all the richness of its martial imagery: territories, invaders, defenders, and weaponry; charges, feints, and retreats. But Atwater's words did more than capture the ephemeral discussion of a decade; with astonishing clarity they also forecast fifty years of activity at Princeton on the theological ramifications of natural science. This Battle Plan formed the context in which Princeton College and Seminary addressed the evolution question.

Reconnaissance

Atwater exhorted his compatriots in the citadel of faith to "watch, detect, and expose" the enemy — to identify the nature of the threat he posed, to discern his location and his movements, to flush him out of his places of hiding. Already in the 1860s several articles in the *Princeton Review* embarked on that mission of military intelligence. Before Darwinism became a serious scientific concern in America — that is, before 1870 — the Princetonians had assembled a very clear profile of the en-

2. Like college president John Maclean, Atwater in the 1860s was deeply concerned to preserve and extend the unique services Presbyterian higher education had to offer. Lyman H. Atwater, "A Plea for High Education and Presbyterian Colleges," *BRPR* 34 (1862): 635-68.

3. Among those articles the following are noteworthy (all appearing in *BRPR*): "The Logical Relations of Religion and Natural Science," by James R. Eckard (1860); "Reason and Faith," a review of James McCosh's book *The Intuitions of the Mind Inductively Investigated* and three other books, by Atwater (1860); "Knowledge, Faith, and Feeling, in Their Mutual Relations," by Atwater (1861); "The Scepticism of Science," by Joseph Clark (1863); "Man's Mental Instincts," by Walter H. Lowrie (1864); "Herbert Spencer's Philosophy; Atheism, Pantheism, and Materialism," by Atwater (1865); "Rationalism" and "McCosh on J. S. Mill and Fundamental Truth," by Atwater (1866); "A Philosophical Confession of Faith," by astronomer Stephen Alexander (1867); "Materialism — Physiological Psychology" (1869).

emy they faced.[4] His name was philosophical materialism, though he used many aliases; his tactic was invasion of the mental and moral sphere under the guise of natural science. Often his scientific garb was woven of evolutionary threads — but the enemy beneath the cloak was materialism.[5]

The "development hypothesis," as we have seen, predated Darwinism and received a mixed welcome at antebellum Princeton. On the one hand, Chambers's fatalistic evolutionary monism met swift repudiation from the *Princeton Review*. On the other hand, Guyot's beatific vision of God-guided development, together with astronomer Stephen Alexander's calculations supporting the nebular hypothesis,[6] christened a form of cosmological evolutionism at Princeton well before the publication of the *Origin*. Guyot's work carried developmentalism into the realm of life in a goal-directed, grand scheme of progressive creation as lilting as a poem and as concrete as the fossil record. His view might even be called "evolutionary," by analogy with the cosmical evolutionism he imbibed from Laplace — evolutionary, but not transmutationist. Princeton was proud of its scientists and partook of that nineteenth-century fascination in past developments that Maurice Mandelbaum has called "historicism": a fascination with directed change, animated by the desire to find a fixed pattern of progress in the very nature of things — a fascination linking transmutationism with social and anthropological evolutionisms and even with the dialectical materialism of Marx and Engels.[7] Within this

4. Geoffrey Cantor dates "the strong version of the Conflict Thesis" to the 1870s, when "science became a weapon to be wielded in public attacks on religion." Geoffrey Cantor, "What Shall We Do with the Conflict Thesis?" in *Science and Religion: New Historical Perspectives*, ed. Thomas Dixon, Geoffrey Cantor, and Stephen Pumfrey (New York: Cambridge University Press, 2010), p. 294. But clearly a rich battle imagery, in American discourse at least, existed in the 1860s.

5. Charles Hodge devoted fifty-three dense pages of his *Systematic Theology* to a discussion of materialism. Of the other antitheistic theories, pantheism came in second, at thirty pages. Charles Hodge, *Systematic Theology* (New York: Scribners, 1872-73; reprint, Grand Rapids: Eerdmans, 1993), 1:246-99. Cf. Charles D. Cashdollar, *The Transformation of Theology, 1830-1890: Positivism and Protestant Thought in Britain and America* (Princeton: Princeton University Press, 1989). Cashdollar argues that positivism, not Darwinism, was the chief challenge to theology in the nineteenth century. Hodge and the Princetonians regarded positivism as a latter-day variety of materialism.

6. See chapter 1, note 56.

7. Maurice Mandelbaum, *History, Man, and Reason: A Study in Nineteenth-Century Thought* (Baltimore: Johns Hopkins University Press, 1971), cited in Peter J. Bowler, *The*

dazzlingly wide array of developmental theories were some the Princetonians found quite gratifying, and many they did not.

We should bear in mind Princeton's selective approval of developmental views, lest the coincidence of the battle cry with the publication of the *Origin* mislead us to conclude that the ruckus was about Darwinism, or even about evolution. The Princetonians did roundly repudiate the doctrine of transmutation until 1868, usually dismissing it as a scientific hypothesis lacking sufficient evidence; but even at the height of their martial rhetoric in the 1860s they propounded a variety of progressionist views and did not hesitate to employ the term "evolution" in a welcoming way. William Henry Green, the seminary's Old Testament specialist, espoused the "evolution" of language; another contributor faulted Kant for approaching the study of mental apparatus in terms too static — Kant erred, he said, in treating the mature mind only, rather than exploring mental *development,* the mind's interaction with its environment as the seeds of its capabilities came to life and grew.[8] Stephen Alexander in 1867 argued the philosophical impossibility of life evolving *out of* nonlife — that is, by some endowment of its own — but he left open the possibility of life evolving *from* nonlife by the addition of a new, external force (i.e., by a miracle). He also discussed evolution *within* species even as he asserted the lack of existing evidence for evolution *between* species.[9]

That same year Charles Hodge identified what he thought really mattered in the doctrine of creation. He was discussing the confessional guarantees that he and other Old School Presbyterians would require of the New School as a precondition of the impending denominational re-

Non-Darwinian Revolution: Reinterpreting a Historical Myth (Baltimore: Johns Hopkins University Press, 1988), p. 133.

8. William Henry Green, "Modern Philology: Its Discoveries, History, and Influence," review of *Modern Philology,* by Benjamin W. Dwight, *BRPR* 36 (1864): 640; Walter H. Lowrie, "Man's Mental Instincts," review of *Francis Bacon of Verulam; Realistic Philosophy, and Its Age,* by Kuno Fischer, *BRPR* 36 (1864): 599. The latter article argued that Bacon himself, had he applied his method to mental nature, would have taken a developmental view of epistemology (p. 594).

9. Alexander, "Philosophical Confession of Faith," pp. 435-36. Observing that "it *is* true that there are evidences of a wonderful *development* of *plan,*" he finds no satisfactory evidence of the development "of the more exquisitely organized and endowed, *out* of the inferior, or even lifeless, which preceded them. . . . But," he adds, "this will not prevent great modifications, by special development, within far narrower limits, of that which *is* alive."

union — a touchy issue, requiring extreme precision of statement. Hodge believed confessional subscription did not mean unswerving acceptance of every single proposition in the creeds of the church, but acceptance of the system as a whole. That system, however, rested on certain basic doctrines "no one of which can be omitted without destroying its identity." Among those foundational doctrines was creation, and Hodge took pains to explain what "creation" could and could not include. Creation meant "that the universe and all that it contains is not eternal, is not a necessary product of the life of God, is not an emanation from the divine substance, but owes its existence as to substance and form solely to his will — and in reference to man that he was created in the image of God, in knowledge, righteousness, and holiness, and not *in puris naturalibis,* without any moral character."[10] Noticeably absent from Hodge's detailed list of the sine qua nons of creation was any denial of transmutation. He jealously guarded the distinction of the Creator from his creation, to avoid pantheistic monism. He also contradicted the Roman Catholic view of natural man as all of earth and none of heaven, for in the Reformed view the first great mystery of humankind was the bridging of mind and matter, and even fallen humanity bore the image of God. On both counts he asserted the confessional necessity of metaphysical dualism — and left the evolution question moot.

When evolution did draw Princeton's fire, it was usually because of its philosophical associations. Occasionally an article harangued scientific contradictions of the Bible, as when Robert Patterson in 1868 railed against "the atheistic folly of a boastful mushroom science, denying the heavenly Father of mankind, asserting our self-education without a revelation from God, and denying the Bible account of God's dealings with the world before the flood." Such vituperations anticipated the tone fundamentalists would later use toward science, but were not characteristic of Princetonian discourse.[11] In general Princeton was content to "wait

10. Charles Hodge, "The General Assembly," *BRPR* 39 (1867): 509. Note that this came just a few years after the publication of Huxley's *Man's Place in Nature* and the *BRPR*'s pointed answer to it (1864). On confessional subscription and the historic Old School position, see the excellent study by S. Donald Fortson III, *The Presbyterian Creed: A Confessional Tradition in America, 1729-1870* (Milton Keynes, U.K.: Paternoster, 2008).

11. Robert Patterson, "The Antiquity of Man," *BRPR* 40 (1868): 606. Patterson was pastor of the Jefferson Park Presbyterian Church in Chicago, the pulpit Francis Patton occupied when he rose to fame in the heresy trial of David Swing. He was not, by the way, a Princeton man.

and see," to learn from the lesson of Galileo. But suspending judgment on the scientific particulars of transmutation did not mean suspending judgment on the philosophical views that made use of it. New scientific facts, once duly authenticated, might require some reinterpreting of the Bible, but that was in everyone's best interest as far as the Princetonians were concerned. They were willing, they had long asserted, to bow to the authority of scientists within their proper domain. They were *not* willing, however, to let men of science, who often had little expertise in philosophical matters, tell them what the philosophical and theological ramifications of their findings ought to be.

There was one great exception to the hands-off rule: anthropology. Even in the 1850s Princeton set aside its talk of cozy confidence in science to combat polygenism. The doctrine of man — theological anthropology — was a point of crucial contact between religious and scientific claims. Princeton, dissenting in principle from the Schleiermachian divorce of scientific and historical truth from religious truth, maintained the union by calling for patience and making a clear distinction between what the Bible itself intended to teach regarding this-worldly realities, and what interpretations fallible humans had attached to its words. Even issues like the transmutation of brute species were arguably beyond the intention of scriptural teaching. The Bible was not a call-in answer service, ready to deliver the informational goods on any subject the caller might find interesting. But the nature and origin of man were much nearer to the religious purposes of Scripture; here this-worldly truth claims had material bearing on the grand doctrines of the *imago*, fall, and redemption through the resurrected Christ. Not surprisingly, then, the scientific discussions of the 1860s that most interested the *Princeton Review* had to do with humankind: man's nature and his place in God's creation.

Peter Bowler has shown that evolutionary anthropology constituted a separate, pre-, and decidedly *non*-Darwinian stream of evolutionary doctrine that historians and scientists after the so-called Darwinian revolution have mistakenly conflated with the tale of Darwin's triumphs. A whole spectrum of cultural or social evolutionisms (Mandelbaum's "historicism"), from Spencer and Huxley to Hegel, Comte, and Marx, flourished in the decades immediately before and after the *Origin*. In the English-speaking world, the new science of anthropology was the main channel of such historicist interest. In common with the social evolutionisms inspired on the Continent by post-Kantian idealism, British and American anthropology from the 1850s onward exhibited a deep interest in goal-directed progress over time, "the ascent of a more or less rigidly preordained hierarchy of cultural stages" from savagery to barbarism to civilization. Archeological research abetted this tendency with its discovery of the antiquity and original primitiveness of the human race. It was at this time that the familiar three-age system of human prehistory was devised, based on the use first of stone, then of bronze, then of iron tools. Bowler notes that anthropologists and archeologists have long resisted the "Darwin industry's" claim that the *Origin* was responsible for their interest in the primitive state of early humans.[12]

The *Princeton Review*'s treatment of evolutionism in the 1860s came not in response to Darwin's book, but in response to British and American works in this largely separate, progressionist vein of anthropology and sociology. Charles Hodge contributed an article that answered polygenism with the assertion of what we would today call human microevolution;[13] Chester Dewey of the University of Rochester reviewed Louis Agassiz in "The True Place of Man in Zoölogy" and, in another review, Huxley's *Man's Place in Nature;* Walter H. Lowrie discussed "man's mental instincts"; Atwater treated Herbert Spencer's evolutionary sociology; Robert Patterson of Chicago discussed "the antiquity of man"; and two anonymous articles examined physiological psychology and Agassiz's polygenism.[14]

12. Bowler, *The Non-Darwinian Revolution,* pp. 133-38. He points out that the linear, teleological progressionism of the anthropologists and archeologists was basically orthogenetic rather than Darwinian.

13. Charles Hodge, "Diversity of Species in the Human Race: Examination of Some Reasonings against the Unity of Mankind," *BRPR* 34 (1862): 450. He argued for wide variation within a unified human species, the result of external causes and climatic influences. This he probably took from Arnold Henry Guyot, *The Earth and Man: Lectures on Comparative Physical Geography, in Its Relation to the History of Mankind,* trans. C. C. Felton (Boston: Gould, Kendall, and Lincoln, 1849). In the same article Hodge made his first published mention of Darwin (p. 461): the highly speculative hypothesis of the *Origin,* he said, minimized the differences between man and brute, contrasting so glaringly with the polygenist doctrine that he felt safe to conclude that science had evidently not yet reached a verdict theologians had to worry about.

14. The subjects of short notices carried in the *BRPR* for the 1860s stood in fairly striking contrast to the subjects of full-length review articles. Works on anthropology and sociology merited whole essays, as listed above; works on Genesis and geology and even natural theology received only brief notice: for example, in 1859, *The Primeval World: A Treatise on the Relations of Geology to Theology,* by Paton Gloag, and *Popular Geology,* by Hugh Miller; in 1861, *The Physical and Moral Aspects of Geology,* by William Barbee; in 1863, *Man-*

These articles objected to transmutationism and occasionally associated anthropological and sociological evolutionism with Darwin's name — they, too, found the name a convenient label, and so contributed to the fog of imprecision that seems always to have surrounded the evolution question. But their biggest guns were reserved for their most formidable foe, the master to whom evolution theory was sometimes a servant.

Dewey's article praised Agassiz for his firm defense of the fixity of species,[15] but objected to his classifying man as a mere animal. A moral nature was humanity's most distinguishing feature; how could any comprehensive system of classification leave that out of the picture? In the ability to think, mankind differed from the brute only in degree, Dewey admitted, citing Locke's "power of abstraction" as the key difference; but in *moral* nature humans were entirely unique in the creation. It was as *natural* for a human to discern right and wrong by conscience, as for a dog to bark. To ignore that fact in a scheme of natural classification, he contended, degraded man from his high position as the image-bearer of God. It undid the good that Agassiz's approach to classification offered. The Harvard naturalist had argued that laws of the material world could never produce life — for laws are dead, and life is alive — his very approach thus ruling out the "desolate theory which refers all to the laws of matter, . . . and leaves us with no God but the monotonous, unvarying action of physical forces, binding all things to their inevitable destiny." In making this observation, Dewey intimated that one's approach to the classification of living things could itself prejudice the outcome. He faulted Agassiz for failing to fulfill the promise of his powerfully nonmaterialistic approach to classification, by limiting his consideration of humanity to our animal nature.[16]

---

ual of Geology, by James Dana, and *The Relations of Christianity and Science,* by N. L. Rice; in 1864, *The Great Stone-Book of Nature,* by David Anstead, and *Textbook of Geology,* by Dana; in 1867, *The Reign of Law,* by the Duke of Argyll.

15. Agassiz was the great exception among American naturalists, never yielding to the doctrine of transmutation. Like his friend Guyot, Agassiz espoused what Bowler calls the "new progressionism" that had its roots in German *Naturphilosophie* — "a divine plan with a symbolic purpose," progressive and developmental but nontransmutationist. Bowler, *The Non-Darwinian Revolution,* pp. 57-58.

16. Chester Dewey, "The True Place of Man in Zoölogy," review of *Contributions to the Natural History of the United States of America,* by Louis Agassiz, *BRPR* 35 (1863): 114-23. Dewey preferred the system of classification James Dana offered in his *Manual of Geology,*

Dewey, and Princeton with him, believed that the divine image was natural in humans, and that natural science ought therefore to take man's moral nature into account. They refused Schleiermacher's separation of moral and religious from physical and historical reality, a separation the materialistic approach to science either assumed or unwittingly abetted.[17] To insist on considering only physical things, as natural science was beginning to do, was to truncate reality, lopping off its top, its highest and noblest component — and such truncation was especially consequential in the study of man, where the Horrible Vision of materialism severed him violently from his God.

Dewey continued this concern in his review of Thomas Henry Huxley's *Man's Place in Nature* (1863). Here the limitation of the science of man to his animal nature took up evolution for an explanation of human origins. Huxley, the brilliant and winsome comparative anatomist who as "Darwin's bulldog"[18] popularized the theory of evolution, and whose debate with Bishop Wilberforce in 1860 cast an early pall of stark oppositionism over the Darwinian controversies, propounded human evolution explicitly. "It is the object of Professor Huxley," Dewey explained, "to prove that man is so related, in structure and other physical aspects, to the ape-tribe, that both are to be placed in the same division of the great class of mammals," and further to prove that man "was *developed* from the ape family by some fortunate operations of the laws that direct the changes of matter." The review took up those two themes at length. Harking back to Dod's review of the *Vestiges*, the article treated evolution (even human evolution) as an old, recurrent theory — but observed that each time the theory recurred, our consciousness of a

---

for it placed man in a subclass by himself (p. 346). Dewey was a friend of Princeton College professor Joshua Hall McIlvaine, and through that connection became a contributor to the *BRPR* (see index volume, 1871-72).

17. Recalling Hodge's objection to the Roman Catholic doctrine of humankind *in puris naturalibis,* it would seem that the issue was the separation of nature from grace, something that long predated the Enlightenment and Schleiermacher's response to it.

18. Despite Huxley's own self-understanding as a Darwinian and his crucial role in propagating the notion of a Darwinian revolution, Bowler contends that he was in fact a "pseudo-Darwinian" (*The Non-Darwinian Revolution,* pp. 72, 76-80). Quite a claim, yet he argues it persuasively. On Huxley's role as "Darwin's bulldog," see James R. Moore, *The Post-Darwinian Controversies: A Study of the Protestant Struggle to Come to Terms with Darwin in Great Britain and America, 1870-1900* (Cambridge: Cambridge University Press, 1979), pp. 58-65, and Gertrude Himmelfarb, *Darwin and the Darwinian Revolution* (1959; reprint, Chicago: Ivan R. Dee, 1996), pp. 263-66.

nobler place for humankind intervened. The common person's repugnance to the idea of brute ancestry was usually enough to overturn it,
the reviewer said, and in so doing common sense was a reliable guide,
"the voice of God in the consciousness of men." When people are faced
with the theory of human evolution, the "chasm" between man and
brute "is seen and felt, and men stop before the yawning gulf." Consciousness, as Dod had said, decided the question; people could feel the
difference a moral nature made.[19]

But moral appeal to the Horrible Vision or to the common sense of
mankind seemed rather out of place in scientific discourse, where
careful accumulation of observable facts guided and verified inquiry.
Was there no way of joining the testimony of consciousness with natural science? Here was the rub — if the moral sphere could be subjected
to the same kind of inductive inquiry that had opened up such impressive vistas in physical science, while yet retaining the fundamental distinction between the two spheres, nature would be seen to include
spirit, and science would not become coextensive with materialistic
monism.[20]

Walter H. Lowrie's article "Man's Mental Instincts" attempted to answer this question. It began by tracing the truncation of nature back to
none other than Francis Bacon. The father of inductive philosophy himself was guilty of "an unnatural and arbitrary limitation" of its sphere: he
restricted human knowledge to external experience of physical nature,
allowing the investigating mind "no natural laws, tendencies, faculties,
or capacities" of its own. Precisely here, Princeton believed, science had
taken a wrong turn. Physical science had flourished under the inductive
philosophy, but mental and moral science suffered degradation at the
hands of a long list of Enlightenment greats: "Hobbes, Locke, Berkeley,
Hume, Bayle, Voltaire, Condillac, Holbach, Helvetius, and others of the
materialist school." They carried Bacon's fatal oversight to its logical
metaphysical conclusion: materialism. Not only did Bacon's wrong turn
yield in due course the materialistic metaphysic that so assaulted
nineteenth-century believers, it also produced the epistemological skep-

19. Chester Dewey, "Man's Place in Nature," *BRPR* 36 (1864): 276-97. Charles Hodge argued similarly from the facts of consciousness to refute all materialism, in his *Systematic
Theology*, 1:276-80.

20. The fantastic popularity some thirty years later of Henry Drummond's *Natural
Law in the Spiritual World* (1883) evidenced the same concern. Within a year the book was
in its tenth edition; within a decade, its twenty-ninth edition.

ticism of Hume, for in the empirical philosophy the study of subjectivity never found adequate ground.[21]

These two fruits of a too-narrow induction — skepticism and materialism — came together in the grand vision of Herbert Spencer. He, more than any other scientist or philosopher in the 1860s, alarmed orthodox academics and set them to planning an adequate line of defense. Spencer had been fascinated by the organic development of things long before Darwin's *Origin*. By his own confession he had since his childhood found miracles increasingly unbelievable, and looked to evolution as a naturalistic alternative to miraculous creation. His latent evolutionism became explicit in the early 1840s after reading Charles Lyell's uniformitarian classic, *Principles of Geology*. Unlike Darwin, he did not much concern himself with the origin of species; rather, his chief interest lay in human social relations. Josiah Royce characterized Spencer's life's work as the attempt to combine a unitary evolutionary process, accounting for all reality, with a doctrine of individual freedom and rights. He found the key in the theory of use inheritance. It was evident that functions remained vigorous only when used, whether in nature or in human society; proper adaptation to either environment required the free exercise of individual powers in the struggle to survive.[22] It was in this connection that Spencer coined his famous phrase, often mistakenly connected with Darwin, "the survival of the fittest." Borrowing from the embryological researches of the German scientist Karl von Baer, Spencer theorized that all evolution proceeded "from an indefinite incoherent homogeneity to a definite coherent heterogeneity through a continuous differentiation and integration."[23] All of reality, from stardust to religion and ethics, was but the unfolding of the potentialities of an unknown and unknowable Force. This was "evolution," literally the unrolling of po-

21. Lowrie, "Man's Mental Instincts," p. 585. In the Princetonians' eyes, Kant's answer to Humean skepticism was unsuccessful; most of them (Guyot was a notable exception) turned instead to the Scottish school to bridge the gap between subject and object. It was a founding aim of the Scottish philosophy to establish just that inductive science of mind that Bacon had neglected. James McCosh, soon to be president of Princeton College, attempted it in his *Intuitions of the Mind, Inductively Investigated,* 3rd ed., revised (New York: Robert Carter and Bros., 1872; orig. 1861).

22. Josiah Royce, *Herbert Spencer: An Estimate and Review* (New York: Fox, Duffield, and Co., 1904), pp. 63-67.

23. Herbert Spencer, quoted in James McCosh, *Development: What It Can Do and What It Cannot Do* (New York: Charles Scribner's Sons, 1883), p. 12.

tentiality into actuality.[24] (It was Spencer's work, not Darwin's, that popularized the word.)

In points of unorthodoxy this theory was remarkably similar to Chambers's. Like the *Vestiges,* Spencer's work espoused a metaphysical monism, harking back to Spinoza. It severed mankind from any meaningful relationship with God. It blurred the distinction between man and beast, calling into question the divine image in humankind. In points of scientific doctrine, too, it echoed Chambers. Its analogy from embryology recalled the image of "the universal gestation of nature." It understood evolution to proceed on the inheritance of acquired characteristics. But it went beyond Chambers, for it made evolution not just the law of life, but (together with a counterbalancing law of dissolution) the law of *everything.* Behind it was no designing God, but an utterly inscrutable Force. If Chambers's theory was deistic (as was Darwin's, by the way), Spencer's was pantheistic and agnostic at the same time.

It was in a review of several of Spencer's works that Lyman Atwater sounded the battle cry in 1865. Despite the significant differences between Darwinism and Spencerism, he identified the enemy as "a positive and semi-positive school, with their allies, under the lead of such men as Huxley, Darwin, Spencer, and Mill."[25] In his judgment the essence of positivism was that fateful combination of skepticism and materialism, a pairing the thinkers he named all shared. It was just the natural consequence of Bacon's oversight. The ultimate enemy was not any theory of evolution, nor was it Spencer or any group of scientists; it was truncated inductivism and the philosophical mistakes it led to. People might indeed "appear to be assailing the fundamental, moral, and religious convictions of men from the scientific side, with weapons claimed to be forged in the laboratories of

24. Royce pointed out that Spencer was interested in decidedly different questions from those most scientists at the time were asking. Scientists usually wanted to know such things as whether Darwin had positively confirmed transmutation, whether Darwinism might be applied outside the animal realm, and what the line of human ancestry was. Spencer, by contrast, was interested in finding a formula general enough to cover all evolutionary phenomena — in finding a universal cause of evolution. His evolutionary theory, Royce adds, was methodologically most unlike Darwin's, for it was "no result of scientific induction. It was simply a consequence of his now settled habit of believing in the existence of a natural cause for everything." In other words, Spencer's presupposed antisupernaturalism determined his evolutionism (Royce, *Herbert Spencer,* pp. 71-75).

25. Lyman H. Atwater, "Herbert Spencer's Philosophy; Atheism, Pantheism, and Materialism," *BRPR* 37 (1865): 269.

physical science,"[26] but they were only the dupes of Bacon's error, led astray, like him, by an unnatural limitation of inductive science they failed to see. Princeton tried to affirm the positive value of their science while fixing a critical gaze on their forays into philosophy — and to convince all sides that science itself was not the problem, but indeed the answer.

With such charity to persons Princeton prepared for war against the error itself, especially when it appeared in connection with the study of man. Scientists were sovereign in their respective fields, free to pursue their inquiries unhindered by theological a prioris about their conclusions — but when natural scientists supposed that material nature was the sum total of reality, they in effect invaded the realms of philosophy and theology. Duping even themselves, they strayed outside their legitimate realm of expertise and acted instead as insinuating agents of false philosophy, dressed up with the garlands science ought rightfully to bring to religion. They adorned materialism with the prestige of science. They furthered a distinct philosophical program under the guise of natural science. It was, said the Princetonians and many like them, a case of gross imposture — presumption — usurpation.

An article in 1869 entitled "Materialism — Physiological Psychology" declared that the principles materialism fostered "cannot be too strongly reprobated," for, the author claimed, its proponents aimed at nothing less than to revolutionize science, education, religion, and society under its influence. Physical science was only "too prone in its intense search after truth in its own domain, to shut the eye of reason and faith against the realms of the spirit." It slipped into Bacon's mistake; it admitted only material data, and, seeking to explain human psychic nature in physiological terms, identified mind with matter — and so reduced man to the level of the beast. Science became an "enemy" when it served this infidel master — but the master, not the servant, was the real enemy. Having exposed him, this article called for his destruction in battle. There could be no compromise with this foe.

> In its very nature, [materialism] is degrading and demoralizing. It is destructive of religion, which has its seat in our spiritual nature, and must worship God, who is a spirit, in spirit and in truth. Materialism has ever been, and must be, the implacable foe of Christianity and spiritual religion. It is the ally and support of sensuality and vice. It

26. Atwater, "Herbert Spencer's Philosophy," p. 269.

gravitates toward the level of the brutes that perish, and cries out from the sty of Epicurus, "Let us eat and drink, for tomorrow we die." It now comes in as a flood under the pressure of positive philosophy, and other forms of crude science or philosophy falsely so-called. May the Spirit of the Lord lift up a standard against it![27]

Tactics

The development of the evolution question in the 1860s tied its answer ever more closely to the philosophical battles Princeton had engaged in for decades. In the identification of the philosophical enemy behind objectionable evolutionisms and in the analysis of the underlying methodological causes of enemy strength, one would expect the work of formulating a strategy for victory — fulfilling Atwater's call to "confront and overpower" the enemy — to be largely accomplished. To know one's enemy was the better part of knowing how to fight him. If incomplete induction was the problem — if a science of mind[28] was the missing piece to a completed scientific perspective that would put material science in its place — then establishing mental and moral science among the physical sciences would seem to be the obvious solution. But that was not such an easy task, nor was a science of mind so simple a concept.

Like many other schools, Princeton had already established a chair of mental and moral science. Atwater held that post at the College of New Jersey since its creation in 1854.[29] But the presence of a philosopher with the title of "scientist" did not persuade many naturalists of the "positive school" that mental "science" was any such thing. Anthropology *among* the sciences was fast becoming the problem rather than the solution. Naturalists like Huxley and Spencer were already undertaking to study mental and moral phenomena scientifically; but for them "science" carried the assumption of an essential continuity between man and beast

27. "Materialism — Physiological Psychology," *BRPR* 41 (1869): 616, 624-25.

28. Writers at the time routinely interchanged the titles "Science of Mind," "Mental and Moral Science," and "Science of Man." They also used the term "psychology" to denote the same thing. The direction this new science of psychology would take was precisely the issue. Since psychology now denotes a science vastly unlike the one the Princetonians conceived, I do not employ that term here.

29. Thomas Jefferson Wertenbaker, *Princeton, 1746-1896* (Princeton: Princeton University Press, 1946), pp. 273-74.

that could account for everything in man without recourse to the supernatural. Naturally, their results were far from what the orthodox wanted. The notion of a method in "the science of man" that was meaningfully continuous with the method in physical science and yet did not treat mental and moral phenomena in material terms, was clearly fraught with tension. So vast were the differences between the inward phenomena of mind and the outward phenomena of matter that any talk of a common method seemed to obscure more than it illuminated.

From the point of view of Princeton's dualistic metaphysic, however, the coexistence of matter and mind was fundamental, and science ought to confirm it. Surely an open inquirer would recognize the duality of matter and mind, the irreducible reality of each sphere in actual experience. A candid collection of all phenomena connected with humanity, body and soul, was all Princeton meant by a complete induction. But the combination of a dualistic metaphysic with a unitary method proved less attainable in practice than in theory.

Two main tactical options presented themselves. First and most obviously, Princeton could devote its energies to cultivating that "science of man," elevating it to a rank the other scientists would esteem as one of their own. This had been a pet project of the Scottish Common-Sense philosophers for almost a century, since the days of Thomas Reid. Unfortunately, no one had yet succeeded in doing it. Still, Atwater (and later James McCosh) pursued that task at Princeton, assured that as the physical sciences had taken centuries to develop, so the uncertain state of inductive mental science was, in light of its relative youth, undaunting. In the meantime the great vogue of natural science made a second tactic more immediately necessary: to embrace material science and to demonstrate its continued compatibility with orthodox belief.

The *Princeton Review* of the 1860s carried several articles exploring the possibilities and pitfalls of this latter strategy. Once again the authors used military metaphors to bring vividness and clarity to their discussion. Two telling phrases summarized their conception of the task. First, the defender of the faith, while embracing natural science as a friend, would have to "stand his ground" against the materialistic truncation of reality. Second, he must "seize and master the weapons of attack," fully persuaded that science as science, the knowledge of God's truth, would serve the cause of faith better than the cause of infidelity.

The language of standing one's ground appeared in Atwater's article on rationalism in 1866. To embrace natural science, he observed, "it is often said that we must meet sceptics or sceptical scientists on their own ground." But he cautioned against the tactical blunders that such an approach might lead to. It all depended on what "ground" meant. "Whether and how far we ought to meet sceptics of any class on their own ground, depends entirely on how far that ground is tenable and gives either party a safe foothold or resting-place." It was a practical question as much as a theoretical one. Many points could be conceded safely for the sake of argument, but others were so fundamental, so determinative of the outcome of the debate, that to yield them was practically to surrender altogether. It was the momentous task of the defender of the faith to discern what ground was precious and what was expendable. "We are to meet them on the ground of truth, not falsehood: we are to abide by this truth and call on them to abide by it, by whatever evidence supported, whether natural or revealed. And whichever party refuses this issue does so at its peril. We will not meet sceptics or others on their own ground, in any sense which requires us to leave the rock and fortress of truth, and go down to be swamped in the ditches and quicksands of falsehood and delusion."[30] Atwater urged believers in their forays into natural science to take care not to concede the underlying philosophical prejudices of naturalism. They were to stand their ground, not to leave the fortress of truth for the slough of skepticism — namely, an assumed neutrality that practically surrendered the stronghold. In particular they must retain an open esteem for the truth value of revelation, the Bible.[31] The metaphor of "ground," then, referred to "prejudgments, or prejudices, as are involved in our most intimate and well-founded beliefs or convictions as Christians, scientists, or rational beings." The faithful must meet false science with true science, and in that sense fight on science's ground — but they must beware lest in the attempt they should yield as irrelevant any real testimony that materialistic science in its limited vision did not esteem. That would be to grant the very point at issue, to make natural science into a metaphysic.

30. Lyman H. Atwater, "Rationalism," *BRPR* 38 (1866): 351-52.

31. Notice the cautionary word that *either side* neglects the Bible at its peril. The Princetonians believed that only biblical faith could ultimately ground philosophical certitude, for faith in a good God who made the world, and who made our minds to know it, was the only logical guarantee for knowledge. (It can be viewed as a kind of positive counterpart to Descartes's "evil deceiver" argument in his *Discourse on the Method*.) Thus the doctrine of creation had foundational value for epistemology. This side of Princeton's Common-Sense Realism has not received adequate attention.

As a case in point, Atwater considered the evolution question: "If the development theory, or the doctrine of the impossibility of supernatural intervention be urged on scientific grounds," he wrote, "let us endeavour to show them false on scientific grounds." This was basic Princetonian policy. But the attempt at scientific reasoning might fail. The adversary might prove "too uncandid and bigoted to appreciate the evidence," or he might refuse "to place himself upon any reasonable ground which will afford a premise in argument" — or perhaps it might for the time being lie "out of our power to master the reasonings and allegations urged on the scientific side so as to be able to silence our adversaries." In any of these scenarios, Atwater declared, the believer must not yield the high ground of faith in God and in the Bible. As for the skeptic who did not admit heavenly light as evidence, "If he refuses to come upon ground where he can see it and follow it, . . . so much the worse for him." "In this aspect we cannot consent to meet upon their own ground those who so darken their souls that for them the light shineth in darkness and the darkness comprehendeth it not. Let God be true, but every man a liar."[32]

The tone of exasperation in this statement suggested a possible parting of the ways, a separation of scientific from religious discourse, a surrender of the guiding principle of the unity of truth as known and discussed. This was a last resort in the face of adverse but temporary circumstances, a statute of limitation to the principle that science should guide scriptural interpretation — not a declaration of normal operating procedure. Still, it evidenced a suspicion that reasoned argument might not always suffice to convince people of the Princetonian position on science and faith.

Another article, written three years earlier, betrayed a similar suspicion. In "The Scepticism of Science" Joseph Clark of the University of Pennsylvania applauded material science's sovereignty within its borders, urging theologians to avoid the folly of fighting scientific theories with biblical proof texts. So far he was in perfect accord with established Princetonian precedent. But he went on to treat the respective territories of science and religion as epistemically *foreign* to each other in the sense that each domain was characterized by a distinct *mode of thinking*.

---

32. Atwater, "Rationalism," p. 352. This whole section of the article, by the way, raises interesting considerations about Princetonian evidentialism. Atwater discussed the impossibility of reasoning without prejudgments (presuppositions?) on p. 351, and thought the attempt to reason men to spiritual truth from the grounds of unbelief was bound to fail (p. 352).

This was something different from the usual orthodox view that faith involved knowledge but was more than knowledge, that faith was knowledge of the gospel *plus* trust, affection, and repentance. Clark argued that the skeptical tendency of science, though deplorable when science trespassed outside its boundaries, was actually good and necessary within them — for *doubt*, he argued, was a proper fundament of scientific thinking. The "scientific habit of mind" discriminated between facts and semblances of facts; it scrutinized and verified truth claims against empirical experience. This was the genius of the inductive method. But as religion involved knowledge claims grounded in authority (that is, revelation) — sometimes, but not always, overlapping with empirical knowledge and inviting empirical verification — it entered a fundamentally distinct realm of epistemic justification. In science, truth was established by accumulated probability or mathematical demonstration, and expressly not by authority. "We beg leave to say, on behalf of the votaries of science, that they cannot possibly, as scientific men, accept authority under any such form" as the dictates of Scripture. "Should science accept a statement of Scripture on a scientific matter as authoritative and exhaustive, it would be so far forth no longer science at all." In such a case, Clark argued, the Bible would become to science what the Koran was to Islamic law, and there could be no progress of scientific knowledge.[33]

It was the skeptical "habit of mind" that made "the pathway of science steady and sure," Clark stated. "But it is easy to see how it may operate disastrously upon a traditional faith when carried over into the sphere of man's religious life." The walls between domains were methodologically solid. Clark was in effect (if not in intent) denying the unity of method upon which Princeton so far had staked its response to issues in science and theology, and to the evolution question in particular.

Not surprisingly, Clark's article occasioned some controversy, enough to reach the pages of the *New York Observer*. Someone charged him there with compromising the authority of the Bible. But Charles Hodge wrote a letter to the editor in Clark's defense, identifying his position with "the doctrine maintained by the Princeton Review for nearly forty years" — namely, "that the Bible is infallible but is to be interpreted in all matters relating to the external world, by the well ascertained facts of science.... It is the weakness of our faith in the infallibility of the Scriptures, which makes us afraid of science, or unwilling that scientific men should pursue

33. Clark, "The Scepticism of Science," pp. 56, 57.

their investigations according to their own methods. If we firmly believe that the Bible cannot err, we should be satisfied that the well authenticated facts of science can never contradict its teachings."[34]

Clark assured his readers of the unity of truth in God even as he distinguished it, implicitly, from the unity of method in induction Atwater and others had proclaimed. Indeed, he sided with Atwater in attributing material science's tendency to become a metaphysic — its trespassing, invading ways — to "a one-sided culture." Exclusive devotion to empirical science, given its Baconian limitation to the material realm, was bound to spread the assumption that only material reality was knowable; this was evident in the many current instances "when men of science ignore or disregard the moral or religious considerations which legitimately bear on the decision of scientific questions." Clark agreed with Atwater that such considerations rightfully belonged in the human decision of scientific questions, just as humans were more than a collection of the material parts science investigated. Given two theories equally capable of explaining a certain set of data, the one consistent with Scripture and the other not, Clark observed that naturalists tended either to grant no weight to biblical authority — to assume an attitude of "indifference" to the Bible — or to "prefer decidedly, and defend with zeal, the anti-scriptural theory, for the very reason that it is anti-scriptural." But in either case naturalists acted "irrationally," Clark charged, for "viewing the matter coolly as a mere philosophical question, the moral considerations, in the case supposed, are entitled to controlling weight." He offered a parallel case to expose the principle: "Sometimes the facts of science seem to conflict with the facts of history. In such cases, is the man of science authorized to wave the historian off of the field, and tell him he must let science take its course? . . . That all truth is consistent, is an axiom which works both ways. If it proves that revelation cannot contradict science, it no less assuredly proves that science cannot contradict

---

34. Charles Hodge to the editor of the *New York Observer*, 14 February 1863 (Hodge MSS, Princeton University, Letters, box 11). Hodge made his position very plain: "The Scriptures teach no error in religion, morals, history, geography, anthropology, or any other department of knowledge. If any man however asserts that the Bible teaches that the earth is a plane round which the sun revolves, because for five thousand years men understood the Bible so to teach, he degrades the Word of God & does all he can to undermine its authority." The letter is published in Charles Hodge, *What Is Darwinism? and Other Writings on Science and Religion*, edited with an introduction by Mark A. Noll and David N. Livingstone (Grand Rapids: Baker, 1994), pp. 51-56.

revelation."[35] The claim was clear: the same relation obtained between science and revelation as between science and history. So far Clark affirmed the premise of a unified field of truth as known in the full sweep of human experience, natural and religious. Truth was truth, and the arrow of influence between science and theology must point both ways.

But for all these affirmations of continuity, Clark accorded to moral and religious truth claims only a very limited place in scientific theorizing. The scenario he presented was hardly usual; he allowed moral and religious intrusions into scientific argument only in borderline cases. The general rule left science free to pursue its course unhindered by moral or religious precommitments, free to doubt and scrutinize as it ought to. Clark's approved article betrayed an ambivalence at Princeton about the proper place of moral and religious "data" in natural science, owing, it appears, to an uncertainty as to the universal applicability of the inductive method. This underlying tension in Princetonian apologetics would become obvious only after decades of trying to apply the strategic battle plan Atwater, Clark, Hodge, and others conceived in the 1860s.[36]

In addition to employing the martial imagery of battles within or across boundaries, Princeton issued an equally martial call to "seize and master the weapons of attack." To declare the unity of truth was not enough; it also required demonstration. The best defense was a good offense. To "mold the age," to shape the intellectual climate, not just to react to the movers and the shakers, but to work on the cutting edge with them — this was the culmination of Princeton's strategy. As educational institutions, the college and seminary committed themselves to shaping, not just reacting to, academic culture.

Clark argued that churchly suppression of scientific investigation

35. Clark, "The Scepticism of Science," pp. 61-63.

36. With the arrival of F. L. Patton (see chapter 6) and B. B. Warfield (chapter 7), Princeton devoted more overt attention to its apologetical evidentialism. Historians often view that interest as mainly a response to the Dutch presuppositionalists Herman Bavinck and Abraham Kuyper, contrasting Princeton and Amsterdam on apologetics. They tend to downplay the awareness of presuppositions in Baconian inductivism and Common-Sense Realism, the very philosophical underpinnings they treat as so determinative of American evidentialism. See, for example, Hendrick Hart, Johan van der Hoeven, and Nicholas Wolterstorff, eds., *Rationality in the Calvinian Tradition* (Lanham, Md.: University Press of America, 1983). For recent scholarship that seeks to correct that view, see chapter 2, note 45.

was the surest way to bring Christianity into disrepute, then added, "Besides, the freedom which we would accord to science is the surest way to secure the correction of its own errors." Religious people could trust the scientific community to patrol itself. Bad science would in the end "be convicted at its own tribunal"; it was not only the most appropriate way, but the most conclusive. To fight science with theology would only demonstrate bad faith. "Unless we suppose that scientific men are specially leagued in conspiracy against the Scriptures, we must bid them Godspeed, knowing that they will ultimately give us truth."[37]

Thus Clark argued forcefully for freedom of scientific inquiry. He grounded it in the methodological distinction we have just observed, but it was also both good public relations and good politics. It would avoid embarrassing the church, and it would win. Princeton agreed with this principle of freedom (though not precisely for Clark's reasons), and chose to trust science as religion's "twin daughter of heaven" to pursue its own course. Despite Atwater's language of a "fearful host arrayed against the truth," scientists as a class still had Princeton's confidence. The enemy was not science, but materialistic monism, using science's prestige to advance its cause. Science was not the problem; indeed, science was the answer. To those religionists who railed against "science falsely so-called,"[38] who countered scientific theories with doctrinal and biblical statements, Clark gave a brave answer, one that Princeton hailed as its own. Sometimes, Clark allowed, science was a sham, a front for a far-reaching philosophical program, the stuff of "ignorant pretenders, sciolists, and vain boasters." "Very well," he said; "give a fair field, and they will be foiled at their own weapons. Real attainment will put to shame pretension, and genuine discovery will silence empty boasting."[39]

37. Clark, "The Scepticism of Science," pp. 64-65.

38. See Jon H. Roberts, *Darwinism and the Divine in America: Protestant Intellectuals and Organic Evolution, 1859-1900* (Madison: University of Wisconsin Press, 1988), chapter 2.

39. Clark, "The Scepticism of Science," p. 65. So different is this high confidence in science from the attitude historians once expected to find among the allegedly proto-fundamentalist Princetonians that Clark's article was interpreted as an aberration from the norm. Joseph E. Illick III, "The Reception of Darwinism at the Theological Seminary and the College at Princeton, New Jersey," *Journal of the Presbyterian Historical Society* 38 (1960): 152-65, 234-43; Dennis Royal Davis, "Presbyterian Attitudes toward Science and the Coming of Darwinism in America, 1859-1929" (Ph.D. diss., University Illinois/Urbana-Champaign, 1980). Davis's dissertation is particularly flagrant in its ascription of anti-intellectualism to various Princetonians. Newer works on the Princeton theology have laid those errors to rest.

And so Princeton, long committed to the unity of truth in God and the universal applicability of inductive method for the human discovery of truth, committed itself nevertheless to a principle of autonomy in each field of knowledge. The map of God's truth, material and spiritual, was divided into separate realms of study, each characterized practically by what we might call "state sovereignty." This principle had far-reaching implications for the battle Princeton thenceforth waged to save the union of science and theology.

In the principle of state sovereignty Princeton affirmed a position apparently similar to the liberal tradition in theology. *Like* Schleiermacher and Kant, the Princetonians held a principle of autonomy in each field of study. But their metaphysical and epistemological reasons for that practical decision were poles apart. Princeton's principle of state sovereignty for natural science rested on a common method across realms and on the continuity or unity of truth. Creation, ultimately, grounded the unity of truth, for God was the source of all things. Induction, the marvelous method of science since Bacon, grounded the division of labor, for by its careful, painstaking ways science reached sure, well-authenticated conclusions untarnished by the musings of the individual scientist. State sovereignty built on both principles, according a legitimate domain to science and to religion, a division of territory such that specialists in each field would recognize the dignity and prerogatives of the other. Yet Clark gave reasons for dividing the map of truth into separate domains that undercut the continuity of method Princeton prized, and Hodge's endorsement of Clark's article betrayed an ambivalence or a lack of resolution — or perhaps a lack of clarity — in Princetonian inductivism.

In the meantime, the Princetonians were sure that state sovereignty did not mean refusing the battle. One of the great benefits of induction was its accessibility: the subject matter of natural science might be complicated and abstruse to the novice, but with a careful reading the theologian or pastor could arrive at a sound understanding of scientific claims, and he had every right to form judgments as to the soundness of the conclusions. The theologians at Princeton were not about to defer abjectly to a professional class of scientists. The methods and materials of science were open to all — was this not the glory and good of enlightenment, whatever the irreligious excesses of Enlightenment rationalism? Science was the opposite of priestcraft. Let the defender of religion vanquish the foe with his own weapons, for he would find them more appropriately *his* than his enemy's. Clark observed, "In every attack which has been made upon Christianity by hostile human learning, from the days of the apostles to the days of Dr. Strauss, the assailing party have been thwarted and vanquished by the church seizing and mastering the weapons of attack. The sons of the church have become learned in the learning of their adversaries, and have not only sustained the attack, but have succeeded in bringing from every newly opened field of inquiry something to strengthen the citadel of their faith."[40] Science was a bulwark of truth; it would serve the cause of the Creator of all truth better than the cause of false philosophy. Looking to the future, the church should seek out its members, especially its youth, "who have special adaptations of mind to scientific pursuits. These ought to be assiduously cultivated. They ought to be held to be special gifts of God in this age." It was the business of the church to educate its leaders in *both* sides of "the great scientifico-religious problem now pending between revelation and science," for theologians and pastors were the shapers of "the religious mind of the age." A new and pressing task faced the seminaries: to master the science/religion problem "on its scientific side," to meet the challenge of natural science head-on. This was the need of the hour. It required creative, novel response. "When will it be considered at least quite as important to furnish students with weapons to contend with living foes, as to arm them against antagonists who have been dead a thousand years?" Clark cried. It was high time to upgrade the arsenal. "An enemy who brings against us new and formidable weapons, must be met by weapons equal or superior. A contest against iron-clad ships can be sustained successfully only by iron-clad ships, or something better."[41]

This was the Battle Plan at Princeton for defending the faith: to unmask the real enemy as infidel philosophy for all to see; to stand on the

40. Clark, "The Scepticism of Science," pp. 67-68.

41. Clark, "The Scepticism of Science," pp. 65-67. Clark's "seize and master" strategy in the *BRPR* echoed the charge given to William Henry Green at his inauguration at Princeton Seminary in 1851. Reminding the new professor of the mantle he was taking up from Charles Hodge and Joseph Addison Alexander, Rev. Samuel Beach Jones said, "Your predecessors in this department have led the way, and laid the Christian world under obligations, by the fruits of their labor. Like the conquerors of Napoleon, they learned the art of modern warfare from the enemies of truth, and then vanquished them by their own tactics and weapons." "Discourses at the Inauguration of the Rev. William Henry Green, as Professor of Biblical and Oriental Literature in the Theological Seminary at Princeton, N.J., Delivered at Princeton, September 30, 1851, Before the Directors of the Seminary" (Philadelphia: C. Sherman, 1851), p. 31, PTS Special Collections.

solid ground of faith in revealed, supernatural religion against a skeptical, materialistic truncation of reality; and positively to storm the enemy
arsenal, seizing and mastering the weapons of attack, turning them to
their proper use in fortifying the citadel of faith.[42]

The Princetonians found martial imagery helpful in their consideration of both the theoretical and practical aspects of "the scientifico-
religious problem" of which evolutionism was a part. By it they expressed
a remarkably clear, apparently simple counteroffensive that affirmed the
freedom of science even as it assured believers that science was their ally,
not their foe, in the battle with materialistic philosophy. But in the metaphor of enemy ground there inhered an uncertainty as to the universality
of method that undergirded the Princetonians' apologetical understanding. Perhaps the counteroffensive would not prove so simple after all.

---

42. James R. Moore (*The Post-Darwinian Controversies,* p. 348) points out that
Thomas Henry Huxley made extensive use of a similar seize-and-master strategy. His "favorite ploy in controversy was to turn his opponents' 'guns' upon themselves: to play off
Suarez against Mivart on evolution, Genesis against Gladstone on geology, and Jesus
against Principal Gore on the Deluge. This was a clever and effective device, and by no
means entailed any commitment to the opposing views." The idea of turning the guns was
very much in the air. But while Huxley turned the guns to show inconsistency within an
enemy position, not holding to the opposing views thus used, the Princetonians viewed
much of the seized weaponry as *true* weaponry, rightfully belonging to God.

CHAPTER FOUR

McCosh and Hodge

Whether there may not be a new species developed out of the old, is a question for science to settle. And, whichever way it is settled, there is room for irreligion — I am sorry to say; but there is room also for religion.

James McCosh, 1871[1]

What is Darwinism? It is atheism.

Charles Hodge, 1874[2]

---

1. James McCosh, *Christianity and Positivism* (New York: Robert Carter and Bros., 1871), p. 39. For biography, see William Milligan Sloane, *The Life of James McCosh* (New York: Charles Scribner's Sons, 1896), and J. David Hoeveler Jr., *James McCosh and the Scottish Intellectual Tradition: From Glasgow to Princeton* (Princeton: Princeton University Press, 1981).

2. Charles Hodge, *What Is Darwinism?* (New York: Scribner, Armstrong, and Co., 1874), pp. 176-77. For older Hodge biography, see Archibald Alexander Hodge, *The Life of Charles Hodge* (New York: Charles Scribner's Sons, 1880); Charles A. Salmond, *Princetoniana: Charles and A. A. Hodge, with Class and Table Talk of Hodge the Younger* (New York: Scribner and Welford, 1888); John Oliver Nelson, "Charles Hodge: Nestor of Orthodoxy," in *The Lives of Eighteen from Princeton,* ed. Willard Thorp (Princeton: Princeton University Press, 1946), pp. 192-211; and Leonard J. Trinterud, "Charles Hodge: Theology — Didactic and Polemical," in *Sons of the Prophets: Leaders in Protestantism from Princeton Seminary,* ed. Hugh T. Kerr (Princeton: Princeton University Press, 1963), pp. 22-38. Two new biographies do an excellent job of contextualizing his life and analyzing his work in light of current historical and theological interests. They are Paul C. Gutjahr, *Charles Hodge: Guard-*

Great Surprise and Consternation?

On a brisk, overcast October day in 1868 the College of New Jersey inaugurated James McCosh as its eleventh president. Despite the clouds, it was a day of bright hope and rejoicing, for Princeton had found her man — a man to lead her with confidence into a promising future, a warrior to defend the faith with both erudition and piety. Trustees, faculty, students, and alumni thronged to welcome the illustrious Scotsman, newly arrived from Belfast, as the embodiment of Princeton's aspirations for excellence and Christian influence.

Never in the history of the college had an academic election received such universal approval.[3] Yale and Harvard sent the customary congratulations and bestowed their highest honorary degrees upon the new president. While the academic community hailed his arrival with high hopes for the progress of American education, the "friends of religion" (as Princeton was fond of saying) looked forward especially to McCosh's role in the defense of the gospel.

Charles Hodge, head of the seminary and senior member of the college board of trustees, welcomed McCosh on their behalf, exhorting him to protect the faith and to keep it at the center of a Princeton education. "We would in a single word state what it is we desire. It is that true religion here may be dominant; that a pure gospel may be preached, and taught, and lived; that the students should be made to feel that the eternal is infinitely more important than the temporal, the heavenly than the earthly."[4] The religious aims of the trustees could not have been more plain. Hodge proclaimed both the unity of piety and learning and the supremacy of religion over natural knowledge. He used Pauline imagery to convey the paramount importance of that sphere of existence that natural science tended to ignore or deny.[5] Princeton cherished a commit-

---

ian of American Orthodoxy (New York: Oxford University Press, 2011), and W. Andrew Hoffecker, *Charles Hodge: The Pride of Princeton* (Phillipsburg, N.J.: P&R, 2011).

3. Hodge, in Sloane, *Life of James McCosh,* p. 187. McCosh was not the first man to receive the offer — the trustees had first elected William Henry Green, professor of Old Testament in the seminary, but Green had declined. Thomas Jefferson Wertenbaker, *Princeton, 1746-1896* (Princeton: Princeton University Press, 1946), pp. 290-91.

4. Charles Hodge, "Address of Welcome" on behalf of the board of trustees, in "Inauguration of James McCosh, D.D., LL.D., as President of the College of New Jersey, Princeton, October 27, 1868" (New York: Robert Carter and Bros., 1868), pp. 10-12.

5. Hodge was alluding to 2 Cor. 4:18: "While we look not at the things which are seen,

ment to these things, a commitment any new administration must share. In a tender and telling benediction Hodge combined blessing with admonition: "We commend you to the grace of God, and the guidance of our great God and Savior, Jesus Christ, for whom this College was founded, and to whom it inalienably belongs."

There was an unusual urgency in Hodge's articulation of the college's familiar religious commitment. "We are deeply convinced that all forms of knowledge without religion become Satanic," he said flatly, citing "the revealed purpose of God, that those who refuse to acknowledge him, he will give up to a reprobate mind."[6] These words implied that providential direction of the advance of learning was something Hodge and the trustees no longer took for granted. It was God's prerogative to grant or to withhold knowledge of the truths that mattered most, perhaps even true knowledge of earthly things. Only through reverent dependence on God would knowledge make progress worthy of the name; without it there might be movement, but movement toward a godless goal. Hodge betrayed a sense of crisis even as he proclaimed his old-fashioned assurance that "religion and learning are twin daughters of heaven." It was imperative that Princeton cling to the gospel; the alternative was not neutrality but hostility toward God.

With this sense of momentousness Hodge and the trustees joined the academic community at large in an expression of high hopes for academic improvement under the new administration. Princeton must keep up with the advance of science, must master scientific weaponry, in order to serve a greater good. But progress without piety, Hodge implied, would spell disaster, strengthening the enemy's arsenal with the vigor of Princeton men.[7]

McCosh did not need admonishing on this topic. Like the trustees, he was convinced that in higher education a combination of progress and orthodoxy was the crying need of the hour. Other colleges were be-

---

but at the things which are not seen: for the things which are seen are temporal; but the things which are not seen are eternal" (KJV).

6. Charles Hodge, "Address of Welcome."

7. At the end of his life Hodge wrote, "There is no danger to the truth from 'currents of thought.' The only danger is from the decline of piety. Men do not firmly adhere to doctrines of which they have not experienced the power." Quoted by Henry Boardman in "In Memoriam: Charles Hodge; Discourses Commemorative of the Life and Work of Charles Hodge" (Philadelphia: Henry B. Ashmead, 1879), pp. 42-43. The passage came from Hodge's last printed article, *Independent*, 9 May 1878.

ginning to make an opposition of the two terms, choosing to drop their religious commitments in favor of academic advancement, but Princeton resolved to preserve the old union of piety and learning even as it joined the breakneck drive in Gilded Age America for university status.[8] In his inaugural address, "Academic Teaching in Europe," McCosh pledged to bring the best of European university education to Princeton while retaining the college's commitment to religious truth. He also expressed a deep pastoral concern for his young charges, a concern that was to guide his entire administration. "I rejoice that my lot calls me to labor among young men," he testified. "I wish to enter into their feelings, to sympathize with them in their difficulties — with their doubts in these days of criticism, to help them in their fights, and rejoice with them in their triumphs."[9] With old Princeton, McCosh was eager to do battle for influence in the world and also to nurture the individual human soul. His tenure would be marked by a constant concern for the welfare of his "boys," especially for the security of their Christian faith.[10]

The inauguration ceremonies presented a great display of solidarity, as inaugurations almost always do. But according to T. J. Wertenbaker, writing in 1946 as the university's bicentennial historian, Princeton's joy soon turned to mortification. "Great was the surprise and consternation," he said, when McCosh let it be known during his first week in Princeton that he "had accepted the theory of evolution." "For years many Princeton men had been denouncing Darwin, had proclaimed that his theories were at direct variance with the Bible, that if evolution were accepted Christianity would fall. Yet here was the new president, himself a leading minister, calmly proclaiming that Darwin was right."[11]

McCosh's public avowal of a baptized evolutionism was indeed dra-

---

8. Hoeveler, *James McCosh,* p. 250.

9. McCosh, "Academic Teaching in Europe," in "Inauguration of James McCosh, D.D., LL.D., as President of the College of New Jersey, Princeton, October 27, 1868," p. 96.

10. See, for example, his "How to Deal with Young Men Trained in Science in This Age of Unsettled Opinion," *Report of the Proceedings of the Second General Council of the Presbyterian Alliance,* ed. John B. Dale and R. M. Patterson (Philadelphia: Presbyterian Journal Co., and J. C. McCurdy and Co., 1880), pp. 204-13.

11. Wertenbaker, *Princeton, 1746-1896,* p. 311. Hoeveler perpetuates this view, writing of the trustees' "wrathful reaction" against McCosh's evolutionism (*James McCosh,* p. 276) and making such opposition a key interpretive point for his treatment of McCosh's administration.

matic. He came to the decision during his ocean voyage from Belfast to America, literally in the act of crossing over. Onboard the ship he pondered the question of going public with his views, weighing their likely impact on fellow religious leaders and especially on the young college men soon to be under his care. He had no wish to unsettle anyone's faith, but he also believed firmly that religion had nothing to fear from truth. In his own words, "I decided to pursue the open and honest course, as being sure that it would be the best in the end." Within a week of his arrival in Princeton he intimated to the upperclassmen "that I was in favor of evolution properly limited and explained."[12] In so doing he became the first prominent American Protestant religious leader to espouse evolutionism.[13] He soon offered "A Series of Lectures to the Times on Natural Theology and Apologetics" at Union Seminary in New York, detailing his evolutionary views and their religious bearings. The lectures were published under the title *Christianity and Positivism* in 1871. Thereafter McCosh became a celebrated Christian evolutionist, publishing a host of books and articles on the topic: "On Evolution" in *Wood's Bible Animals* (1875), *Ideas in Nature Overlooked by Dr. Tyndall* (1875), *The Development Hypothesis: Is It Sufficient?* (1876), *The Conflicts of the Age* (1881), *Development: What It Can Do and What It Cannot Do* (1883), *The Religious Aspect of Evolution* (1888), and many more.

McCosh's Princeton was most grateful for his campaign to keep God in the origin of species. Faculty and alumni reminiscences are full of testimonials to that effect. His writings "averted a disastrous war between science and faith," said George Macloskie, professor of natural history, "and in 'his' college, men have studied Biology without discarding their religion." Macloskie ventured to add, "I suspect that future writers will represent this as the best service that Dr. McCosh or any other Christian apologist has rendered in our day"[14] — and from a historiographical point of view, his prophecy proved quite true.

But while the college president was proclaiming "room for religion"

---

12. James McCosh, *The Religious Aspect of Evolution* (New York: Putnam, 1888), pp. x-xi. Hoeveler appears to doubt the story, suggesting that McCosh's views on evolution may already have been known in America, however dimly, at the time of his call to Princeton. Hoeveler, *James McCosh,* p. 278.

13. James R. Moore, *The Post-Darwinian Controversies: A Study of the Protestant Struggle to Come to Terms with Darwin in Great Britain and America, 1870-1900* (Cambridge: Cambridge University Press, 1979), p. 245; Hoeveler, *James McCosh,* p. 274.

14. George Macloskie, quoted in Sloane, *Life of James McCosh,* p. 124.

in the theory of evolution, senior seminary professor Charles Hodge undertook his own appraisal of the question and in 1874 reached a conclusion whose baldness and economy of words made it the single most famous statement of clerical antievolutionism ever uttered. "What is Darwinism?" he asked. "It is atheism."[15]

On the face of it, then, there is much to commend Wertenbaker's tale of "great surprise and consternation." Alumni recollections support it. It makes a good story, too (perhaps one reason for the alumni recollections?). Generations of historians and controversialists have relished the dramatic contrast afforded by McCosh and Hodge, leaders of college and seminary, influential Presbyterian educators, colliding head-on over the religious bearing of evolution. The two men offer a handy personification of liberalism and dogmatism. McCosh's transformation of the college into a university, together with his openness to evolution, bespeaks progress, enlightenment, and infusing a breath of enlivening European air into stuffy, parochial Princeton. Hodge's seminary, with its reputation for confessional orthodoxy, its biblical inerrantism, and its declared purpose to defend the faith from scientific assault, fairly beckons the historian to account it the true heir of pre-Enlightenment dogmatism and forebear of fundamentalism. Since the days of Andrew Dickson White, the dichotomy of McCosh and Hodge has served to illustrate the two sides of religious response to evolutionism: open-minded accommodation and obscurantist opposition.[16]

Histories of the college routinely represent McCosh's arrival as a major break from Princeton's past, thus doing their part to abet the polarization of McCosh and Hodge. Many alumni reminiscences of college days propagated this view of McCosh's administration, such as the following from Francis Speir: "Shortly after the election of Dr. McCosh to the presidency of the College, Princeton awoke from a long sleep and shook off the lethargy that had settled down at the beginning of the Civil War. Through the energy of Dr. McCosh interest was aroused, movement

---

15. Charles Hodge, *What Is Darwinism?* pp. 176-77.

16. See chapter 2, note 16. Even George Frederick Wright, noted Calvinist evolutionist, author in later years of *Scientific Confirmations of Old Testament History* and professor of the Harmony of Science and Revelation at Oberlin, believed that "such opponents [of evolutionism] as Hodge and Dawson . . . have made matters still worse" than "the infidel class of Darwinian expositors" had. Wright to Asa Gray, 26 June 1876, cited in Cynthia Eagle Russett, *Darwin in America: The Intellectual Response, 1865-1912* (San Francisco: W. H. Freeman, 1976), p. 28.

and progress appeared, and a new Princeton was born."[17] McCosh clearly made a deep impression on his students, and their tendency to ascribe the college's progress solely to him was quite natural. Even B. B. Warfield, Class of '71, successor to the chair of the Hodges at Princeton Seminary, called McCosh "distinctly the most inspiring force which came into my life in my college days." William Berryman Scott '77, Guyot's successor as professor of geology, called McCosh's inauguration "the beginning of the Renaissance."[18] In many ways this picture is correct: McCosh greatly elevated the level of academic competence in the faculty, revamped the curriculum, instituted graduate study in several fields, and, largely by courting the alumni, greatly increased the college's endowment. When he took office there were 264 students and ten professors in the college; when he was about to step down in 1887, there were 603 students and thirty-seven professors — an almost threefold increase of the student body, and of the faculty almost fourfold.[19] McCosh's energies and skills were of inestimable value in bringing Princeton College again to the forefront of American education — no mean feat in an era of sink-or-swim competition and academic professionalization.[20]

17. Francis Speir, "Personal Recollections of Princeton Undergraduate Life: V. The College in the Seventies," *Princeton Alumni Weekly* 16, no. 30 (3 May 1916): 701. (Speir was one of the students of '77 who organized Princeton's first scientific expedition to gather fossils in Wyoming — see chapter 5.) White called McCosh a "deus ex machina." Andrew Dickson White, *A History of the Warfare of Science with Theology in Christendom,* 2 vols. (New York: D. Appleton and Co., 1896), 1:80.

18. Benjamin Breckinridge Warfield, "Personal Recollections of Princeton Undergraduate Life: IV. The Coming of Dr. McCosh," *Princeton Alumni Weekly* 16, no. 28 (19 April 1916): 652; William Berryman Scott, *Some Memories of a Palaeontologist* (Princeton: Princeton University Press, 1939), p. 23.

19. McCosh, Report to the Trustees (1887) containing his resignation, McCosh MSS, PU Archives, AM 13392.

20. Francis Landey Patton, McCosh's successor as president, gave this picture of McCosh the skillful executive: "In matters of administration Dr. McCosh, without being in any sense autocratic, managed to exercise a good deal of authority. . . . He had the insight to know when the trustees were more important than the faculty, and when the faculty were wiser than the trustees; and he belonged to both bodies. He was shrewd, sagacious, penetrating, and masterful. . . . The students loved him and he loved them. He was faithful with them; spoke plainly to them; as a father with his sons he was severe; and also as a father he was tender and kind" (quoted in David Murray, ed., *History of Education in New Jersey,* no. 23 of U.S. Bureau of Education, Circular of Information No. 1, 1899: Contributions to American Educational History, ed. Herbert B. Adams [Washington, D.C.: Government Printing Office, 1899], 282 n. 2). William Berryman Scott reported on McCosh's balance-of-

But the histories underplay the degree to which McCosh was following a directive given him at the time of his election. His hiring was no mistake. The Princetonians had chosen him carefully; he was their idea of a defender of the faith par excellence. McCosh carried out the strategic directive for offensive battle the *Princeton Review* had elaborated in the 1860s. He was, in short, the new point man in Princeton's battle against positivism — positivism in evolution as elsewhere. During his presidency Princeton Seminary paralleled and even collaborated in many of his attacks on materialist science. If the military metaphor has had unfortunate historiographical consequences, surely one of them is the misleading picture of McCosh and Hodge, college and seminary, at war with each other over the evolution question in the 1870s.[21]

While it is clear that some alumni and trustees were indeed "hidebound conservatives" staunchly opposing McCosh's policies,[22] and that some professors believed evolutionism to be a more fundamental threat than others did, the picture of a Princeton deeply divided over the evolution question is incomplete and misleading. The Princetonians considered the evolution question in the context of their larger and older battle with materialism — and behaved in the McCosh years in a way remarkably consistent with the battle plan they had drawn up before his arrival. Instead of presenting a radical break from Princeton's past, the McCosh years show how Princeton put its earlier plans into action.

There was even a substantial continuity between McCosh's and

---

power politics somewhat less delicately: "When [McCosh] came to Princeton in 1868 he found both Faculty and Board of Trustees so full of hidebound conservatives, that he could carry out his reforms only by playing off Board and Faculty against each other and coercing one body by threats of what the other would do. He had to keep this up through most of his administration" (Scott, *Some Memories*, pp. 132-33).

21. Only one historian so far, Gary Scott Smith, gives any considerable attention to the broad agreement between McCosh and Hodge on evolutionism: Gary Scott Smith, "Calvinists and Evolution, 1870-1920," *Journal of Presbyterian History* 61 (1983): 335-52. Even Hoeveler's biography of McCosh plays up the alleged "wrathful reaction to his views" on evolution within the Princeton circle, though he does admit that "McCosh's relations with the seminary . . . were never so strained as some of the extreme remarks might suggest." Hoeveler, *James McCosh*, pp. 277, 279.

22. Scott recalled an anti-McCosh party among the New York alumni. Some of them felt McCosh had been discourteous to them; others disliked his boastfulness about the great progress the college was enjoying under his early administration. In the winter of 1876-77, the *New York Tribune* began carrying attacks on Princeton College. Scott, *Some Memories*, p. 53.

Hodge's ideas on the evolution question itself. They disagreed as to whether the transmutation of species was a fact; they disagreed as to the necessary consequences of Darwinism for the design argument — but they agreed on nearly everything else connected with the question of evolution and religion.

Solidarity

McCosh's sudden, unexpected avowal of evolutionism likely brought the issue to the fore at Princeton, but subsequent events at both the college and the seminary belie Wertenbaker's story of "great surprise and consternation." More accurate is McCosh's own recollection of the opening years of his administration. From the first, Princeton's many friends assured him of their financial and moral support. He recalled with satisfaction the many voices of encouragement that greeted his early efforts at the college.[23]

McCosh already had a strong reputation for scientific doxology, unfolding to his readers the glories of God in creation. A personal friend of Hugh Miller, he undertook serious amateur study of the mode of God's providence in nature while a pastor in rural Scotland. In 1850 he published *The Method of the Divine Government*, earning such high acclaim that Queens College, Belfast, promptly offered him a professorship. The book systematically described God's method of ruling the world through divinely ordained secondary causes. Some years later he coauthored *Typical Forms and Special Ends in Creation*, again emphasizing the evidences of God's design everywhere and drawing on Goethe's philosophy of nature.[24] McCosh's interest in the natural world, and his doxological presentation of it as God's evident handiwork, were well known and well appreciated in Princeton. In *The Supernatural in Relation to the Natural* (which, incidentally, received only partial praise in the *Princeton Review*) he took on Herbert Spencer outright.[25] The Princetonians knew whom

23. McCosh, in Sloane, *Life of James McCosh*, p. 191.

24. McCosh acknowledged his debt to Goethe for *Typical Forms* in a later article, "Is the Development Hypothesis Sufficient?" *Popular Science Monthly* 10 (1876): 98.

25. James McCosh, *The Supernatural in Relation to the Natural* (New York: Robert Carter and Bros., 1862), briefly noted in *Biblical Repertory and Princeton Review* (hereafter BRPR) 34 (1862): 361. The reviewer believed McCosh inadvertently taught a pantheistic doctrine in calling God "the actor in all action."

they had hired, and when he announced that he found nothing necessarily atheistic in the doctrine of evolution "properly limited and explained," some may have balked, but they certainly did not raise a battle cry. Instead, they calmly set about defining what was and was not objectionable about the theory, much as McCosh himself had done.

That Princeton had not conclusively made up its mind about the evolution question by the time of McCosh's arrival we have already seen in the *Princeton Review* of the 1860s. A number of events in the years immediately following McCosh's arrival again testify to a less polarized situation than many have been led to believe existed at Princeton. First, in 1869 the *Review* ran an article occasioned by six recent books on the fundamentals of morals, among them McCosh's *Present State of Moral Philosophy in Great Britain in Relation to Theology*. Here, at the outset of his presidency, and very shortly after the announcement of his views on evolutionism, the *Review* lauded McCosh's "great good judgment" concerning questions of mental science, theology, and morality — and that in direct connection to the social and moral ramifications of the theory of natural selection. The writer observed that the theory, "as some hold it, logically demands the extinction, and not the merciful protection, of the feeble and helpless portion of our race" — a reference no doubt to Spencer — and in answer asserted, "Here our views are fully expressed by Dr. McCosh" on the insufficiency of natural moral philosophy apart from the Bible.[26] The *Review*, in other words, still under the control of Charles Hodge and Lyman Atwater, explicitly used McCosh as its spokesman against what came later to be called social Darwinism.

A year later, in 1870, the faculty of the seminary approached the directors to ask that a permanent fund be set up to provide a secure basis for the continuation of a lecture series on "scientific subjects which are intimately related to a theological course." College professors Atwater and Guyot had been giving this series for several years. Funds since the Civil War had been very tight, but the seminary was happy to continue using the college professors for these extracurricular lectures delivered "so usefully and successfully for some years past." That is to say, the seminary was happy to continue its close collaboration with the college in the matter of science and religion — now, in the McCosh years. When insufficient funds prevented the lectures from continuing in 1868-69, the

26. "Some Recent Discussions on the Fundamental Principles of Morals," *BRPR* 41 (1869): 179, 180.

faculty lamented the loss. When in 1870 the money was raised to reinstitute the lectures, the faculty asked McCosh himself to join Atwater and Guyot — and promptly requested the directors to put the funding for the series on a permanent basis.[27] Here was an explicit sanction of McCosh's views on science and religion.

Yet more revealing is the content of McCosh's seminary lectures. No notes or reports of them survive, but according to seminary records, McCosh gave "a series of lectures to the times on Natural Theology and Apologetics" in the academic year 1870-71.[28] This description, word for word, formed the subtitle to *Christianity and Positivism,* McCosh's momentous avowal of evolution "properly limited and explained." With the publication of that book in 1871, McCosh became the first major religious leader in America to promote a form of the evolution theory. His attitude to evolutionism contrasted sharply with Hodge's denunciations of Darwinism in *Systematic Theology* (1872-73) and *What Is Darwinism?* (1874). Although the preface to McCosh's book refers to the Ely Foundation Lectures he gave at Union Seminary, New York (Princeton's chief rival), it appears that McCosh first expounded his epochal views at Princeton Seminary, by invitation — and only later at Union and in print.[29]

Christianity and Positivism's very title indicated McCosh's agreement with old Princeton as to the nature of the battle they were waging. Just as Atwater had identified positivism as the foe behind Darwinism, now McCosh attacked that philosophical opponent directly — and in the process argued that evolutionism need not carry with it the desolations of materialism and agnosticism. He treated the transmutation of species as an established or nearly established scientific fact, and in that particular differed from previous Princetonian opinion. But in so doing McCosh actually put into practice the Princetonian plan for reconnoitering the enemy and turning his own biggest guns against him. McCosh now seized

27. PTS Directors Minutes, 27 April 1868, 27 April 1869, and 26 April 1870, PTS Special Collections.

28. PTS Faculty Minutes, 25 April 1870, PTS Special Collections.

29. The front matter and preface of *Christianity and Positivism* credit only Union Seminary and its Ely Foundation, probably because of the prestige of such endowed lectures. As a consequence, their original use — namely, to benefit Princeton seminarians — has gone unnoticed. It now appears that McCosh drafted the substance of *Christianity and Positivism* for his extracurricular lectures there. However, the appendix, where McCosh treats Darwin directly, appears to have been added only at the time of publication — it contains three "articles," whereas the other chapters are listed as "lectures."

even evolutionism — a most formidable weapon in the positivist arsenal — for the cause of Christian supernaturalism.

In the course of this sweet turning of the guns McCosh argued his case along familiar Princetonian lines. Like Dod's review of the *Vestiges* a quarter of a century earlier, *Christianity and Positivism* made a poignant appeal to moral sensibilities, by quoting a poignant passage from Owen Meredith's epic poem *The Siege of Constantinople.* It was the most moving instance of the Horrible Vision yet issued from Princeton.

> An immense solitary spectre waits:
> It has no shape, it has no sound; it has
> No place, it has no time; it is, and was,
> And will be; it is never more nor less,
> Nor glad nor sad. Its name is Nothingness.
> Power walketh high; and misery doth crawl;
> And the clepsydron drips; and the sands fall
> Down in the hour-glass; and the shadows sweep
> Around the dial; and men wake and sleep,
> Live, strive, regret, forget, and love, and hate,
> And know it. This spectre saith, I wait,
> And at the last it beckons and they pass;
> And still the red sands fall within the glass,
> And still the shades around the dial sweep;
> And still the water-clock doth drip and weep.
> And this is all.

"This," said McCosh, "is *Positivism.*" He traced its spirit to Diodorus of ancient times, "for it is recorded of him that he wrote a treatise on the Awful Nothing and died in despair."[30]

This positivism, this "spectral figure" of "lean and haggard form, spreading like death a shivering feeling wherever it goes," waited patiently for inexorable logic to drive into its clutches anyone who built his intellectual house on less than solid philosophical ground. "This, then, is the gulf to which we have come."[31] In his first published avowal of Christian evolutionism McCosh presented an ultimate and stark choice in

30. McCosh, *Christianity and Positivism*, p. 166; Owen Meredith (pseudonym for Edward Robert Bulwer Lytton), "The Siege of Constantinople," in his *New Poems* (Boston: Ticknor and Fields, 1868), 1:295.

31. McCosh, *Christianity and Positivism*, p. 178.

philosophy: realism, with its assurance of both natural and religious knowledge, or the sinking nescience and spiritual emptiness of positivism. McCosh did not upset Princeton's cart; if anything he threw the established Princetonian position into high relief.[32]

Darwin's book, and its remarkable inroads into the scientific community in the decade since its publication, had convinced McCosh that the transmutation of species was a fairly well established fact. He was fond of telling his undergraduates that no reputable naturalist under the age of thirty rejected evolution. Before Darwin published the *Origin,* McCosh's own work in natural philosophy had sought method and mechanism in the divine production of the variety of life, predisposing him toward an evolutionary view. His botanical investigations in the 1840s and 1850s had led him to question the idea of millions of fiat creations of separate species.[33] Darwin, Huxley, and Spencer drew agnostic or atheistic conclusions from evolution, but McCosh, agreeing with them as to transmutation's factuality, opposed them bitterly as to its religious and metaphysical entailments. He advocated *limiting* and *explaining* evolution — keeping a biological theory within its proper sphere, and opposing any invasion outside it. This was, in principle, just what Princeton had understood the need of the hour to be.

"I admit the existence of evolution," McCosh said, "but I oppose the theory that would account for every production by evolution."[34] He limited the theory in two crucial ways. First, he refused to allow evolution to extend to the human race. This he did largely on the grounds that the facts of the case — the fossils — were extremely meager, but also on philosophical and religious grounds. Humanity's moral and spiritual side could never be accounted for by the operations of physical force, McCosh insisted: to attempt to do so was to assume materialism at the outset, to reduce mind to a phenomenon of matter. Consciousness recoiled from the claim, giving the lie to it.[35] These were familiar Prince-

32. The *Princeton Review,* under the editorship of Lyman Atwater, commended McCosh's book highly, making no objection to his evolutionism. It praised McCosh's clear philosophical insight, his aptitude for both physical and metaphysical science, his mastery of the literature, and his witty eloquence. *BRPR* 43 (1871): 444-48.

33. James McCosh, *The Development Hypothesis: Is It Sufficient?* (New York: Robert Carter and Bros., 1876), p. 89.

34. McCosh, *Christianity and Positivism,* p. 353.

35. "I am inclined to urge that the very circumstance that man has a consciousness of something within, which separates him from the brutes, that he claims to have a higher

tonian themes. Secondly, McCosh rebuked the arrogance of scientists who deemed themselves fit to pontificate on matters outside their expertise. They were not qualified to speculate on other sciences or on history, much less "to settle or unsettle for ever all the questions bearing on the relations of the universe to its Maker." McCosh commented dryly, "For this work, some of them seem to me to have no aptitude and no calling."[36] This, too, was a familiar Princetonian position.

On the affirmative side, McCosh admitted natural selection, but he found in it only another instance of secondary causation (natural laws) carrying out the will of God, the great First Cause. Darwin's theory of the mechanism of evolution threatened religion no more than Newton's theory of gravitation did. Each removed some of the mystery of the cosmos, perhaps, but revealed to humankind the beautiful intricacies of natural law — law whose order, beneficence, and evident purposefulness glorified its Ordainer. Never mind that Darwin disavowed any providentialist rendering of natural selection; Darwin was a fine scientist, but a poor philosopher. McCosh believed he had rescued a good scientific theory from the scientist's own unphilosophical conclusions.[37]

With Guyot and with Hodge's *Review*, McCosh maintained that evolution "could not do" what Darwin, Spencer, and Mill claimed for it — it could not bridge the gap between nonlife and life, or the gap between body and spirit. Natural selection carried out God's purposes, but neither natural selection nor any other powers in brute nature could produce mind. If McCosh was a "providentialist" regarding the laws of nature, he was enough of an "interventionist" to require a divine infusion of wholly new principles at the creation of life and of man.[38] That, together with his doctrine of the utter inability of natural law to do its work apart

origin, is a consideration of some value in determining the question. Man's very feeling is a presumption in favor of his having a noble lineage." McCosh, *Christianity and Positivism,* p. 351.

36. McCosh, *Christianity and Positivism,* p. 174. Darwin himself was among the trespassers McCosh arraigned. "Mr. Darwin's theory of the origin of our moral ideals is one of the loosest and most unsatisfactory, — altogether one of the weakest ever propounded" (p. 353). "It is clear that he is not at home in philosophical and ethical subjects, as he is in questions of natural history" (p. 359).

37. McCosh found evolution to strengthen his philosophical case for design, revealing as it did a marvelous "collocation" of causes in intricate interrelations. Hoeveler, *James McCosh,* p. 161.

38. McCosh, *The Development Hypothesis;* cf. his *Development: What It Can Do and What It Cannot Do* (New York: Charles Scribner's Sons, 1883). See also note 78 below.

from the constant activity of God in and through it, led his philosophical successor Alexander T. Ormond to classify McCosh as a fundamentally nonevolutionary thinker.[39]

Like Atwater and the *Princeton Review*, McCosh turned to words of war when it came to the materialistic uses of evolution. "We are on the eve of a conflict with a physico-philosophy, which would account for all mental action and ideas by molecular motion, or some form of material agency."[40] Man must continue to be recognized as distinct from the beasts, created in the image of God; and reality must not be reduced to the material sphere only. In all these arguments McCosh approached the evolution question precisely as the Princetonians had approached other scientific issues connected with enemy philosophies in the 1860s. As if to underscore their solidarity, in the very year of the publication of *Christianity and Positivism* the seminary elected McCosh to its board of directors, the highest decision-making body in the institution.[41]

Princeton's relative openness to the evolution question in the early 1870s may also be seen in the hiring of Charles Augustus Aiken as the seminary's first professor of Christian ethics and apologetics. No stranger to Princeton, Aiken had been a frequent contributor to the *Princeton Review* since the 1850s, and in 1866 had come from Dartmouth to teach Latin language and literature at Princeton College, leaving three years later to assume the presidency of Union College. Charles Hodge's personal papers mention social interaction with Aiken and his family rather frequently; apparently they were fairly close friends. When in 1870 former seminary trustee Stephen Colwell provided in his will for the establishment of the new Archibald Alexander chair, the faculty recommended Aiken for the job.[42] The professorship was originally intended to cover ethics only, but Colwell hoped that it might be enlarged to include the defense of revealed religion from assaults made "on the side of material science, metaphysical speculation and historical criticism." The faculty reported to the directors

39. Alexander T. Ormond, in Murray, *History of Education in New Jersey*, pp. 275, 277 n.
40. McCosh, *Christianity and Positivism*, p. 101.
41. PTS Directors Minutes, 25 April 1871. So much for the persistent claim, even from as good a historian as Edward Larson, that Charles Hodge "raised an alarm against teaching evolution, particularly within seminaries and denominational colleges." Edward J. Larson, *Summer for the Gods: The Scopes Trial and America's Continuing Debate over Science and Religion* (New York: Basic Books, 2006; orig. 1997), p. 18.
42. *BRPR* index volume (1870-71); Wertenbaker, *Princeton, 1746-1896*, p. 284; PTS Directors Minutes, 25 April 1871.

that "the subject, when brought to the attention of various friends of the seminary, awakened so lively an interest that it was judged advisable to seek the immediate creation of the chair." Among the supplemental contributors to the cause was the seminary's Old Testament expert, William Henry Green. The choice of Aiken for the post was "especially acceptable to those who have taken part in endowing this proposed chair."[43] His hiring, then, was deliberate and well informed. In this light Aiken's position on the evolution question offers another valuable gauge of Princeton's view of the matter shortly after McCosh's arrival.

Aiken's appointment was Princeton Seminary's first exercise of its increased autonomy since the reunion of the Presbyterian Church in 1869.[44] Under the terms of the reunion agreement, the seminary could now nominate and elect its own faculty, subject only to the General Assembly's veto. The infusion of the more liberal-tending New School into the General Assembly therefore had nothing to do with the seminary's choice for filling the new chair. Yet we find that Aiken's position toward evolution was at least as tolerant as McCosh's. In his inaugural address as president of Union College, a published copy of which is held in the seminary library, Aiken presented the by now familiar Princeton line about seeking knowledge of not only the material world but also the intellectual and spiritual. But in the course of this standard line of argument Aiken made a surprising statement suggesting the possibility even of *human* evolution. "If we are to confess ourselves kindred to or descended from the apes, and, more remotely, other lower orders of being," he said, "we demand the right to study the things in which we differ from our kin as well as the things in which we agree with them." Echoing Guyot's account of progressive creation, Aiken urged the study of "the new elements that have strangely come in during the progress of this de-

43. PTS Directors Minutes, 25 April 1871. Lest we ascribe Aiken's hiring to McCosh's arrival on the Seminary Board of Directors, it is worth pointing out that McCosh actually protested the establishment of Aiken's chair, "so far as to reserve all legal rights of the said College under the will of the late Stephen Colwell." And it was former college president John Maclean — who objected in the 1860s to Aiken's appointment to the college on the grounds that he was a Congregationalist and not a Presbyterian (Wertenbaker, *Princeton, 1746-1896,* p. 284) — who motioned for the approval of Aiken's appointment to the new chair.

44. Joseph H. Dulles, in Murray, *History of Education in New Jersey,* p. 331. The seminary's prerogatives were widened as a result of the General Assembly's decision to standardize its relations with all the seminaries, Old School and New School.

velopment — thought, freedom, conscience." "Man, the lord of the terrestrial creation," must not be neglected in the rush for knowledge of the natural world. "We will investigate . . . that part of man's being with which his lordship is connected, as well as that part through which he claims affinity to his own subject realm."[45] The call for a "science of man" again echoed old Princeton, but Aiken connected this familiar theme with the possibility of human bodily evolution — an astonishing thing to allow in 1870, even before Darwin had published *The Descent of Man*. Yet within a year the faculty at Princeton Seminary chose him as their new professor of apologetics! After Aiken's first year at Princeton, an examining committee reported very favorably on "the results already accomplished in the new department of Christian Apologetics" and on its potential to do great service to the church "in fitting her ministers to meet the assaults of infidelity in all its phases, whether old or new."[46]

The "great surprise and consternation" theory is hard pressed to account for these events, which make it very difficult indeed to maintain that Hodge's Princeton was aghast at McCosh's evolutionism. At the outset of McCosh's presidency Princeton clearly took a far more open attitude toward evolution than Wertenbaker and others have supposed. The actions of Hodge's seminary indicate a unity of purpose, a sense of comradeship with McCosh in their common battle. McCosh's hiring, his seminary lecture series, his appointment to its board of directors, the publication of his views on evolution — as well as Aiken's appointment to teach apologetics — all constituted positive steps to implement Princeton's battle plan against materialistic naturalism. Despite differences of opinion, there were solidarity and mutual esteem within the citadel of faith.

45. Charles Augustus Aiken, inaugural address, in "Exercises Connected with the Inauguration of Rev. Charles A. Aiken, D.D., as President of Union College, Schenectady, New York, Tuesday, June 28, 1870" (Albany: Joel Munsell, 1870), pp. 26-27. Aiken's evident flirtation with the idea of human evolution may have been due to his insistence on the solidarity of the human race in Adam, in view of the debates over polygenism at the time. In an article he wrote for the *Princeton Review* in 1868, Aiken asserted his conviction that the Scriptures demand a brotherhood of man resting on fleshly relationship: "We are quite certain that the 'fleshly relation' which the Scriptures assert, stands in vital connection with the moral condition of our race. The problem of one Adam's fall is quite enough for us in itself and its consequences. And happily for our deliverance we are not invited to trust a Saviour who assumed the nature of some one among several sinning and ruined races co-existing upon earth, but one who stands related by a simple single bond, to every human being that needs his salvation." Aiken, "Whitney on Language," *BRPR* 40 (1868): 292.

46. PTS Directors Minutes, 23 April 1872.

What Is Darwinism?

Those differences of opinion, however, do require explanation. The published statements of McCosh and Hodge on the evolution question certainly appear to indicate disagreement. While we have seen that McCosh did not simply say, as Wertenbaker would have it, that "Darwin was right," his assurances that evolution left "room for religion" do seem to contradict Hodge's equation of Darwinism with atheism.

Hodge made his famous statement in the last book he published, a little volume called *What Is Darwinism?* (1874). An examination of the road to its publication will set that book in its context, helping us to understand what Hodge did and did not mean.

Hodge began work on *What Is Darwinism?* in the autumn of 1873, shortly after returning home from the Evangelical Alliance Conference in New York City. Protestant leaders had assembled from all over the world at this illustrious weeklong general council to hear papers on a wide array of salient topics. One historian described the conference as "a Protestant counterpart to Vatican I."[47] It was there that a prolonged discussion of evolutionism prompted Hodge to write *What Is Darwinism?*

At the Philosophical Section meeting Hodge heard papers by Guyot and McCosh, respectively, on the correspondence of Genesis 1 to geology and the "religious aspects of the doctrine of development."[48] John William Dawson, principal of McGill College in Montreal, also spoke. A renowned paleontologist, president of the Natural History Society of Montreal, vice president of the American Association for the Advancement of Science (AAAS), and head of its natural history section, Dawson was fast becoming, according to his biographer, "something of an anti-Darwinian celebrity" since his presidential address to the Natural History Society of Montreal in 1872. He argued (in distinct agreement with Princeton) that Darwinism had a tendency to prostitute natural history to the service of a shallow philosophy. If unchecked, he urged, it would bring about "the destruction of science, and a return to semi-barbarism." He had issued

---

47. John T. McNeill and James Hastings Nichols, *Ecumenical Testimony: The Concern for Christian Unity within the Reformed and Presbyterian Churches* (Philadelphia: Westminster, 1974), pp. 189-90.

48. Arnold Guyot, "The Biblical Account of Creation in the Light of Modern Science," in *History, Essays, Orations, and Other Documents of the Sixth General Council of the Evangelical Alliance,* ed. Philip Schaff and S. Irenaeus Prime (New York: Harper and Bros., 1874), p. 276.

this warning two months previously, at the AAAS.[49] At the Evangelical Alliance he limited his remarks to a discussion of the scientific evidence for the scriptural account of man as opposed to the doctrine of "the more extreme evolutionists" that man was evolved from the brute.[50]

The session was a convivial gathering of like-minded men: evangelical scientists, philosophers, and theologians interested in the evolution question and especially in the McCoshian task of considering what it "could and could not do." The speakers all agreed that progress and development (not necessarily transmutation) were facts of natural history. Most agreed that an admission of animal evolution posed no insurmountable obstacle to an orthodox reading of the Bible. Most drew the line, however, at human evolution — in the words of one speaker, "the theory of the amiable, but I think mistaken, Professor Darwin, . . . that man, as he is, came from clots of animated jelly." In this inquiring but not very controversial atmosphere Hodge might well have sat contentedly by, but instead he arose and addressed the assembly.

> I don't stand here to make any speech at all. I rise simply to ask Dr. Brown [the second speaker] one question. I want him to tell us what development is. That has not been done. The great question which divides theists from atheists — Christians from unbelievers — is this: Is development an intellectual process guided by God, or is it a blind process of unintelligible, unconscious force, which knows no ends and adopts no means? In other words, is God the author of all we see, the creator of all the beauty and grandeur of this world, or is unintelligible force, gravity, electricity, and such like? This is a vital question, sir. We can not stand here and hear men talk about development, without telling us what development is.[51]

Hodge was issuing a call for definition. "Development" or "evolution" was an imprecise term that might apply as easily to an atheistic, materialistic worldview as to a Christian one emphasizing design and providence. It

49. Charles F. O'Brien, *Sir William Dawson: A Life in Science and Religion* (Philadelphia: American Philosophical Society, 1971), pp. 131, 117-18.

50. John William Dawson, "Primitive Man and Revelation," in *History, Essays, Orations, and Other Documents of the Sixth General Council of the Evangelical Alliance*, pp. 272-75.

51. "Discussion on Darwinism and the Doctrine of Development," in *History, Essays, Orations, and Other Documents of the Sixth General Council of the Evangelical Alliance*, pp. 317-18.

might mean a blind process or an intellectual one — a universe wandering by chance, or a universe guided by God. The contrast was stark, but the language completely covered it over. Hodge felt uneasy about discussions of "development" that might persuade the undiscerning to admit principles that, carried to their conclusions, would ungod the world.[52]

In another open discussion later that day, Dawson distinguished between Darwinism and Spencerism — the latter evolving all forms of life, and life itself, from matter and force, while the former "takes up only one branch of these speculations, that relating to the transmutation of species, and says if you will give me two or three species of plants or animals, I will show you how all species of plants and animals are evolved out of them."[53] In truth, Darwin had already paralleled Spencer in extending the principle of evolution to human cultural and spiritual attainments. Hodge, however, was interested not in the question of scope, but of cause. He responded, "My idea of Darwinism is that it teaches that all the forms of vegetable and animal life, including man and all the organs of the human body, are the result of unintelligent, undesignating forces. . . . It excludes God; it excludes intelligence from every thing. Am I right?" Dawson agreed: while Darwin himself might not say so much, that was in fact the logical tendency of the theory.[54]

McCosh had accepted both the transmutation of species and Darwin's account of it, natural selection, with the understanding that natural selection *was* divine design. Hodge knew these points well from McCosh's seminary lectures and from *Christianity and Positivism*. At the Evangelical Alliance he heard others discussing the religious bearings of "Darwinism," sometimes meaning an evolution by God's design through the instrumentality of a divinely ordained law called "natural selection," sometimes meaning an evolution by blind chance, God rendered unnec-

52. Hodge took Huxley as a prime example of the dangers involved in admitting evolution unwarily. On the strength of his scientific reputation, Huxley merged metaphysics into physics, all the while crying *"Irenicum"* ("peace, peace") to religious people, urging them "to let science alone." Hodge would not stand for Huxley's double standard. "Do he and his associates let metaphysics and religion alone? . . . Professor Huxley tells the religious world that there is overwhelming and crushing evidence (scientific evidence, of course) that no event has ever occurred on this earth which was not the effect of natural causes. Hence there have been no miracles, and Christ is not risen. . . . Huxley's Irenicum will not do. Men who are assiduously poisoning the fountains of religion, morality, and social order, cannot be let alone." Charles Hodge, *What Is Darwinism?* pp. 135-37.

53. Charles Hodge, *What Is Darwinism?* pp. 319-20.

54. Charles Hodge, *What Is Darwinism?* p. 320.

essary. Hodge tolerated the first kind of "Darwinism" but deeply abomi-
nated the second. The second, he believed, was Darwinism itself; the
first was something else again, even if it did employ Darwin's phrase
"natural selection." In short, Hodge wrote *What Is Darwinism?* to expose
the theological consequences of Darwinism, not McCoshism.[55]

Upon his return to Princeton from the New York conference, Hodge
entered a contented note into his memoranda. "October 2d. Went to
New York with Mrs. Hodge to attend the meetings of the Evangelical Alliance, and returned home on the 7th; having been greatly delighted and
edified by what we saw and heard."[56] About three months later he presented at "the Club" (a gathering of Princeton professors) a paper of his
own on Darwinism. Three months after that, *What Is Darwinism?* was in
print.[57] Hodge had decided that the issue he raised at the conference was
momentous enough to warrant a book on the topic, and he brought his
ideas to his colleagues for discussion before publishing them. McCosh
may well have been present at that meeting. The entire sequence of
events suggests a certain urgency of purpose, but also a sense of openness and collaboration with his colleagues. *What Is Darwinism?*, then,
was not a protest against McCosh-like attempts to reconcile evolution

55. Hodge's colleagues clearly understood this at the time. The *Princeton Review* (now
Presbyterian Quarterly and Princeton Review [hereafter *PQPR*], a combined Old School
and New School organ) paired its review of *What Is Darwinism?* with a review of Alexander
Winchell's *Doctrine of Evolution,* endorsing Winchell's McCosh-like argument "that the
production of species by evolution, no less than by immediate creation, requires a personal, All-wise and Almighty God." The reviewer read Hodge's thesis as centering on the
issue of supernaturalism — the "intervention of supernatural power" in the evolutionary
process. Darwinism was atheism in its exclusion of God from the world process; deistic
views of evolution were just as bad, for they shared Darwin's exclusion of supernatural intervention from the process even if they admitted design by involution at the start. Theistic evolution of Winchell's variety, however, "may be safely conceded." The issue was precisely supernaturalism. "Contemporary Literature," *PQPR* 3 (1874): 558-59.

56. Charles Hodge, MS Memoranda, 6:143 (PTS Special Collections). On other occasions Hodge was quite ready to record his dissatisfaction with things he had heard. For example: "Club at Dr. McDonald's. Heard it said there that there are no intuitive truths; no
second causes; no substance; and that all power is God-power" (6:126).

57. Charles Hodge, MS Memoranda, 6:150. Apparently happy with his accomplish-
ment and eager for some feedback, Hodge left a copy of *What Is Darwinism?* on the New
York City doorstep of James Lenox, his personal friend and a benefactor of the college and
seminary (and of the New York Public Library, which bears his name on its façade). James
Lenox to Charles Hodge, 8 May 1874 (Hodge Family MSS, PU Library, Letters, box 12). The
two men exchanged lighthearted jokes and riddles about evolutionary descent.

with design, but a pointed definition of what Hodge found objectionable — and unavoidable — in Darwin's peculiar version of evolutionism. To repeat his remarks at the conference, "The great question which divides theists from atheists — Christians from unbelievers — is this: Is development an intellectual process guided by God, or is it a blind process of unintelligible, unconscious force . . . ?"

We are now in a position to sketch Hodge's views on Darwinism in particular, and on evolutionism in general, in some detail. We have already seen in the pages of the *Princeton Review* that Hodge allotted to science a major role in theological construction, routinely recalling the lesson of the Galileo affair, that science must interpret Scripture. Divine revelation was not given to teach science, but as the word of God it spoke truth in all its assertions. Insofar as the Bible touched on scientific and historical matters, it did so truthfully; hence Hodge held both the "conservative" belief that Scripture must agree with natural knowledge and the "modernist" belief that the arrow of influence ran from science to Scripture more readily than in the other direction. Natural knowledge in Hodge's view illumined the true but casual references Scripture made to natural matters in the course of pursuing its religious aims.

But Scripture was not the whole issue anyway. Hodge and his seminary approached the evolution question not from a generic commitment to the Christian Scriptures, but rather from a particular version of Reformed, or Calvinistic, theology. They made sense of biblical and natural-theological concerns through a fully systematized Calvinism and a solemn commitment to uphold the "system of doctrine" contained in the confessional standards of the Presbyterian church, namely, the Westminster Confession of Faith. Unlike twentieth-century Christian antievolutionists, for whom the direct biblical connections of the evolution question loom largest, Hodge focused his attention on the theological system he had spent a lifetime building and defending.

Hodge's specifically theological concern comes as no surprise given Princeton's commitment to professional boundaries. Hodge the theologian assessed the evolution question in terms of his theology — his whole theology. His comments on the issue were an exercise in proper specialist activity, a theologian drawing theological conclusions from scientific positions, and reserving the right to do so.

At the time he wrote *What Is Darwinism?* Hodge had just finished giving his theological system its final form in his magnum opus, the three-volume *Systematic Theology* (1872-73). For this work, the culmination of a lifetime of seminary teaching, he disavowed any originality, claiming in an oft-quoted (and oft-abused) remark that no "original idea in theology" had ever originated in Princeton Seminary.[58] He phrased this strange claim deliberately, for rhetorical effect. He did not mean that the Princeton theology owed nothing to the minds of that seminary or to the currents of the nineteenth century, but simply that he and his seminary cherished a high regard for the system of doctrine they inherited from Calvin, the Westminster divines, and the Continental tradition of Reformed dogmatics, especially Francis Turretin. It was a claim to stand in a developmental line. Whatever additions or refinements Princeton made were, he believed, simply attempts to carry that system of theology into his contemporary situation, enhancing and correcting it according to the progress of knowledge in his time, but leaving its essence intact.

Hodge's treatment of the evolution question in his *Systematic Theology* hinged on several venerable principles from that tradition. In interpreting Genesis 1 he followed Calvin's understanding that the language of the passage was observational — an "accommodation to our perspective," given in terms a human observer of the process would use.[59] As such, the words of the creation narrative were deliberately sketchy, so as to communicate effectively to people in all times and at all levels of sophistication — leaving much latitude for interpretation by the clearer light of science for those who cared to know such particulars. Hodge followed Augustine's distinction between first and second, or immediate and mediate, creation. "The one was instantaneous, the other gradual; the one precludes the idea of any preëxisting substance, and of coöperation, the other admits and implies both." In the beginning God created the formless original matter of the universe by instantaneous fiat, out of nothing; thereafter the entire creation narrative gave "an account of the progress of creation." Hodge concluded that "forming out of preëxisting matter comes with the Scriptural idea of creating."[60] His antievolutionism was therefore not a matter of stasis versus flux; he read the creation narrative as an account of secondary causes effecting the decree of almighty God in a progressive creation. So far he was in perfect agreement with both

58. Charles Hodge, *BRPR*, index volume (1870-71), 1:11.

59. Charles Hodge, *Systematic Theology* (New York: Scribners, 1872-73; reprint, Grand Rapids: Eerdmans, 1993), 1:569-70, citing John Calvin's *Institutes of the Christian Religion* 1.14.3.

60. Charles Hodge, *Systematic Theology*, 1:556-58, citing Augustine's *De Genesi ad Literam* 5.45.

Guyot and McCosh, and with them may be classed as holding a developmental (i.e., progressive) view of God's creative activity.[61]

However, Hodge also insisted upon a theological distinction between God's creation, preservation, and government of the natural order — the last two terms together constituting divine providence. This old distinction presented a barrier to any baptized evolutionism, for to say that secondary causes, the laws of nature as established by God, brought about the progressive creation of life-forms seemed practically to say that all mediate creation was a category of providence. The impenetrable mysteries of divine sovereignty and creaturely free agency were numbing enough when posed in terms of God's providence; to refer all history and all coming-to-be to God's creative activity would eliminate sin, righteousness, and judgment entirely — or rather ascribe them all, almost directly, to God. Hodge devoted several pages to a painstaking dissection of various erroneous views of providence, views that slid easily into either deism or pantheism. He was sure that God did not uphold the natural world by acts of "continued creation" (thus dissenting from both the doctrine of *concursus* his esteemed theological forebears held and an understanding of the world as a *de novo* creation at each instant in time). Hodge's treatment of the mode of God's providence was distinctly negative; after refusing the several explanations ventured by theologians and philosophers, he concluded simply that God's providence was universal, powerful, wise, and holy — and that beyond those scriptural assertions the attempt to delve into the mysteries of how providence worked only led people into insoluble and useless puzzles. Strikingly, he listed the question of "the relation between [God's] agency and the efficiency of second causes" as a mystery comparable to the age-old question of divine sovereignty and human freedom. Only "as philosophers insist upon answering" such impossible questions did it become "necessary for theologians to consider their answers," mainly to expose

61. This versus Lefferts A. Loetscher's contention that "evolution substituted change for fixity as the law of all things." Loetscher, *The Broadening Church: A Study of Theological Issues in the Presbyterian Church since 1869* (Philadelphia: University of Pennsylvania Press, 1954), p. 9; cf. Theodore Dwight Bozeman, *Protestants in an Age of Science: The Baconian Ideal and Antebellum American Religious Thought* (Chapel Hill: University of North Carolina Press, 1977), p. 169. John Oliver Nelson makes fixity one of Hodge's most characteristic personality traits, observing his "phenomenal resistance to any sort of change" and calling it "almost pathological." Hodge's opinions, orthodoxy, and worldview are understood to follow suit. Nelson, "Charles Hodge," pp. 205-6.

the many ways they so often contradicted scriptural doctrine. In other words, Hodge preferred to leave the metaphysical "how" of divine providence an unfathomable mystery. As a scientific question of efficient causation only, the "method of divine government" held keen interest for him. As a theological question of the relation of those efficient causes to divine agency, God's providence was, as the Puritans used to say, strange and beyond knowing. Hodge preferred simply to bow to it; he addressed it theologically only as rushing fools made a mess of things in their impertinence, and then only negatively.[62]

Such was the unhappy case when Hodge felt himself compelled to write *What Is Darwinism?* His aims were far from lofty. All he set out to do was to expose the atheistic gall of a scientific theory that plunged into a divine mystery so deep that Hodge himself, a career theologian, dared not to venture in. He made no attempt to construct a theistic explanation of the relation of the putative collection of secondary causes, together called evolution, to the ways of God. Darwin's heaven-shaking announcement that chance and chance alone guided the world of living things simply required exposure. That was what Hodge set out to do. He had, in fact, already done so in the second volume of his *Systematic Theology*. *What Is Darwinism?* was essentially a restatement and expansion of those views, prepared for a wider audience.[63]

Hodge's assessment of Darwinism followed rather predictably. He reiterated his commitment to the principle of interpreting Scripture by the facts of science. Hodge was insistent upon this point — but he was equally insistent that theology would do itself a grave disservice if it hoisted its sails to every wind of theory that came along. Darwinism was in Hodge's mind a theory to account for certain facts. He admitted the facts — fossils, glacial deposits, and so forth — and welcomed as a fact the grand progression in the history of life. But he regarded transmutation as a still tenuous theory to account for those facts.[64] Until the the-

62. Charles Hodge, *Systematic Theology*, 1:578-80.

63. Charles Hodge, *Systematic Theology*, 2:12-19. On the background to and principal aims of Hodge's book, see Mark Noll and David Livingstone's helpful introduction to their new edition of *What Is Darwinism? and Other Writings on Science and Religion* (Grand Rapids: Baker, 1994), pp. 11-47. I find a bit more continuity between Hodge and B. B. Warfield than they do.

64. In *What Is Darwinism?* Hodge wrote, "Religious men believe with Agassiz that facts are sacred. They are revelations from God. Christians sacrifice to them, when duly authenticated, their most cherished convictions.... Religious men admit all the facts con-

ory received sufficient proof, Hodge was not about to revise a theological structure hammered out over centuries and possessing, in his view, highly compelling evidences of its own. To his mind Calvinism stood on footing far more sound than Darwinism did. He felt no embarrassment in labeling evolutionism "not proven" — and until it was, he felt no need to adjust his theology or his reading of the Bible to it.

In the early 1870s Hodge still had at his disposal such illustrious names in American science as Louis Agassiz, Arnold Guyot, and James Dwight Dana as experts skeptical of transmutation. His treatment of the question of factuality depended on their testimony. In keeping with the principle of professional boundaries, he cited those men, rather than McCosh, on the status of evolution as fact or theory.[65] And yet, in keeping with the idea of the perspicuity of nature and the universal accessibility of truth in careful reflection, Hodge ventured also to declare his own impression of the evolution theory as highly incredible on the face of it. "It shocks the common sense of unsophisticated men," he wrote in his *Systematic Theology*, "to be told that the whale and the humming-bird, man and the mosquito, are derived from the same source." Such an assault on our natural sensibilities was for Hodge a strong argument against a theory. More forceful yet was the essentially a priori conviction that "the theory in question cannot be true, because it is founded on the assumption of an impossibility" — namely, "that matter does the work of mind." These were familiar themes, predating the Darwinian controversies, but they were to Hodge and his fellows the most telling ones. While he devoted many pages to strictly scientific arguments against spontaneous generation and the transmutation of species (ancient doctrines, he noted, and traceable to heathen philosophies), the moral and metaphysical case against evolution was for Hodge the strongest. Darwin's doctrine, he said, citing the British scientist and evolution enthusiast John Tyndall, traced all phenomena, from nebulae to human culture, to natural causes without the intervention of mind. "No man can believe

---

nected with our solar system; all the facts of geology, and of comparative anatomy, and of biology. Ought not this to satisfy scientific men? Must we also admit their explanations and inferences? If we admit that the human embryo passes through various phases, must we admit that man was once a fish . . . ? It is to be remembered that the facts are from God, the explanations from men; and the two are often as far apart as Heaven and its antipode" (pp. 131-32). Page numbers in this note and following refer to the original edition.

65. Hodge sketched and sanctioned Dana's stripped-down version of Guyot's day-age theory in *Systematic Theology*, 1:572-73.

this, who cannot also believe that all the works of art, literature, and science in the world are the products of carbonic acid, water, and ammonia." The baldest statement of the theory served as its best disproof, for it unmasked its patent absurdity and its moral repugnance to the reader.[66]

These philosophical observations, however, were mere trifles when compared to the religious implications of Darwin's theory. The idea of a world process not guided by intelligence was worse than philosophical nonsense; it was rank atheism. Like Laplace a few generations earlier, Darwin had no need of the theistic hypothesis. Worse than Laplace, Darwin carried his godless developmental process to the present moment. Since the creation aeons ago of perhaps a handful of primordial germs, "God has no more to do with the universe than if He did not exist." Providence vanished altogether. Hodge concluded, "This is atheism to all intents and purposes, because it leaves the soul as entirely without God, without a Father, Helper, or Ruler, as the doctrine of Epicurus or of Comte."[67]

The burden of *What Is Darwinism?* was to show the atheism of the theory. Hodge distinguished between evolutionism and Darwinism, defining Darwin's theory as evolution plus natural selection, minus divine design.[68] He rejected evolution itself as incredible and unproven, but allowed the possibility of theistic evolutionisms. He repeated his commitment to interpreting Scripture by the facts of science and his conviction that evolution had yet to pass muster as scientific fact. He drew his famous conclusion that Darwin's denial of design made the theory inherently atheistic, supporting his reading with the opinions of Darwin's supporters as well as his opponents.[69] Even that climactic equation of Darwinism with atheism was not Hodge's own; he cited Darwin's chief American apologist and would-be baptizer, Asa Gray, as prime witness to the fact. Darwin himself and his proponents agreed with Hodge: the

66. Charles Hodge, *Systematic Theology,* 3:8-10, 14-15.

67. Charles Hodge, *Systematic Theology,* 2:16.

68. Charles Hodge, *What Is Darwinism?* p. 141.

69. Remarking on the contrast between the acceptance of Darwin and the rejection of Chambers, Hodge wrote, "There is only one cause for the fact referred to, that we can think of. The 'Vestiges of Creation' did not expressly or effectually exclude design. Darwin does. This is a reason assigned by the most zealous advocates of his theory for their adoption of it." Hodge ascribed Darwin's success not to any new facts he had marshaled in support of the evolution theory, but to a change in the climate of opinion. Darwin's denial of design "happens to suit a prevailing state of mind." Charles Hodge, *What Is Darwinism?* pp. 145-46, 149.

theory excluded God. "We have thus arrived at the answer to our question, What Is Darwinism? It is Atheism. This does not mean, as before said, that Mr. Darwin himself and all who adopt his views are atheists, but it means that his theory is atheistic; that the exclusion of design from nature is, as Dr. Gray says, tantamount to atheism."[70]

As historians have differed over the essence of Darwinism, they have differed over Hodge's little book. Bruce Kuklick and Peter Bowler agree with the old theologian — not on the rejection of evolutionism, but on the identification of Darwinism with goallessness, and thus its incompatibility with theism.[71] Darwin himself certainly regarded his doctrine as ateleological, and said so explicitly in *Variation of Animals and Plants under Domestication* (1868). There he avowed the impossibility of believing that "an Omniscient Creator" had foreordained the evolutionary process by preprogramming the laws of nature so as to bring about a desired outcome.[72] In effect, Darwin disowned deism as well as theism, despite his hypothesis of a handful of originally created primordial germs from which all life evolved. He never denied the existence of God, but his theory left no room for even a deistic providence that foreordained the course of the

✦

70. Charles Hodge, *What Is Darwinism?* pp. 176-77. Notice that Hodge uses Gray, a defender of "Christian Darwinism," to make his point — turning the guns.

71. Peter J. Bowler, *The Non-Darwinian Revolution: Reinterpreting a Historical Myth* (Baltimore: Johns Hopkins University Press, 1988); Bruce Kuklick, *Churchmen and Philosophers: From Jonathan Edwards to John Dewey* (New Haven: Yale University Press, 1985), p. 193.

72. In a famous passage Darwin asked, "Did He ordain that the crop and tail-feathers of the pigeon should vary in order that the fancier might make his grotesque pouter and fantail breeds? Did He cause the frame and mental qualities of the dog to vary in order that a breed might be formed of indomitable ferocity, with jaws fitted to pin down the bull for man's brutal sport? But if we give up the principle in one case . . . no shadow of reason can be assigned for the belief that variations . . . [in nature] were intentionally guided. However much we may wish it, we can hardly follow Professor Asa Gray" in his attempt to find teleology in the process. Charles Darwin, *Variation of Animals and Plants under Domestication,* quoted in Benjamin Breckinridge Warfield, "Charles Darwin's Religious Life: A Sketch in Spiritual Biography," in his *Studies in Theology,* in *The Works of Benjamin B. Warfield,* ed. Ethelbert D. Warfield et al., vol. 9 (New York: Oxford University Press, 1932; Grand Rapids: Baker, 1991), pp. 566-67. Cf. Ronald L. Numbers, *The Creationists: The Evolution of Scientific Creationism* (Berkeley: University of California Press, 1993), pp. 4-5. Note that Darwin's disavowal of teleology focused not on natural selection, but on variation. This may have been the basis of Hodge's distinction between natural selection and the denial of design in his definition of the component parts of Darwinian doctrine (evolution plus natural selection minus design).

world from the beginning and then set it in motion, let alone a theistic providence that intervened in the laws of nature along the way. That, to Hodge, as to Darwin's friend Gray, was plainly "tantamount to atheism."

McCosh agreed with Hodge that Darwin's version of evolutionism ruled God out of his creation. In *Christianity and Positivism* he freely acknowledged that there was "room" in the evolution theory "for irreligion." He hastened to add that Christians could and should separate Darwin's science from Darwin's metaphysics — but in this, too, he concurred with his theological colleague. In other words, McCosh's declaration of "room for religion" did not contradict Hodge as flagrantly as first appears. Both men believed that the religious issue in evolution hinged on the question of divine design in the progress of earth history. It is not too much to say that Hodge and McCosh agreed almost completely on the metaphysical side of the evolution question,[73] and differed chiefly on its scientific side.

A Combined Legacy

Some fourteen years after the publication of *What Is Darwinism?* when Charles Hodge lay ten years in his grave and James McCosh had just retired from his long and eventful presidency, Benjamin Breckinridge Warfield composed a lecture for his students at Princeton Seminary on the evolution question. It began with a comparison of his two great mentors. The energetic, brilliant, and highly orthodox young heir to Hodge's chair, Warfield had been present as an entering sophomore at McCosh's inauguration, graduating in 1871, the year of *Christianity and Positivism*. He studied theology under Hodge at the very time the old man was writing *What Is Darwinism?* By his own confession he had come to Princeton "a Darwinian of the purest water,"[74] but under his venerable professors

73. Hodge and McCosh did differ on certain particulars of theistic proof: see Francis Landey Patton, "Syllabus of Prof. Patton's Lectures on Theism" (Princeton: Princeton Press, 1888), pp. 9-10; cf. David N. Livingstone, "The Idea of Design: The Vicissitudes of a Key Concept in the Princeton Response to Darwin," *Scottish Journal of Theology* 37 (1984): 329-57. But they shared a common commitment to Scottish Realist views of being and knowing, McCosh serving of course as the Princetonian expert in philosophical matters.

74. Warfield, "Personal Recollections," pp. 650-53. Warfield apparently discussed the evolution question with McCosh while preparing his lectures, and enjoyed tweaking him on their point of disagreement. McCosh insisted that no scientist under thirty questioned transmutationism. Warfield replied: indeed — only in his thirties did he "outgrow" it.

he came to mitigate his views and, in the process, to shift his career plans from science to theology. His remarks on the positions of the two men are penetrating and instructive.

Warfield opened his lecture with characteristic directness and clarity. "There are three general positions," he declared, "which may be taken up with reference to the various development or evolutionary hypotheses now so common." The first position viewed evolutionism as "an adequate philosophy of being," combining the nebular hypothesis with spontaneous generation and the transmutation of species to present a complete package accounting for both the origin and the present state of the universe. In a phrase whose source is clearly recognizable, Warfield declared this position "tantamount to Atheism" and called it "but a new form for the expression of an atheistic philosophy." Having just read the newly published *Life and Letters of Charles Darwin,* Warfield observed that although the great naturalist had posited an original creation of primordial germs and had written the *Origin* at a time when he was still "feeling theistically," "the theory as held by him was essentially atheistic, as Dr. Charles Hodge asserted" — and the proof of the pudding was Darwin's own drift away from theism as his thinking ran in channels more and more defined by his theory.[75]

The second position viewed evolution as an established scientific discovery, a matter of fact as to how — under what order and conditions — living species came into being. "In this form the theory is not made to *account* for anything more than other second causes account for," Warfield asserted. As a second cause, evolution implied a first cause. This view of it is not only consistent with theism, but "implies & presupposes theism." And, he added, "this is the form in which Dr. McCosh holds it."

In two brief paragraphs Warfield had affirmed both the difference and the unanimity between McCosh and Hodge on the evolution question. As a world-philosophical explanation, evolution practically presupposed atheism,[76] for it was "only another form for the presentation of the

---

75. Warfield, MS Notes on Anthropology (Systematic Theology course, junior year), PTS Special Collections. Warfield had just published "Charles Darwin's Religious Life: A Sketch in Spiritual Biography" (1888), based on Darwin's *Life and Letters.*

76. This observation comports well with John Corrigan Wells's thesis that *What Is Darwinism?* presented a theistic argument not *from* design, but *to* design — that Hodge indicted Darwin's theory for its premises more than its conclusions. Wells's main argument is that Hodge believed in design because of a precommitment to belief in God, and

old problem of the materialistic philosophy." Warfield identified this insight with Hodge, no doubt because of *What Is Darwinism?* — but he might have included McCosh's name as appropriately. As a putative discovery of science regarding the history of speciation, the theory carried no necessarily irreligious philosophical baggage; indeed, its elucidation of secondary causation only served, as had the discoveries of the first scientific revolution, to magnify the wonders of divine design. This understanding Warfield identified with McCosh. The two views were polar opposites on the philosophical question, but the two views did not represent the two men. Rather, Warfield showed that Hodge had *negatived* the first view, while McCosh *affirmed* the second. The two men agreed philosophically but chose different weapons and trained them on different targets.

The first position — the one Hodge opposed — had two components: it viewed evolution "as a *fact &* as itself the sufficient account of the phenomena: both as demonstrated fact & as the all-sufficient force & cause." The second position — the one McCosh propounded — also had two components: the affirmation of evolution "as demonstrated fact but as *only* supplying the method through which the true force & cause works." McCosh and Hodge agreed on position two, part two, but disagreed on part one of both positions. That is, they agreed that if evolution had happened it was at best a secondary cause requiring a first cause; but they disagreed as to whether evolution (i.e., the origin of species by whatever form of descent) had indeed happened — whether it was indeed a fact.[77] These convolutions inherent in the evolution question made it likely indeed that the relations of their opinions would be misunderstood.[78]

---

his belief in God was not premised on the evidence of design. Wells, *Charles Hodge's Critique of Darwinism: An Historical-Critical Analysis of Concepts Basic to the 19th Century Debate* (Lewiston, N.Y.: Edwin Mellen Press, 1988).

77. Warfield, MS Notes on Anthropology.

78. David Livingstone, drawing on Peter Bowler's account of the "idealist version" of the argument from final cause, ascribes McCosh's and Hodge's differences over evolution to differing concepts of design: Hodge's was, he says, essentially Paleyan, focusing on particular fittedness to environment and function, whereas McCosh's was Owenian or idealist, focusing on the grand scheme of natural law, the vision of orderly progress that implied an Ordainer (Livingstone, "The Idea of Design"). Denis O. Lamoureux suggests that what divided them was their respective views on the mode of relation of the supernatural to the natural: McCosh, a "providentialist," saw divine activity in natural law, whereas Hodge required certain breaks in natural law in the course of natural history (as Guyot

For his part, Warfield affirmed Hodge's negative and negatived McCosh's affirmative — evolution as world philosophy was simply recycled materialism, tantamount to atheism; but evolution was not a demonstrated fact. He preferred to view it "as a more or less probable, or a more or less improbable conjecture of scientific workers as to the method of creation": that is, as "a working hypothesis which is at present on its probation." In this he followed Hodge more than McCosh, warning that "we dare not adjust our theology to what is as yet a more or less doubtful conjecture."[79] But on the other hand he affirmed McCosh's most famous declaration, that there was room in evolutionism for religion. Darwin was wrong, but Darwin was perhaps right — wrong certainly on philosophy, right perhaps on science. Maybe species did come by descent; if so, materialism (or positivism, or naturalism) could not account for it. Scientific investigation into natural history was to be encouraged; scientific trespassing into philosophy and religion was to be steadfastly opposed, and those who cherished holy ground must patrol the border. This remained the position of every Princeton theologian until the reorganization of the seminary in 1929. Historians have pondered the question of whose legacy Princeton perpetuated, McCosh's or Hodge's. The answer is — both.

---

did, and indeed as McCosh did) — which Lamoureux calls "interventionist" (Lamoureux, "Between 'The Origin of Species' and 'The Fundamentals': Toward a Historiographical Model of the Evangelical Reaction to Darwinism in the First Fifty Years" [Ph.D. diss., Toronto School of Theology, 1991]). I find both positions on both sides. McCosh and Hodge each understood the difference between Paleyan and Owenian design, and believed in both; each required a providence of both general superintendence and particular intervention at crucial points. Theologically and philosophically they were remarkably united. Their remaining point of disagreement was simply on the factual question.

79. Warfield, MS Notes on Anthropology. "As to whether species have in any way come by descent, I am more of a pure agnostic." He concluded, "The upshot of the whole matter is that there is no *necessary* antagonism of Xty to evolution, *provided that* we do not hold to too extreme a form of evolution" (emphasis in original). Specifically he guarded God's prerogative to work apart from law in miraculous interventions, in the introduction of radically new principles in creation (such as life, sentience, and mind), in the creation of each individual soul, and in the regeneration of believers by the Holy Spirit. Provided these things, "we may hold to the modified theory of evolution and be Xians in the ordinary orthodox sense. I say we may do this. Whether we ought to accept it, even in this modified sense, is another matter, and I leave it purposely an open question" — and then he quoted James Russell Lowell: "With faith enough to bridge the chasm / Twixt Genesis and protoplasm."

CHAPTER FIVE

To Mold the Age

Our country needs her College men;
  She calls to them for timely aid,

To bring fair Honor back again
  From cloisters where she long has stayed;
To lend their educated might
To guide a youthful nation right.

"The world needs Christians:" heed her call,
  You who will crowd her crowded streets;
Go, let your light be seen by all
  Where Life's great heart most strongly beats.
Go show the world that Christian men
Can live beyond an abbot's ken.

> Class poem, Princeton College, 1881

As the spirit of the age is, is a maxim tried and true,
Whether it shall mold your future rests, my comrades,
  but with you.

> Class poem, Princeton College, 1878[1]

1. B. B. Blydenburgh Jr., "Class Poem," *Nassau Herald* (1881), p. 44; George R. Gaither Jr., "Class Poem," *Nassau Herald* (1878), pp. 15-17. PU Archives.

From Defense to Offense

James McCosh believed himself a man of destiny. From his assumption of the presidency of Princeton College at age fifty-seven, he felt the thrill of new vigor, new victories to win, new vistas awaiting. "In those days," he recalled with gusto, "I was like the hound in the leash ready to start, and they encouraged me with their shouts as I sprang forth into the hunt."[2] Alumni often said he was the dreamer of one dream, the glory and advancement of Princeton. He was sure that he could fashion the old place into a leading institution in the fullest sense of the term — both topnotch and cutting edge. He judged America still a young country, and while he assured his compeers of his real regard for the distinctive spirit of the American college and its peculiar fitness for American soil, he was sure the American college had not yet quite found itself. European standards of research and a European atmosphere of open collegiality were goods McCosh hoped to introduce to the old and faithful College of New Jersey, thus producing a kind of institution unparalleled in the Old World or the New, one characterized by the potent combination of piety and active research. In adolescent America, with all its potential for good or ill, McCosh dreamed of shaping Princeton into a university that would "mold the age" philosophically, scientifically, and religiously.[3]

McCosh had good cause to believe in his ability to shape his world. As a young country preacher he took part in the great Disruption that gave rise to a strong and evangelical Free Church of Scotland. When he turned his hand to writing on science and religion, the meteoric success

2. James McCosh, in William Milligan Sloane, *The Life of James McCosh* (New York: Charles Scribner's Sons, 1896), p. 191.

3. See J. David Hoeveler Jr., *James McCosh and the Scottish Intellectual Tradition: From Glasgow to Princeton* (Princeton: Princeton University Press, 1981). Hoeveler does a good job of emphasizing both the Enlightenment and evangelical motives of the man. Indispensable is Paul C. Kemeny's thorough and well-documented study, *Princeton in the Nation's Service: Religious Ideals and Educational Practice, 1868-1928* (New York: Oxford University Press, 1998). The first two chapters treat McCosh's administration, aspirations, and public relations in lavish detail. George M. Marsden's magisterial *Soul of the American University: From Protestant Establishment to Established Nonbelief* (New York: Oxford University Press, 1994) locates Princeton's story in the larger story of American higher education, stressing its unique stance for the older evangelical ideal in the age of the university. "If a more traditionalist Protestant intellectual alternative to the emerging definitions of American academia was to survive at any major school, Princeton was the foremost candidate" (p. 196).

of his first book earned him a professor's chair in the United Kingdom's newest college. On his first visit to the United States in 1866, he appeared as the honored guest of both General Assemblies of the Presbyterian Church, Old School and New School, and now Princeton had called him to sit in the chair of Edwards and Witherspoon, two men whose combinations of Calvinism and philosophy McCosh admired and sought in his own way to emulate. McCosh was naturally decisive and visionary, his ego legendary. He proudly referred to Princeton, in his Scottish accent, as "me college." A student once observed him strolling about the campus, fondly surveying each path and building added during his tenure. The student told a companion, "Look at old Jimmy, saying to himself 'This is great Babylon that I have builded.'"[4] McCosh himself would admit no likeness to Nebuchadnezzar; he believed himself rather a soldier of the faith, a willing arm of God's providence. On at least one occasion he pounded his fist on the table and grunted that a certain proposal he was fighting for was "the will of God" — to which his wife, Isabella, retorted, "Indeed, I'll be thinking it's the will of James McCosh."[5]

McCosh's experience in his new homeland soon convinced him of the tactical importance of Princeton College in American academia. At first he spoke merely of the college's "civilizing and humanizing influence" upon young men entering positions of power, and through them reaching "down to the provinces,"[6] but by the early 1870s he began to emphasize Princeton's unique spiritual mission in higher education. Harvard, the nation's leading college and the example of excellence he strove to follow academically, impressed him as a spiritual desert. So did the vast majority of state colleges. In his own student days at Glasgow and Edinburgh McCosh had become convinced that the neglect of moral and religious oversight in colleges and universities was a great evil, for the students needed a guiding hand to keep them from the dissipations so tempting to youth and from developing bad habits as well as loose beliefs. He was determined that the college now under his care would preserve its spiritual heritage for the sake of "his boys." In grave earnest, and

4. Bill Annin, quoted in William Berryman Scott, *Some Memories of a Palaeontologist* (Princeton: Princeton University Press, 1939), p. 72.

5. Hoeveler, *James McCosh,* p. 270, quoting Philip Ashton Rollins, "Reminiscences of Mrs. McCosh," an informal address (1935), PU Archives.

6. James McCosh, "Academic Teaching in Europe," "Inauguration of James McCosh, D.D., LL.D., as President of the College of New Jersey, Princeton, October 27, 1868" (New York: Robert Carter and Bros., 1868), pp. 51-52.

not merely as a sop to the conservative trustees to carry his reforms, McCosh told the board in 1875 that Princeton must foster "all the intellectual activity of such Colleges as Harvard, while we continue to impart the sound religious instruction for which our College has been distinguished. If this is not done," he warned, "our abler youth will be tempted to turn towards the Colleges in which the intellectual faculties are stimulated, even though there be no encouragement to true religion."[7] His heart ached for those devout parents whose sons heard of nothing but Harvard in the New England prep schools, only to lose their faith once they got there.[8] The problem was not intellectual pursuit as such, but intellectual pursuit to the neglect of religious life. Princeton's cherished spiritual commitment, together with its venerable place among America's oldest colleges and its growing network of influential and monied alumni, gave it a potential for good that outstripped other religiously committed institutions like Amherst or Bowdoin. To build Princeton was to build a bulwark for true religion in a secularizing academic terrain. This conviction of McCosh's only grew with time. He frequently adverted to the edifying effects of a Princeton education, claiming at the end of his twenty-year tenure that he knew of only a handful of his students who had forsaken Christianity, and that he had personally won many a wandering youth back to the faith.[9]

But McCosh wanted to build something more than a spiritual haven. His admonitions to keep up with Harvard included a grander vision, one of lasting influence on the culture at large. He believed great institutions were the shapers of society. Great academic institutions in particular shaped the way a whole nation thought. McCosh's highest goal was to produce at Princeton the leading thinkers of the generation to come, both in natural science and in philosophy. Princeton's chosen captain for the faith's academic defense, McCosh took his mandate a step further and prepared to mount an offensive.

The tales of hostility between McCosh and the trustees find their explanation not in a fundamental difference over the evolution question, but in the extent and rapidity of the real, structural changes

7. Hoeveler, *James McCosh,* p. 46; McCosh, President's Report, 22 December 1875, PU Trustees Minutes, PU Archives.

8. Thomas Jefferson Wertenbaker, *Princeton, 1746-1896* (Princeton: Princeton University Press, 1946), p. 314; Hoeveler, *James McCosh,* pp. 302-3.

9. McCosh, "Twenty Years of Princeton College," in Sloan, *Life of James McCosh,* pp. 228, 231-33.

McCosh carried out in preparation for his great offensive. He "sprang forth into the hunt" immediately upon taking office, introducing a limited elective system where no electives had been allowed before, adding alongside the revamped academic curriculum a second one for engineering, and launching a building campaign that included a handsome brownstone library, a dormitory, and an imposing neo-Gothic laboratory building to house the new John C. Green School of Science. So many and so visible were the changes that McCosh came under criticism for devoting his attention mainly to expanding the campus with monuments to his administration.[10] In 1873 he answered those charges by announcing to the trustees that the time had come for a second wave of reforms, this time aiming to cultivate a more serious spirit of study, both scientific and literary, among the students. "I am afraid that in this respect we are inferior to other Colleges in Europe and even in America — Colleges striving to raise young men who will mould the thoughts of their age, and advance the learning, the science, and philosophy of their country."[11] McCosh wanted a Princeton that not only followed the leading thought of the day, but also advanced it and shaped it. It was not enough to keep abreast of the latest research and speculation, even for the purposes of taming it and tempering its possibly deleterious effects on orthodoxy. McCosh wanted to gather around him men who would act, not just react — men who with him would shape the nation's intellectual life and "mold the age."

To foster such a spirit of serious inquiry McCosh introduced a system of academic prizes and fellowships in natural science and philosophy. With Arnold Guyot's grateful collaboration and the generosity of William Libbey Sr. (whose son and namesake was a Princeton undergraduate interested in science), McCosh greatly expanded the college's small natural history museum and made it a campus centerpiece, housing it in the faculty room of Nassau Hall.[12] The new collection embraced

10. Wertenbaker, *Princeton, 1746-1896*, pp. 297-98. The criticisms became very public in a prolonged exchange of letters to the editor of the *New York Tribune* prompted by an editorial in December 1876. The controversy raged until February 1877.

11. McCosh, President's Report, 17 December 1873, PU Trustees Minutes, PU Archives.

12. McCosh, "Twenty Years," p. 194; PU Trustees Minutes, 22 June 1874; Arnold Guyot, "The Museum of Geology and Archaeology," in *The Princeton Book* (Boston: Houghton, Osgood and Co., 1879), p. 264. It was Guyot who requested the Faculty Room for the museum's new location, the library having been housed there previously. In setting up the fossil display, Guyot intended "that they should strike the eye as an open book in which the

thousands of species, including a cast of the recently discovered *Hadrosaurus,* the first mounted dinosaur skeleton in the world (Philadelphia, 1868). Princeton thus became the first college anywhere to display a dinosaur.[13] In connection with hands-on laboratory work in the School of Science, the splendid new museum presented a powerful draw to scientific investigation. Student response to such opportunities was immediate. McCosh was especially proud of a group of students who demonstrated by their own initiative the soundness of his belief that an atmosphere of open inquiry would encourage intellectual zeal. In 1876 three seniors — one of them Charles Hodge's grandson — requested permission to organize an expedition to the fossil beds of the West, having read in a magazine of such an expedition from Yale. That fall, to drum up wider participation, they founded the Nassau Scientific Society. Soon the club proposed a course of lectures on the evolution question in the wake of Huxley's American tour. As their spokesman explained in the campus newspaper, the students believed their college campus afforded a more open and evenhanded environment for the discussion of scientific questions than did the press, their only other source for current debates.[14] It was a sterling testimony to McCosh's reforms and to the science faculty, especially Guyot and astronomer Stephen Alexander. The fossil hunt in the summer of 1877 was a tremendous success, launching a long series of near-annual expeditions that built the college museum into one of the leading collections of vertebrate paleontology in the world. Three members of the original expedition became leading evolutionary scientists themselves: William Berryman Scott (Hodge's grandson) and William Libbey Jr. as professors at Princeton, and Henry Fairfield Osborn as professor at Princeton and

---

student can read, at a glance, and in real forms, the history of the creation, from the dawn of life to the appearance of man" (p. 265). Princeton Seminary soon elected Libbey to its board of trustees, where he served from 1876 to 1895. *Biographical Catalogue of Princeton Theological Seminary,* vol. 1, 1815-1932, comp. Edward Howell Roberts (Princeton: Trustees of the Seminary, 1933), p. xviii.

13. Donald Baird, director of the museum, in a letter to the *Princeton Alumni Weekly* 85 (30 January 1985): 2. Even at its founding in 1874, the "E. M. Museum" (named after Libbey Sr.'s wife Elizabeth Marsh Libbey) was no small affair; the college catalogue for 1875-76 boasted of a *Megatherium* skeleton cast and several other "large fossil animals, American, European, and Asiatic," as well as "several thousand species of smaller fossils." *Catalogue of the College of New Jersey,* 1875-76, 35, PU Archives.

14. *The Princetonian,* 30 November 1876. Unfortunately no records survive of the lectures themselves.

Columbia and highly influential director of the American Museum of Natural History in New York City.[15]

Such developments earned McCosh a reputation as a scientific liberator and educational progressive. But that is only half of the story. McCosh was equally concerned to foster religious commitment among the students, believing in no uncertain terms that the faculty and college officers stood *in loco parentis*. Early in his administration he took upon himself the responsibility for Bible instruction, making it more rigorous, not less, than it had been.[16] He prided himself in never violating a student's private right of conscience or seeking to persuade non-Presbyterians to join his denomination, but he made real effort to know the spiritual state of his "boys" and to woo any skeptical wanderers back to the faith. These efforts, like his efforts in curricular enhancement, paid off. At the same time as student interest in science and evolution began to climb, so did religious earnestness. The winter of 1875-76 saw one of the most extensive revivals the college had ever experienced — and it was the students who began and carried out most of the work, with the president, faculty, and local seminarians giving assistance. The revival culminated in a campus-wide communion assembly of some 260 trustees, professors, and students kneeling together as brothers in thanksgiving to God. McCosh called it "one of the most solemn, tender, impressive scenes I have ever witnessed."[17] In the 1880s, when Harvard dropped all mandatory religious attendance, Princeton still stood on its commitment to the active encouragement of religion. McCosh engaged Harvard president Charles W. Eliot in a public debate, widely reported, on the place religion should occupy in colleges, and repeatedly urged his faculty to share his commitment to

15. Scott, *Some Memories*, chapters 5 and 6.

16. McCosh, President's Report, 16 December 1868, PU Trustees Minutes. In the mid-1870s he gave part of the responsibility for Bible instruction back to the clerical members of the faculty, but watched over it carefully. In 1876 McCosh actually scolded the trustees for the "utterly inadequate" provision they had made for religious instruction of underclassmen (President's Report, 9 November 1876). As of 1877 the students were required to attend morning and evening prayers daily, morning chapel and evening prayer on Sundays, and regular instruction in the Bible — McCosh taught the seniors in Old Testament history and the book of Romans. Class prayer meetings, which were optional, were held twice a week, and optional college prayer meetings three times a week (President's Report, 8 November 1877). McCosh summarized his efforts in religious instruction in "Twenty Years," pp. 227-28.

17. McCosh, President's Report, 26 June 1876.

religious *in loco parentis* policy.[18] Out of Princeton's student religious life in those years were born two enormously influential evangelical organizations, the Intercollegiate YMCA and the Student Volunteer Movement for world missions.[19]

Graduation orations and class poems reveal how deeply McCosh's students were beginning to feel the thrill and the gravity of being called upon to mold their age. A graduate in 1875 declared, "We must believe science, and we enter life intending to accept all that science proves, regardless of consequences" — but he confessed "the need of a pilot to steer the vessel whose sails are filling by science, whose engines are constructed by science, whose furnace fires are fed by science." That pilot was the Christian faith; and the student rejoiced to observe that Guyot and Alexander, "two of the most practical and most daring of scientists[,] hold the same faith that our old fashioned fathers hold, and pray the same prayers our mothers taught us."[20] Class poems especially showed that the leading students had got the activist message McCosh so wanted to convey. The poet of 1878 asked his fellow graduates to consider whether they would accept the stamp of their age or place their stamp upon it, and proceeded in a rather bumpy rhapsodic epic to describe the enemy, his telltale philosophical fundaments, and his spiritual desolation, in distinctly old-Princetonian tones. Standing over against the new graduates he pictured

18. McCosh told the board, "It would simply be an iniquity for this College to allow young men of from 15 to 20 years of age from their homes, hundreds, it may be thousands of miles away, and take no care of them" with regard to character and conduct (President's Report, 19 June 1882). Cf. his report of 16 June 1884 concerning Harvard.

19. McCosh, "Twenty Years," p. 231. In the 1880s some of the younger, professionalizing faculty did chafe under their obligations for religious and moral oversight, regarding them as distracting nonacademic chores. Scott, *Some Memories*, p. 136; W. Bruce Leslie, *Gentlemen and Scholars: College and Community in the "Age of the University," 1865-1917* (University Park: Pennsylvania State University Press, 1992), p. 76.

20. J. P. Coyle, "Memorial Oration," *Nassau Herald* (1875), pp. 25-26. Hoeveler mistakenly claims that two other science professors at Princeton, astronomer Charles Augustus Young and physicist Cyrus Fogg Brackett, "had no commitment to religion" — basing his inference on the students' nickname for the neighborhood where the two scientists lived, "atheists' corner" (Hoeveler, *James McCosh*, pp. 244-45). But the nickname was only a joke. In fact, Young, an authority on the sun and a pioneer in spectrum analysis, perpetuated the antebellum tradition of doxological science, lecturing at PTS on "God's glory in the heavens." The lecture was printed as a pamphlet (Cranbury, N.J., 1894) and is preserved in PTS Special Collections. Brackett came to the College of New Jersey from a ten-year career at Bowdoin, a highly religious college. Alexander Leitch, *A Princeton Companion* (Princeton: Princeton University Press, 1978), pp. 64, 534.

an infidel army under the crimson banner of atheism — "Positivists, Sceptics, Scoffers." The cohorts of "Evolution" marched behind them, guarding their rear — indicating the theory's subservience to prior philosophical commitments, namely, the limitation of knowledge to empirical experience and the denial of innate mental apparatus. From this paucity of epistemic endowment infidelity made a great theoretical leap,

> Whereby all that is in Nature is evolved from that below,
> And we rise through endless series to the last creation — Woe:

a fitting name for the new humanity, no creation in the image of a good and holy God, but a mere evolved aggregation of passions and wants, a changeling at the mercy of "Fates and hellish Furies." Morality, human aspiration, certain knowledge, and spiritual blessedness were all threatened by the infidel host and its godless form of evolutionism, as the passage concluded:

> They would take from earth its Eden,
>   they would springs of life destroy,
> They would take from soul its conscience,
>   they would render Nescience joy.[21]

Princeton College, its museum cases filled with fresh discoveries from the fossil beds of Colorado and Wyoming, its brightest sons about to un-

---

21. George R. Gaither Jr., "Class Poem," *Nassau Herald* (1878), pp. 15-17. Some students, of course, were not nearly so grave. A graduating senior in 1875 used all the talk about scientific infidelity to poke fun at a few classmates. He presented a fictitious award for "Our Man of Science" as follows: "Science, ladies and gentlemen, is no longer the innocent moral thing that our fathers and great grandfathers once supposed. It is now very dangerous. It believes in all manner of strange and heterodox things. Adam and Eve have been banished by it from the Garden of Eden; instead we find two monkeys chattering in the 'forest primeval.' In order to be scientific at college, you must read all the infidel books you can lay your hands on, must say you don't believe in anything not established by scientific method, must talk about Darwin and Huxley and Tyndall and Protoplasm all the time, must scowl when Dr. Atwater annihilates them, and you must talk continually of theological bias, say that the Bible and Hodge may be very good, but for your part you prefer the Descent of Man and Darwin. Such a line of conduct and conversation will not fail to secure to the average student a 'scientific' reputation, and such a line of conduct and conversation has been pursued by our Man of Science.... [He is] none other than Samuel, *alias* Huxley, Miller, of Philadelphia. Will this compound of modern infidelity and science, falsely so-called, please advance...." "Presentation Address," *Nassau Herald* (1875), pp. 25-29.

dertake graduate study of evolutionary biology in Europe, had certainly not lost sight of the Horrible Vision.

Anti-Darwinian Citadel

As the class poem of 1878 showed, evolution still sometimes served as a dirty word on the Princeton College campus. Certainly the students knew their college president was intent upon wresting evolution from infidel hands, confident that there was "nothing atheistic about the theory, properly limited and explained."[22] McCosh encouraged his students to face the evolution question openly, to read Huxley and Spencer and Mill — and to heed his own exposure of their philosophical shortcomings. He busied himself in the middle years of the decade with pointed attacks on the philosophical ineptitude of the more flagrantly positivistic evolutionary scientists (Huxley and Tyndall), drawing repeated attention to the limits of material and efficient causes: their inability to account for the human mind or indeed to account for the world of brute nature without reference to causes higher than themselves.[23] McCosh's activities to tame and Christianize the theory were well known. But then, as now, the terminology hid huge differences in metaphysical opinion, so that the historian looking over the sources, finding "evolution" and related terms used with favor and disfavor, is tempted to divide the Princetonians into neat pro- and antievolutionary camps (or, what is more misleading, into evolutionist and creationist camps). *Everyone* on the college and seminary faculty, it is safe to say, appreciated in some measure the *process* of divine activity in the natural world. All held a common belief in the growth analogy, the perception of an ascending order in the creaturely realm, both over time (long geological ages) and up the ladder of being. In this sense they were all developmentalists, and all non-Darwinians — as indeed were many of their philosophical foes among scientists, including even Thomas Huxley and Ernst Haeckel.[24] But de-

22. James McCosh, *The Religious Aspect of Evolution* (New York: Putnam, 1888), pp. x-xi.

23. James McCosh, *Ideas in Nature Overlooked by Dr. Tyndall: Being an Examination of Dr. Tyndall's Belfast Address* (New York: Robert Carter and Bros., 1875), and *The Development Hypothesis: Is It Sufficient?* (New York: Robert Carter and Bros., 1876).

24. On Huxley and Haeckel as non-Darwinians, despite their eager advocacy of evolution under Darwin's name, see Peter J. Bowler, *The Non-Darwinian Revolution: Reinterpreting a Historical Myth* (Baltimore: Johns Hopkins University Press, 1988), pp. 76-90.

spite sharing with them a belief in the growth analogy of development, the Princetonians held a line of united metaphysical opinion against materialistic evolutionism. Perhaps a good umbrella term for 1870s Princeton would be "dualistic, developmental anti-Darwinism."

Location under this umbrella was far and away the most important Princetonian concern in the evolution question. But beneath the umbrella real differences existed: not only over the obvious issue of transmutation in general, but also as to whether human descent from simian ancestors was even theoretically admissible and whether any ultimately subversive principle of interpretation or argument was involved.[25] During the mid-1870s Princeton displayed both a concerted anti-Darwinian effort (in the technical meaning of the phrase) and a touchy uncertainty about other particulars of the evolution question. It is this period that has prompted historians to view the evolution question at Princeton as a battle between McCosh and Hodge, liberalism and fundamentalism. But another reading is not only possible but more compelling.

The mid-1870s were a momentous time for the fortunes of evolutionism in the American scientific community. In a few short years a climate of uncertainty gave way dramatically to near-unanimous acceptance. When Charles Hodge finished his *Systematic Theology* in 1873, his claim that evolution was unproven still reasonably described the case, for such

---

Bowler treats their views, as well as those of other "Darwinian" luminaries including Othniel C. Marsh and Francis Balfour, under the rubric of "pseudo-Darwinism."

25. Mathematics professor John T. Duffield warned that human evolution absolutely contradicted the Bible, whatever the status of the question scientifically and whatever the origin of other forms of life. He issued this warning in a chapel sermon entitled "Adam, the Son of God," which the new, nontheological *Princeton Review* published by invitation (Theodore Cuyler, in "In Memoriam: John Thomas Duffield" [pamphlet, 1901, PTS Special Collections]); Duffield, "Evolutionism Respecting Man, and the Bible," *Princeton Review* 1 (1878): 150-57. Dissatisfied with printing errors in the edited version of his essay, Duffield issued it again in pamphlet form: "Anthropology of Evolutionism and the Bible" (Princeton: Princeton Printing Establishment, 1878). In the latter version he rejected all transmutationism, not just human evolution. Hoeveler confuses Duffield's biblical literalism with Old School dogmatism (*James McCosh*, pp. 238-39, 276: "a hardened defender of the Old School ways") — but, as a premillennialist and an advocate of confessional revision, Duffield disagreed with the Old Schoolers at the seminary on two watershed issues (B. B. Warfield MSS, file on Premillennialism, PTS Special Collections; "In Memoriam: John Thomas Duffield"). David Livingstone has made a suggestive exploration of the relation between various millennial views and belief or disbelief in evolution — see his "Evolution, Eschatology and the Privatization of Providence," *Science and Christian Belief* 2 (1990): 117-30.

estimable scientists as Louis Agassiz of Harvard and James Dwight Dana of Yale, not to mention Princeton's Arnold Guyot, ranged their scientific prestige against transmutation.[26] But as McCosh had pointed out, the younger scientists all favored the theory, and they held the future. Agassiz died in 1873, leaving almost no antievolutionist followers among his many disciples; and in the following year Dana conceded "the derivation of species from species" in the second edition of his definitive textbook, *Manual of Geology.* While the older generation of naturalists was either passing from the scene or making its peace with transmutationism, a host of younger men remained aloof from the religious controversy and simply pursued their studies in paleontology, embryology, and morphology, finding the hypothesis of derivation very fruitful.[27] By 1877 paleontologist O. C. Marsh of Yale ventured to announce to the American Association for the Advancement of Science, "I need offer no argument for evolution, since to doubt evolution is to doubt science, and science is only another name for truth."[28]

Marsh's triumphant declaration was more bravado than statement of fact, however, for the supposedly unanimous chorus of evolutionist scientists was in fact deeply divided over what evolution meant, even as a purely scientific theory. Dana, for example, admitted derivation of species from species, but only by saltation ("abrupt transitions") — a mechanism that upon inspection was utterly inscrutable, and thus nigh unto miraculous — and he remained convinced that no natural evolutionary

26. Guyot, Agassiz, and Dana were close friends, by the way. James Dwight Dana, "Biographical Memoir of Prof. Arnold Guyot" (pamphlet reprint from the *Smithsonian Report* for 1886-87 [Washington: Smithsonian Institution, 1889]).

27. Ronald L. Numbers, *The Creationists: The Evolution of Scientific Creationism* (Berkeley: University of California Press, 1993), pp. 6-8; Paul F. Boller Jr., *American Thought in Transition: The Impact of Evolutionary Naturalism, 1865-1900* (Chicago: Rand McNally, 1969), pp. 12-18; Denis Oswald Lamoureux, "Between 'The Origin of Species' and 'The Fundamentals': Toward a Historiographical Model of the Evangelical Reaction to Darwinism in the First Fifty Years" (Ph.D. diss., Toronto School of Theology, 1991), p. 160. Numbers relates that Agassiz's successor in the zoology chair at Harvard, John McCrady, an anti-Darwinist of strong religious convictions, was forced to resign by President Eliot in 1877. McCrady blamed the move on local favoritism (he was a southerner), his religious conservatism, and his open stance against "Darwinism, Huxleyism, and Spencerism" — and on Asa Gray's efforts to oust him. With McCrady's dismissal Harvard forsook its increasingly uncomfortable legacy of antitransmutationism.

28. Othniel Charles Marsh, quoted in John William Dawson, "Evolution and the Apparition of Animal Forms," *Princeton Review* 1 (1878): 665.

process could produce humanity from the brute without divine intervention. Many other leading American evolutionists held equally un-Darwinian views. Joseph Le Conte of the University of California, a former student of Agassiz who in 1872 avowed a very reluctant transmutationism but within a few years called himself "an evolutionist, thorough and enthusiastic," retained his belief in "paroxysmal" change and the inheritance of acquired characters, as well as his interest in connecting the process with religion. Vertebrate paleontologist Edward Drinker Cope adopted a similarly "Lamarckian" interest in use inheritance, probably from reading Spencer, observing pointedly that Darwin's theory of natural selection left unexplained the *origin* of the fittest. The scientific community's much-touted wholesale conversion to evolutionism in the 1870s was hardly a unified, let alone a Darwinian, affair. Only by reading "evolution" as the barest transmutationism can we speak of any near-unanimous conversion to the theory — or rather to the idea, for the theory behind the idea varied enormously.[29]

Nevertheless, Marsh and many others triumphantly noised abroad the scientific certification of "evolution." At the end of the decade, the *New York Independent* challenged its rival religious newspaper, the *Observer,* to name more than two "working naturalists of repute" in the United States and Canada who were not "evolutionists." The *Observer* could not do so. Only Arnold Guyot of Princeton and John William Dawson of McGill remained[30] — and by the time of Guyot's death in 1884, Dana felt it appropriate to characterize his old Swiss friend as a limited transmutationist after all.[31]

29. Boller, *American Thought in Transition,* pp. 15-18; Bowler, *The Eclipse of Darwinism: Anti-Darwinian Evolution Theories in the Decades around 1900* (Baltimore: Johns Hopkins University Press, 1983), pp. 123-24. The American Association for the Advancement of Science even elected Dawson, the supposed lone voice against evolutionism in the scientific community, its president in 1882 — five years *after* Marsh's triumphant speech.

30. Numbers, *The Creationists,* p. 7. However, in 1880 Dawson claimed the French paleontologist Barrande as a fellow antitransmutationist — if true, that makes three, though not all in North America. Barrande was the foremost expert on the Paleozoic era, according to Dawson, and "certainly labored to overcome his doubts [about transmutation] with greater assiduity than even many of the apostles of the new doctrine," but "the stubbornness of the facts" — the abrupt appearance of complete forms in the fossil record — prevented him. John William Dawson, "The Antiquity of Man and the Origin of Species," *Princeton Review* 6 (July-December 1880): 396.

31. Dana, "Biographical Memoir of Prof. Arnold Guyot." It appears that Guyot's view had not changed, but Dana wished to emphasize the points of friendly contact between

In this turbulent climate of scientific opinion, the Princetonians determined not to twist helplessly in the wind like a weathercock, nor to shutter their windows against it, but rather to direct it: to take an active part in the development of natural history. To channel that study in its proper theistic direction was one of McCosh's main goals in his call to "mold the age." He proposed a chair of natural history as part of the plan of the School of Science that the board approved in 1871. But filling the post proved difficult. McCosh's inability to find a suitable candidate went down in the annals of American education as a prime illustration of clerical obstruction of scientific progress, on the assumption that the ministerial faction on the board of trustees, led by Charles Hodge, blocked McCosh's every move to bring a working evolutionist to Princeton. A brief look at the history of that appointment is in order.

The proposed chair embraced natural history, geology, and botany. In 1871 Guyot requested relief from his duties in geology, wishing to concentrate his ebbing energies on physical geography alone. The establishment of a School of Science provided the opportunity. When McCosh, as head of the appointments committee, went prospecting for suitable candidates early in 1873, Joseph Henry, a member of the committee, former professor at Princeton, and first director of the Smithsonian Institution, recommended young Edward Drinker Cope for the job. A committed Quaker, Cope had already published a paper on use inheritance to explain the origin of the variations upon which natural selection operated. This so-called Lamarckian explanation of variation by individual adaptation to environmental changes preserved an element of purpose in a wholly natural, scrutable process, thus satisfying both scientific and religious desires. The organism was itself responsible to adapt or lose out in the struggle for existence; thus a moral and goal-directed category survived in the evolutionary process — blind chance was not the ultimate driving force.[32] Much as this view might have commended Cope to Princeton and to McCosh in particular, the president himself nixed Cope's candidacy. In a letter to his father, the young scientist claimed McCosh objected to his evolutionism, "for those views are much condemned at Princeton."[33] Other candidates

---

Guyot's idealistic developmentalism and progressive evolutionism — considerable points, as I have argued above.

32. Bowler, *The Eclipse of Darwinism*, p. 54.

33. Edward Drinker Cope to Alfred Cope, 6 March 1873, in Nathan Reingold, ed., *Science in Nineteenth-Century America: A Documentary History*, American Century series (New York: Hill and Wang, 1964), pp. 245-46 (orig. in O. C. Marsh Papers, Yale University).

made it through committee but were not appointed. They included Theodore Gill, noted zoologist, librarian of the Smithsonian Institution, and author of over 140 papers mostly on new fish species, and Charles Frederick
Hartt, professor of geology and physical geography at Cornell and a student of Louis Agassiz. Gill felt mishandled by Princeton, claiming that
McCosh had made a definite offer that the trustees then refused to confirm because he was "a Darwinian." Hartt passed the trustees but refused
the offer because the salary offered him was too little. The trustees appeared unwilling to appoint a transmutationist, whatever his metaphysics, either by refusing him outright or by making a salary offer so small that
he was bound to refuse. Two decades after the Scopes trial, retired Princeton biologist Edwin G. Conklin attributed the logjam to a strong and definite antievolutionist sentiment among the trustees, evidenced by the appearance of Hodge's *What Is Darwinism?* at about that time. Inasmuch as
Hodge was president of the college board and senior professor at the seminary, the entire affair looked like a religious attempt to limit scientific inquiry — a resolute "No!" to McCosh's evolutionism and to his plan to make
Princeton a leading center of baptized evolutionary science.[34]

But McCosh's breaking off of negotiations with Cope, at least, may
not have owed solely to the board's objections. Cope's evolutionism,
however welcome for its scientific preservation of teleology, was clearly
too radical for McCosh. Not only did humankind definitely evolve from
the beasts in it, but it also destroyed the biblical story of the Fall by explaining original sin as vestigial brutishness. Cope's view threatened the
boundaries between biology and psychology — matter and mind — and
denied the absolute distinctiveness of the human spirit.[35] McCosh
viewed these matters with grave concern. In a similar way the limits of
another candidate's evolutionism were wider than McCosh himself allowed. When Asa Gray recommended Joseph Le Conte for the job,
McCosh did not so much as mention him to the board.[36] As to the paltry

34. PU Trustees Minutes, 17 December 1873; Edwin Grant Conklin, "Biology at Prince-
ton," *Bios* 19 (October 1948): 156. According to Willard Thorp et al., "McCosh had run head-
on against the 'Princeton Theology,'" still strong on the board, whose refusal to confirm
Gill's nomination was "possibly meant as a rebuke to McCosh for his advanced views" (*The
Princeton Graduate School: A History* [Princeton: Princeton University Press, 1978], p. 19).
On Hartt, see *National Cyclopedia of American Biography*, 11:260-61.

35. Short notice of *Half-Hours with Modern Scientists*, in *Presbyterian Quarterly and
Princeton Review* 1 (1872): 614.

36. On Gray's recommendation of Le Conte, see James R. Moore, *The Post-Darwinian*

salary offered Hartt, it may be explained by the uncertain economic conditions surrounding the Panic of 1873, exacerbated by the college's building spurt. Only the awkward affair with Gill remains as positive testimony to a sense of opposition over evolution between McCosh and the trustees. Since, as we have already seen, McCosh and Hodge and their respective faculties did not range their forces against each other on the evolution question, it is likely that any stiff-necked and categorical opposition to evolutionism on the board — evidenced in the failure to confirm Gill — owed not to the influence of the seminary faculty but to the prejudices of other, unfortunately nameless, trustees.[37]

Upon recommending Gill, McCosh told the board frankly that despite extensive travel and correspondence he had found it disappointingly hard to find a suitable candidate.[38] Such a statement did not convey great enthusiasm about the nominee. When the nomination failed, McCosh looked overseas and with remarkable ease brought in a former Belfast student of his, George Macloskie, recent pastor of a Presbyterian church and current secretary of the Bible Society of Ireland. Macloskie held degrees in philosophy and law (with special honors) and enjoyed the amateur study of plants and insects. He was surprised by Princeton's offer, according to Conklin, doubting his fitness for the position. But having wanted for some time to see America, he accepted the job "and thought he might learn enough natural history on the way over to keep ahead of the boys." In time he published a textbook of elementary botany (1883) and a few papers on insect morphology, and even prepared several charts for the *Atlas of Biology* by Huxley and Howes. Macloskie was hardly the new breed of professional scientist McCosh had hoped for — but he was competent enough, and he was certainly no antievolutionist. For the next

---

Controversies: A Study of the Protestant Struggle to Come to Terms with Darwin in Great Britain and America, 1870-1900 (Cambridge: Cambridge University Press, 1979), pp. 225, 385-86 n. 81; cf. Joseph Le Conte, *The Autobiography of Joseph Le Conte*, ed. William Dallam Armes (New York: D. Appleton and Co., 1903).

37. Hoeveler names one trustee, George W. Musgrave, who in 1877 called McCosh an "evolutionist — a sneaking heretic." But Hoeveler also notes that Musgrave changed his mind after reading one of McCosh's books (Hoeveler, *James McCosh*, p. 277). Musgrave served also as vice president of the seminary board of directors and president of the Presbyterian Alliance in Philadelphia (*Biographical Catalogue*, p. 43). The nonresident directors and trustees of both Princeton institutions appear to have been more extreme in their opinions than the faculty members were. Cf. seminary director Henry J. Van Dyke's speech at F. L. Patton's inauguration in 1881 (see chapter 6 below).

38. McCosh, President's Report, 22 June 1874, PU Trustees Minutes, vol. 5.

three decades he propounded a McCosh-like theistic evolutionism in successor journals to the old *Biblical Repertory and Princeton Review*.[39] It seems likely that it was Macloskie's reliable, Presbyterian devoutness that the more intransigent trustees had missed in the other candidates.[40]

Macloskie's appointment was a stopgap measure, not a permanent solution. Guyot continued to teach geology and to request relief from that responsibility. Meanwhile, as the American scientific profession entered its period of most rapid conversion to transmutationism, certain British scientists made public forays into metaphysical questions on the basis of their evolutionisms. Thomas Henry Huxley toured the United States in 1875 to popularize not only the theory of transmutation but also a positivistic philosophy that claimed sure knowledge for material things but no knowledge, properly speaking, for metaphysical things such as ultimate causes and God.[41] John Tyndall caused a great stir promoting similar views in an address before the British Association in Belfast in 1874.[42] Against these prominent evolutionists who used their scientific prestige to commend nasty philosophical notions, McCosh arose with all his martial fervor to defend the foundations of belief.[43] The bat-

39. Edgar Sutton Robinson, ed., *The Presbyterian Ministerial Directory* (1898) (Cincinnati: Armstrong and Fillmore, 1899), p. 414; Conklin, "Biology at Princeton," pp. 156-57; David N. Livingstone, *Darwin's Forgotten Defenders: The Encounter between Evangelical Theology and Evolutionary Thought* (Grand Rapids: Eerdmans; Edinburgh: Scottish Academic Press, 1987), pp. 92-96.

40. PU Trustees Minutes, 28 October 1874. The push to maintain a distinctly Presbyterian identity at Princeton under McCosh's predecessor, John Maclean, is well known. See Wertenbaker, *Princeton, 1746-1896*, pp. 283-84.

41. Thomas Henry Huxley, *American Addresses* (New York: D. Appleton and Co., 1877). Already in 1860 Huxley had railed against "the cosmogony of the semi-barbarous Hebrew" and against those who tried "to force the generous new wine of Science into the old bottles of Judaism." These statements prompted his famous debate with Bishop Wilberforce. Moore, *The Post-Darwinian Controversies*, p. 60.

42. For an account of the Tyndall affair, with instructive comparisons between Princeton, Belfast, and Edinburgh on the evolution question, see David N. Livingstone, "Science and Religion: Foreword to the Historical Geography of an Encounter," *Journal of Historical Geography* 20 (1994): 377. Cf. Livingstone, "Darwinism and Calvinism: The Belfast-Princeton Connection," *Isis* 83 (1992): 408-28; and Livingstone, "Science and Religion: Towards a New Cartography," *Christian Scholar's Review* 26 (1997): 270-92.

43. McCosh's treatments of evolutionism in the 1870s came mainly in the form of rebuttals to the positivists: *Christianity and Positivism* (New York: Robert Carter and Bros., 1871); *Ideas in Nature Overlooked by Dr. Tyndall;* and *The Development Hypothesis*, his answer to Huxley's American tour. Plainly McCosh's ire was up: he scornfully described "a

tle was exactly what Atwater, Clark, and others had been predicting for over a decade. But there was an element of surprise, too, for the Princetonians before McCosh had not expected transmutationism to conquer the scientific community. When Marsh declared before the American Association for the Advancement of Science that "evolution," "science," and "truth" were interchangeable terms, he declared more than the certification of transmutationism; he made science the supreme (if not sole) category of truth. What was this but the brazen trespassing Princeton had vowed to prevent? Princeton would not allow scientists like Huxley, Tyndall, and Marsh to corner the market on truth. Transmutation was one thing; evolution as a world philosophy was quite another.[44]

But former Bible Society secretaries were not the sorts of warriors to do battle with science's big guns. Within a few years of Macloskie's appointment, Princeton made a concerted effort to woo John William Dawson away from Montreal, offering him a dual position in paleontology at the college and the relations of science and religion at the seminary. Since Agassiz's death the mantle of antitransmutationism had fallen on Dawson's shoulders. McCosh, Hodge, Guyot, and seminary Old Testament professor William Henry Green all wrote to Dawson in 1878 urging him to come join them in their battle to save the union of science and religion.[45]

It was a striking move. Never before had the college and seminary

---

mutual admiration society — who are ever quoting each other as infallible authorities, — . . . [Tyndall,] Professor Huxley, Mr. Herbert Spencer, Mr. Darwin, and Mr. Bain, and a whole host of inferior men who have assisted the leaders in getting the British Association very much under their management" (*Ideas in Nature*, p. 3). This view of enemy machinations must have influenced McCosh's resolution to organize the faithful in a counteroffensive, not leaving it to the positivists to mold the age.

44. The College of New Jersey's two biggest evolutionists in the 1880s, Scott and Osborn, perpetuated the battle against Marsh, siding with Edward Drinker Cope in the famous Cope-Marsh "battle for the bones," the rush for new fossil discoveries and ultimately for supremacy in the American paleontological community. Marsh was a Darwinian, Cope a neo-Lamarckian. Marsh won. See Henry Fairfield Osborn, *Cope: Master Naturalist* (Princeton: Princeton University Press, 1931).

45. Dawson was a friend and comrade of Princeton already — in 1874 he had given a series of six lectures at the seminary on "the relations of science and religion." PTS Faculty Minutes, 3 September 1874. For the most recent biography of Dawson see Susan Sheets-Pyenson, *John William Dawson: Faith, Hope, and Science* (Montreal: McGill-Queen's University Press, 1996).

jointly called a professor. McCosh informed Dawson that the trustees had "set their hearts" on him and were prepared to offer a salary of $3,000 plus a house. The seminary offered an additional $1,000, bringing Dawson's salary to a par with McCosh's.[46] He would have a free hand in forming the young School of Science — in effect, Dawson would join McCosh as cohead of the college, McCosh heading the academic course and Dawson the scientific. "But," McCosh hastened to add, "your influence would extend over our whole academic department, where we graduate 100 a year, and over the rising ministry of the Presbyterian Church." Remarking on the "concurrence of all parties in this place," McCosh wrote, "We give you this call. It looks to me as if it were a call from God." "The College and the Seminary unite in you not only cordially, but with intense eagerness and earnestness. The friends of religion, anxious about the cause of Christ in these critical times[,] will rejoice to hear of your acceptance."

As remarkable as the joint call itself was the reason McCosh gave for it. "The fact is that if you decline, which I hope you may not, we do not know where to look for a geologist of repute who is not a Darwinian."[47] Here is a real problem for the historiography that pits McCosh *against* Hodge, the trustees, and the seminary on the evolution question. McCosh was supposed to be fighting against these others to admit a theistic version of evolution into Princeton, yet here we find him working earnestly *with* them, begging the most renowned antitransmutationist of the day to take over McCosh's pride and joy, the School of Science, on the grounds of his anti-Darwinism. To explain this anomaly James R. Moore suggests that Hodge, as senior trustee and therefore McCosh's "employer," put the president up to it.[48] McCosh's own words certainly contradict that. He described the invitation as "a call from God," something about which an ordained minister of the gospel would not likely dissemble. He avowed, "It is surely a providence that both the College and the Seminary have been able unanimously to unite on you" — not because of any warfare between the two institutions, but because together they could offer a package deal worthy of the eminent scientist, in money and in influence.

46. For helpful context on academic salary levels, see Leslie, *Gentlemen and Scholars,* chapter 3.

47. McCosh to Dawson, 23 March 1878, Dawson MSS, McGill University Archives, Montreal.

48. Moore, *The Post-Darwinian Controversies,* p. 385 n. 81.

McCosh pressed the Canadian on the matter of influence. "Vast consequences depend on your decision," he wrote. Dawson would have "more weight over public opinion" from Princeton than from Montreal or from any British position. "The United States are not after all as wild as England is. You might help to keep us stable on this Continent." McCosh beckoned him with the prospect of nearness to other leading scientists, fully underwritten fossil expeditions to the West, collaboration with Guyot, and a hand in shaping the rising ministry of the church.[49] This call was not something McCosh was coerced into issuing; it fit beautifully his plan to mold the age.[50] With characteristic self-importance he saw Princeton as the best hope for religion among the American intellectual leadership, and America as the best hope for the world.[51]

Dawson declined the call but expressed a strong sense of solidarity in battle. "We have here also those beginnings of materialism which are threatening you," he wrote, "and it seems impossible to desert the friends also who have fought with me." McCosh was terribly disappointed. So unwilling was he to "part with the hope" that he reopened the offer twice in the next two months.[52]

There are indications in those letters that the call of Dawson was possibly to have provided the basis for an even closer collaboration between college and seminary than had existed before McCosh's time — another blow to the conventional interpretation. McCosh wrote, "I regarded it as a great triumph when we got the two institutions to agree on you — there will [be] no attempt now to combine them." Again: "the understanding between College and Seminary is dissolved and each will look out for itself, our promise of an endowment for the College being no

49. McCosh to Dawson, 23 March 1878 and 4 April 1878, Dawson MSS.

50. Guyot wrote Dawson, "If I had thought it possible for you to leave the high & useful position you now occupy, to take charge of our College Course, your name would have been brought forward long ago. Dr. McCosh thought he had ground for more hope." McCosh appears to have been an initiator in the process, not a man coerced. Guyot to Dawson, 3 April 1878, Dawson MSS.

51. On the former point — Princeton's unique position among American colleges as the best hope for the evangelical college ideal — McCosh's pride was somewhat justified. Marsden, *Soul*, p. 196.

52. Dawson to Charles Hodge, 16 April 1878, Hodge Family Papers, box 12; McCosh to Dawson, 25 April 1878 and 3 June 1878, Dawson MSS. Dawson would indeed continue to work with Princeton on the evolution question, publishing six articles in the *Princeton Review* between 1878 and 1881.

longer binding." When Dawson refused a second time, McCosh lamented, "I am entirely *out* in my plans for the present."[53] He called them "my plans." It appears that McCosh himself engineered the joint call of Dawson, hoping even for some kind of combination of the two institutions. He probably had a financial rather than an administrative combination in mind, perhaps to pool the endowments each institution was able to draw from its peculiar constituency and to avoid competition between them for the money of the great Presbyterian benefactors such as the Green, Stuart, and Lenox families.[54] In any case, McCosh's scheme to "combine" the college and seminary fairly demolishes the usual story that he set out to free the college from denominational or specifically seminary connections. The evolution question, far from dividing the two institutions, brought them together in a joint attempt to establish an "anti-Darwinian citadel" at Princeton.[55]

At first glance it seems bizarre that McCosh should want to bring to Princeton the last of what he routinely told his students was a dying breed, the antitransmutationists. But to focus on transmutationism is to miss the issues in the evolution question that the Princetonians considered far more fundamental. To the college and seminary the most important matters in "Darwinism" were not scientific, but philosophical — not the mutability of species, but materialistic monism, positivism, and antitheism. On those matters McCosh and Hodge agreed heartily. They agreed as well on a basic approach to meeting the philosophical challenge that veiled itself beneath a scientific theory: they would meet it openly, expose its hubris, and embrace the truths it contained, assured that God's works could not ultimately contradict his revealed word. But to do so they needed to find faculty who were both scientific experts and pious, reflective believers (preferably Presbyterians). This was as much

53. McCosh to Dawson, 25 April 1878, Dawson MSS.

54. On Princeton's benefactors, see Hoeveler, *James McCosh*, pp. 281-82.

55. Charles F. O'Brien, *Sir William Dawson: A Life in Science and Religion* (Philadelphia: American Philosophical Society, 1971), pp. 18-22. The phrase "anti-Darwinian citadel" is O'Brien's (p. 21). McCosh's Old World background is important to remember in connection with the Dawson call. At Glasgow and Edinburgh theological and scientific courses existed side by side. McCosh held no particular brief for the institutional isolation of theology. Indeed, what he objected to in the Scottish universities was the *neglect* of religion, especially of religious and moral oversight (see Hoeveler, *James McCosh*, p. 46). Only *after* the academic revolution of the late nineteenth century did the separation of religion from university study come to be widely considered a given (on this see especially Marsden, *The Soul of the American University*).

McCosh's initial strategy for molding the age as it was the older Princetonians' strategy for defending the faith. They stood in close agreement on both goals and tactics. Were McCosh trying to free academic inquiry from churchly control or to establish a beachhead at Princeton for theistic evolution, his united effort with the seminary would make no sense. But if he saw himself as the chosen captain of Princeton's company of soldiers, fighting common philosophical foes who bid to undermine their religion and indeed their whole worldview — and who had no intellectual right to do so, because they entered the realms of philosophy and theology as trespassers and usurpers — then McCosh's "active collusion" with the seminary, even in calling the last great antievolutionist scientist, presents no puzzle at all. It becomes, rather, an illustration of what mattered most in the evolution question at Princeton.[56]

The Bright Young Men

Out of the failed call to Dawson grew one of McCosh's most famous policies, the identification and cultivation of promising students to assume professorships at their alma mater. In the first half of his administration McCosh had deliberately sought appointments from outside the Princeton fold, declaring the college too inbred. But now, after 1878, his policy shifted. His educational reforms were bearing fruit in a crop of promising, ambitious students eager to do their part to mold the age by participating in the explosion of American academic research and the formation of academic professions, especially in the sciences.

The classes of 1877 and 1879 showed particular promise, as evidenced by their initiation of the Princeton Scientific Expeditions. McCosh encouraged a number of them to remain at the college for an additional year of laboratory research, then sent them off to Europe to earn doctorates under the leading researchers in their fields. By 1880 the

---

56. Peter Bowler observes that "'theistic evolutionism' flourished in the 1870s as the most vocal source of *opposition* to Darwin's theory" (*The Non-Darwinian Revolution*, p. 182, emphasis mine). The call of Dawson to Princeton illustrates Bowler's point beautifully. McCosh the theistic evolutionist felt completely at home with Dawson the antitransmutationist, precisely because both were anti-Darwinists. Their common commitment to design discernible in the creation and to the growth analogy outweighed their differences on transmutationism.

first of them were ready to bring the best of modern science back to Princeton, "under God," as McCosh admonished one of them.[57] Of the nineteen appointments McCosh made after 1880, ten were Princeton graduates — McCosh's own students, of whom he boasted endlessly in his Scottish accent as "me bright young men."[58] Fully two generations his junior, this group of young professors formed the nucleus of the new Princeton that under Woodrow Wilson (himself a Bright Young Man of '79) became a full-fledged, leading center of graduate as well as undergraduate education.

Previous histories of Princeton have rightly emphasized the importance of McCosh's Bright Young Men policy, but they have overlooked its tactical continuity with old Princeton, unaware of the common Battle Plan — or they have treated it as a political maneuver on McCosh's part to subvert the intransigence of conservative faculty and trustees. According to the latter reading, exemplified in J. David Hoeveler's biography, McCosh "needed new political allies, and he would pluck them directly from the ranks of his own students." McCosh's "honeymoon" years had ended and a "reaction against evolution and other liberal tendencies" had "set in against him." In hiring the Bright Young Men McCosh accomplished a great coup against the board, his recompense for the botched Gill appointment to the natural history chair.[59] A letter from McCosh to Dawson in early 1880, however, argues otherwise. After Dawson had turned down Princeton's offer, McCosh asked him for advice in finding a suitable candidate to succeed Guyot, who by this time was in his seventies. Dawson suggested several British scientists, but the trustees were hesitant to appoint someone unknown to them to a post so central to the currents of contemporary thought. McCosh wrote, "At last they said pretty decidedly to me *'You must raise your own man.'*" It was the trustees, not the president, who first suggested the policy that became McCosh's greatest asset in modernizing the college.[60] And one of the first Bright Young Men to return to Princeton, having seized and

57. McCosh to Scott, 14 May 1880, McCosh MSS, PU Archives.

58. Hoeveler, *James McCosh*, p. 285.

59. Hoeveler, *James McCosh*, p. 285. Clearly there was trouble for McCosh after 1878, but to attribute it to his evolutionism is a mistake. As evidence of the alleged antievolutionary backlash, Hoeveler cites Hodge's *What Is Darwinism?* and Duffield's article for the *Princeton Review,* "Evolutionism Respecting Man, and the Bible." On Duffield see note 25 above.

60. McCosh to Dawson, 5 February 1880, Dawson MSS, emphasis mine.

mastered materialism's most formidable weapon of attack, evolutionary science, was the favorite grandson of Charles Hodge himself: William Berryman Scott, Class of '77.

Willie Scott (from college on he preferred "Wick") lived for seventeen years with his brother and widowed mother under the great theologian's roof on the Princeton Seminary campus. He called Hodge "the only father I ever had." Hodge delighted in his grandson's quick mind. Scott recalled receiving from him his first lesson in paleontology. "Not far from where we were standing, a wagon was unloading coal and he said to me: 'Do you know what that is?' 'Why! yes; it's coal.' 'No; it's wood,' was the puzzling rejoinder. The old gentleman made no attempt to explain the paradox, which long continued to bewilder me, but he planted a seed which in after years bore fruit."[61] It was Willie Scott who at the age of sixteen, while a student at the college, corrected the proofs of *What Is Darwinism?*[62] Hodge followed his grandson's participation in the Princeton Scientific Club and the Scientific Expeditions with warm interest.[63] Here, surely, was the kind of youth Princeton had been hoping to send into the scientific fray — bright, eager, impeccably brought up, and sound in the faith.

Hodge died while Wick was out west on the Scientific Expedition of 1878. His uncle, A. A. Hodge, conveyed the sad news to him by mail.[64] When the expedition returned, Scott found Princeton all astir after the theologian's passing, and his own future plans quite up in the air. After

---

61. Scott, *Some Memories*, p. 22.

62. Scott, *Some Memories*, p. 49.

63. Hodge noted with pride in his MS Memoranda, 21 June 1877, "Willie graduated with the first honor and received ye fellowship for Natural Science. In the evening he left home with fourteen other students in an exploring expedition in the far west" (6:220, PTS Special Collections). Willie wrote him from Fort Bridger, Wyoming, full of the joy of discovery. His letter begins, "I thought perhaps that you would like to hear something from your wild Injun grandson. . . ." Scott to Charles Hodge, 5 August 1877, Hodge Family MSS, PU Library, Letters, box 12.

64. On hearing the news, Scott confided, "Dear Uncle Arch, you can't tell how grateful I am to you for your remembrance of me at that solemn hour. Please keep me always in your prayers; for, although I have given myself to the Saviour, and my end in my life is to make the world somewhat 'better for my having lived in it' by striving to advance his kingdom, yet dark clouds of doubt and distress are continually settling down over me, and I need all the help I can get." Scott to A. A. Hodge, 1 July 1878, Hodge Family MSS, Letters, box 12. Despite this intimation of a sometimes shaky faith, McCosh and the Hodges sent Scott off to face the big world of scientific experts alone.

two western expeditions and a year of graduate research, he had largely exhausted the scientific training the College of New Jersey had to offer. In the confused situation that summer, his elders decided it would be best to grant the youth's wish to study in Europe. To hear Scott tell the story — and he had a knack for making a story flavorful — it was a very poorly thought-out plan:

> This fortunate turn was very much more "by good luck than good management." As I look back, I am fairly aghast at the foolishness of my whole scheme and am wholly at a loss to understand how such experienced and sagacious men as my uncles [A. A. Hodge and Caspar Wistar Hodge], Dr. Guyot and Dr. McCosh, all of them deeply interested in my welfare, could have sanctioned so absurd a plan. I, a boy of twenty, who had never in his life been away from home entirely on his own responsibility, was expected to start out with no definite destination. Nor was any institution or teacher agreed upon in advance; even the subject of my studies was left entirely vague. Practically, I was told: "Go to England and study something with somebody, and then go on to Germany and study something else with some other body," as Dr. McCosh would have said. That this absurd undertaking should actually have worked out so well was due to no one's wisdom or foresight, but to the happy chance of Leidy's having given me a letter to Huxley and my having presented it promptly upon my arrival in London.[65]

Perhaps the plan really was as half-baked as Scott remembered it, but perhaps not. McCosh's letter to Dawson in 1880 reported Scott's appointment as the fulfillment of the trustees' directive to "raise your own man." "We have such a one in view trained under Guyot," he said — and after listing Scott's extensive European and American qualifications, McCosh described him as a man "with a profound philosophical mind and sound in his religious opinions."[66] McCosh presented Scott as a homegrown Princetonian paragon, the kind of man they had tried unsuccessfully to bring in from outside. Scott was a bright young Princetonian sent out to garner the best science the world had to offer, then brought back to teach it at believing Princeton, to train young men in paleontology within a sound philosophical and theological framework. The whole episode fits beautifully with the twenty-year-old

65. Scott, *Some Memories,* p. 85.
66. McCosh to Dawson, 5 February 1880, Dawson MSS.

Princetonian plan to seize and master the weapons of attack, bringing them back into the citadel of faith. While the particulars of Scott's European training may indeed have been left largely to his own devising, that does not necessarily negate the overall intention of raiding the infidel camp. It might be read instead as a profound (if naïve) expression of Princeton's trust in Scott's preparation under their care. Perhaps young Scott simply did not fully recognize the plan.

In any event, it is indeed remarkable that this prize of a young Princetonian, Charles Hodge's very flesh and blood, should show up one day on Huxley's doorstep. We must remember that the Princetonians professed a glad acceptance of good science, and reserved the right to separate scientific fact from explanatory speculations or theories — so they viewed Huxley's agnosticism as a foreign element brought in illicitly to his laboratory work, as something not native to science. In this light Huxley, *as a scientist,* was no enemy of the truth. The remarkable thing is not just the irony of Hodge's grandson coming under Huxley's wing, but what a radical demonstration it was of the Princetonians' brave confidence in their rhetoric about the twin daughters of heaven. Their confidence was real — they fully expected that the scientific method would produce truth harmonious with good theology; that religion truly had nothing to fear from well-authenticated scientific facts.

Scott enjoyed the hospitality of the Huxley family and the close personal attention of his new mentor. Huxley himself went through Scott's notebooks from his laboratory course at the Royal School of Mines, correcting any errors he found.[67] Scott remembered fondly the interest the great scientist took in him; from the time Huxley invited him to attend his course in London, "my troubles were over, for I had put myself into thoroughly competent hands and every step in my European education was taken at Huxley's advice."[68]

67. Scott, *Some Memories,* p. 90. The notebooks are held in the PU Library (MSS Division).

68. Scott, *Some Memories,* p. 85. An example of how thoroughly Huxley took young Scott under his wing is found on p. 87: "Some days before the Christmas holidays began, and after a meeting of the Royal Society, the great man came up to me and, putting his hand on my shoulder, said: 'What are your plans for New Year's Day?' 'I haven't any, Sir.' 'Then come and take dinner with me, won't you?' 'Thank you very much, Sir, I shall be delighted.' This, every one assured me, was an unprecedented honor." Earlier that fall Scott had written his future wife, "every one with whom I have come in contact from Huxley down or up, whichever way you choose to count, has treated me in the kindest & most

The young Princetonian immersed himself eagerly in his work. Having devised a kind of shorthand of his own, he captured virtually every word of the great scientist's lectures. Dutifully recopying them each evening, he produced twenty to thirty pages at a time. The students spent several hours each day in the laboratory using microscope and scalpel to make detailed anatomical and taxonomical observations of the whole sweep of animal life from invertebrates to mammals. Saturday afternoons took Scott to the British Museum, where he worked in the fossil mammal collection. The sheer volume of material, presented in impressive detail and without dogmatic speculation, soon convinced Scott of the truth of the evolution theory. It was not argued directly; rather, it was the assumed framework of all his studies, the plain consensus of the great scientific men under whom he worked. Later in life Scott recalled, "By degrees my anti-evolutionary beliefs seemed to drop away from me; no one argued on the subject, but every one took evolution so completely for granted, it was so obviously the best and most probable explanation of the facts of nature, that before I was well aware of it, I had become a fully convinced evolutionist and, needless to say, have remained even such an one until this day."[69]

At the conclusion of Huxley's course the "eminent man" urged Scott to go to Cambridge and study embryology under Francis Maitland Balfour, a dashing young prodigy of science who, while mountain climbing a few years later, would meet a tragic, early death. Balfour's thrilling career, his derring-do, and his unaffected friendliness captivated the younger American. In Cambridge Scott was joined by Princeton classmate Henry Fairfield Osborn, whose father was helping to finance Scott's European work, and at Balfour's suggestion the two set to work on the embryology of the common newt. Their 1879 article reporting their findings earned them an early reputation on both sides of the ocean.[70] ·

A letter of introduction from Huxley took Scott from Cambridge to Heidelberg, to study under Carl Gegenbaur, an eminent embryologist. "It was the fame of the universities that took me to Germany," he wrote. "In those days, not to have studied in Germany was to confess oneself

---

cordial way. All the scientific men have been especially warm in their welcome." "Memoirs; Materials for an Autobiography," Scott MSS, PU Library.

69. Scott, quoted in Leonard Huxley, "An American Student in Huxley's Laboratory: From the Letters of Professor W. B. Scott," *Cornhill Magazine* 149 (1934): 686-87.

70. Scott, *Some Memories*, 97-100; Leonard Huxley, "An American Student," p. 692.

unprepared for the higher kinds of work in one's own field." One of Gegenbaur's assistants, a Dr. Calberla, had recently died after four years of collecting observations on the lamprey eel, "a creature which is far more primitive and lower in the scale than any fish," and hence of great evolutionary interest. Calberla's unfortunate death provided Scott with a tremendous opportunity: a hot topic and a few years' head start on his research.[71] McCosh, with Professor Sloane and Princeton benefactor Libbey, told Scott it was "imperative" that he take a degree. He applied himself to his studies with characteristic fervor and discipline, earning a Ph.D. in 1880.[72]

His dazzling European tour completed and top-notch doctorate in hand, Scott returned to Princeton in the fall of 1880 and began teaching that winter. McCosh had been assuring him of a post for some time, and when the way was clear he wrote with evident satisfaction, "I think you have a fine opening under God at Princeton."[73] Having garnered the best scientific education the world had to offer, Scott now returned home to teach paleontology "under God." He brought the latest in comparative anatomy, zoology, and paleontology to his alma mater, and he brought great prestige as well. A review in the London *Lancet* of one of Scott's papers had heaped exaggerated praise on the young American, saying he occupied a position in his country much like Huxley's in England. Of course, that was patently false, but as Scott recalls, "When I remonstrated [the reviewer] for printing such preposterous stuff about me, he replied that that was what his New York correspondents were telling him."[74]

Just what did it mean to teach paleontology "under God" at Princeton? Arnold Guyot wrote his young protégé a fatherly letter shortly after

71. Scott, *Some Memories,* pp. 107-8, 126. Gegenbaur was a friend of Ernst Haeckel, one of Hodge's prime targets in *What Is Darwinism?* In keeping with his grandfather's sentiments, Scott felt Haeckel "should have been a poet and not a man of science, for he lacked a regard for the truth," and had "a charlatan streak" (p. 109).

72. Scott, *Some Memories,* pp. 113, 122. That year Scott published some of his Heidelberg work in the *Morphologisches Jahrbuch* and the *Zoologischer Anzeiger* (p. 125).

73. McCosh to Scott, 14 May 1880, McCosh MSS. Earlier McCosh had written, "You are aware that the Trustees and all your friends here are resolute in keeping the College a religious one. You have passed through varied scenes since you left us in London, in Cambridge and now in Germany. If a man has the root in him he will only be strengthened in the faith by such an experience. It will be profitable to me to find how you have stood all this" (McCosh to Scott, 15 December 1879, McCosh MSS).

74. Scott, *Some Memories,* p. 135.

McCosh's, spelling out his concerns and expectations. Guyot explained that it was he himself who had "long urged on Dr. McCosh the propriety of giving you a chance to try your fitness . . . in teaching Geology." While it was the president's place to set the conditions of the post, Guyot wrote to add his own admonitions. "In my turn I would say that in accepting you, my dear young friend, as my substitute, I take for granted" two enumerated points. First, "That nothing in your studies of Nature has been able to disturb your belief in that grand, supernatural work, into which we enter by faith, live by love, and abide in peace in the bosom of our Saviour. Your mind is not shallow enough to allow you, while admiring Nature, to seek in it what God never put in it, & to believe, as too many do, that true Science is possible when we confine our view to the narrow field of this lower domain." On warm religious grounds Guyot urged the distinction between nature and supernature. Science must never forget its limits. Notice that he conceived those limits as inherent in the subject itself, not imposed from outside. Science must not forget the existence of a higher domain beyond its reach — the spiritual and moral. Second, Guyot wrote, "I hope also that you will consider it a first duty, when teaching young beginners in the Science of Nature, to give them essentially only the undoubted, well observed facts, leaving the yet doubtful doctrines out of view. You understand that I hint at the doctrine of evolution in its extreme forms." Here the aged geologist gave a brief manifesto of his own views on evolution near the time of his retirement. It was still too early, he wrote, "to determine its proper place, its sound limitations, and to sift the true from the false. The deeper minds see it & become more & more cautious." But he was quite sure of the metaphysical foundation beneath the question of physical means: "There is a vast difference between a *plan*[,] an *idea,* realized *by means* of matter, or matter *shaping itself &* growing into a well connected, intelligible system of living forms." This difference he urged Scott to make clear. He left the ascertaining of facts — including the question whether species descended from other species — to Scott's responsibility, asking him to avoid not evolution in general but "its extreme forms," those in which matter did the work of mind.[75]

The Princeton set were delighted with their young scientist — they

75. Guyot to Scott, 11 February 1880, Hodge Family MSS, emphasis in original. Here Guyot specified nothing new for Princeton. For a good ten years, in print, at the college, and even at the seminary (those extracurricular lectures), McCosh had taught the factuality of evolution by divine design. Scott did, however, go a step beyond Guyot in affirming speciation by descent in addition to the older developmentalism.

even sent him back to Heidelberg for another summer in 1881.[76] His lectures at Princeton plainly taught the evolution of animal species, but concluded that the whole of natural history evidenced God's design. He wrote in his manuscript notes for 1882,

> We have now followed the globe in its history fr earliest times till introduction of our own race. Have seen how fiery mass cooled & assumed shape; how in earliest interactions [?] a certain plan was sketched out; how yt plan was gradually elaborated through long series of ages. Have seen yt history is one grand connected whole w. no breaks & no abrupt transitions & yt all yse mighty changes have been brought about by slow & ceaseless operation of causes wh. are still at work. . . . In all ys we have seen yt whole has been under steady domain of law, yt it has been unfolding a grand & uniform design, wh. has been carried out in an infinite diversity of ways, fitting the earth for the habitation of Man, in whose appearance & destiny we find the final step; the culmination of geological history.[77]

Scott taught a non-Darwinian form of evolution, an evolution that explicitly left room for religion. With Cope and Osborn he espoused a variety of neo-Lamarckism, which later lost out to the neo-Darwinism of Marsh and his followers. Neo-Lamarckism enjoyed a vogue in America during the 1880s and 1890s, in large part because its doctrine of the inheritance of acquired characters suggested purposive development rather than development by blind chance. When the new science of genetics dashed that view, Scott "remained anti-Darwinian and retreated from his cautious neo-Lamarckism without finding anything to replace it, so that evolution for him became simply inexplicable."[78] In his lifelong

76. Scott, *Some Memories,* 138-39. The purpose of the trip was to finish up his work on the lamprey eel — his dissertation had by no means exhausted the material. On the way he paid a visit to Huxley in London, spending a Sunday evening at his house at his invitation.

77. Scott, MS "Lectures on Geology to the Junior Class, 1882-3," Scott MSS, 2:47-48. It is interesting to compare Scott's concluding statements with Guyot's *The Earth and Man,* written some thirty-five years earlier. Many of the themes remain the same. In Scott's abbreviation system, "yt" = "that," "yse" = "these," etc.

78. Edward J. Pfeifer, "The Genesis of American Neo-Lamarckism," in *Science in America since 1820,* ed. Nathan Reingold (New York: Science History Publications, 1976), pp. 221-32; S. S. Simpson, "Biographical Memoir of William Berryman Scott, 1858-1947," in *National Academy of Sciences of the United States of America, Biographical Memoirs* 25 (1948): 190. Numbers contests the idea "that American scientists who accepted evolution divided into

anti-Darwinianism Scott continued in the tradition not only of McCosh but also of his grandfather, Charles Hodge.

McCosh brought other Bright Young Men back to Princeton in 1880 — nine in all, most notably Henry Fairfield Osborn and William Libbey Jr.[79] A similar if less dramatic story could be told of some of them, especially Osborn. But Scott's odyssey best illustrates how the College of New Jersey implemented its old plan of seizing and mastering the weapons of attack, taking the best that science had to offer and bringing it back "under God" at Princeton. On a plan of laying sound philosophical foundations, training up young men in piety and scholarship, and sending them out into the emerging professions — bringing the best men back to their alma mater to reproduce after their kind — Princeton placed its bid to mold the age.[80]

---

opposing camps of neo-Lamarckians and neo-Darwinians." Virtually no American scientist belonged to the latter category before the twentieth century, while in the meantime a host of other theories attracted adherents. Ronald L. Numbers, *Darwinism Comes to America* (Cambridge: Harvard University Press, 1998), pp. 23, 33-40.

79. The nine were: Theodore W. Hunt, William Milligan Sloane, William Libbey, Samuel R. Winans, Henry F. Osborn, Allan Marquand, Henry B. Fine, William F. Magie, and Scott. From Scott's obituary in the *Princeton Alumni Weekly,* 11 April 1947.

80. "The danger is not in speculation, but in a bad bias; and we ought to encourage the right kind of men to unfettered investigation of branches of science, which are pushing their way into philosophy and faith, as well as affecting our secular interests." George Macloskie, "Scientific Speculation," *Presbyterian Review* 8 (1887): 618.

The original building of Princeton Seminary, Alexander Hall, in the early 1880s.
Miller Chapel is on the left (*Encyclopaedia of the Presbyterian Church in the United
States of America: Including the Northern and Southern Assemblies,* ed. Alfred Nevin
[Philadelphia: Presbyterian Encyclopaedia Publishing, 1884])

Albert B. Dod, Princeton College Professor of Mathematics and a close friend of Charles Hodge, penned Princeton's spirited response to *Vestiges of the Natural History of Creation.* **Portrait by Edward Ludlow Mooney, ca. 1840** (Princeton University Archives, Department of Rare Books and Special Collections, Princeton University Library)

Arnold Guyot, Professor of Geology and Physical Geography at Princeton College. This portrait by Daniel Huntington, ca. 1850, recalls Guyot's roots in German Romanticism. (Princeton University Archives, Department of Rare Books and Special Collections, Princeton University Library)

Charles Hodge, Professor of Didactic and Polemical Theology at Princeton Seminary, in midcareer, ca. 1850 (Author's private collection)

Lyman Hotchkiss Atwater, Professor of Mental and Moral Science at Princeton College, was Charles Hodge's right-hand man in the editing of the *Biblical Repertory and Princeton Review*. This portrait was taken in December 1860. (Princeton University Archives, Department of Rare Books and Special Collections, Princeton University Library)

Princeton Seminary Faculty, 1871. Left to right: James Clement Moffat (Church History), Alexander Taggart McGill (Pastoral Theology), Caspar Wistar Hodge Sr. (New Testament), Charles Augustus Aiken (Apologetics), Charles Hodge (Systematic Theology), William Henry Green (Old Testament) (Special Collections, Princeton Theological Seminary Library)

James McCosh, pious and energetic President of the College of New Jersey, 1868-88
(Charles A. Salmond, *Princetoniana: Charles and A. A. Hodge, With Class and Table
Talk of Hodge the Younger [New York: Scribner & Welford, 1888])

A composite picture featuring the new buildings added to Princeton College under the McCosh administration. (*Encyclopaedia of the Presbyterian Church in the United States of America: Including the Northern and Southern Assemblies*, ed. **Alfred Nevin** [Philadelphia: Presbyterian Encyclopaedia Publishing, 1884])

Benjamin Breckinridge Warfield looking ready for battle at age thirty-six. Taken in his first year as Professor of Didactic and Polemical Theology at Princeton Seminary, 1888 (Special Collections, Princeton Theological Seminary Library)

The E. M. Museum of Science in 1886, housed in Nassau Hall. Princeton's *Hadrosaurus*, the tall skeleton in the front, was one of the first mounted dinosaur skeletons in the United States. The college's Scientific Expeditions greatly increased the collection over the years, thanks especially to the direction of **Prof. Scott** (Princeton University Archives, Department of Rare Books and Special Collections, Princeton University Library)

The Princeton Scientific Expedition of 1882, with young Professor William Berryman Scott (wearing pince-nez) seated in the middle (Princeton University Archives, Department of Rare Books and Special Collections, Princeton University Library)

Archibald Alexander Hodge, jovial and incisive successor to his father in the chair of Didactic and Polemical Theology at Princeton Seminary (Charles A. Salmond, *Princetoniana: Charles and A. A. Hodge, With Class and Table Talk of Hodge the Younger* [New York: Scribner & Welford, 1888])

Francis Landey Patton at about the time of his appointment as Princeton Seminary's first Stuart Professor of the Relations of Philosophy and Science to the Christian Religion, 1881. He went on to serve as President of Princeton University (1888-1902) and of Princeton Seminary (1902-12) (Princeton University Archives, Department of Rare Books and Special Collections, Princeton University Library)

John Maclean, President of the College of New Jersey, 1854-68. This portrait was taken ca. 1865, near the time of his run-in with Prof. Shields (Princeton University Archives, Department of Rare Books and Special Collections, Princeton University Library)

Charles Woodruff Shields, Princeton College's adamantine Professor of the Harmony of Science and Religion, photographed ca. 1875 (Princeton University Archives, Department of Rare Books and Special Collections, Princeton University Library)

Princeton Seminary Faculty, 1896. Nicknames given on the back by an alumnus: Standing, left to right: Shorty [George T.] Purves, Jack [John D.] Davis, [Geerhardus] Vos, Benny [B. B.] Warfield, Brenty [William Brenton] Greene [Jr.], [Joseph Heatly] Dulles (Librarian), [Henry Wilson] Smith. Front row, left to right: Francis Landey Patton, Billy [William Miller] Paxton, [Chalmers] Martin, Rabbi [William Henry] Green (Pres.), Johnny [John] DeWitt. Only Patton escaped without a nickname or sur-name-only appellation (Special Collections, Princeton Theological Seminary Library)

Caspar Wistar Hodge Jr., grandson of Charles Hodge and Warfield's successor in the chair of Didactic and Polemical Theology, photographed when a young assistant professor, 1906 (Special Collections, Princeton Theological Seminary Library)

A young J. Gresham Machen, ca. 1910s. H. L. Mencken nicknamed him "Dr. Fundamentalis" for his erudite defense of historic Christianity (Special Collections, Princeton Theological Seminary Library)

Henry Fairfield Osborn with the counsel for the defense in the Scopes Trial, 1925

(Image #311029, American Museum of Natural History Library)

Edwin Grant Conklin, Princeton University Professor of Biology, photographed in the 1920s. Conklin and Osborn championed liberal Christianity as the religion of science (Princeton University Archives, Department of Rare Books and Special Collections, Princeton University Library)

CHAPTER SIX

Theism and Evolution

True philosophy has God as its postulate; true science reaches God as its conclusion.

Francis Landey Patton, 1888[1]

Princeton and the Woodrow Affair

Eighteen eighty-one was a banner year for the evolution question at Princeton. In January the first cohort of McCosh's Bright Young Men began teaching evolutionary anatomy, embryology, and paleontology at the college. In April, A. A. Hodge and B. B. Warfield published their famous article, "Inspiration," in the *Presbyterian Review,* contending against Charles Briggs for the inerrancy of the original manuscripts of the Bible, including any incidental affirmations of scientific and historical fact.[2] And in the fall term Francis Landey Patton entered upon his duties as the Stuart Professor of the Relations of Science and Philosophy to the Christian Religion, a new chair endowed specifically as a platform for theistic argument.

With these three events Princeton committed itself simultaneously

---

1. Francis Landey Patton, inaugural address, in "The Inauguration of President Patton" (New York: Gray Bros., 1888), p. 42, pamphlet, PTS Special Collections.

2. Archibald Alexander Hodge and Benjamin Breckinridge Warfield, "Inspiration," *Presbyterian Review* 2 (1881): 225-60.

to evolutionary science, an inerrant Bible, and a highly reasoned theism. In our century, when fundamentalism, liberalism, and neoorthodoxy have each decisively severed this three-stranded cord, the Princetonian combination appears surprising, even self-contradictory. Fundamentalists reject evolution; liberals reject biblical inerrancy; the neoorthodox reject both biblical inerrancy and natural theology. But to Princeton College and Seminary in the 1880s the combination made eminent sense; for them each strand, when properly understood, actually supported the others. Princeton had "made its peace" with evolution; if they were not sure whether species came by descent, the Princetonians were at least sure that the origin of species did not undo their religion. In their hands evolution even strengthened theistic reasoning.

Princeton was the oldest, the largest, and the most influential seminary in the Northern Presbyterian Church (PCUSA). It was also the most conservative. If Princeton could make peace with evolution "properly limited and explained," traditionalists could rest assured their Bible and their creed need not suffer on evolution's account. "At length all over America a happy *modus vivendi* has been reached," George Macloskie wrote around 1890, crediting McCosh's Princeton with calming not just the church but the nation. "Whilst the intelligent public are not sure whether Evolution is sound or erroneous, they are convinced that it is not dangerous to Christianity."[3] Macloskie and the Bright Young Men at the college, zealous for the memory of their great mentor, ascribed this victory to McCosh alone. Historian James R. Moore gives the seminary a share in the glory: when Charles Hodge's son and successor, Archibald Alexander Hodge, wrote an introduction for Joseph Van Dyke's *Theism and Evolution* in 1886, it marked, according to Moore, "a turning point for the acceptance of evolution among American Protestants." Hodge assured his readers that evolution "when strictly confined to the legitimate limits of pure science . . . is not antagonistic to our faith as either theists or christians."[4] Sitting in the venerable chair of Didactic and Polemic

3. George Macloskie, in William Milligan Sloane, *The Life of James McCosh* (New York: Charles Scribner's Sons, 1896), p. 124.
4. James R. Moore, *The Post-Darwinian Controversies: A Study of the Protestant Struggle to Come to Terms with Darwin in Great Britain and America, 1870-1900* (Cambridge: Cambridge University Press, 1979), pp. 242, 245; A. A. Hodge, introduction to *Theism and Evolution: An Examination of Modern Speculative Theories as Related to Theistic Conceptions of the Universe,* by Joseph S. Van Dyke (New York: A. C. Armstrong and Son, 1886), pp. xv-xxii. Hodge's essay was less of a sanction of theistic evolution than a statement of its al-

Theology at Princeton Seminary, Hodge wielded considerable authority; even this very tentative and circumscribed allowance of evolution functioned as a virtual "imprimatur" on a book on theistic evolution.[5]

Moore's date for this so-called imprimatur is actually about eight years too late. In the second edition of his celebrated *Outlines of Theology* (1878), a handy question-and-answer compendium of his father's theological system, Hodge had gone on record to allow what amounted to McCosh's view of evolution: transmutation by natural law under God, reserving direct divine intervention for the origination of matter and the appearance of life (plants), consciousness (animals), and spirit (humankind).[6] This was, of course, only a mildly evolutionized version of the progressionism Guyot had taught at Princeton College and Seminary for over two decades. Still, Hodge did not endorse this view; he merely allowed it. Theologically, Princeton's peace with transmutationism was highly tentative.

The date of Hodge's "imprimatur" is important because of subse-

---

lowable limits. He flatly refused to render judgment on transmutation, for he considered evolutionary science to be still "in its hypothetical stage." Any attempted reconciliations would be premature and crude. Hodge took as his task to establish "certain boundary lines which the scientific doctrine of evolution must not pass; and the passing of which can alone be regarded as casus belli by the christian church." These included: the recognition that the agencies and laws of evolution could not be accounted for by the process of evolution; respect for the proper place of philosophy, especially "the universal causal judgment," in interpreting the meaning of evolution; the fundamental duality of mind and matter, entailing a radically unique place for humankind in the web of life; allowance for God's activity in natural and human history, including "redemptive providence" — miracles, the incarnation, and "the gracious operations of the Holy Ghost."

5. Moore, *The Post-Darwinian Controversies*, p. 242. He borrows the term "imprimatur" from Deryl Freeman Johnson, who dates it to Hodge's 1880 review of Asa Gray (Johnson, "The Attitudes of the Princeton Theologians toward Darwinism and Evolution from 1859-1929" [Ph.D. diss., University of Iowa, 1968], p. 149).

6. Archibald Alexander Hodge, *Outlines of Theology,* 2nd ed., "re-written and enlarged" (New York: Robert Carter and Bros., 1878), pp. 245-46, 298; cf. a selection from Hodge's "table talk" in C. A. Salmond, *Princetoniana: Charles and A. A. Hodge, with Class and Table Talk of Hodge the Younger* (New York: Scribner and Welford, 1888), pp. 139-40. Salmond recorded the table talk while a student at PTS, 1877-78. In the *Outlines* (1878) Hodge defined evolution against "mediate creation" in a way B. B. Warfield later followed (pp. 238-39; cf. chapter 8 below). In a review of Asa Gray in 1880 Hodge stated, "we have no sympathy with those who maintain that scientific theories of evolution are necessarily atheistic" (quoted in Johnson, "Attitudes," p. 147). Johnson traces changes in Hodge's terminology from 1878 to 1886 (pp. 147-52), changes that in my view only muddy the waters. The development Johnson traces is mainly a matter of words rather than meanings.

quent events in Princeton's sister denomination, the Southern Presbyterian Church (PCUS). There the evolution question was not nearly as peaceful a matter as in the North. A painful and protracted controversy over the evolutionary views of a seminary professor wracked the Southern denomination in the 1880s. The difficulty concerned James Woodrow, since 1861 the Perkins Professor of Natural Science in Connection with Revelation at Columbia Theological Seminary, South Carolina (and, incidentally, an uncle of Woodrow Wilson). The Woodrow affair represented the first instance of outright church controversy over the evolution question in the Presbyterian church, and called forth from Princeton some revealing statements about evolutionism in general and human evolution in particular.

Financial hard times had closed Columbia Theological Seminary around 1880. An announcement of the seminary's reopening in 1882 rejoiced in the better fortunes of a school "manned by those who are too honest to secretly impugn the verbal inspiration of any part of the original Scriptures, or to covertly teach evolution and other insidious errors that undermine the foundation of our precious faith."[7] This statement prompted the scrupulous Woodrow to apprise the board of directors that he believed evolution might be true. The following year the board asked Woodrow to make a full statement of the views he taught concerning the evolution of lower animals and man, to be published in the *Southern Presbyterian Review*. Woodrow delivered his opinions in person in an annual Alumni Address in May 1884, which he titled simply "Evolution." While preparing for the address, he said, he had come to the conviction that Adam's body probably evolved from brute ancestors. He maintained the complete authority of the Scriptures, even using the word "inerrancy," but asserted that the Bible was indifferent as to the evolution of animals and of Adam's body (but not Eve's).[8]

The board allowed Woodrow his views — but when they appeared in the *Southern Presbyterian Review* in the summer of 1884, they inflamed the Synod of South Carolina and soon the entire denomination for three arduous years. Before it was over Woodrow was asked to resign, was dismissed, was reinstated, was dismissed again, and was tried for heresy

7. J. B. Mack, quoted in Robert K. Gustafson, *James Woodrow (1828-1907): Scientist, Theologian, Intellectual Leader* (Lewiston, N.Y.: Edwin Mellen Press, 1995), p. 134.

8. William Childs Robinson, *Columbia Theological Seminary and the Southern Presbyterian Church, 1831-1931* (Decatur, Ga.: Dennis Lindsey Printing Co., 1931), pp. 173-76.

but not defrocked. The seminary closed temporarily for a second time, and the church found itself wrestling with not just the multifaceted doctrine of evolution, but a whole tangle of political questions concerning denominational control of seminaries and ecclesiastical prerogatives over academic freedom.[9] When we remember that the Woodrow affair beset the Southern Church at the very time that the first of McCosh's Bright Young Men were returning from Huxley's laboratory to teach the latest developmental biology "under God" at Princeton, it comes as no surprise that Princeton in later years prided itself on having "averted a disastrous war between science and religion."[10]

The Woodrow affair brought Hodge's published allowance of evolutionism, limited and tentative though it was, back to haunt him. When the Synod of South Carolina officially disapproved the teaching of evolution in 1884, the Northern Church looked on with considerable alarm. The Old School faction, which the Civil War had severed from its large Southern constituency, still felt close theologically to its Southern brethren. The majority of Old School newspapers called for Woodrow's resignation, believing human evolution subversive of the old "federal" theology. The Princetonians, whose whole effort in matters of science and religion had aimed at maintaining the union between those "twin daughters of heaven," found themselves in a delicate position between their Old School constituency and a fellow professor's plight.

Princeton's discomfort soon increased. Woodrow suggested in his own defense that the views for which he was suffering persecution were shared by such orthodox Northern Old Schoolers as Samuel H. Kellogg of Western Theological Seminary (Allegheny, Pa.) and A. A. Hodge of Princeton. He had in his possession a private letter from Kellogg bearing witness to that claim. Soon the letter was printed in the *Presbyterian Banner* of Pittsburgh.[11]

---

9. Robinson, *Columbia Theological Seminary*, pp. 168-93; T. Watson Street, "The Evolution Controversy in the Southern Presbyterian Church with Attention to the Theological and Ecclesiastical Issues Raised," *Journal of the Presbyterian Historical Society* 37 (1959): 232-50; W. S. Plumer Bryan, review of *My Life and Times, 1810-1899*, by John B. Adger, *Presbyterian and Reformed Review* 11 (1900): 181-85. Adger, a colleague and supporter of Woodrow at Columbia, devoted a 250-page chapter in his autobiography to the Woodrow affair. See also Gustafson, *James Woodrow (1828-1907)*, and Fred Kingsley Elder, *Woodrow: Apostle of Freedom* (Two Harbors, Minn.: Bunchberry Press, 1996).

10. George Macloskie, quoted in Sloane, *Life of James McCosh*, p. 124.

11. *Presbyterian Banner*, 19 November 1884.

Kellogg was Hodge's successor at Allegheny — Hodge having left in 1877 to take his father's place at Princeton — and a colleague there of young B. B. Warfield. In a private letter to Warfield, Hodge explained that Kellogg had tried unsuccessfully to persuade him to come out on Woodrow's side. Hodge did "not want to be mixed up in any way" with the controversy — "but unhappily for me," he complained, Kellogg's letter to Woodrow, now published, implicated him in the affair further than he believed the facts warranted. The letter claimed that Kellogg and Woodrow "agreed *entirely* with A. A. Hodge." Hodge now felt it necessary to define his views on evolution more precisely, stating not just what he *allowed* but what he *believed*.[12]

Hodge's letter to Warfield reveals how far he was from endorsing evolutionism on its possible theistic merits. Should the need arise — for Warfield was teaching at Allegheny and might be called upon to discuss his friend's views — Hodge wished "to be allowed distinctly to say" what he thought of evolution. And distinctly he did say it, far more distinctly than in any published work. He began, "I think modern science is preposterously far off from proving anything as to the evolution of the lower species, . . . and far more emphatically so as to the evolution of the human species." Speciation by descent was a theory still on its probation; theology had no call to accommodate it yet. This statement placed the younger Hodge squarely with his father. But he went on to consider whether human evolution, even as a theory, was theologically acceptable. Hodge reasoned that the theory would require a series of female as well as male ancestors — and since Genesis gave a detailed account of the creation of Eve from Adam's side, a Christian interpretation of the evolution of Adam's body would require "a series of almost human beings being arrested by the giving of Adam a soul & the killing off of his natural female & the production of his non-natural wife by miracle" — a pretty incredible scenario. The conclusion: "All, without exception, who admit all that Woodrow & Kellogg say they are

12. Hodge to Warfield, 19 November 1884, Warfield MSS, PTS Special Collections. Woodrow himself had passed from mere allowance to belief in the *likelihood* (not yet considering it *proven*) that Adam's body came by descent from lower forms (Robinson, *Columbia Theological Seminary*, p. 174). Hodge did get involved publicly, writing for the *Southern Presbyterian* (Columbia, S.C.) on the evolution question alongside Patton and Dawson. See Ronald L. Numbers, *Darwinism Comes to America* (Cambridge: Harvard University Press, 1998), p. 65.

ready to admit, must get ready to give up the account of the Genesis of Eve."[13]

This brief letter sheds new light on Hodge's position. In public he pronounced evolution compatible with theism, under certain conditions; but in private he believed evolution to be far from established scientifically, and the evolution of humankind frankly incompatible with Scripture. Hodge kept quiet his own conjectures on human evolution and the Bible because in the 1880s human evolution was a mere extension of evolutionary theory, attested mostly by analogy, not by any hard data to speak of. Eugene Dubois's discovery of Java man *(Pithecanthropus erectus)*, the first alleged "missing link" between man and apelike ancestors, was still seven years off.[14] Hodge expected no such discovery and saw no point in provoking a damaging battle between science and religion where no actual antagonism existed. For that reason he refused to be dragged into the Woodrow affair.

But Princeton did not ignore Woodrow's plight. Two months after Kellogg's attempt to draw Hodge into the controversy, Hodge's junior colleague Francis Landey Patton contributed a brief but momentous article entitled "Evolution and Apologetics" to the *Presbyterian Review*. Its close parallel to Hodge's private letter suggests that the two men conferred on the matter. Patton occupied at Princeton a chair much like Woodrow's own, a chair concerned with the relations of science and religion. Hodge, then coeditor of the *Review*, seems to have deferred to his colleague's specialization in such questions. In the space of six pages Patton issued a terse manifesto of the Princeton position on the evolu-

13. Hodge to Warfield, 19 November 1884. This letter conclusively answers Johnson's uncertainty as to Hodge's view on the evolution of Adam's body (Johnson, "Attitudes," pp. 170-71). In identifying the origin of Eve as the main barrier in the Genesis narrative to an evolutionary reading, Hodge appears to have been influenced by the Stone Lectures given at Princeton by Dartmouth's president Samuel C. Bartlett in March 1882. Bartlett, *Sources of History in the Pentateuch* (New York: Anson D. F. Randolph and Co., 1883), pp. 36, 62. Woodrow himself held that Eve was created by a miracle — agreeing with Hodge that the scriptural text required it. Warfield, MS Notes on Anthropology, Warfield MSS; Robinson, *Columbia Theological Seminary*, p. 177; Numbers, *Darwinism Comes to America*, p. 62.

14. Neanderthal man was discovered in 1856, but, being understood to be a member of the human species, was not considered a missing link evidencing human evolution. Thomas Henry Huxley and Charles Lyell famously argued for human evolution in the 1860s, but without claiming any fossil evidence. Jon H. Roberts, "Religious Reactions to Darwin," in *The Cambridge Companion to Science and Religion*, ed. Peter Harrison (New York: Cambridge University Press, 2010), p. 84.

tion question both in theory and in practice, alluding unmistakably to Woodrow's case.[15]

The Bible taught no doctrine of the origin of species in general, Patton averred. The question was a purely scientific one, as far as efficient causation, that is, the mode of origination, was concerned.[16] However, Scripture did give a particular doctrine of the origin of man by special creation: here Patton repeated Hodge's arguments from the account of Eve's creation, the solidarity of the race in Adam's fall, and Paul's description of Christ as the second Adam (Rom. 5). With Hodge, Patton professed an inability to reconcile the Bible to human evolution, even an evolution of Adam's body alone. With Hodge, too, he felt no particular call to bother trying, in view of the dearth of hard evidence.[17]

As to evolution and theism, Patton stated flatly, "A more egregious blunder is hardly conceivable than that of assuming that Evolution and Atheism are synonymous." At first glance this looked like a frank repudiation of Charles Hodge's verdict in *What Is Darwinism?* but Patton was employing what was for him a characteristic rhetorical strategy, making a bold and pithy remark certain to win the approval of his more liberal hearers or readers, then qualifying it in such a way as to persuade them

15. Jon H. Roberts, in his usually very good *Darwinism and the Divine in America: Protestant Intellectuals and Organic Evolution, 1859-1900* (Madison: University of Wisconsin Press, 1988), unfortunately gets Patton's position on evolutionism quite wrong. He treats Patton as a "Biblicist" in the chapter on staunch antievolutionists, "Get Thee Hence, Satan" (treating Patton on pp. 220-21), on the strength of Patton's statement that nonscientists have a right to evaluate scientific opinions. Roberts says such biblicists reserved the right to judge science in order to assert special creation in the face of a growing scientific consensus to the contrary. Surely this misrepresents Patton, as seen below. Again, Roberts numbers Patton among those who believed the Bible was "the source of all valid theological ideas" (p. 221) — an especially unfortunate misconstrual of this Princetonian champion of natural theology. It is one thing to say Scripture is the sole theological *standard* (which Patton, a good Protestant, would gladly aver), and quite another to say it is the sole *source*.

16. This was exactly Woodrow's long-expressed and well-known contention. See Woodrow's inaugural address (1861), digested in Robinson's *Columbia Theological Seminary and the Southern Presbyterian Church, 1831-1931* and printed in full in *Dr. James Woodrow as Seen by His Friends; Character Sketches by His Former Pupils, Colleagues, and Associates*, ed. Marion Woodville Woodrow (Columbia, S.C.: R. L. Bryan Co., 1909).

17. Francis Landey Patton, "Evolution and Apologetics," *Presbyterian Review* 6 (1885): 141, 144. On the solidarity of the race in Adam and its soteriological significance, see Patton, "The Two Adams," Doctrinal Series, #10 (Chicago: T. T. Jones, 1879), a sermon pamphlet in PTS Special Collections.

of his more conservative position. So here: Patton went on to introduce Hodge's all-important distinction between evolutionism in general and Darwinism in particular, affirming with him that Darwin's theory "was really a theory of chance" that would destroy the teleological argument if goallessness were proved true. When the old theologian called Darwinism atheism in this sense, he "was right." But Patton, unlike the elder Hodge, had at his disposal new and constructive theories of evolution that did not carry with them "the Epicurean doctrine" of randomness. McCosh's young scientists Scott and Osborn were fast becoming leaders of an "American School" of evolutionists, offering neo-Lamarckian and orthogenetic views of what their camp liked to call "the *origin* of the fittest." In their theories the tendency to vary was not indefinite and directionless, but lawful, following a plan.[18] Thus, Patton argued, "there is a teleology immanent in the very nature of the organisms, providing for the existing order of biological development." Far from being synonymous with atheism, evolution was theism's friend; "instead of being antagonistic to the theistic proof which builds upon design, the idea of design is woven into the very web of nature."[19] Patton drew McCosh, Hodge, and the young Princetonian teleo-evolutionists together in one cozy circle.

But theism was one thing; the Christian doctrines of creation and providence were another. Was evolution, whatever its brand, inherently hostile to them? Some said so, Patton observed, but they were mistaken. As to creation, "the gradual genesis of the existing cosmos" was an account of form, not of substance — in McCosh's (Aristotelian) terms, it was a matter of material and efficient cause, not formal and final cause. As to providence, many and varied were the views excellent Christian thinkers had entertained of that doctrine in the course of history. Jonathan Edwards, for example, construed providence as continued creation; each instant in the phenomenal world constituted an immediate exercise of divine power. Edwards's view was well suited to modern evolutionism, Patton claimed. He would quite reasonably and defensibly have been inclined to regard evolution as "simply a word that expresses the uniform mode of God's manifestation." Yet no one would question

18. Peter J. Bowler, *The Eclipse of Darwinism: Anti-Darwinian Evolution Theories in the Decades around 1900* (Baltimore: Johns Hopkins University Press, 1983), chapter 6; cf. my chapter 7 below.

19. Patton, "Evolution and Apologetics," pp. 140-41.

Edwards's Christianity on account of his "reverent habit of contemplat-
ing the world" and the world's flux.[20]

It was not the doctrine of speciation by descent, but the "metaphysical complement" certain evolutionists attached to their theory, that
made them antitheists, Patton wrote. "Some will say, of course, that matter is eternal, and add that there is no Creator; but that is because they
are materialists, not because they are evolutionists." Let Christians be
discerning. Some scientific particulars of evolution carried religious or
irreligious import, especially the mode of variation. But more often the
real culprit was a precommitment to an antitheistic metaphysic. With
obvious reference to Woodrow's misfortune, Patton pleaded,

> Some of the most conspicuous defenders of evolution hold a material-
> istic or pantheistic metaphysic, and those who know the hypothesis of
> evolution only as it is expounded by these anti-theistic thinkers are
> very apt to suppose that a theory of evolution that is at once theistic
> and Christian is impossible. For the sake of truth, as well as for the
> sake of those who may be brought under unjust suspicion because of
> their known sympathy with some phases of the evolution hypothesis,
> this mistake ought to be corrected.[21]

Patton did not endorse theistic evolution as proven, nor yet likely,
but he did urge toleration of certain forms of the theory. Echoing
McCosh, he said that "wise dealing in this question" would involve consideration not only of how to defend Christianity's philosophical foundations, but also of how to avoid pushing evolutionists away from the faith.
Meanwhile the Princeton apologist was sure that right reason was on the
side of religion. "Evolutionists can be consistently hostile to Christianity
only by being Atheistic," he proclaimed — "and they can be Atheistic only
by being illogical."[22]

It was Patton, not A. A. Hodge, who gave Princeton Seminary's public answer to the Woodrow affair — Patton, the voice of philosophical
foundations, not Hodge, the voice of systematic theological conclusions.
The seminary went on record answering the evolution question from the

20. Patton, "Evolution and Apologetics," p. 141. For a discussion of the Princeton theology's relation to Edwards, see Bruce Kuklick, *Churchmen and Philosophers: From Jonathan Edwards to John Dewey* (New Haven: Yale University Press, 1985), chapter 5.
21. Patton, "Evolution and Apologetics," p. 144.
22. Patton, "Evolution and Apologetics," p. 144.

viewpoint of apologetics, not systematics — from the beginnings, not the conclusions, of theological inquiry. Systematic theology, the queen of the sciences, drawing upon their duly ascertained data and relating them to God and to the drama of redemption in Christ, had no call to answer the evolution question. Just as McCosh said, the derivation of species was a question for natural science to settle. But where the evolution question carried a "metaphysical complement," there theology had an interest from the first, under the rubric of apologetics. It was the business of apologetics to establish the groundwork of theology, to consider the questions of being and knowing in religious perspective. Evolution's "metaphysical complement" had everything to do with that task.[23]

Thus, while the case for evolution and *scriptural theology* was pending, the case for evolution and *theism* was not. Darwin's blow to the evidence of divine design, widely regarded nowadays as the coup de grâce to natural theology,[24] actually provoked an explosion of theistic literature — so much so that we might call the period from the 1880s to 1910 the "heyday of theism." With the fragmentation of the evolutionist front into rival theories during the "eclipse of Darwinism," public attention

23. The classic Princetonian statement of the foundational place of apologetics in theological encyclopedia (the classification of theological knowledge) is Benjamin Breckinridge Warfield, "The Idea of Systematic Theology" (1896), in his *Studies in Theology,* in *The Works of Benjamin B. Warfield,* ed. Ethelbert D. Warfield et al., vol. 9 (New York: Oxford University Press, 1932; Grand Rapids: Baker, 1991), pp. 49-87. I discuss this in chapter 7 below.

24. Cynthia Eagle Russett, *Darwin in America: The Intellectual Response, 1865-1912* (San Francisco: W. H. Freeman, 1976), pp. 35-36, is characteristic, crediting Hume with the fatal blow to theistic proofs, and Darwin with the finishing empirical touch. Gillispie made quite a point of this, seeing pre-Darwinian geological controversies as evidencing a contest *within* the empirical-doxological tradition, between the impulse to glorify God through the discovery of natural law and the need to retain some immediate providential divine activity in the material world. "From the standpoint of the providentialist interpretation of nature, *On the Origin of Species* was a *coup de grâce* rather than an entering wedge." Charles Coulston Gillispie, *Genesis and Geology: A Study in the Relations of Scientific Thought, Natural Theology, and Social Opinions in Great Britain, 1790-1850* (New York: Harper Torchbooks, 1959; orig. 1951), p. 220. William Hallock Johnson described Darwin's blow as the widely recognized coup de grâce as early as 1908 in "Pragmatism, Humanism and Religion," *Princeton Theological Review* 6 (1908): 546. The idea traces back to Thomas Henry Huxley, who in 1864 wrote that when he first read the *Origin* he was forcibly struck with "the conviction that teleology, as commonly understood, had received its deathblow at Mr. Darwin's hands." Huxley, "Criticisms on 'The Origin of Species,'" in his *Lay Sermons, Addresses, and Reviews* (New York: D. Appleton and Co., 1870), p. 330.

shifted from specific evolution theories to their philosophical entailments and to the philosophical evolutionisms that had been obscured by
all the attention to biology and geology. Religious academics, too, turned
their eyes to the profound questions they had said all along were the real
issue in evolutionism — the character and knowability of the God who
created and governed his world, perhaps by evolutionary processes.[25]

Among the Princetonians the new theistic concern after Darwin
was only natural: not only had he stirred up the question of theism
again, but they in the meantime had located their battleground in philosophy, not science. Here were the fountains of current thought, the
foundations that set the limits of all that could be built upon them, the
forms of thought that would mold the age. Here was the eye of the
storm. It is no wonder that philosophical theism became a focus of attention among these men who so consciously reconnoitered the field
and so carefully assessed their arsenal and honed their plan of defense.
During the heyday of theism Princeton launched the counteroffensive it
had been calling for since the 1860s. It aimed its guns at the enemy's
capital city, not at his munitions factories — at antitheism, not the evolutionist cohorts at his disposal. In the course of that assault Princeton's
own philosophical foundations grew more explicit than before, subtler
in some places, starker in others. Out of this discussion arose the full-
blown evidentialist apologetic for which the Princeton theology became famous. Its immediate roots lay in the work of Charles Hodge,
Lyman Atwater, and James McCosh; its fullest flower was the work of
B. B. Warfield; but the first to devote full attention to its formulation
was Francis Landey Patton.

---

25. Jon H. Roberts is one of the few historians to take note of the explosion of theistic
literature in the wake of Darwin — see his *Darwinism and the Divine*, pp. 99, 120, 288 n. 8.
Charles D. Cashdollar is another: see his very fine book, *The Transformation of Theology,
1830-1890: Positivism and Protestant Thought in Britain and America* (Princeton: Princeton
University Press, 1989), p. 342. A common commitment to theism, I would argue, connected conservative and liberal Protestants in the latter half of the nineteenth century.
Neoorthodoxy, arising in the twentieth century, repudiated both liberalism and conservatism on this point, as did other movements less interested in orthodoxy at all — and as did
many evangelicals. Few people are left who find theism interesting. For this reason, I expect, and perhaps because of a fondness for Kant, historians commonly assume theistic
reasoning should have been dead after Darwin — or as good as dead, enough so as not to
merit attention.

The Shields Affair

On 27 October 1881 Patton was inaugurated as the first Stuart Professor of the Relations of Philosophy and Science to the Christian Religion. His longtime friend Henry J. Van Dyke[26] delivered the customary "Charge" on behalf of the board of directors. Van Dyke's words at this auspicious occasion were striking indeed. They stand as the high-water mark of what we might call "the Dare": Princeton's open challenge to the world of scholarship on behalf of the truth value of its creed.

Truth was unchanging, Van Dyke proclaimed in standard Princetonian tones — but human knowledge of the truth was progressive, "and such progress must always be through conflict." "We need not tremble at the noise of the battle," he cried. The facts of science "are divine revelations as truly as the Bible." Princeton must not ignore science and philosophy, even when their progress seemed to contradict orthodox doctrine. Modern scholarship was indeed fraught with dangers for religious faith, for modern scholars often made quite a show of contradicting traditional doctrines in the name of science; but in high martial tones Van Dyke proclaimed, "to repudiate science and despise philosophy would be to vilely throw away the sword and shield of the mighty in the interest not of orthodoxy but of superstition." To shun investigation would serve only ignorance and fear; to allow investigation would dispel all fears and confirm God's truth. "The best way to lay a ghost is not to flee from it, nor to use any magical incantations, nor even to pray without works," Van Dyke argued; "the best way is in God's name to go after it into the darkness, to grapple with it, and see what it is made of."[27]

These were familiar themes in familiar forms. But Van Dyke went considerably beyond them when he declared, "Let all ascertained and accepted facts, all demonstrated truth, be cast into the furnace, and if our creed cannot walk in it without the smell of fire on its clothes *let it be*

26. Henry J. Van Dyke (1822-91) was the father of Henry van Dyke (1852-1933), who was professor of belles lettres at Princeton University and a very popular author in the genteel tradition. Van Dyke Sr. held a Brooklyn pastorate near Patton's in the early 1870s. He would later champion the revision of the Westminster Confession, much to the chagrin of the Princeton theologians.

27. Van Dyke, "The Charge," in "Addresses at the Inauguration of the Rev. Francis L. Patton, D.D., LL.D., as Stuart Professor of the Relations of Philosophy and Science to the Christian Religion . . ." (Philadelphia: Sherman and Co., 1881), pp. 6, 14-15, pamphlet, PTS Special Collections.

burned.... [W]e are prepared to adjust our interpretation of Scripture to the demonstrated truth; or if that cannot be done, to give up our confidence in the infallibility of Scripture."[28] Now this was quite a shocking thing to say. Although Princeton's theology stood for the inseparability of faith from doctrine — the union of head and heart in true religion — and although many a polemical article had appeared in Princeton's journals proclaiming confidence in the unity of God's works with his Word, never had anyone gone as far as this. It was one thing to affirm the harmony of science and religion, to sing with the psalmist that the heavens declared the glory of God (Ps. 19), to say with the apostle that all people knew God's eternal power and deity from observing the creation (Rom. 1). It was quite another thing to offer science the judge's seat, daring her to try revelation at her bar. Science became the superior, revelation the inferior, in Van Dyke's imagery. Human knowledge became the standard by which to measure biblical Christianity; what failed to measure up would be discarded. What was this but precisely the position of the deists a century before, the very party against whom Princeton Seminary originally aimed its apologetical guns?[29]

Van Dyke's Dare might suggest that Princetonian apologetics after the Hodges took a radical turn toward rationalism — something not a few historians have argued without benefit of the corroborating evidence of this speech. Rationalism here means that the Princetonians made religion chiefly a matter of knowledge and proof, all in the name of defending it from modern scientific, historical, and philosophical contradiction. In so doing they not only did violence to the distinction between faith and sight, robbing religion of the profundity of mystery and making it over in the image of Enlightenment notions of truth, but they actually set up both Christian and theistic belief for a very bad fall. They publicly put Bible, creed, and the natural knowledge of God to the test of the fiery furnace, and when the academic world smelled smoke on the clothes, unbelief scored a mighty victory. The Princetonians and their fellow travelers, on this telling, unwittingly abetted the enemy by accepting the challenge to do battle on enemy ground.[30]

28. Van Dyke, "The Charge," pp. 15-17, emphasis in original.

29. On the seminary's antideistic impetus at its founding, see chapter 7, note 54, below.

30. James Turner, *Without God, without Creed: The Origins of Unbelief in America* (Baltimore: Johns Hopkins University Press, 1984), is the best instance of this line of argument. See especially p. 193: "It was, after all, theologians and ministers who had welcomed this secular visitor into the house of God. It was they who had most loudly insisted that knowl-

Van Dyke's charge encapsulated one logical extreme of Princeton's battle plan. The whole notion of taking up enemy weaponry assumed the essential neutrality of scientific inquiry — for the enemy was a set of metaphysical precommitments, and science just the tool — and lent itself to rhetorical boasts of objectivity, even falsifiability. Surely it seemed a noble thing to be willing to follow truth wherever it might lead, and a craven thing to have so little faith in the reality of one's religion as to refuse to subject it to scrutiny. But on the other hand, to *subject* one's religion to scrutiny was to elevate some other truth claim or some other method *above* it as its judge. To suggest actual falsifiability was to court treason against the ultimacy and totality of faith commitment. Here was a real dilemma.

The Princetonians were very much alive to this quandary, more so than they are usually given credit for. In fact, they had already wrestled with it for fifteen years, in a very tangible form: a long, cold war between the major Princetonians and a renegade colleague at the college. Charles Woodruff Shields, since 1866 the Professor of the Harmony of Science and Religion, systematically and persistently assumed just the posture of neutral scrutiny that Van Dyke charged Patton to take — and earned for himself the hearty *opposition* of his peers. The Shields affair, by presenting a potent counterexample to the major Princetonian figures, provides important context to Patton's hiring and the development of the Princeton apologetic.[31]

An alumnus of both Princeton institutions, Shields was a classmate of A. A. Hodge at seminary (1847). While pastor of the Second Presbyterian Church of Philadelphia, which Charles Hodge's brother Hugh attended, Shields conceived a scheme for reconciling the apparent conflict between science and religion, published in 1861 under the title *Philosophia Ultima*. The philosophical spirit of impartiality, Shields argued, was the key to bringing all parties in the division of intellectual labor to realize the ultimate unity of truth. He called for a rethinking of science and theology under a "final philosophy" that would unite them

---

edge of God's existence and benevolence could be pinned down as securely as the structure of a frog's anatomy — and by roughly the same method." In this the Princetonians serve as Turner's prime examples.

31. For an admiring sketch of Shields and his project, see Henry William Rankin, "Charles Woodruff Shields and the Unity of Science," *Princeton Theological Review* 13 (1915): 49-91; cf. Rankin, "In Behalf of a Philosophia Christiana," *Princeton Alumni Weekly*, 26 April 1929.

both. The book did not attempt to deliver the goods, but merely to point the way, sketching the proper theoretical configuration of all the sciences under one grand head — philosophy — and urging all pursuers of knowledge to find their place in its schema. Under this guidance — and provided that each participant agree to do his work not as a partisan but in a philosophical attitude of impartiality — an atmosphere of cooperation and mutual forbearance might replace the too-frequent enmity between the sciences of the spirit and the sciences of the physical world.[32]

Shields's book presumably came to the attention of Princeton by way of the Hodges. The *Biblical Repertory and Princeton Review* reviewed it favorably, but did not rave.[33] College president John Maclean, however, responded with more enthusiasm. Since the mid-1850s Maclean had hoped to establish a chair of science and religion to benefit both institutions at Princeton. The strength of Shields's objectivity claim impressed Maclean; the college soon awarded Shields an honorary D.D. and, with the help of some of his wealthy friends in Philadelphia, created a new professorship for him in 1865.[34]

Interestingly, Shields's chair was the Princeton equivalent of Woodrow's position — the Perkins Professorship of Natural Science in Relation to Revealed Religion, established in 1861 at Columbia Theological Seminary — and, like Woodrow, this Princetonian harmonizer became an object of controversy. (A fruitful study might be made of the ill-starred attempts at creating such "harmony chairs" in Britain and America.) Since before midcentury it had become common in orthodox circles to register the need for a "new Paley" who would update the evidences of divine design in light of such new sciences as geology.[35] Guyot's idealist progressionism answered the need in part, but Maclean hoped for a thorough systematization that would relate philosophy as well as science to God and the Bible. But this idea, seem-

32. Charles Woodruff Shields, *Philosophia Ultima* (Philadelphia: J. B. Lippincott and Co., 1861).

33. Short notice of *Philosophia Ultima*, by Charles Woodruff Shields, *Biblical Repertory and Princeton Review* 33 (1861): 576.

34. Thomas Jefferson Wertenbaker, *Princeton, 1746-1896* (Princeton: Princeton University Press, 1946), pp. 284-85; Addison Atwater, "The Faculty," in *The Princeton Book* (Boston: Houghton, Osgood and Co., 1879), p. 150; PU Trustees Minutes, 20 September 1865, PU Archives.

35. For example, A. A. Hodge, in Salmond, *Princetoniana*, p. 142.

ingly so straightforward, was a very tall order. Not only did it involve an enormous mass of material from the two great realms of mind and matter, but its goals mingled what had previously been two distinct projects, natural theology (reasoned proofs of God's existence and attributes) and the "Christian evidences" (reasoned proofs of the divine origin of the Bible). Foreshadowing the trouble soon to come between Maclean and his new professor, a local paper, the *Princeton Standard*, questioned "the wisdom . . . of establishing a chair with such exalted prerogatives and supreme jurisdiction."[36]

The question of supremacy soon erupted. When the spring term opened in 1866, the president decided to sit in on Shields's introductory lecture. He was surprised and appalled by what he heard. Shields told his students he was laying aside his ministerial robes and taking on the garb of a philosopher. He declared, "I am not here as a Theologian, or even as an Apologist for the True Religion" — a most unwelcome statement coming from a man commissioned, as Maclean understood it, to demonstrate the harmony of natural knowledge with revelation, and one whose post had been originally considered for the seminary.[37] The president spoke privately to Shields, but the professor would not budge. Shields was no fool; Maclean's objection undermined his whole project. He had made his views plain enough in print already, after all, and the college had given him only praise for them. To Maclean's mind, however, and to several professors who sided with him, a terrible mistake needed decisive remedy. So the president took his case to the board. Shields "has greatly misapprehended the design of his appointment," he reported at the June meeting; "his views of his Professorship are not in all respects such as will command the approval of the Trustees."[38]

According to Maclean's report, Shields had disposed of the apologetics textbooks previously in use — Butler and Paley — finding them written "too much in the interest of religion" and "not well adapted to the liberal view of religious culture called for, he imagines, by the Charter of the College" and by the purposes of his chair.[39] Worse, he offered his final

---

36. Quoted in Wertenbaker, *Princeton, 1746-1896*, p. 285.

37. John Maclean, draft of a fund-raising letter dated 17 February 1860, Maclean MSS, PU Archives; cf. Wertenbaker, *Princeton, 1746-1896*, pp. 272-73.

38. John Maclean, in PU Trustees Minutes, 25 June 1866.

39. Maclean, in PU Trustees Minutes, 25 June 1866. About this time Maclean drafted a proposed set of amendments to the college charter to establish the college as a distinctly Christian institution (undated, untitled MS, 1860s, John Maclean MSS, PU Archives). In his

philosophy as the "umpire" between science and religion — "thus, in appearance at least, exalting the teachings of philosophy above the teachings of Revelation." Maclean believed the board had intended Shields to take a distinctly apologetical stand, to position himself squarely within the circle of faith — not to assume an air of neutrality, and certainly not to make human reason the judge of divine revelation. He expected him to teach "the Evidences of Natural and Revealed Religion," not some neutral philosophy purporting to rise above them both. Shields's posture was too deistical; he stood too comfortably on enemy ground, and bade his students to do likewise. Right reason supported revelation, but reason had no right to sit in judgment over the Word of God.

The president and the professor actually shared a broad area of agreement. They both believed that the "book of nature" corroborated the book of revelation — that science and the Bible both taught truth — and therefore, to the extent that they overlapped, they were sure to agree with each other. Where differences appeared, both men anticipated a reconciliation of the two accounts by the application of human inquiry. Both agreed that the paramount method of inquiry for assuring factual results was the inductive method of Francis Bacon.[40] Both agreed that the Christian religion concerned not just doctrines and feelings, but factual events — especially creation and the resurrection, the bases respectively for the order of nature and the order of redemption. Both agreed that theology should take account of the discoveries of science, and that science should respect the truths of religion. Both held to the dualism of mind and matter.

But Maclean and Shields differed strikingly as to their expectations of philosophy. While Maclean granted the existence and importance of "fundamental truths of philosophy," he did not grant that discipline the

---

view the charter lacked reference to the founders' clear religious aims only because of the accidental historical context of its drafting under an Anglican governor already suspected of too much sympathy with the Presbyterians. See his richly detailed *History of the College of New Jersey, from Its Origin in 1746 to the Commencement of 1854*, 2 vols. (Philadelphia: J. B. Lippincott and Co., 1877), vol. 1, chapters 1 and 2.

40. In answer to Tyndall's fictional dialogue between Bishop Butler and a Lucretian, personifying the antagonism between religion and science, Shields wrote a script of his own, adding Lord Bacon himself as the umpire between the two. In fact, he attributed his original notion of a final philosophy to Bacon's suggestion of a "summary, universal science" to which all others were tributary. Charles Woodruff Shields, *Religion and Science in Their Relation to Philosophy: An Essay on the Present State of the Sciences* (New York: Scribner, Armstrong and Co., 1875), pp. 51-52.

exalted prerogative of deciding between science and religion when they disagreed. Maclean found Shields's "umpire" indistinguishable from a judge. Shields protested that in his system philosophy posed not as a tribunal, but as a mediator in a contest among equals. He had chosen the umpire analogy very deliberately. Maclean, however, found the effect to be the same in either case: philosophy had the last word, and that simply would not do. Philosophy was science's foundation, not its apex; Shields's umpire idea unseated religion as both the final authority and the goal of learning, enthroning human philosophy in its place.[41]

Only because Charles Hodge intervened did Shields retain his job. As both a friend and a member of the college board of trustees, Hodge spent hours with him in an attempt to find a compromise. But Shields behaved badly, publishing and distributing the offensive lecture far and wide — thus provoking not just the president but a significant number of the faculty at both institutions, none of whom could have been too pleased that their most junior colleague had gone public with an internal dispute. Maclean was set on removing the upstart, but Hodge persuaded him instead to propose to the trustees an official change of title and duties so as to direct Shields in no uncertain terms to "lay aside the garb of a philosopher, & assume that of a champion of Christianity."[42] It took some doing, but in the end Maclean recommended, and the board passed, a set of resolutions along the lines Hodge suggested.

> *Be it resolved* — (1) That in establishing the Professorship of "The Relations of Science & Religion & Philosophy," it was *not* the intention of the Trustees to establish a Professorship of the Philosophy of Science and Religion; nor was it their design to have Philosophy set forth, in the teachings of the Professorship, as the *umpire* between Science and Religion.
>
> (2) That it was the design of this Professorship to defend Revelation

41. Charles Hodge to Hugh Lenox Hodge, 26 April 1866, Hodge Family MSS, Letters, box 11, PU Library.

42. Charles Hodge to Hugh Lenox Hodge, 26 April 1866. The theologian expressed disappointment at the character traits the man he called "our friend" now exhibited. Shields had disregarded the advice of the assembled "club" of college and seminary professors, to whom he had submitted the offending lecture before publishing it. They regarded the publication as "an open challenge" to the president. Hodge lamented, "He is, I believe, crude & unsettled in his views, although he would consider that equivalent to saying the Sun is a dark lantern. My hope is, that if let alone, he would find his level, & would do a good work."

from the assaults of those who maintain that the discoveries of Science and the fundamental truths of Philosophy are at variance with the teachings of revealed truth; and also to shew that all the established facts of Science, having any bearing upon the matters in question, confirm what the Scriptures teach respecting God and his works.

(3) That the title of the Professorship be so changed that the Professor in this Department shall be hereafter known as "Professor of the Harmony of Science & Religion."

(4) That the Professor in this Department is expected to conform his instructions to the views presented in these resolutions.[43]

Maclean had his way, and Shields at least had a job. So far Hodge's compromise worked. But no one was particularly happy with the outcome. Shields's academic freedom was severely curtailed, his ego bruised. He now taught the old standards, Butler and Paley, instead of his own "final philosophy." His course remained a requirement even in McCosh's revamped curriculum, but it presented only a quaint sideshow, a relic of the old days, compared to the line of development from the natural history chair to the Bright Young Men. When the seminary revived its extracurricular lectures in science, philosophy, and religion, McCosh was invited to join Guyot and Atwater — yet the professor of the Harmony of Science and Religion was not.[44]

It seems, then, that the trustees of Princeton College did experience "great surprise and consternation" over science and religion in the late 1860s after all — but their alarm concerned Shields, not McCosh; the prerogatives and limits of philosophy, not the theory of evolution. In the light of the Shields affair, the events of the McCosh years take on a new aspect. McCosh's own hiring, the creation of Aiken's apologetics chair at the seminary, the natural history chair, the joint call of Dawson, the Bright Young Men plan, and the creation of Patton's professorship now appear as a long series of attempts to secure adequate instruction in the relations of science and religion — and philosophy's place in the equation — after the failure of Shields's Harmony Chair to live up to its promise.[45]

43. PU Trustees Minutes, 25 June 1866.
44. PTS Directors Minutes, 27 April 1868 and 27 April 1869, PTS Special Collections.
45. Paul C. Kemeny's fine study, *Princeton in the Nation's Service: Religious Ideals and Educational Practice, 1868-1928* (New York: Oxford University Press, 1998), unfortunately can give quite a different impression of Shields, claiming that Shields initiated the change of title for his chair and that his courses in natural theology and science and religion were

Certainly a major part of the problem was that Shields himself rejected — or rather postponed indefinitely — the harmony project. He did not compare the "facts" or authenticated teachings of science with the "facts" or received doctrines of Reformed Christianity; he believed that task too enormous for an entire generation of thinkers, and the present state of both natural and theological science far too provisional even to bother making the attempt. Instead of harmonizing the end results of science and theology, Shields was interested in the *structure* of any such projected harmony — the structure of the sum total of human knowledge. Like Spencer and Comte, the hated positivists, he aimed at a science of the sciences, a New Organon of knowledge in fulfillment of Bacon's ideal. He saw himself as an architect, not a builder, in the relations between scientific and religious knowledge.[46]

Princeton's censure of Shields's grand project left him undaunted. He remained at his post, despite its strictures, for more than thirty years,[47] devoting his scholarly energies on the side to the final philosophy. He simply took his pet project to more sympathetic audiences elsewhere. In 1875 he published an utterly unrepentant little book, *Religion and Science in Their Relation to Philosophy: An Essay on the Present State of the Sciences,* based on a lecture he gave at the Philosophical Society of Washington.[48]

"critical to sustaining the evangelical Protestant faith of students," omitting any mention of the flap over Shields's teaching in the 1860s (pp. 44-49). Further on in the book Kemeny does better, taking extensive note of later in-house criticisms of Shields, who in the 1890s "felt that he was 'perpetually exposed to a cross-fire' from the Princeton theologians on one side and the college scientists on the other" (pp. 104-5).

46. James R. Moore notes a striking parallel between Shields and Herbert Spencer, in career and aims. Moore, *The Post-Darwinian Controversies*, p. 358 n. 79. For a careful treatment of Shields's relation to positivism, see Cashdollar, *Transformation of Theology*, pp. 119-20, 334-38. Cashdollar credits Shields with being one of the earliest American theologians to treat Comte extensively (p. 116). Cf. Robert Flint, "Classification of the Sciences," part 2, *Presbyterian Review* 7 (1886): 532-34, who observed that Shields followed Comte on the notion of "'a general science of all the other sciences, based upon their historical and logical evolution'" (Shields's words, from his *Order of the Sciences, an Essay on the Philosophical Classification and Organization of Human Knowledge,* 1882).

47. Why did Princeton tolerate Shields for so long? For one thing, Shields married his daughter into the Stockton family (Princeton's most venerable) and actually bought back Morven, the Stockton mansion, for his financially strapped son-in-law. Charles Hodge's second wife was a Stockton; Shields was now law-kin to the Hodges. Interview with longtime Princeton resident and local historian William K. Selden, February 1993.

48. With obvious reference to Maclean, Shields wrote, "It is to be regretted that a prejudice should exist in some minds against a word of such noble significance" as philos-

In 1877 an enlarged version of his original project appeared with the English title *The Final Philosophy*, followed in 1882 by *The Order of the Sciences*. The renegade of Princeton stolidly developed and defended the "umpirage of philosophy" for which the trustees had reprimanded him, indulging in a few digs at his naysayers at home.[49]

Laying the Foundations

To Princeton's great relief, another son of the seminary arose to cross swords with the upstart Final Philosopher, carrying the argument beyond the old impasse over philosophy's titular headship, offering a detailed discussion of the particular apologetical dangers in Shields's approach. The new critic also presented a constructive alternative. This knight in shining armor was Francis Landey Patton, by many accounts the brightest young intellectual star in the Presbyterian firmament and, happily for Princeton, an ardent defender of Old School orthodoxy. In 1878 young Patton enjoyed the highest distinction of the church, serving as moderator of that year's General Assembly. In 1879 he wrote a searching critique of *The Final Philosophy* for the *Princeton Review*.[50] The following year Princeton created for him "the Professorship of the Relations of Philosophy and Science to the Christian Religion," plainly echoing the original title of Shields's chair.[51] This sequence of events strongly suggests that Patton was entrusted with the project Shields had so wished to define. His appointment marked Princeton's answer to Shields, Princeton's decisive step in defining the relations of human knowledge to revealed religion. His criticisms of Shields, then, are ex-

---

ophy, the actual, the only available, and the only desirable umpire between science and religion. Shields, *Religion and Science*, pp. 53-55.

49. Shields classified Hodge and Dawson among "an exclusively biblical or dogmatic anthropology which would deliberately shut its eyes to all the discoveries of ethnologists, linguists and antiquarians," "resisting all the light" of science. Their approach, he said, was one of "hasty prejudgment." While he applauded McCosh's position on evolution, he dismissed the Scot's philosophy as a lower stage in the development of realism, superseded by Lotze. Shields, *The Final Philosophy; or, System of Perfectible Knowledge Issuing from the Harmony of Science and Religion* (New York: Scribner, Armstrong and Co., 1877), pp. 176-77, 289.

50. Francis Landey Patton, "The Final Philosophy," *Princeton Review*, 1879, part 1 (January-June): 559-78.

51. See note 64, below.

tremely important in determining Princeton's "official" position on these matters.

Patton's answer to Shields in the *Princeton Review* identified the excesses of the "final philosophy" and suggested ways to avoid them. It is worth noting that those excesses consisted mainly in carrying certain Princetonian themes in science and religion to their extremes. As a result, it is difficult to draw rigid contrasts between Shields and the others. Quite possibly this was one reason why the major Princetonians found him so exasperating; in many ways Shields was just a particularly stark Princetonian. But the prolonged Shields affair shows at least that the Princetonians were aware of the possible excesses of their positions, and on guard against them.

In the first place, according to Patton, Shields confused philosophy with apologetics, making apologetics the whole raison d'être for his work.[52] Here certainly was a classic Princetonian tendency. Concern to maintain the unity of truth, the union of God's works with his word, had guided the Princetonian response to such matters as evolution for decades. Giving a reasoned defense of the faith was among the three cardinal purposes of Princeton Seminary at its founding. But apologetics was not everything, Patton urged. Structuring one's philosophy according to apologetical needs tended to at least two evils: to intensify the atmosphere of conflict between science and religion, and to divert attention from the fundamental philosophical issues at stake. Patton faulted Shields for making "very liberal use of military language," opening each chapter with a picture of battle, and thus putting religion in a more precarious position than it really occupied. Thus Shields exposed Christian belief "to the varying fortunes of war." Failing to discriminate between questions of science-and-religion, science-and-Christianity, and science-and-the-Bible, Shields's work would have Christians "live in a state of chronic alarm," for the gospel might fall with every attack on some little fact of Scripture. By magnifying the contest between science and religion, Shields inflated the importance of his final philosophy, but recklessly endangered the Christian's sense of intellectual security. Philosophy was important; indeed, epistemological and metaphysical questions lay behind all the hubbub about the scientific contradiction of Christianity — this Princeton had maintained from the outset. But to articulate the "battle" between science and religion in minute detail, and

52. Patton, "The Final Philosophy," p. 577.

then to ask "philosophy" to arbitrate the inflated conflict, did little service to belief — and even less to philosophy, for it called that discipline to divert its attention from the roots of the tree of knowledge, where it properly belonged, to its outermost twigs.[53]

Like Maclean before him, Patton objected to Shields's definition of philosophy as an utterly neutral, dispassionate spirit of inquiry — a naked, careless curiousness devoid of precommitments. Princetonian rhetoric did tend in this direction, for in emphasizing knowledge as a component of faith it suggested not only a *common* ground of discussion but also an *objective* ground. Claims to objective truth tended to involve appeals to a neutral inquirer. Was not Shields, in rhetorically exchanging ministerial for philosophical robes, simply acting out the objectivity claim? Was not this the whole thrust of Butler's and Paley's time-honored texts? Patton thought not, for Shields made neutrality into something neither the theologian as theologian, nor the scientist as scientist, could claim. He made theologians and scientists *advocates* for their respective sides, not impartial inquirers; only an impartial philosophy could settle the contest. Shields's philosophy, structured for apologetical aims, now foreswore apologetics. This Patton found both absurd and insulting: absurd for founding a philosophy upon an impulse it ruled unphilosophical, and insulting for alleging that theologians and apologists (or scientists, for that matter) had no business on the borderlands of their own disciplines. Worst of all, for Patton, Shields set objectivity against religious commitment — as though to believe in God were to take something less than the broadest view.[54]

The practical effect of Shields's "umpirage of philosophy," Patton argued, was to forbid absolutely any border crossing between science and religion. Here again was a familiar Princetonian position carried to an extreme. Atwater and others had made quite a stink about science trespassing into theological matters; McCosh perpetuated the tradition in his invectives against the incompetence of Tyndall and Huxley outside their fields. But surely someone had to do it, as Atwater, McCosh, and Guyot had done in their extracurricular lectures at the seminary. The "no tres-

53. Patton, "The Final Philosophy," pp. 559-60, 577.

54. Patton, "The Final Philosophy," pp. 571-72. The answer to this dilemma seems to lie in the difference between commonality and neutrality. Princeton resolved to meet the enemy on "his" ground so long as it was *common* ground, ground the believer could stand on as well. Objectivity meant not the absence of commitments (i.e., neutrality), but *truth* or *reality* (ground common to all).

passing" rule could not hold absolutely; it flew in the face of necessity and offended the perspicuity of both the Bible and science. One had to look for people competent across fields, such as George Frederick Wright; or for experts in science, sympathetic to religion, to draw general conclusions, like Dawson or Guyot; or for experts in theology to draw provisional conclusions from science, like Hodge and Patton. The "final philosophy," however, awaited the finalization of facts and dogmas: until the fullness of times for both science and religion, no sense could be made of the two together. Thus the Princetonian call for patience, the refusal to adjust theology to hypotheses yet unproved, became absolute. This especially Patton could not abide. It left, he argued, no alternative but "nescience" or "agnosticism" — the doctrine of the hated positivists.[55]

More concretely, Patton complained that Shields's "umpirage of philosophy" had no real referent. Shields identified it with a philosophical spirit, not with any group of people — but again using the evolution question as an example, Patton noted that Shields ruled out of court all "theological geologists" or "geological theologians" as mere "eclectics." *The Final Philosophy* classed Guyot and Dawson among a group Shields described as "'specious,' 'partial,' 'illogical,' 'unscientific,' 'narrow,' 'premature,' 'visionary,' and 'vague.'" The only remaining alternative, Patton observed, was to identify the umpirage of philosophy with the final philosophy — but who knew how long it would be until that "broad, comprehensive, and summative science," mute and helpless until the finalization of all facts, made its actual appearance? "If this is what the umpirage of philosophy means," he remarked, "agnosticism is the only position open to any man who would not be an infidel or a bigot."[56]

Finally, Patton faulted Shields for a weighty sin of omission. For all his attention to the end results of inquiry, Shields had neglected the

55. Patton, "The Final Philosophy," pp. 566-67, 570. Note the importance here of a moral dimension of knowing: one had to commit to belief in the face of some uncertainty. For Patton this did not entail a compromising of objectivity.

56. Patton, "The Final Philosophy," pp. 570, 572. Shields's answer to this charge was not very comforting. His "advice to the 'unfortunate inquirer' might be, 'Stick to your Bible and to your creed, and let philosophy alone. You can be a good Christian and even a sound divine without being a philosopher.'" Shields, "Philosophy and Apologetics," *Princeton Review*, 1879, part 2 (July-December): 203. Observing Shields's repudiation of all current attempts at harmony and his taking refuge in an unfounded belief in a grand harmonization wholly future, Wertenbaker went so far as to classify him as a "fundamentalist"! Wertenbaker, *Princeton, 1746-1896*, pp. 312-13, 420.

foundations. He and Patton shared the belief that the apparent conflict between scientific hypotheses and religious dogmas owed to errors of interpretation, not to any "actual disagreement between the facts of nature and the truths of Scripture." But Patton observed, "This, however, is a belief which the author entertains in spite of his argument, and if his argument is sound his belief has no good reason for its existence; for a supernatural revelation is one of the dogmas which stand opposed to scientific hypotheses, and it is one which, according to the author's specific averment, cannot be regarded as settled."[57] According to Patton, Shields believed in the truth of the Bible but never substantiated the claim, despising the work of "Christian Evidences" as unphilosophical. By *assuming* rather than establishing the Bible's truth, Shields left a wide, soft flank open to attack. Without regard to finding solid ground he wanted to begin erecting a magnificent building, a "summative science" that upon its completion would demonstrate the harmony of science and religion. Patton accepted the idea of a summative science as entirely laudable; indeed, he registered the urgent need for believers to build such a system, so as not to leave to unbelievers the privilege of framing the grandest structure of knowledge.[58] But the way to build up a summative science was not to foreswear all harmonization attempts until some great day of finality when all "facts" of science and religion would be duly confirmed and lo! scientists and theologians would at last perceive the unity of truth plainly demonstrated in the facts before them.[59] No, the way to build up a summative science was to start with the foundations, to establish the unity of truth in principle, and only then to affirm one's confidence that the results would eventually confirm it.

57. Patton, "The Final Philosophy," p. 567.

58. Patton, "The Final Philosophy," p. 576. "The work of building up the scattered elements of knowledge is one of great importance, and there is no reason why the Positivists should monopolize it. It is time that some should undertake to do, from the standpoint of Theism and in the interests of Christianity, what Fiske and Lewes and Spencer are doing in the interests of Positivism; and it is gratifying to know that there is at least one Christian thinker whose mind is turned in this direction."

59. Shields concluded *Religion and Science* with this image: ". . . the most extreme investigators are now but groping through the darkness toward some central point where, at length, they shall meet as in a focus of light. Only, we may be sure, they will meet there, not like those two rash knights at their first encounter, not like those eager champions who are now filling the air with challenges and criminations, but rather like exhausted and bleeding warriors, after having fought their way into a recognition of each other's truth and virtue, to clasp hands as friends who had but mistaken themselves for foes" (p. 66).

One could then get on with the business of constructive synthesis, something much larger than the apologetical task Shields had made his focus.

Here Patton offered his alternative vision of a "comprehensive philosophy." It would start at the beginning, not at the end, dealing first with questions of epistemology and metaphysics. It would undertake "a critical study of the conditions of human knowledge — an inquiry concerning human understanding"[60] that would reveal the reality of a priori ideas and ground "the inevitable dualism of mind and matter." Upon these philosophical foundations, duly established rather than dogmatically assumed, the summative science would stand. As to its name, "philosophy" would serve as an indication of its interest in truth; "science" would do to highlight its systematic exhibition of what is known — but "its most appropriate title will be Theology. A comprehensive philosophy must regard the spheres of moral and material order under some unifying category. That category is God."[61] The queen of the sciences, the apex of syntheses, would be, in this self-consciously modern sense, theology.[62]

Patton's answer to Shields pleased the Princeton theologians so much that the seminary created a new professorship expressly for him to expound "the relations of philosophy and science to the Christian religion."[63] His stated task was precisely what he himself had charted out in the debate with Shields: to secure the philosophical foundations of a summative worldview under the category of God. It was in this respect

60. N.b. the clear allusion to Hume and Kant.

61. Patton, "The Final Philosophy," p. 577.

62. However, for Patton the *scientia scientiarum*, "the doctrine of science" — the philosophical framework for classifying and relating the sciences — was not the apex but the fundament of the whole system. Philosophy rightly held that place. Shields's mistake, according to Patton and the Princetonians who followed him, was to confuse this *philosophia prima* with the *philosophia ultima*. Cf. Robert Flint's assessment of Shields in "Classification of the Sciences," p. 534. Princeton, especially Patton, thought very highly of Flint, who delivered the Stone Lectures at PTS in 1880-81.

63. PTS Directors Minutes, 26 April 1880 and 8 September 1880; PTS Trustees Minutes, 10 September 1880 and 27 October 1880, PTS Special Collections. The latter minutes list specific doctrinal requirements binding the Stuart Professor, the violation of which would cause the deed ($100,000) to pass to the American Bible Society. Stuart also gave $100,000 to the college, rescuing McCosh from the only debt problem of his administration (James McCosh, "Twenty Years of Princeton College," in Sloane, *Life of James McCosh*, p. 212). See A. A. Hodge to Henry A. Boardman, 4 June 1880 (PTS Special Collections) for a remarkable expression of how completely Princeton Seminary had fixed its future hopes on Patton.

precisely the opposite of Shields's approach; it began at the bottom rather than the top of the edifice of knowledge. It regarded the "harmony of science and theology" not as a conclusion to be demonstrated by comparing the end results of each discipline, but as a principle to be established by philosophical argument and, that being done, as a matter of adjustments in each department, unperturbed by the necessity of tweaking here and there — not calling the entire enterprise into question afresh at the discovery of each little glitch. The harmony project became not a dull task of cataloguing corroborations, but the more needful task of making adjustments in order to complete the big picture. Patton separated apologetics from the harmony project as Shields had conceived it, giving apologetics the *first* place — a very important place — but emphatically not the *final* place.[64]

Patton left the harmony project for others to do, defending their right to make tentative explorations even where scientific knowledge was hypothetical at best. (He did, however, on assuming the presidency of Princeton College in 1888, demote Shields's science-and-religion course from a requirement to an elective, substituting his own evidences course as the requirement!)[65] While "wait and see" remained Princeton's watchword with regard to matters of science and religion (and the evolution question in particular), provisional attempts to make sense of the "two books" were welcome.[66] In the meantime, Patton set about his spe-

64. Dennis Royal Davis, "Presbyterian Attitudes toward Science and the Coming of Darwinism in America, 1859-1929" (Ph.D. diss., University of Illinois/Urbana-Champaign, 1980), first alerted me to the debate between Patton and Shields (p. 120). Unfortunately Davis grossly misconstrues Shields's significance, portraying him as an ally of McCosh in a battle against the Princeton theologians (pp. 147-48), whom he caricatures as hostile to science. Davis misses the essential friendliness to science, even evolution, entailed in Princeton's wait-and-see policy, paints Patton as a stern antievolutionist (p. 111), and reverses the positions of Patton and Shields on the value of contemporary efforts to reconcile science and religion (p. 120). Davis expects any evolutionist to be a theological liberal, and any theological conservative to be an antievolutionist. This is what comes of assuming that in religion "liberal" meant "friendly to science" and "conservative" meant "hostile to science," not to mention the assumption that the evolution question was simply scientific.

65. Kemeny, *Princeton*, p. 104. Ten years later, still during Patton's administration, Princeton University dropped the curricular requirement for the president's course on evidences. An elective course in apologetics remained (p. 106).

66. Witness, for example, Princeton's favorable appraisal of the work of George Frederick Wright, the occupant of yet another harmony chair at Oberlin. In 1904-5 Wright delivered the Stone Lectures at Princeton Seminary, with Patton now installed in the presi-

cial calling to secure the foundations of a theistic worldview in epistemology and metaphysics.[67]

A Fundamental Choice

At his inauguration to the Stuart chair Patton must have winced at the
rhetorical excesses of his old Brooklyn friend. The inflated Dare that Van
Dyke gave in his "Charge" smacked of everything Patton had opposed in
Shields: excessive claims of objective neutrality, a posture of willingness
to abandon the dearest commitments of faith, the rhetorical subjection
of religion to reason. The new professor's own gifts of oratory served him
well that day. His inaugural address steered smoothly away from Van
Dyke's unwitting caricature of his project, offering in its place a compelling argument for his own view. In place of a *Dare,* Patton posed a stark
Choice between two fundamental, mutually exclusive worldviews: either
you must believe in a creator God, distinct from his creation — in a word,
theism — or you must hold some form of pantheistic or atheistic "automatism."[68]

Early in his speech Patton forthrightly rejected the Shieldsian posture
of assumed neutrality, in language distinctly recalling Shields's run-in
with Maclean. "It may occur to some," he said, "that as the apologete is the
professed *advocate* of Christianity the occupant of this chair may very
properly act in the capacity of a *judge,*" endeavoring "to divest himself of
all dogmatic bias" so as to approach the relations of science and religion
with the impartiality of blindfolded Justice herself. It seemed a gratifying
prospect, Patton admitted, but "candor requires me to say that it is not
true." Princeton Seminary required its professors to subscribe in good

---

dent's office. The lectures were later published as *Scientific Confirmations of Old Testament
History,* 2nd ed. (Oberlin, Ohio: Bibliotheca Sacra Co., 1907).

67. While Shields was the near antagonist against whom Patton charted his system,
the whole idea of building up a science of the sciences recalled the grand attempts of the
positivists, especially Comte. Shields, Patton, and Flint (not to mention Warfield) all recognized this. See, e.g., Flint, "Classification of the Sciences," p. 533; and in general on the relations of positivism to nineteenth-century theology, see Cashdollar, *The Transformation
of Theology, 1830-1890.*

68. Patton seems to have come up with this term in a series of sermons he preached
in Chicago a few years earlier. Patton, "Thoughts on the Theistic Controversy," Doctrinal
Series, 1:6.

faith to the system of doctrine contained in the confessional standards of the Presbyterian church. The seminary stood squarely on "Westminster orthodoxy," and Patton took that commitment seriously. Therefore, "I do not see that there is any way whereby I can avoid the charge of approaching my subject with foregone conclusions." After all, "A man should have made up his mind respecting the place of Christianity in the world before taking the position of a teacher in a school of divinity." It would be positively immoral to hold a seminary chair while consciously out of sympathy with the church's purpose to propagate a particular system of belief.[69]

But Patton went on to argue that this frank admission of bias, this conscious "dogmatic attitude," did not contradict the "philosophic spirit." To hold a precommitment did not disqualify one from defending it, nor did it necessarily blind one to its difficulties. Precommitments were, in fact, unavoidable; *neutral* ground as such was a dream. Fair and open discussion required not the pretense of utter objectivity, but the establishment of *common* grounds of argument — "common intellectual conditions and common objective evidence." Such commonality could coexist quite well with varying individual precommitments, though neutrality could not. Along these lines Patton argued for the continued importance of argument in religious questions. "Argument is not unavailing. It was useful in the deistic battle of last century; it is needed in the theistic battle of this."[70]

Patton thus coupled an emphatic awareness of the importance of presuppositions and subjectivity with a firm endorsement of reasoned argument. "Common intellectual conditions" (the reasoning powers common to all humanity) and "common objective evidence" (the facts admitted as such on all sides) provided him with all he needed, he believed, to persuade people of the reasonableness of belief in God, and from there to persuade them of the truth of Christianity. Whether they then came to personal trust in Christ was, of course, another matter. On the basis of common grounds of argument, Patton bid to drive any interlocutor to the admission of a great, fundamental metaphysical Choice — to the admission, that is, that there really was no neutral ground. Either there was a God above nature, a distinction between Creator and creature, or the universe was a vast automaton. Each thinker had to choose

69. Patton, "Inaugural Address," in "Addresses at the Inauguration of the Rev. Francis L. Patton . . ." (1881), pp. 22-23 (emphasis in original).
70. Patton, "Inaugural Address" (1881), pp. 26-27.

on which ground he would build. A theistic worldview or one of the various automatistic worldviews, materialistic or pantheistic: these were the options, short of rank skepticism.[71]

But the Choice was not an arbitrary one. Patton argued that the theistic alternative alone could explain the realities of experience, external and internal. God alone was the sufficient ground of all knowledge and all being; without him they could neither exist nor be known. In God alone the moral and emotional life found satisfaction. Deny God and you lost all grounds of confidence in your reasoning powers. Identify God with the universe and you lost all grounds of separate personality and individual freedom. Either of these alternatives meant intellectual suicide, dividing the mind against itself. For good reasons, then, subjective and objective, theism was the better choice. The proof was in the trying.[72] To this end Patton redeployed the Horrible Vision as a powerful weapon against an antitheistic metaphysic. Inviting the affections to experience the desolation of godlessness, he took materialism as an example: "Consistent materialism is egoism. The self is a solitary tenant of a lone universe. It has no logical right to call any other self its companion, for of that other self it has no knowledge. The soul is a caged bird, and it is the function of a true theory of knowing and being to open the doors of that gilded cage, and when this is done, with little help from us, but under the irresistible tendency of an instinct born in heaven, this poor, pining, imprisoned thing will fly away to God."[73] The liberator of that caged bird,

71. Before his appointment Patton wrote to A. A. Hodge, "I believe that a man can be driven into nihilism or into an admission of the evidences for the supernatural." Patton to Hodge, 19 May 1880, PTS Special Collections.

72. In a baccalaureate sermon at the college Patton admonished each graduate, "It may be that Christ has come from God; that he is the propitiation for our sins; that he holds in his hands the gift of eternal life, and that you have but to trust him to enter into the full heritage of the kingdom of God. Give faith a chance today, my friend.... You have tried to give up the supernatural in Christ and cling to Christ, and you find you cannot.... See, then, if you do not find a better theory of the world and a better philosophy of life in Peter's bold avowal: 'We believe that Thou art the Christ, the Son of the living God.'" Patton took John 6:67-69 as his text: "Then said Jesus unto the twelve, Will ye also go away? Then Simon Peter answered him, Lord, to whom shall we go? thou hast the words of eternal life ..." (KJV). Patton, "Baccalaureate Sermon Preached before the Class of 1894" (pamphlet apparently excerpted from "A Report of the Exercises at the Opening of Alexander Commencement Hall," PTS Special Collections), pp. 48-49.

73. Patton, "Inaugural Address" (1881), pp. 41-42. "It makes no difference how my personality is obliterated, whether by pantheism or materialism; the effect is just the same" (p. 40) — echoes of Dod.

the "true theory of knowing and being," was theism. Theistic argument was but the "little help" Patton offered, guiding the soul to its own "instinct born of heaven." Argument merely led the mind to contemplate truths that, once discovered, shone with their own brightness.[74] In contrast to them, how deep the darkness of unbelief!

This, then, was the fundamental metaphysical Choice people faced. Patton painted it in the starkest colors possible, to emphasize the radicalness, the mutual exclusivity of the options — two and only two. We "must decide between a metaphysic that leads to an absolute vacuum in knowledge, absolute irresponsibility in morals, absolute mechanism in life," on the one hand, and "a metaphysic that will secure the separateness, the sovereignty, the morality, the immortality of the soul" on the other.[75] Patton returned to this theme repeatedly in both classroom and chapel, employing the old Horrible Vision to enlist our God-given moral feelings against the desolations of modern unbelief. In a college chapel sermon in 1894 he quoted Tennyson's poignant poem "Vastness," to depict for the students "the inclined plane down which some of you have slipped from faith in God to loss of faith in man":

Many a hearth upon our dark globe
    sighs after many a vanished face,
Many a planet by many a sun
    may roll with the dust of a vanished race;
Raving politics never at rest —
    as this poor earth's pale history runs —
What is it all but a trouble of ants
    in the gleam of a million million of suns?
. . . .
What is it all, if we all of us end
    but in being our own corpse — coffins at last,
Swallow'd in vastness, lost in silence,
    drown'd in the deeps of a meaningless Past?[76]

---

74. It is worth remarking here how far Patton was from claiming airtight proof or indubitability for his line of theistic argument, or for founding religion on reason. Cf. Paul Kjoss Helseth, *"Right Reason" and the Princeton Mind: An Unorthodox Proposal* (Phillipsburg, N.J.: P&R, 2010).

75. Patton, "Inaugural Address" (1881), p. 45.

76. Alfred Lord Tennyson, "Vastness" (1885), quoted in Patton, "Baccalaureate Sermon," pp. 47-48.

The sense each of us has of individual personality, responsibility, and immortality — and the impulse to ground them adequately — provided the common ground on which Patton believed he could press a successful case for belief in a personal Creator distinct from the creation, God the ground of truth, goodness, and freedom. That theistic worldview supplied a solid foundation for the edifice of theology (and, indeed, for science and philosophy as well). "With the soul assured, the way to God is plain. And if God is[,] a revelation of God may be. With the possibility of a revelation conceded, the proofs are sufficient. And with a proved revelation before us" — the Bible — well, the whole system of Westminster orthodoxy followed from there, point by point, until at last we beheld the glorious vision that in Christ "are hid all the treasures of wisdom and knowledge, and that by Him all things consist."[77]

In his turn to the foundations Patton made a point of demonstrating his continuity with the old Princeton theology. His new emphasis on careful philosophical grounding smacked distinctly of current concerns, as Patton well knew; he reveled in the contemporary relevance he felt his work possessed. But he built his whole presentation outright on distinctions and concepts Charles Hodge had used in his definitive *Systematic Theology*. After a six-chapter treatment of prolegomena, Hodge began his theology with a chapter entitled "Origin of the Idea of God," followed by "Theism" and "Anti-Theistic Theories."[78] Already in Hodge these themes stood at the base of systematics. Patton's course simply delved into them in greater historical and philosophical detail. The opposition between theism and antitheism was patent in Hodge's very terminology; Patton pushed it for apologetical purposes to the brink of a radical presuppositional dualism,[79] but without stepping over the edge. He maintained that it was possible to argue a person to the admission that one had a fundamental choice to make: a choice between a theistic and an antitheistic

77. Patton, "Inaugural Address" (1881), pp. 45-46.

78. Charles Hodge, *Systematic Theology* (New York: Scribners, 1872-73; reprint, Grand Rapids: Eerdmans, 1993), 1:ix-x.

79. Here I refer to Abraham Kuyper's later theory of two radically distinct scientific epistemes, the Christian and the non-Christian, based on the possession of two equally fundamental sets of presuppositions — a theory the Princetonians are renowned for opposing. See Warfield's review of Herman Bavinck's *De Zekerheid des Geloofs* (The certainty of faith), and especially Mark Noll's note introducing it, in Noll, ed., *The Princeton Theology, 1812-1921: Scripture, Science, and Theological Method from Archibald Alexander to Benjamin Breckinridge Warfield* (Grand Rapids: Baker, 1983), pp. 302-7.

metaphysic. But he also maintained that it was possible to show that the theistic alternative was the better choice — more satisfying to the intellect and to the feelings. Patton's emphasis on a fundamental Choice thus followed Hodge, yet overtook him.

Patton's actual lectures on theism, a "syllabus" or summary of which survives in pamphlet form, opened with a distinction between theism as a personal religious belief and theism as a "philosophy of the universe." The former presented the religious-epistemic aspect of theism, the latter its metaphysical aspect. Following this distinction Patton discussed the historical development of theistic argument, then compared the theistic "philosophy of the universe" with vying antitheistic alternatives.

Patton's epistemology of theism was frankly modern, tracing the development of theism as a locus of study and acknowledging his special debt to Descartes and Locke on the matter of radical choice. Theistic argument began with the Greeks, he said, but "the conditions did not exist in the ancient world for the production of a reasoned Theism and of elaborate treatises in Natural Theology." Those conditions were the possession of the Bible, introducing the distinction between natural and revealed religion; the systematization of dogmatic theology, making the question of God's existence a locus of careful discussion; and, not least, "the polemic relations of Theism to anti-theistic theories."[80] Only over time, then, in connection with systematics and often in response to opposition, did theistic study develop. In the modern period the salutary role of opposition became especially prominent, so that in Patton's view the church owed a debt of gratitude to the hand of Providence for allowing antitheistic philosophical challenges to drive believers to penetrate deeper into the truths of theism. This was a philosophical correlate to the time-honored notion that dogma, the human attempt to encapsulate revealed truth, developed progressively in response to the challenges of heresy. Here was an affirmation of the constructive role of history in the unfolding human understanding of unchanging truth.

Patton appreciated Descartes for his grounding of all knowledge in the knowledge of God. "Rightly or wrongly," he observed, "Descartes was as sure of God's existence, as of the truths of geometry." But instead of faulting Descartes for making excessive epistemic demands of faith,

---

80. Francis Landey Patton, "Syllabus of Prof. Patton's Lectures on Theism" (Princeton: Princeton Press, 1888), pp. 15-16, pamphlet, PTS Special Collections.

Patton applauded him for tying all certitude to "the theistic hypothesis." The certitude of geometry stood not as the measure of all knowledge claims, but as itself a knowledge claim dependent on belief (not necessarily saving faith) in God. "That is, he sees that the reasonings in geometry are true, on the supposition that there is such a thing as truth, and that this postulate conditions them." Affirming the necessity of *presupposing* God, Patton queried, "Is not this Cartesian position our own position in the debate of to-day? The theistic hypothesis is the only guarantee, in other words, of our intellectual integrity. We can cast discredit upon all processes of thinking, by a theory of knowledge that destroys the possibility of knowledge; or we can make belief in God the presupposition and postulate of all knowledge."[81]

Patton found a similar effect in Locke's theistic argument from the existence of the human mind. Locke reasoned that either "there has been a knowing being from all eternity, or else there was a time when there was no knowledge"; furthermore, "if there was a time when there was no knowing being, it is impossible that any knowing being ever could have been." But we are knowing beings, and we exist — therefore there has been a knowing being from all eternity: God. This rather peculiar argument Patton found quite compelling. It amounted to the familiar declaration that "only mind can be the cause of mind." But it presented the case in such a way as to pose "a choice of hypotheses": "the choice between Theism and the most thorough-paced Agnosticism."[82] Patton liked this presentation of stark alternatives, for it harnessed the horrors of godlessness in the service of belief.

Patton's lectures on theism did not make a very clear distinction between belief in God as a philosophical postulate and belief in God as an act of faith — that is, between natural theology and religious belief. But that was because he did not construe natural theology particularly naturally. Again following Charles Hodge (and, in this instance, *not* James McCosh),[83] he taught that an individual's belief in God originated in

---

81. Patton, "Syllabus," pp. 19-20; cf. Charles Hodge, *Systematic Theology,* 1:50. Patton added, "This is not reasoning in a circle." He rejected Scottish philosopher William Hamilton's claim that (in Patton's words) "confidence in our knowing powers must condition confidence in our knowledge of God" — calling Hamilton's position "a palpable fallacy" and a clear specimen of circular reasoning, which Descartes avoided.

82. Patton, "Syllabus," p. 22.

83. Like Hodge, McCosh believed belief in God to be universal among normal minds, but unlike Hodge, he traced its origin to inference, not intuition. Patton, "Syllabus," p. 9.

intuition — "that we have a constitutional tendency or impulse toward belief in God." But instead of construing that intuition as some kind of rapid, unconscious inference, as he said Hodge did, he ventured the theory that "the idea of God may be God's testimony to His own existence" — "that it is through the Spirit of God within, and not merely by arguments without, that we derive our first belief in God." In other words, individual theism (not, notice, saving faith) arose by an immediate work of the Holy Spirit on the individual, in conjunction perhaps with external arguments. For Patton, all knowledge of God, whether natural or revealed, whether salvific or merely philosophical, owed at least in part to the "direct relation to the soul" of the Spirit of God.[84] This connection of faith with philosophy, far from naturalizing faith, supernaturalized philosophy.[85]

Indeed, this was the whole tendency of Patton's emphasis on the Choice between a theistic and an antitheistic metaphysic: either you admitted God and built your world upon belief in him, or you denied the constitutional tendency of your own mind and sank yourself in the delusion of independence from God, denaturing your very soul. Intellect and will, morality and belief were bound together, ultimately, in natural as well as in religious knowledge. Epistemics and metaphysics

84. Patton, "Syllabus," p. 11. Patton's view here was not without its difficulties for traditional Calvinist understandings. It posited an immediate, supernatural instance of what was in effect a work of "common grace," although that term usually denoted God's providential goodness to all people through natural law. In addition, it might lead to a Wesleyan, non-Reformed doctrine of "prevenient grace" (God's preparation of the sinner's heart and mind to receive the gospel) or perhaps to founding theism on mysticism. Francis R. Beattie, another Reformed apologist contemporary with Patton, expressed reservations about this aspect of Patton's theism in a letter to B. B. Warfield, 6 September 1890, Warfield MSS.

85. Patton, "Syllabus," pp. 10-11. Patton liked this reason-and-Holy-Ghost explanation because it preserved the importance of traditional theistic argument, yet avoided the pitfalls associated with mere argumentation. External arguments by themselves fell short because they conditioned belief in God "by the probability of inductive proof," while the belief itself required something better than mere probability. Internal arguments from intuition or a priori reasoning fell into a vicious circle, never able to ground their conviction in something outside the self. This immediate relation of the soul to God overcame those obstacles, yet without doing away with the mind in the process. And, important for distinguishing Patton's presuppositionalism from Abraham Kuyper's, this view of the cooperation of the Holy Spirit with arguments "makes it unnecessary to establish a schism between Adam and his posterity, as to the mode of knowing God."

met at the bottom floor; all knowing and all being were grounded in God.[86]

What folly, then, to suppose that evolution, "God's way of doing things" (to quote John Fiske), undid belief in God. A mode of causation could not alter a worldview; rather, it presupposed one.[87] The question was simply which worldview to presuppose: one that maintained the distinction between Creator and creation, grounding the objective world and the canons of rationality, or one that did not. For Patton there was only one logical choice. But in either case "evolution" was merely a mode, a tool, for explaining the universe in terms of one's underlying metaphysic. The antitheist used it to explain the universe in monistic terms; the theist used it to explain the procedure of a supernatural God in fashioning and governing the world.

Patton's Choice carried on the old battle against positivism, mixing positivism with other foes — materialism, idealism, pantheism, atheism — as Atwater and the *Biblical Repertory and Princeton Review* had done two decades before. In this his rationale was the same as theirs: these isms all shared a denial of the distinction between God and his creation, and between mind and matter. But in the intervening decades these vying worldviews had come together in the constructive task of building a system to rival the theistic one, a world explanation presenting a fully articulated alternative view of nature and history devoid of divine intervention. To leave any distinctive activity of God out of the picture was, as Charles Hodge had said, tantamount to atheism; depending on which aspect he wished to emphasize, Patton called it antitheism, or automatism, or naturalism, or nescience, or nihilism. "Antitheism" stressed its philosophical status as a negation of and negative alternative to the theistic worldview, "automatism" stressed its denial of moral freedom, "naturalism" its denial of a power above and distinct from nature, "nescience" its impotence for finding meaning, and "nihilism" its desolating emotional consequences. It oscillated between a monism of spirit (idealism) and a monism of body (materialism).[88] It assumed many forms, each distinct from the others in important ways — but increasingly it took as its mode of explanation the consuming idea of the nineteenth century, the concept on which rival theories converged: evolution. Cou-

86. Cf. Patton's teacher, Charles Hodge, *Systematic Theology,* 1:52.
87. Patton, "Syllabus," pp. 37-38.
88. Patton, "Inaugural Address" (1881), pp. 39-42; cf. his "Baccalaureate Sermon," p. 42.

pled with a theistic metaphysic, evolution was benign; but apart from a theistic metaphysic, evolution was malignant indeed. One's philosophical foundation made all the difference in the world.[89]

89. Patton, "Evolution and Apologetics," p. 144. "It is not evolution in its scientific aspect so much, but rather the metaphysical complement of evolution that is especially hostile to the gospel." Biologist George Macloskie would continue this line at Princeton, repeatedly, into the 1900s. See, for example, his "Outlook of Science and Faith," *Princeton Theological Review* 1 (1903): 597-615.

CHAPTER SEVEN

Natural Religion

*When will the Church at large awake to the fact that the problem
which "the newer religious thinking" is putting before her is simply
the old eighteenth-century problem in a fresh form? Is Christianity
a natural religion, the crown and capstone it may be of natural religion, but only natural religion for all that? Or is Christianity a supernatural religion — supernatural in origin, in sanctions, in
power and in issue?*

Benjamin Breckinridge Warfield, 1895[1]

The Changing of the Guard

James McCosh left the presidency of the College of New Jersey on 20 June
1888, after two full decades of service. He was seventy-seven years old.
His hope in a body of Bright Young Men to carry Christian fidelity into
the upper ranks of professionalizing academia, and so to mold the age,
now faced its truest test: the test of succession. Princeton was not alone
in facing a change of administrations; in the late 1880s, at prominent colleges all across America, aging presidents were retiring and a new group
of leaders was replacing them. It was a remarkable generational phe-

---

1. Benjamin Breckinridge Warfield, short notice of *"The Ascent of Man": Its Note of
Theology,* by Principal Hutton, *Presbyterian and Reformed Review* (hereafter *PRR*) 6 (1895):
367.

nomenon, as Burton Bledstein has observed — a momentous changing of the guard.[2]

Amid much pomp and circumstance the aged president handed the college keys and charter to none other than Francis Landey Patton, that champion of theistic foundationalism. According to T. J. Wertenbaker, the election was a matter of some controversy, for the bulk of the alumni wanted most of all an able administrator, a man of the world — but a conservative faction of the trustees overruled them, securing instead a man of the cloth. Patton's election, in this view, was a disappointing setback to the process of liberalization McCosh had begun, a reassertion of the seminary's restrictive power over the college. Some said the new president, McCosh's junior by a generation, seemed a century older.[3] Wertenbaker tells a good story: Patton, pale and monkish, wearing side whiskers and a frock coat, represented to the newer alumni all the somber reserve and dreary ecclesiasticism their alma mater was just escaping. His only connection to the college was as a lecturer in theism; he was neither a son of Old Nassau nor even an American citizen. But the Bermudian clerical president-elect put his magnificent gift of oratory to good use at a meeting of liberal New York alumni, melting "an atmosphere of cold hostility" so effectively that by the end of his speech "his enemies were standing on tables, waving napkins and yelling in a frenzy of enthusiasm."[4] In the event, the alumni's initial unease proved well

2. Other college presidents retiring in the 1880s were Noah Porter of Yale (1871-86), Andrew Dickson White of Cornell (1868-85), Frederick A. P. Barnard of Columbia (1864-89), William Watts Folwell of Minnesota (1869-84), and John Bascom of Wisconsin (1874-87). Three other notables who assumed office about 1870 remained there into the next century: William Eliot of Harvard (1869-1909), Daniel Coit Gilman of Hopkins (1876-1902), and James Burrill Angell of Michigan (1871-1909). Bledstein makes much of the striking similarity of the terms of office of these men, focusing attention on them rather than on their successors. Burton J. Bledstein, *The Culture of Professionalism: The Middle Class and the Development of Higher Education in America* (New York: Norton, 1976), p. 129. Cf. George M. Marsden, *The Soul of the American University: From Protestant Establishment to Established Nonbelief* (New York: Oxford University Press, 1994).

3. Laurence Veysey, quoted in Howard Segal, "The Patton-Wilson Succession," *Princeton Alumni Weekly,* 6 November 1978, p. 21; Thomas Jefferson Wertenbaker, *Princeton, 1746-1896* (Princeton: Princeton University Press, 1946), pp. 344-46; J. David Hoeveler Jr., *James McCosh and the Scottish Intellectual Tradition: From Glasgow to Princeton* (Princeton: Princeton University Press, 1981).

4. William Berryman Scott, quoted in Wertenbaker, *Princeton, 1746-1896,* p. 345; cf. P. C. Kemeny, *Princeton in the Nation's Service: Religious Ideals and Educational Practice, 1868-1928* (New York: Oxford University Press, 1998), pp. 87-89.

founded, for the brilliant rhetorician soon showed himself to be a decid-edly uninspired administrator. In 1902 he was politely but plainly re-moved from office by a band of McCosh's own Bright Young Men — and seated in a more appropriate place as president of Princeton Seminary. Patton's college administration serves in standard accounts of American educational history as an instructive interlude — a churchly counterexample to the history of educational liberation — between the towering figures of McCosh and his truer heir, Woodrow Wilson.[5]

Patton's lackluster presidential performance notwithstanding, his views on science and religion made him, in one sense at least, a fitting heir to McCosh. What seems anomalous to the history-of-education mainline, dominated as it is by the theme of the blessings of seculariza-tion, is just what the leading Princetonians thought best for progress: the union of religion with academic distinction. Patton's transfer from the Stuart chair to the office in Nassau Hall fit well with McCosh's own fond-est hopes for Princeton's influence on the religious tone of academia. Here was a philosopher like himself, a man well versed in "first and fun-damental truths" (to echo the title of one of McCosh's own books) and possessed of a dazzling knowledge of the leading issues of the day, a man who addressed the questions of science and religion at their roots and made God the foundation for the life of the mind. We need read no dis-simulation into McCosh's hearty endorsement of his successor.[6]

If Patton's administration did not live up to its promise, this was due to the new president's too-easy liberality, not any religious clampdown on free inquiry. His tenure was in fact notorious not for tight strictures, but for laissez-faire. His enemies on the faculty faulted him not for intol-erance, but for indolence. James Mark Baldwin, professor of psychology under Patton and toward the end of his life a man quite out of sympathy

5. Laurence R. Veysey, *The Emergence of the American University* (Chicago: University of Chicago Press, 1965), p. 52; Alexander Leitch, *A Princeton Companion* (Princeton: Princeton University Press, 1978), pp. 354-57. Wertenbaker's chapter titles are revealing: on McCosh, "The Birth of a University"; on Patton, "Expansion and Inaction."

6. "I am to be succeeded by one in whom I have thorough confidence. . . . Possessed of the highest intellectual powers, he will devote them all to the good of this college. With unrivalled dialectic skill he will ever be ready to defend the truth. I am not sure that we have in this country at this moment a more powerful defender of the faith. . . . I am partic-ularly happy when I think that philosophy, and this of a high order, and favoring religion, is safe in his hands, and will be handed down by him to a generation following." James McCosh, in William Milligan Sloane, *The Life of James McCosh* (New York: Charles Scribner's Sons, 1896), p. 238.

with Princeton's creed, found it utterly baffling that his president, an ardent dogmatician in church matters — a heresy hunter, even — could so casually accord full freedom to the college faculty on scientific matters like evolution and physiological psychology.[7] But the reason is not far to seek. Patton actually believed in the Battle Plan: he believed that scholarship undertaken by faithful men, founded on theistic presuppositions, offered the safest road to both the preservation and the progress of truth. In this he personified exactly the two sides of McCosh, the academic liberal and the religious conservative.[8] Unfortunately he lacked McCosh's energetic activism and political savvy. He was not cut from administrative cloth — but that had nothing particularly to do with his clerical collar.

Patton was so impressed with the importance of well-laid foundations that he trusted logic and reason to build a sound edifice upon them without any intervening religious guidance. Here was the key to the seeming paradox of the Patton years. Religious allegiance and freedom of thought need not oppose each other, provided that the common grounds of the knowledge of God and the world were secure. The free development and interchange of ideas, on such a basis, would naturally discover and strengthen the structure of objective truth, of which God was the ground and goal.[9] Because Patton believed theism the most rationally justified worldview, the project of building upon theistic foundations was, for him, arguably more a case of open inquiry than of prescribed boundaries. In its own way this was a rather daring venture, entrusting the college's most cherished spiritual commitments to an

7. James Mark Baldwin, *Between Two Wars, 1861-1921: Being Memories, Opinions, and Letters Received by James Mark Baldwin* (Boston: Stratford Co., 1926), 1:56-57. Patton gained national notice in 1874 for his prosecution of Chicago pastor David Swing for heresy. Baldwin thought him "a case of divided personality or rather of divided interests" who "condemns his fellows by the most approved Calvinistic formulas of original and persistent sin, on Sundays when in the pulpit," but during the week "manifest[s] the largest charity to sceptics and other intellectual sinners." Baldwin freely called him "Patton the liberal and wise President of Princeton," depicting Wilson, by contrast, as an enemy of modern science (1:59).

8. On these two sides of McCosh see Hoeveler, *James McCosh and the Scottish Intellectual Tradition*, and Marsden, *Soul*, chapter 12; on Patton see Marsden, chapter 13.

9. At his inauguration Patton said, "True philosophy has God as its postulate; true science reaches God as its conclusion." Francis Landey Patton, inaugural address, "The Inauguration of President Patton" (College of New Jersey) (New York: Gray Bros., 1888), p. 42, pamphlet, PTS Special Collections.

open atmosphere of intellectual work on the basis of mere theism, not confessional Christianity, assured that such a basis sufficed for the triumph of truth.[10]

Theism became the watchword of Patton's Princeton, with a variety of beneficial side effects. Besides offering unprecedented academic freedom (by Princetonian standards) to scientists within their fields, it afforded Patton latitude to please the growing body of non-Presbyterian, mainly Episcopalian, alumni. In his smashing speech in New York he first won his audience with the declaration that "Princeton is too big to be sectarian." Theism also meant that religion would permeate a Princeton education in ways mere chapel observance could not. In the same speech Patton proclaimed, "When an Episcopalian comes to us and is under the supervision of his rector on Sunday, he shall not hear a philosophy taught him on Monday that undermines his faith in God. We mean that he shall have the universe opened to his view and that he shall deal with the facts and problems of life under theistic conceptions; this is something more than daily prayers in chapel, though we shall have them, too."[11] Harnessing the momentum of theism's heyday, Princeton

10. Patton was eager to avoid any appearance of academic stricture in this institutional commitment to theism. When Woodrow Wilson was elected professor of political economy and jurisprudence in 1890, Patton was plainly embarrassed to have to apprise him of criticisms he had heard of Wilson's published work. "Two or three parties" had complained "that in your discussion of the origin of the state you minimise the supernatural, & make such unqualified application of the doctrine of naturalistic evolution" — note well the qualifier — as to slight the hand of Providence and the reforming influence of Christianity. "I do not mention these matters as expressing my own judgment," Patton hastened to add; but he felt it his duty to inform Wilson of the scruples of the trustees. "They would not regard with favour such a conception of academic freedom or teaching as would leave in doubt the very direct bearing of historical Christianity as a revealed religion upon the great problems of civilization." He expressed hope that Wilson would appreciate Patton's responsibility, pardon the intrusion, "and put the proper interpretation upon my motive." *The Papers of Woodrow Wilson,* vol. 6, 1888-1890, ed. Arthur S. Link (Princeton: Princeton University Press, 1969), pp. 526-27. I am indebted to Dr. Link for bringing this letter to my attention. I differ with his reading of it, however: he saw it as a clampdown by Patton on evolutionism, a religious stricture on academic freedom; I see it as confirmation of Patton's distaste for any religious patrolling of scholars' views once a common foundation in theism (and thus supernaturalism) was secured. Cf. Marsden, *Soul,* p. 220.

11. Patton, in "Speech of Prof. Francis L. Patton, D.D., LL.D., President-Elect of Princeton College, at the Annual Dinner of the Princeton Club of New York, March 15, 1888" (pamphlet, PTS Special Collections), p. 5.

under Patton would become less distinctly Presbyterian but, he hoped, more pervasively religious.[12]

George Marsden, examining Patton's administration in light of larger trends in higher education, has observed that the college in the 1890s occupied "a peculiar hybrid position" in that it attempted "to maintain a national atmosphere congenial to Christian faith, without establishing particular Christian tenets." This was peculiar in light of the college's distinctly Presbyterian identity just a dozen years before Patton, and also because Patton made conservative Princeton look remarkably like the liberal Protestantism that reigned at most other schools. Marsden pulls no punches, calling it a "functional Unitarianism" — which, in view of the epigraph to this chapter, is a rather ringing condemnation.[13]

In any case, with Patton's theism as their philosophical fundament, the college's faculty of Bright Young Men took active part in the development of their various disciplines under the leitmotif of evolution. In biology and geology Princeton men gained special prominence. William Berryman Scott's evolutionary textbook, *An Introduction to Geology* (1897), became a standard in colleges across the country, passing through many editions over the next two decades. The student fossil expeditions grew in size and scope; in 1896 Scott sent out the first of several expeditions to Patagonia, which brought back enough prize finds of tertiary mammals to fill eight published volumes.[14] Scott's classmate, colleague, and close friend Henry Fairfield Osborn left Princeton in 1891 for a joint appointment as professor of comparative anatomy at Columbia University and curator of vertebrate paleontology at the American Museum of Natural History. There he enjoyed a position of enormous popular and scholarly influence, with huge sums of money at his disposal — making the museum one of the world's best, planning the Bronx Zoo, sending fossil expeditions around the world, and publishing

12. Repeating this theme at his inauguration, Patton urged that opportunities for formal worship were "not enough," for they served only those students already inclined toward religion. "There should be a distinct, earnest, purposeful effort to show *every man* who enters our College Halls the grounds for entertaining those fundamental religious beliefs that are the common heritage of the Christian world." Theism thus would serve even an evangelistic function. Patton, "Inauguration of President Patton" (1888), p. 43, emphasis mine.

13. Marsden, *Soul*, p. 221.

14. William Berryman Scott, *Some Memories of a Palaeontologist* (Princeton: Princeton University Press, 1939), p. 224.

profusely.[15] In Princeton's School of Philosophy — focal point of Mc-Cosh's hopes for shaping the American mind — James Mark Baldwin (class of 1884 and professor from 1893 to 1903) pioneered empirical research in physiological psychology, having studied under W. M. Wundt in Leipzig. In 1894 he founded the pathbreaking *Psychological Review.* Also in that year he published *Mental Development in the Child and the Race,* tracing the "evolution" of the ethical self in children. Baldwin's best-known work, *Social and Ethical Interpretations in Mental Development* (1897), continued the theme, using what he called "the Darwinian account" to connect the development of the individual conscience to the social evolution of morality — explaining the origin of ethics as a natural adjustment to the environment.[16] On the basis of Pattonian theism, then, Princeton not only tolerated but took active part in the proliferation of evolutionisms in the 1890s.

When McCosh died in 1894, Patton extolled his predecessor's wisdom in handling the potentially destructive evolution question, affirming with him that as an explanation of the origin of species, evolution was neither necessarily atheistic nor irreconcilable with the Bible.[17] When the college celebrated its sesquicentennial anniversary in 1896, officially changing its name to Princeton University, a guest lecturer from the Netherlands traced man's ancestry back to the tarsier, a tiny prosimian[18] — while Patton, with no sense of dissonance, endorsed economics professor Winthrop More Daniels's statement that the new university "stands for a theistic metaphysic."[19]

15. Scott, *Some Memories,* pp. 220-21; Ronald Rainger, *An Agenda for Antiquity: Henry Fairfield Osborn and Vertebrate Paleontology at the American Museum of Natural History, 1890-1935* (Tuscaloosa: University of Alabama Press, 1991).

16. Cynthia Eagle Russett, *Darwin in America: The Intellectual Response, 1865-1912* (San Francisco: W. H. Freeman, 1976), pp. 114-16. Baldwin based his theories on experiments he conducted on his two young daughters — granddaughters, through their mother, of Princeton Seminary's Old Testament professor William Henry Green.

17. Francis Landey Patton, "James McCosh: A Baccalaureate Sermon," *PRR* 6 (1895): 658.

18. The lecturer was A. A. W. Hubrecht, professor of zoology at Utrecht and recipient of an honorary degree at the sesquicentennial. The seminary's journal was not persuaded by Hubrecht's account of human ancestry, but did not dispute the propriety of his lecture as part of the university's celebration. Short notice of *The Descent of the Primates,* by A. A. W. Hubrecht, *PRR* 9 (1898): 780-82.

19. Francis Landey Patton, "Religion and the University," in *Memorial Book of the Sesquicentennial Celebration of the Founding of the College of New Jersey and of the Ceremonies*

Princeton Seminary, to an even greater degree than the college, experienced a momentous changing of the guard around 1890. Its small faculty suffered four deaths in close succession: systematic theologian A. A. Hodge at the end of 1886, church historian James Clement Moffat in 1888, New Testament scholar Caspar Wistar Hodge in 1891, and apologist Charles Augustus Aiken in 1892. With Patton's departure to the college, the total loss came to five men in as many years — five men out of seven. To replenish its ranks the seminary hired six new professors, all alumni from the Battle Plan years: systematic theologian Benjamin Breckinridge Warfield (College of New Jersey, Class of '71; Princeton Theological Seminary, Class of '76), Old Testament archeologist John D. Davis (CNJ '79, PTS '83), New Testament scholar George Tybout Purves (PTS '76), church historian John DeWitt (CNJ '61, PTS '64), apologist William Brenton Greene Jr. (CNJ '76, PTS '80), and biblical theologian Geerhardus Vos (PTS '85). Each new member of the faculty had received careful philosophical grounding at Princeton: Warfield, Purves, and Greene as undergraduates under McCosh and Atwater; Davis and Vos as seminarians under Patton; DeWitt under Atwater at both the college and the seminary. Each took theology from Charles or A. A. Hodge, and (except for DeWitt) apologetics from Charles Aiken. This was the crowning group of Bright Young Men, the theological culmination of Princeton's united front to "mold the age."[20]

Warfield, brilliant and energetic scion of a Kentucky family distinguished in both politics and religion, successor at age thirty-six to the revered chair of the Hodges, led the new vanguard confidently into a bright future. It was he, together with senior professor William Henry Green, who selected the rest of the new cohort.[21] Within a few years of his ar-

---

Inaugurating Princeton University (New York: Charles Scribner's Sons, 1898), p. 38. Daniels's statement is worth quoting in full: "While not denominational, Princeton is definitely and irrevocably committed to Christian ideals. It has, therefore, with reference to certain primary problems already taken a definite position. It stands for a theistic metaphysic. Nor does it claim or desire any reputation for impartiality or open mindedness which is to be purchased by a sacrifice of this, its traditional philosophical attitude. The motto of the new University is that of the old College — *Dei sub numine viget* — under God's guidance it flourishes." Winthrop More Daniels, "Princeton after One Hundred and Fifty Years," *Review of Reviews* 14 (1896): 449-50.

20. *Biographical Catalogue of Princeton Theological Seminary,* vol. 1, 1815-1932, comp. Edward Howell Roberts (Princeton: Trustees of the Seminary, 1933).

21. The Warfield MSS, PTS Special Collections, include many letters pertaining to the

rival in Princeton Warfield founded a new theological quarterly, the *Presbyterian and Reformed Review* (1890-1902), as a platform for the seminary's implementation of the Battle Plan.[22] In the pages of this journal and its successor, the *Princeton Theological Review* (1903-29), the theologians of Princeton and a cadre of like-minded contributors dutifully and painstakingly assessed an astonishing number of the leading books of the day. The reviews and short notices in those volumes, filling page after page in fine print, chronicled the theological and philosophical output of two generations of scholars in Europe and America, in several languages — a vivid demonstration of the Princeton theologians' commitment to currency in scholarship. Typically the reviewers took the opportunity to mark the underlying philosophical ground of the works before them and to point out certain logical entailments for biblical Christianity and Calvinistic orthodoxy. No better single example exists to show the tenacity of Princeton's Battle Plan to "watch, detect, and expose" fundamental principles.[23]

Warfield conceived the journal's "Reviews of Recent Literature" section as much more than a hodgepodge of sundry book notices. He structured the section carefully, according to a scheme of theological encyclopedia he apparently worked out with Patton and the new college librarian, E. C. Richardson.[24] Apologetical theology came first, as the

---

calls to Princeton of DeWitt, Greene, and Purves. The calls of Vos and Davis were presumably left to William Henry Green alone.

22. Previously the Princetonian theologians had worked with Charles A. Briggs of Union Theological Seminary, New York, on the *Presbyterian Review,* a joint organ of the reunited Old and New School branches of the Presbyterian church. But disagreements over biblical inerrancy and confession revision led to a falling out. Now Warfield chose his company, building a network of men dedicated to the Reformed doctrines but crossing denominational lines. See Lefferts A. Loetscher, *The Broadening Church: A Study of Theological Issues in the Presbyterian Church since 1869* (Philadelphia: University of Pennsylvania Press, 1954). Warfield cultivated working relationships with intellectual leaders in the Reformed Church of America, the Christian Reformed Church, the Southern Presbyterian Church (PCUS), the Presbyterian Church of New Zealand, and various Calvinistic denominations in Great Britain. In this he followed a precedent set by the early Reformed councils: the Pan-Presbyterian Council, the World Alliance of Reformed Churches, and the Evangelical Alliance. Here we see the beginnings of what we might call a conservative alter-ecumenism, an interesting sister movement to the liberal one, and one having important bearing later on the transdenominational fundamentalist movement.

23. See the bibliography, section 3, for a selected list of articles and reviews.

24. Ernest Cushing Richardson to Warfield, 12 April 1895 (Warfield MSS). At this time Warfield was writing articles on the structure of theological science. See especially "The

fundament of all that followed; then exegetics and historics, the gatherers of theological data; then systematic theology to synthesize the whole; followed by practical theology, the application of religious truth in the business of living. Last came general literature — novels, secular histories, and other miscellaneous material.[25] This purposeful articulation represented more than a love of order; it manifested Princeton's view of its review effort as a step toward building an encyclopedic theological science highly conscious of its philosophical structure. Following Patton, Warfield measured the foundations in order to build.

The 1890s were the glory days of Princeton Seminary, when enrollment burgeoned, a new dormitory was erected, fellowships for European study were endowed, and the Presbyterian church looked to Princeton for a sure guide in the brave new world of modern thought.[26] With its fresh, young faculty Princeton Seminary answered the call. The decade saw a tempestuous series of General Assemblies at which the distinctives of "Princeton theology" triumphed, becoming established doctrine in the church, thanks to a combination of scholarly efforts and careful maneuvering in church politics.[27] It was Princeton's chance to lead decisively, and Warfield and company rose to the occasion to mold their age,

Idea of Systematic Theology" (1896), in his *Studies in Theology,* in *The Works of Benjamin B. Warfield,* ed. Ethelbert D. Warfield et al., vol. 9 (New York: Oxford University Press, 1932; Grand Rapids: Baker, 1991), p. 74, where Warfield offers a chart of that structure.

25. A division called "Philosophical Literature" sometimes appeared just before "General Literature," as a kind of prolegomenon in the secular realm paralleling the place of apologetics in the theological realm. In 1903 that section moved to the forefront, before apologetics, completing the development of a philosophically articulated review effort. At this time Patton moved to the presidency of the seminary and Warfield ceded the *Presbyterian and Reformed Review* to the faculty, renaming it the *Princeton Theological Review.* Patton's inaugural address as president of the seminary marked the culmination of this movement toward systematization. Patton, "Theological Encyclopaedia," in *Biblical and Theological Studies, by the Members of the Faculty of Princeton Theological Seminary* (New York: Charles Scribner's Sons, 1912), pp. 1-34.

26. Warfield's correspondence contains many letters urging the Princetonians to fight the good fight on behalf of all evangelical Christians, naming Warfield and William Henry Green as special champions. See for example W. C. Stitt to Warfield, 2 January 1894, Warfield MSS, PTS Special Collections.

27. A major theme of Loetscher's history of the Presbyterian church is "the struggles whereby the Church first accepted [in the 1890s] and later rejected [in the 1920s] the Princeton attitude toward the Bible" and, indeed, toward all theology (*The Broadening Church,* p. 21). Loetscher's little book is still the best source for the complicated story of church-political wranglings in that period.

building on the foundation of Pattonian theism. There, as at the college, the Princetonians sought to combine the insights of evolution, so far as they deemed them true, with their religious precommitments. But unlike the college, the seminary did so with a specialist's eye to the peculiar concerns of confessional Calvinistic orthodoxy. The mix proved a very interesting one.

Theological Orthogenesis

With the hiring of Geerhardus Vos in 1892, Princeton Seminary made an explicit, curricular commitment to study Holy Writ under the category of historical development. Vos came not to fill a vacancy but to inaugurate and define a new chair, the professorship of biblical theology — or, as Vos himself preferred to think of his subject, "the History of Revelation."[28] An interest in the Bible's organic nature and structure had characterized the work of William Henry Green, and even that of seminary founder Archibald Alexander before him,[29] but not until the 1890s, with that decade's atmosphere of intense interest in all things evolutionary, did the seminary have the mind or the resources to devote a chair to it. At his inaugural exercises, following the customary and very serious public signing of the form of subscription to uphold Westminster orthodoxy, Vos delivered an address charting his concept of the new chair: "The Idea of Biblical Theology as a Science and as a Theological Discipline."

Vos's articulation of his subject combined the idea of the fixity of truth with the idea of temporal flux in a way that affirmed both ortho-

28. Geerhardus Vos, "The Idea of Biblical Theology as a Science and as a Theological Discipline" (1894), in *Redemptive History and Biblical Interpretation: The Shorter Writings of Geerhardus Vos,* ed. Richard B. Gaffin (Phillipsburg, N.J.: P&R, 1980), p. 21.

29. Marion Ann Taylor, *The Old Testament in the Old Princeton School (1812-1929)* (San Francisco: Mellen Research University Press, 1992), p. 266. Green made clear his commitment to study the Old Testament as "the gradual communication of divine truth. The revelation of God was, after the analogy of most of his works, progressive. . . . It was first the blade, then the ear, then the full corn in the ear." In view of that, the proper method of studying God's progressive revelation in the Bible was to consider each divine communication "separately in its order and considering the time of its unfolding and the place it holds in the gradual advance." "Discourses at the Inauguration of the Rev. William Henry Green, as Professor of Biblical and Oriental Literature in the Theological Seminary at Princeton, N.J., Delivered at Princeton, September 30, 1851, Before the Directors of the Seminary" (Philadelphia: C. Sherman, 1851), pp. 56-57. PTS Special Collections.

doxy and development. The science of biblical theology, he said, dealt with "revelation in the active sense, as an act of God" — and as any science was defined not by the whim of the investigator but by the nature of its object,[30] this science followed the features of God's revealing acts, foremost of which was *historical progress.* "God has not communicated to us the knowledge of the truth as it appears in the calm light of eternity to His own timeless vision. He has not given it in the form of abstract propositions logically correlated and systematized. . . . The self-revelation of God is a work covering ages, proceeding in a sequence of revealing words and acts, appearing in a long perspective of time. The truth comes in the form of growing truth, not truth at rest."[31] Here was an expressly developmental view of Scripture, yet one that preserved its supernatural, personal-revelatory character. Vos taught that God gave us this "growing truth, not truth at rest" as an accommodation to human finitude, a condescension to our ability to appropriate truth only gradually. More important, he said, was the fact that God was redeeming the world in a gradual, progressive way.[32] Vos thus aimed to locate revelation, like redemption, in human history — in the stream of development — showing God to have spoken and acted in this world, but from above.

This biblical theology emphasized both the *variety* in Scripture — variety in authorship, literary form, time and place, and phenomenology (oracles, dreams, events, preachings) — and the traditional idea of overarching scriptural *unity.* Vos connected the two by means of the growth analogy, defining his science as "the exhibition of the organic progress of supernatural revelation in its historic continuity and multiformity."[33] From the first seed of promise in Eden, when God foretold a "seed of the woman" who would crush the serpent's head, through God's covenant with Abraham to make of him a great nation and to bless all the peoples

---

30. This declaration itself sounded a ringing objectivism. Vos confirmed it in saying that the classification of the sciences "has to follow the great lines by which God has mapped out the immense field of the universe," calling them "God-drawn lines of distinction." Yet this very objectivism allowed Vos to say that the various sciences *grew up* by *law.* The rise of biblical theology in the late 1700s "was not a matter of mere accident, nor the result of definite agreement among theologians; the immanent law of the development of the science, as rooted in its origin, has brought it about in a natural manner." Vos, "Idea of Biblical Theology," pp. 4-5.

31. Vos, "Idea of Biblical Theology," p. 7.

32. Vos, "Idea of Biblical Theology," pp. 8, 12.

33. Vos, "Idea of Biblical Theology," pp. 13-14.

of the world, through the Mosaic law, through the promise to David of a descendant who would reign forever, through the great prophecies of a suffering servant and a coming kingdom, God's revelation of his plan to redeem the world grew and grew, until in the New Testament it burst into bloom with the coming of Christ, his atoning death, and his glorious resurrection. Like a plant, God's plan of redemption sprouted, grew, and blossomed, a wonder of unfolding complexity and beauty. As a flower buds and opens only after a long period of development in roots and stalk, so the slow growth of revelation, spanning centuries under the Old Testament, suddenly flowered in the New Testament in the space of one generation. And as the drive of development stops after the plant produces flower and fruit, so after the completion of the New Testament, revelation ceased.[34] Here was a panorama of unfolding redemption worthy of the nineteenth century's attraction to organicism.

But this analogy of organic growth, so strongly suited to fashionable notions, remained inherently conservative. As Peter Bowler has observed in contrasting the evolutionisms of Chambers and Darwin, the growth analogy meant precisely the opposite of randomness: it meant the unfolding of a predetermined plan, development according to design.[35] Vos espoused a "perfect germ" theory of the history of revelation: while the fullness of divine redemption appeared only slowly, over long centuries, the early stages of its growth represented not imperfect strivings in need of correction, but partial adumbrations of the whole. History did not mean relativity or imperfection, when it came to the activities of God. The fact that revelation came in stages did not mean it moved from untruth to truth. For it was God who did the revealing, following the plan of his own good counsel, just as it was God who made things in nature grow according to an inner principle. The sapling and the mature tree were both perfect in their stages. The analogy to growth fit beautifully; Vos even claimed it was the only way the two great facts of Scripture — divine perfection and historical process — could be reconciled.[36]

---

34. Vos, "Idea of Biblical Theology," p. 13.

35. Peter J. Bowler, *The Non-Darwinian Revolution: Reinterpreting a Historical Myth* (Baltimore: Johns Hopkins University Press, 1988), pp. 11-13.

36. Vos, "Idea of Biblical Theology," pp. 10-11. "The truth of revelation, if it is to retain its divine and absolute character at all, must be perfect from the beginning. Biblical Theology deals with it as a product of a supernatural divine activity, and is therefore bound by its own principle to maintain the perfection of revealed truth in all its stages. When, nevertheless, Biblical Theology also undertakes to show how the truth has been gradu-

But mere tactical considerations did not drive Vos to assume an analogy otherwise foreign to the Scripture. Vos found a principle of organic growth in the Bible's teaching itself: not only in the diachronic unfolding of the covenant promises, but in the very process by which God said he was redeeming a sinful cosmos under Christianity. God did not disassemble the world and mechanically fix one part after another, Vos argued; rather, God had chosen to work redemption in a vital way, by "creating within the organism of the present world the center of the world of redemption, and then organically building up the new order of things around this center." The incarnation brought Christ into the world; his church as his body continued and widened this presence, and would go on doing so until its leaven worked through the whole world order. Princeton's postmillennialism thus formed another plank in its developmentalist platform.[37]

This theological growth analogy can be viewed as another application of the Battle Plan to "seize and master the weapons of attack." No doubt the Princetonians saw it that way. Vos took the very fact that the Bible had a history — a fact the liberals used increasingly to mitigate scriptural claims to absolute authority — and, by way of analogy to organic development, made the temporal process of revelation a witness instead to its perfection. This was no attempt at *proving* the Bible's authority; rather, Vos *assumed* it on the basis of theistic and Christian precommitments, and said so. Still, he did regard this work as an effective antidote to what the Princetonians called "destructive criticism" of the Bible — exemplified by the documentary hypothesis of Wellhausen and Kuenen — which, Vos said, served to *dis*organize rather than organize the Scripture. Biblical theology, by showing the organic history of revelation, revealed the destructiveness of destructive criticism. People would be enabled to see its effects and reject it. Vos was proud of this strategy: it went beyond mere negative defense to a positive assertion

---

ally set forth in greater fullness and clearness, these two facts can be reconciled in no other way than by assuming that the advance in revelation resembles the organic process, through which out of the perfect germ the perfect plant and flower and fruit are successively produced."

37. Vos, "Idea of Biblical Theology," p. 12. Note here a radical difference between Princeton's traditional Calvinist view of cosmic redemption and the cataclysmic, distinctly antidevelopmental view of premillennial fundamentalism. See David N. Livingstone, "Evolution, Eschatology and the Privatization of Providence," *Science and Christian Belief* 2 (1990): 117-30.

of truth, and it enabled him, rather than his opponents, to set the theological agenda.[38]

Whether by way of direct influence or by some other route, other Princetonians took up the themes Vos sketched in his inaugural and applied them to current theological contests so as to make the development of the Bible serve the cause of orthodoxy. George T. Purves, Princeton's new professor of New Testament, even used the phrase "the evolution of revelation" to describe God's working "through human media the perfect disclosure of saving truth."[39] Melancthon W. Jacobus Jr., CNJ '77 (classmate of Scott and Osborn) and PTS '81, professor at Hartford Theological Seminary, applied Vos's idea to a specific, hot topic in New Testament criticism. Delivering the Stone Lectures at Princeton Seminary in 1897-98, Jacobus turned evolution's guns on the leading thinker of New Testament "evolutionary criticism," Albrecht Ritschl.[40]

One of Ritschl's most famous contentions was that the teachings of Paul the apostle brought an influx of pagan Greek thinking into the early church, corrupting Jesus' simple gospel of dependence and sonship into a hybrid of religion and metaphysics. In Ritschl's view of the history of nascent Christianity, the developmental arrow pointed downward; Pau-

38. Vos, "Idea of Biblical Theology," p. 22. Biblical theology "thus meets the critical assaults, not in a negative way by defending point after point of the citadel, whereby no total effect is produced and the critics are always permitted to reply that they attack merely the outworks, not the central position of the faith; but in the most positive manner, by setting forth what the principle of revelation involves according to the Bible, and how one part of it stands or falls together with all the others." Vos believed the growth analogy to be taught in the Scripture itself; thus he believed he was building on the foundation of scriptural truth rather than treating the Bible in a way prescribed by the tactics of the enemy.

39. George Tybout Purves, review of *Messianic Prophecy,* by Edward Riehm, *PRR* 3 (1892): 554. "This book thus falls in line with the current method of viewing revelation. Its point of view is historical. It seeks the supernatural in the natural.... None can fail to be helped by thus realizing the evolution of revelation as God wrought through human media the perfect disclosure of saving truth. This broad view of prophecy forms, we think, a more cogent apologetic than that drawn from minute, specific predictions and in its light the character and work of the prophets become more intelligible." These last remarks parallel the nineteenth-century shift in emphasis from Paleyan to Owenian (idealist) evidences of design in natural theology. Cf. David N. Livingstone, "The Idea of Design: The Vicissitudes of a Key Concept in the Princeton Response to Darwin," *Scottish Journal of Theology* 37 (1984): 329-57.

40. The phrase "evolutionary criticism" is Jacobus's, not Ritschl's. Melancthon Williams Jacobus, *A Problem in New Testament Criticism,* Stone Lectures, 1897-98 (New York: Charles Scribner's Sons, 1900), p. 86.

line religion represented a historical line of theological development better characterized as retrogression than progress. It was a theory of degradation, of corruption of type — not of evolution in its usual upward sense. Ritschl's disciple, the enormously influential church historian Adolf von Harnack, carried his teacher's leading idea beyond the New Testament period, indicting the development of orthodoxy itself as a departure from the religion of Jesus. The whole line of doctrinal evolution, from Paul to Augustine to Calvin and beyond — especially the minutely detailed systems of the seventeenth-century "Protestant Scholastics" — represented the outgrowth of a corrupt impulse foreign to Jesus' gospel. Christians had squandered their religious energies on metaphysical squabbles over such abstruse topics as the essential relations among the persons of the Trinity and the mode of Christ's presence in the Eucharist. Harnack called for a definite break in this developmental line, a rejection of the history of doctrine as a sorry tale of degeneration. What was needed, he said, was a new Reformation to return the church to its pristine roots in what Ritschl called the *Lehre Jesu,* the simple, ethical, nondoctrinal teachings of Jesus.[41]

Jacobus limited his Stone Lectures to the New Testament problem Ritschl had introduced: the evolution of doctrine from Jesus to Paul. He did not deny the existence of differences between the two; instead he asked what *relation* they displayed. Did Paul's gospel stand "in developed line with that of Jesus"? If so, far from discrediting Paul, it showed him to be a true follower of his Lord, unfolding the potentialities in the perfect germ of Christ's teaching as the environmental pressures of New Testament church life required Paul to elaborate the gospel in terms of specific issues. Jacobus freely granted the development of Paul's theology over time from simple (the epistles to the Thessalonians) to complex (the prison epistles). The church's theological needs naturally grew in complexity as the seeds of Christ's teaching naturally sprouted into various interpretations, causing dissension. Equally naturally, the apos-

41. For full expositions of Ritschlism from an orthodox Reformed point of view, see Benjamin Breckinridge Warfield, *Perfectionism,* vol. 1, in *The Works of Benjamin B. Warfield,* ed. Ethelbert D. Warfield et al., vol. 7 (New York: Oxford University Press, 1931; Grand Rapids: Baker, 1991), and James Orr, *The Ritschlian Theology and the Evangelical Faith* (London: Hodder and Stoughton, 1897). Harnack's call to complete the Reformation suggests an interesting, perhaps surprising parallel to the defining impulse of Puritanism. Adolf von Harnack, *Lehrbuch der Dogmengeschichte,* 3 vols. (1886-90), translated into English as *History of Dogma,* 7 vols. (1896-99).

tles found themselves obliged to address the resultant controversies. "The development of the Church's needs made the development of the Apostle's thought inevitable," Jacobus asserted. The question was not whether differences existed between Jesus and Paul, or even whether those differences were the result of "evolution" following natural, scrutable causes. The real question, Jacobus argued, was what sort of development had taken place: an evolution "out of line with Christ," or "in line with Christ." If the doctrine of the New Testament developed legitimately from the perfect germ of Jesus' gospel, then its authority was vindicated. An evolution from a perfect germ, in response to environmental pressures, only demonstrated the organic unity of the growth.[42] And if God could effect his plans by natural means in the origin of species, he could do so just as well in the origin of Scripture, without in either case obliterating supernatural superintendence. "If evolution generally can be theistic and yet be evolutionary," Jacobus declared, "Apostolic development specifically can be inspirational and yet be developmental."[43]

B. B. Warfield employed a similar developmentalism in defining his specialty, systematic theology. A New Testament scholar until his call to Princeton in 1887, Warfield had hesitated to accept the chair of the Hodges because of the shift in departments it involved. When he did accept, he felt it his duty to define his new calling as carefully and consciously as possible, with an eye to its relations with the other seminary chairs. This project took several years, overlapping with Patton's interest in charting an up-to-date, philosophical distribution of the departments of theological science. Warfield made this inquiry the subject of his inaugural address at Princeton, "The Idea of Systematic Theology Con-

42. Jacobus, *Problem,* pp. 111-22, 138-41.

43. Jacobus, *Problem,* p. 104. Cf. this explanatory note from p. 122: "The position we have taken is simply that, starting, as the Apostle evidently did, with the essentials of his theology, the experiences of his mission work brought these essentials into such new expression as to constitute, upon the whole, a development of his theology. This, we believe, is what we naturally would expect of any man, and may therefore naturally be held to have been the case with Paul, even though he had to do with supernatural revelations of truth. God reveals his truth, even to inspired men, in accordance with their nature, and it is man's nature to develop his understanding of the truth which comes to him. This is also what we believe Paul's Epistles reveal."

Two decades later, seminary professor J. Gresham Machen would make a similar argument about Paul's true development of Jesus' teaching, in his first book, *The Origin of Paul's Religion* (New York: Macmillan, 1921).

sidered as a Science." After eight years of further consideration he published an expanded version in the *Presbyterian and Reformed Review*.[44]

If Warfield's subject coincided with Patton's interest in the philosophical division of theology, his treatment coincided with Vos's and Jacobus's use of the growth analogy in revelation. Warfield coupled the idea of *system* in theology — a static network of fixed relations — with the idea of historical *development*. This pairing was the essence of the growth analogy. Systematic theology, in Warfield's definition, was a philosophical discipline, investigating theological matters from a philosophical rather than a historical standpoint. Its goal was to discover not what people *held* to be true, but what *was* true, and to reduce those truths to order. But systematic theology, like biblical theology, developed progressively over time. The facts of Christian theology had lain within human reach since the close of the canon, Warfield said, but they awaited systematic arrangement at the hands of theologians. Before the close of the New Testament, progress had occurred in revelation itself, under divine inspiration, whether mediately or immediately. In the church age, progress occurred not in revelation but in the "intellectual realization and definition of the doctrines revealed." The resultant science was systematic theology, "slow but ever advancing" as the church progressively articulated the scriptural deposit of truth in philosophical form.[45]

Warfield did not use the word "evolution" to describe this process, but he freely used the language of development. Theology was an "organic growth," "the ripened fruit of the ages." Following the growth analogy, his guiding idea was not so much transmutation as addition —

44. Benjamin Breckinridge Warfield, "The Idea of Systematic Theology Considered as a Science" (pamphlet, New York: Anson D. F. Randolph Co., 1888), PTS Special Collections; "The Idea of Systematic Theology" (1896), in his *Studies in Theology*, pp. 49-87. Notes here refer to the latter publication. Warfield's other important efforts along this line include an introduction to Francis R. Beattie's *Apologetics; or, The Rational Vindication of Christianity*, vol. 1, *Fundamental Apologetics* (Richmond, Va.: Presbyterian Committee of Publication, 1903) and an article, "Apologetics," for the *New Schaff-Herzog Encyclopedia of Religious Knowledge*, ed. Samuel Macauley Jackson (New York: Funk and Wagnalls Co., 1908), 1:232-38, reprinted in his *Studies in Theology*, pp. 3-21. Patton taught the course "Theological Encyclopedia" at the seminary from 1882; his inaugural address as president of Princeton Seminary treated the same subject. See note 25 above.

45. Warfield, "Idea of Systematic Theology" (1896), pp. 51, 75. James Samuel McClanahan Jr., "Benjamin B. Warfield: Historian of Doctrine in Defense of Orthodoxy, 1881-1921" (Ph.D. diss., Union Theological Seminary, Richmond, Va., 1988), first alerted me to Warfield's progressionist view of church history.

building on the basis of prior growth. Once again we may observe the conservative nature of developmentalism. Progress for Warfield involved standing on the shoulders of past generations, building on truths already established. It was a matter of evolution as opposed to revolution. He thus could treat theological conservatism as the way of progress, and theological radicalism as progress's enemy — even likening theological radicals to flat-earthers.[46]

The seminary's theological uses of the growth analogy present a striking parallel to the evolutionisms of Princetonian scientists Scott, Osborn, and Baldwin in the same period. These three heirs of McCosh and Guyot led the so-called American School of neo-Lamarckism, whose chief interest, according to Bowler, was regularity and linearity; its starting point was the recapitulation theory of Haeckel and Huxley and the German idealists before them. For the Princetonians that interest makes perfect sense: they learned their *Naturphilosophie* at Princeton, straight from Arnold Guyot.[47] Scott and Osborn then pursued their European degrees in the classic fields of growth-analogy evolutionism: embryology and paleontology. Both of these fields focused on morphology, the comparative study of organic structures, as a means to elucidate the relationships among living things. They sought orderly relationships; their goal was to map those relationships in a family tree of life on earth. By background training and career focus Scott and Osborn were thus committed to the discovery of order in the

---

46. Warfield, "Idea of Systematic Theology" (1896), pp. 75-77. Note that Warfield did not use the phrase "perfect germ" to describe the development of doctrine. Though he carried a kind of developmentalism into the church age, he insisted on a fundamental disjunction between biblical and postbiblical times. The "perfect germ" analogy worked in biblical theology precisely because God was the ultimate author of Scripture as well as of nature — but in the church age, God did not inspire theologians; their writings, unlike the Bible, were not infallible. This disjunction was the Princetonians' key point of contention against Harnack and his followers. Warfield made a similar disjunction concerning miracles; see his *Counterfeit Miracles,* Smyth Lectures for 1917-18 (New York: Charles Scribner's Sons, 1918). Cf. David B. Calhoun, *Princeton Seminary,* 2 vols. (Edinburgh: Banner of Truth Trust, 1994, 1996), 2:101-2, pointing out that A. A. Hodge argued *against* Charles Briggs's attempt to describe the history of the Reformed confessions as a pattern of developmental evolution. Briggs was using growth-analogy evolutionary language to justify doctrinal revision — quite the opposite of Princeton's use of the imagery.

47. James McCosh, too, was fascinated by the parallel between ontogeny (embryological growth) and phylogeny (the family tree of the animal kingdom) even in his preevolutionist days, citing Goethe by name. McCosh, "Is the Development Hypothesis Sufficient?" *Popular Science Monthly* 10 (1876): 98.

history of life on earth. No wonder Princeton's philosophers and theologians found it easy to fit theism with evolutionism.[48]

The hallmark of Lamarckism was the link between adaptation and evolution by way of the inheritance of acquired characters. In the classic example, giraffes stretched their necks to reach higher branches and passed this beneficial adaptation to their offspring; after many generations the cumulative effect was the extraordinarily long neck of the modern giraffe. The Lamarckian view appealed to those thinkers who sought purpose in nature, for if it detracted from the idea of an overarching plan of life on earth, at least it preserved purpose in the form of adaptation by each species to its situation.[49] By contrast the Darwinian view not only negated the overall plan, it also negated adaptation as such: what looked like clever adaptation was only happenstance. The organism had not responded to the environment; it had only changed by chance mutation, and those changes happened to line up advantageously with the environment. The element of mutation just described, however, characterizes today's post-Mendelian Darwinism; a century ago genetic theory had not yet linked up with Darwinian natural selection, and the big question was what Cope called "the origin of the fittest." Committed to transmutation, evolutionists were in search of a mechanism. Darwin gave natural selection, but whence the varieties contending for selection? The Lamarckian inheritance of acquired characters was one answer.

But the American School, and the Princetonians in particular, were more interested in overarching linear trends than in a host of particular adaptations. They mingled their Lamarckism with "orthogenesis," a theory of goal-directed change by an inner principle of growth, in keeping with the recapitulation theory. What Lamarckism and orthogenesis had in common was the idea of variation as an *addition* to growth rather than a *disruption* of growth — a point most welcome to theists for its regularity, and to conservatives for its affirmation of the past. On the other hand, Lamarckism and orthogenesis were polar opposites on the matter of adaptation. Lamarckism was all about response to the environment, or adaptive variation, while orthogenesis rendered the environment almost adventitious, for change was directed by a principle within. Ortho-

48. Peter J. Bowler, *The Eclipse of Darwinism: Anti-Darwinian Evolution Theories in the Decades around 1900* (Baltimore: Johns Hopkins University Press, 1983), chapter 6.

49. In this respect Lamarckism has more in common with "Paleyan design" than with "idealist design."

genetic variation followed linear patterns even when nonadaptive. The curious combination of two partially opposing theories marked the American School; what set it apart from "normal" European neo-Lamarckism was the admixture of orthogenetic ideas.[50] In fact, Bowler argues, the orthogenetic element was more fundamental to their conception than Lamarckism ever was. August Weissmann sounded the death knell of Lamarckism with his famous experiment cutting off the tails of generations of mice, who stubbornly continued to produce young with tails. In Weissmann's wake the Princetonians returned, tellingly, to theories more distinctly orthogenetic, willing to give up adaptationism but not their original interest in patterns, regularity, and linearity.[51]

This mixture of adaptationism with a more basic linearism is just what we have found in the new generation of Princeton theologians in the 1890s. Vos spoke forcefully of the development of the Bible's theology from a perfect germ — a plainly orthogenetic image. Jacobus appealed to a changing religious environment in the years of Paul's ministry to explain the apostle's development of Jesus' teaching, all the while interpreting that change as an unfolding of the potentialities inherent in Jesus' message — thus mingling a theory of adaptation to environment with a perfect germ theory. Warfield treated the growth of systematic theology in a similar way. Did the Princeton theology borrow from the evolutionism of the university? Or did the scientists at the university borrow from — or worse, were they constrained by — the seminary? No line of direct influence (much less of constraint) is visible, nor is it particularly necessary to go looking for one. The easiest explanation is the common root in Guyot and McCosh, masters at whose feet both sets of Princeton's Bright Young Men had sat.[52]

---

50. Bowler, *The Eclipse of Darwinism,* pp. 118-20.

51. Scott insisted throughout his long career in paleontology that evolution was goal directed, though after 1894 he was agnostic as to the mechanism. In an attempt to revitalize Lamarckism, Osborn and Baldwin codeveloped a theory of "organic selection" that focused on the role of habit in evolution — it came to be known as the "Baldwin effect." Osborn then turned to a purely orthogenetic theory of brute evolution and worked on it for decades, intent on disproving "the nightmare of Darwinism" (Bowler's phrase) with a demonstration of evolution's regularity. True to his training under McCosh and Guyot, he retained the Baldwin effect as a mental/spiritual factor in human evolution. Baldwin broke with Osborn, converted to Darwinism proper, and promptly left Princeton (1902). Bowler, *The Eclipse of Darwinism,* pp. 130-32; Baldwin, *Between Two Wars, 1861-1921,* 1:69-70; Russett, *Darwin in America,* pp. 114-20.

52. Bowler seems not to have fully realized the importance of Princeton in the American School. The three leaders he names (after Cope and Hyatt) are all Princetonians

"The Naturalistic Evolution of Belief"

There was a certain irony in Princeton's participation in the heyday of theism after Darwin. When Darwin's theory lent scientific prestige and empirical weight to the philosophical denial of natural theology, the Princetonians countered with improved theistic arguments, thanking the opposition for this opportunity to perfect their metaphysical foundations. In their view, theism entered its golden age only in the nineteenth century, thanks in fact to Hume and Kant and Darwin.[53] But an irony lay in this new assertion of the value of natural theology, for one of the seminary's founding purposes was to *restrict* its sphere.

Fifty years before the start of the Darwinian controversies, Princeton Seminary's founders identified the chief enemy of evangelical Christianity as the exclusively "natural religion" of the deists, represented in America by such shining patriots as Thomas Jefferson, Ethan Allen, and Thomas Paine.[54] Allen's *Reason the Only Oracle of Man* (1784) and Jefferson's literal excision of all supernatural elements from his Bible exemplified the core belief of deism: the all-sufficiency of reason in religion, the subjection of revelation to the bar of rationality. The deists anathematized all dreary talk of human moral inability, for in their view it demeaned noble aspira-

---

(Scott, Osborn, and Baldwin), yet he attributes their interest in linearity to the indirect influence of Agassiz's *Naturphilosophie* by way of Cope (*The Eclipse of Darwinism*, p. 131) — apparently unaware of the Princetonians' direct link to German idealism via their own professor of geology, Arnold Guyot. Guyot's role only confirms Bowler's interpretation of the American School as fundamentally orthogenetic. Cf. my exposition of Guyot's developmentalism in chapter 1 above.

53. William Brenton Greene Jr., "Outline Syllabus on Apologetics and Evidences of Christianity," from notes by Frank W. Hill (n.p.: Hill and Roddy, 1894), p. 5, pamphlet, PTS Special Collections.

54. The seminary's Plan specified that by the end of his three-year course each student "must have read and digested the principal arguments and writings relative to what has been called the deistical controversy. — Thus will he be qualified to become a defender of the Christian faith." "Report of a Committee of the General Assembly of the Presbyterian Church, Exhibiting the Plan of a Theological Seminary" (New York: Williams and Whiting, 1810), pp. 4, 14; Mark A. Noll, "The Founding of Princeton Seminary," *Westminster Theological Journal* 42 (1979): 80, 85-93. See also Lefferts A. Loetscher, *Facing the Enlightenment and Pietism: Archibald Alexander and the Founding of Princeton Theological Seminary* (Westport, Conn.: Greenwood Press, 1983). Learned polemics were not the founders' sole aim; their Plan also emphasized personal devotion and practical piety as the lifeblood of evangelical religion. They were seeking to avoid the excesses of revivalistic enthusiasm on the one hand and the dryness of rationalized religion on the other.

tions, lowered expectations of progress, and abetted moral lassitude. Doctrines of atoning sacrifice they rejected as gory superstition unworthy of the dignity and goodness of God. They emphasized instead the benignity and reasonableness of creation, basing all relationship with the Almighty on those grounds. Deism restricted religion to the created order, bidding people to approach their Maker simply as his reasonable and able creatures. For them, "nature's religion" alone was true religion.

To the evangelicals, however, deism represented natural theology run amok. Against its natural gospel they reasserted the primacy of "revealed religion," the gospel of salvation in Christ known only through the Scriptures. Against a religion based solely on the universal principles of the created order, they asserted the need for a supernatural salvation wrought in particular historical events, especially the incarnation, crucifixion, and resurrection of Jesus Christ. Where the deists worshiped only the Creator of nature, the evangelicals worshiped also the Redeemer of history. To them natural theology was important, but not sufficient; indeed, it served only to give sinful man a knowledge of the Creator from whom he was, in natural terms, hopelessly estranged. Natural theology was sufficient to condemn, but insufficient to save.[55]

But common enmity makes strange bedfellows, and the destructive arguments of Hume and Kant against the theistic proofs threw the evangelicals in with the deists on behalf of natural theology. Decades later, Darwin's so-called coup de grâce only intensified theistic study, with Princeton's evangelicals in the thick of it. Theism became, as we have seen, the watchword of the new university, its rallying point for religious commitment in the face of denominational diversity and its foundation for both philosophical and scientific study. Theism also served as the

---

55. See, for example, Charles Hodge, *Systematic Theology* (New York: Scribners, 1872-73; reprint, Grand Rapids: Eerdmans, 1993), 1:22-26, and Benjamin Breckinridge Warfield, "Mysticism and Christianity" (1917), in his *Studies in Theology*, p. 661. The classic text for the idea of natural theology is Rom. 1:18-23: "For the wrath of God is revealed from heaven against all ungodliness and unrighteousness of men, who hold the truth in unrighteousness; because that which may be known of God is manifest in them; for God hath shown it unto them. For the invisible things of him from the creation of the world are clearly seen, being understood by the things that are made, even his eternal power and Godhead; so that they are without excuse: because that, when they knew God, they glorified him not as God, neither were thankful; but became vain in their imaginations, and their foolish heart was darkened. Professing themselves to be wise, they became fools, and changed the glory of the incorruptible God into an image made like to corruptible man, and to birds, and fourfooted beasts, and creeping things" (KJV).

seminary's foundation for both the defense and the construction of a scientific theology.

But just as the Princetonians renewed and intensified their commitment to natural theology, their old enemy, natural religion, returned with a vengeance, strengthened by the fantastic successes of evolutionism in biology and geology. The fields of comparative religion and biblical criticism burgeoned in the 1890s, taking naturalistic development as their leading idea. The prestige of so-called Darwinism clearly bolstered this growth, but these evolutionisms sprang from independent sources dating back well before the *Origin of Species*. Darwin's evolutionism denied natural theology by denying the argument from design — but now this new set of evolutionisms, too often muddled together under Darwin's name, sought to explain religion itself in natural terms, that is, by means of natural development. Evolutionism thus attacked traditional natural theology but aggrandized natural religion, for not only did it occasion a revival of theistic study, it also offered a natural explanation of the religious impulse and its development, extending even to the rise of the Christian Scriptures. Far from destroying natural theology, evolution gave new and compelling force to natural religion, the extreme case of natural theology. It was the eighteenth-century battle all over again, B. B. Warfield observed; only this time natural religion enjoyed the enormous scientific prestige of evolution.[56]

The idea of tracing a natural history of religion harked back to the great positivists, Comte and Spencer, and was nothing especially new to the Princetonians. What was new and alarming was the emergence of such ideas in theological discourse itself. Late in the nineteenth century a barrage of religious-evolutionary theories, some by clerical authors, appeared in print, each duly analyzed and answered in Warfield's *Presbyterian and Reformed Review:* Friedrich Max Müller's *Natural Religion* (1889), Charles Chapman's *Preorganic Evolution and the Biblical Idea of God* (1891), James Macdonald's *Religion and Myth* (1893), Edward Caird's *Evolution of Religion* (1893), David Jayne Hill's *Genetic Philosophy* (1893), Otto Pfleiderer's *Philosophy and Development of Religion* (1894), William Mackintosh's *Natural History of the Christian Religion* (1894), Benjamin

---

56. Warfield, short notice of *"The Ascent of Man,"* p. 367. At a later date he commented, "The Unitarians must seem to themselves to be coming into their kingdom. All the world appears to be now of their way of thinking; the weapons of their warfare are forged to their hand in the traditional workshops of orthodoxy, and they scarcely need even to furbish them to fit them for their polemic." Benjamin Breckinridge Warfield, review of *The Historical Jesus and the Theological Christ,* by J. Estlin Carpenter, *Princeton Theological Review* 10 (1912): 508.

Kidd's *Social Evolution* (1894), and Allan Menzies' *History of Religion* (1895), to name some of the most prominent. Three of these authors (Müller, Caird, and Pfleiderer) enjoyed a dynastic hold on the prestigious Gifford Lectures in Scotland for five years running. With varying degrees of respect for Christianity — some quite high, some very low — these authors attempted to explain religion wholly within nature, by way of continuous development.

These works were highly speculative in character, their details varying considerably. Together, however, they offered the possibility of a composite rendering of religion in natural-developmental terms, a complete (if unpolished) alternative to the traditional biblical doctrines of humanity's origin and essential relations to God. In this respect they furthered Spencer's all-inclusive project of tracing the evolution of all things, from stardust to human society, arts, even religion. This emerging naturalistic and evolutionary alternative bid fair to transform Christian doctrine at several crucial points, replacing man's original innocence with primitive brutishness, his original knowledge of God with primitive superstition, and his fall with the dawn of moral consciousness — so that the "fall" of the orthodox was in fact a great leap forward for the evolutionist of religion. Monotheism developed from ghost-worship through stages of fetishism, animism, and polytheism. The religion of the Hebrews, slowly shedding its primitive conception of a capricious, vengeful God in need of placating by blood sacrifice, transcended itself in the ethical teachings of Jesus. Here was a thorough revolution in the meaning of the Bible. Morality and a high regard for spiritual goods remained intact — but the new story contradicted the system of evangelical religion at such cardinal points as the nature of divine revelation, the dilemma of sin and its cure, and the hope for society.[57]

57. The *PRR* contains many incisive reviews of works on the evolution of society and religion, giving a handy sketch of their arguments and especially of what Princeton found objectionable in them. Notable are the following: Benjamin Breckinridge Warfield, short notice of *Religion and Myth*, by James Macdonald, 4 (1893): 686-88; William Brenton Greene, review of *Natural Religion*, by Friedrich Max Müller, 5 (1894): 95-103; Daniel S. Gregory, review of *Christian Ethics*, by Newman Smyth, 5 (1894): 350-54; Greene, review of *The Evolution of Religion*, by Edward Caird, 6 (1895): 125-33; Henry Collin Minton, review of *The Ascent of Man*, by Henry Drummond, and of *Social Evolution*, by Benjamin Kidd, 6 (1895): 136-42; Warfield, review of *Natural History of the Christian Religion*, by William Mackintosh, 6 (1895): 507-22; George Macloskie, review of *Genetic Philosophy*, by David Jayne Hill, 6 (1895): 573-75; Greene, review of *The Ethics of the Old Testament*, by W. S. Bruce, 7 (1896): 724-25; Vos, review of *De Mozaische Oorsprung van de Wetten*, by Ph. J. Hoedemaker, 8 (1897): 106-9;

Many churchmen hoped to avoid a showdown between science and religion by finding broad commonalities between the spirit of Christianity and the emerging evolutionary view of religion. The most popular of these was Henry Drummond, professor of natural science at the Free Church College in Glasgow and a friend and onetime evangelistic coworker of D. L. Moody.[58] Drummond authored two wildly successful books applying evolutionary ideas to spiritual things: *Natural Law in the Spiritual World* (1883) and *The Ascent of Man* (1894). The former went through twenty-nine editions in ten years. The latter was less remunerative, but attracted wide notice for its attempt to baptize human evolution. Drummond declared it not just conceivable but "inevitable" that human minds arose "by natural genesis from the minds of the higher quadrumana" — but he also assured his audience that this shocking idea, far from unseating cherished Christian beliefs, actually enthroned them. All creation history drove toward the production of man's spiritual nature: far back in our beastly genealogy a spiritual principle, the "struggle for the life of others," began to grow, opposing the morally problematic reign of Darwin's "struggle for life." Altruism arose to counter individualism. Regard for others, in the form of regard for the species, checked regard for self. Evolution was not a tale of "nature red in tooth and claw," but, in Drummond's unabashed effusion, "a love-story."[59]

Drummond was deeply and consciously influenced by Spencer, as

George S. Patton, review of *Moral Evolution*, by George Harris, 8 (1897): 531-41; Greene, review of *An Introduction to the History of Religion*, by Frank Byron Jevons, 9 (1898): 136-39; and Minton, review of *Through Nature to God*, by John Fiske, 11 (1900): 149-52. In a review of *Personal and Social Evolution with the Key of the Science of History*, 1 (1890): 708, Charles Aiken, fed up even before the real blitz began, quipped, "Great is protoplasm, of which this volume is one of the latest and most typical evolutionary developments."

58. James R. Moore, "Evangelicals and Evolution: Henry Drummond, Herbert Spencer, and the Naturalisation of the Spiritual World," *Scottish Journal of Theology* 38 (1985): 383-417.

59. Henry Drummond, quoted in Minton, review of *The Ascent of Man*, p. 137. To make human evolution serve religion was to Drummond a thrilling coup. "If Evolution can be proved to include Man, the whole course of Evolution and the whole scheme of Nature from that moment assume a new significance. The beginning must then be interpreted from the end, not the end from the beginning. An engineering workshop is unintelligible until we reach the room where the completed engine stands. Everything culminates in that final product, is contained in it, is explained by it. The Evolution of Man is also the complement and corrective of all other forms of Evolution. From this height only is there a full view, a true perspective, a consistent world." Henry Drummond, *The Ascent of Man*, 14th ed. (New York: James Pott and Co., 1907), p. 9.

James R. Moore has shown. He set out to Christianize the great positivist's vision of social and religious evolution, something Princeton was certainly not predisposed to do. Yet Drummond's approach actually paralleled Princeton's, particularly Arnold Guyot's. *The Ascent of Man* began as a set of Lowell Lectures in Boston, as had Guyot's book *The Earth and Man* forty years earlier. Guyot and Drummond each presented a beatific vision of the organic and goal-directed connectedness of religion and nature. Each constructed a kind of loose evolutionary Butlerism,[60] showing in current scientific theories of development an "analogy of nature" to revealed religion. Each approached his topic in the spirit of romantic *Naturphilosophie*, articulating less a "proof" by correspondence than a plantedness, an organic unity of natural processes with religious truths — a poetic assurance of the full reality of Christianity by virtue of the fact that its cardinal truths structured not only moral but material reality. Each viewed natural history in profoundly teleological terms, the process finding its earthly culmination and meaning in humankind. What Guyot did with a developmental view of earth history, Drummond now did with the evolutionary theory of religion, giving looser rein to his creative imagination in order to complete the partial picture evolutionary biology had suggested.[61] Evolution was one in spirit with Christianity, for the gospel of love, the full bloom of humanity, was evolution's goal and culmination. "Up to this time no word has been spoken to reconcile Christianity with Evolution, or Evolution with Christianity. And why? Because the two are one. Through what does Evolution work? Through Love.... Evolution and Christianity have the same Author, the same end, the same spirit. ... No man can run up the natural lines of Evolution without coming to Christianity at the top."[62]

Drummond shared with Princeton not only a thoroughly develop-

---

60. Joseph Butler, *The Analogy of Religion, Natural and Revealed, to the Constitution and Course of Nature* (1736), was a standard text in nineteenth-century American colleges. On early Princetonian uses of Butler's antideistic tactics, see Loetscher, *Facing the Enlightenment*, pp. 57-58, 178.

61. "Evolution was given to the modern world out of focus," Drummond declared; by adjusting it to "the whole truth and reality of Nature and Man" he claimed to put the theory in focus for the first time (*The Ascent of Man*, p. vi). Notice Drummond's metaphysical affinity to the Princetonians: he agreed that evolutionism had furthered the materialistic truncation of reality. Like them, he was a metaphysical dualist. But to give due regard to the moral sphere Drummond proposed extending natural law (evolution) into the spiritual world, rather than fencing it in to the material realm.

62. Drummond, *The Ascent of Man*, p. 342.

mental view of evolution — something they both shared with Spencer — but a common strategy for the defense of the faith. He attempted to turn evolution to the service of religion, to hitch Christianity's cart to evolution's still-rising star: precisely the strategy Princeton had advocated in "seize and master" and had put into practice with regard to the development of species and even the development of Scripture.

But Princeton rejected Drummond's arguments, despite many points of commonality, because of metaphysical consequences the Princetonians felt sure would quickly undermine their whole system of theology and the gospel it was meant to elucidate.[63] It was one thing to read a spiritual tale of progress into the creation narrative, as Guyot and McCosh had done — that was a fairly easy task, given the story's sketchiness on scientific matters, its straightforwardly progressive structure, and its simple conclusion in the goodness of the created order. But after creation came the Fall: sin entered in and altered everything. In the expulsion from Eden human history began with a fundamental *discontinuity* from the natural order, a sharp break from natural goodness. Human nature was corrupt; it needed a cure *above* nature.[64] Drummond offered the evolution of altruism as a cure for an ecology "red in tooth and claw," thinking he had thereby cleared evolution of its conflict with divine goodness. Princeton's problem with evolution, however, concerned not nature but *grace* — not creation's natural benignity, but man's unnatural depravity and God's supernatural remedy. Drummond thus addressed the moral dilemma of evolution at the wrong point. He used evolution to vindicate the Creator's goodness — but what about the plight of the sinner who has despaired of attaining a righteousness of his own?[65]

63. Drummond tried to defend the faith "by showing that it could assimilate the doctrine of evolution," but "actually took his dialectic stand, not on Christianity, but on evolution," explained an unnamed reviewer for the *PRR*. In other words, he assimilated Christianity to evolution, rather than evolution to Christianity. "Christians must take their stand on the complete system of Christianity, and work out from that." Anonymous short notice (Warfield?) of *Pseudo-Philosophy at the End of the Nineteenth Century. I. An Irrationalist Trio; Kidd — Drummond — Balfour,* by Hugh Mortimer Cecil, *PRR* 8 (1897): 776.

64. Minton wrote, "Evolution made a wandering prodigal; it was a *revolution* that brought him back to his father's house." Minton, review of *The Ascent of Man,* p. 142, emphasis in original. On Minton's relation to PTS, see chapter 8, note 29, below.

65. George S. Patton (College of New Jersey, Class of '91, Princeton Theological Seminary, Class of '95), assistant professor of biblical instruction at Princeton University under his father's presidency, wrote, "If the Word was God, and if the Word was made flesh, if He was crucified, dead, and buried, and if He rose again from the dead — then it is hard to un-

Here the evolution-of-religion controversies did the gospel a favor, in Princeton's estimation, for they heightened the distinction between natural and revealed religion. This is what Warfield meant when he wrote that the problem the "newer religious thinking" posed to the church was nothing more than "the old eighteenth-century problem in a fresh form." What set revealed religion apart from natural religion was the *revelation* in the Bible of God's grace to sinners in Christ. Older issues in the relations of science and religion had turned Princeton's eyes to questions of underlying philosophy; now, in addition, theories rendering religion as a natural product of human development focused the spotlight on the Bible as the distinctive basis of Judaism and Christianity, setting them apart from all other religions. Other religions might pretend to be based on revelation, but only Old Testament Judaism and New Testament Christianity actually were. Other religions had, then, indeed evolved naturally;[66] Bible religion was the grand exception, and on the validity of Scripture's exclusive claim to divine inspiration the gospel of redeeming grace — grace unknown to nature, that "amazing grace" of sins forgiven by the atoning death of Christ — depended.[67]

In this way the evolution question helped to steer the Princeton theologians into their famous role as champions of the Bible in the 1890s, rejoining and escalating their oldest battle, the battle against deism.[68] Their concern over the evolution question now centered not on the alleged incompatibility of Genesis with geology — unlike most fundamentalistic antievolutionism and scientistic irreligion of the next century —

---

derstand how it is possible to reconcile this with evolution unless we eliminate from the ordinary antisupernaturalistic evolution of science as much of its essence as some modern apologists would eliminate from Christianity." Patton, review *Moral Evolution*, p. 539. Interestingly, young Patton was willing to concede Harris's arguments for human evolution, even the evolution of morality "through the other-regarding instincts," so long as the supernatural character of salvation and the teleological character of evolution were preserved (pp. 536-37).

66. Charles Augustus Aiken, "Lectures on the Relations of Philosophy and Science to the Christian Religion" (MS, ca. 1888, PTS Special Collections), Lecture 1.

67. William Henry Green gave this pithy expression of the Princetonian view: "The reality of the revelation assures the truth of the facts with which it is indissolubly linked." Green, review of *Christ and Criticism*, by Charles M. Mead, *PRR* 5 (1894): 168.

68. On Princeton Seminary's antideistic purpose, see Noll, "Founding of Princeton Seminary," pp. 72-110; "Plan of the Theological Seminary of the Presbyterian Church in the United States of America, Located at Princeton" (Elizabethtown, N.J.: Isaac A. Kollock, 1816), PTS Special Collections.

but on the unique nature of the gospel as a supernatural intrusion into the course of nature, a sequence of occurrences *in* history but *above* nature, restoring the relationship between the Creator and his estranged creatures. Such redemption, historical and yet supernatural, distinguished revealed religion (the gospel) from natural religion (deism old or new) — and it was revealed only in the Bible.

Developmentalism pervaded Princetonian discourse in the 1890s at both the university and the seminary, but it had its limits. The sense of secure foundations in "Christian theism" allowed the Princetonians to explore the explanatory value of evolution without fearing for their faith, but those very foundations drew a definite line beyond which evolutionary explanations were not allowed to go. As a series of secondary causes by which God worked his will in the world, evolution was quite welcome; it magnified the power and plan of God by revealing the progress of his working, even in the events and revelations of the Bible. But evolution remained a tool of one's world philosophy, and if it had theistic and Christian uses, it had infidel uses as well. The same decade that saw a flowering of orthogenetic and adaptive evolutionism at Princeton on the basis of Pattonian theism, saw also a harvest of tares growing up among the wheat in the larger academic world — evolutionisms and even "theisms" that negated both the distinction between Christianity and other religions, and the distinction between the Creator and his creation. These theories obviously offended Princetonian metaphysics, shading easily into pantheism or deism, those old enemies of Calvinistic religion. Worse, in the 1890s they spilled over from sociological discourse into churchly discourse — and from there even into ecclesiastical politics.

This antievolutionary connection is easy to miss. Princeton Seminary of the 1890s is most remembered for some questionable victories within the Presbyterian church: two successful heresy trials against professors at rival seminaries, the defeat of a movement to soften the strict Calvinism of the Westminster Confession, and the official adoption of the doctrine of biblical inerrancy.[69] Northern Presbyterians studiously avoided bringing the transmutation of species to a church tribunal, whether out of regard for the proper domain of science (as in the case of the Princetonians) or, warned by the Woodrow affair, out of a pragmatic

69. See Loetscher, *The Broadening Church,* for a full discussion of the Briggs and McGiffert trials, the Confession Revision controversy, and the Portland Declaration that made biblical inerrancy official Presbyterian doctrine.

regard for denominational peace. Instead of addressing either the concrete question of the origin of species or the grander questions involved in an evolutionary worldview, they seem to many interpreters to have spent a great deal of energy in a misbegotten attempt to fight a movement of the intellect with official pronouncements on niggardly details of theology.

But the battles the Princeton theologians chose to fight in the 1890s actually had a good deal to do with evolution — namely, with what one Princetonian called the "naturalistic evolution of belief." The heresy trials, the Confession Revision controversy, and the issue of biblical inerrancy all involved the nature of Christianity as a religion of God's *supernatural* activity: revealing himself in the Scriptures, working in individual hearts, and guiding church history. Relying on natural development as a sufficient explanation, modern theories of the origin and authority of the Bible, the nature of religious experience, and the history of doctrine contradicted that supernaturalism. Warfield, no foe to organic transmutationism, made the antievolutionary connection in religious matters explicit when he wrote against heresy defendant A. C. McGiffert in 1895, "The Church did not grow up by natural law; it was founded."[70] Princeton's take on confessional orthodoxy and biblical authority was based on just this distinction.

The strategy of securing official pronouncements and expelling those who did not comply with them drew upon historic confessionalism, a complex issue with a long and tangled past.[71] It formed a separate, distinctly ecclesiastical front in the intellectual war the Princetonians were waging. Enforced consensus of basic belief they deemed appropriate in a denominational setting — essential, in fact, to the purpose of denominating — but inappropriate in the republic of ideas outside church affiliations. Unfortunately, this ecclesiastical effort drove a wedge between the two institutions at Princeton, driving a good number of university professors and alumni to a position quite out of sympathy with the Old School Calvinists at the seminary.[72]

Recourse to coercion seems at first blush to betray a lack of confidence in the power of rational argument, or worse, in the rational viabil-

70. Benjamin Breckinridge Warfield, "The Latest Phase of Historical Rationalism" (1895), in his *Studies in Theology*, p. 639.

71. See S. Donald Fortson III, *The Presbyterian Creed: A Confessional Tradition in America, 1729-1870* (Milton Keynes, U.K.: Paternoster, 2008).

72. Kemeny, *Princeton*, p. 96.

ity of the position one wishes to defend. But the use of heresy trials and official pronouncements shared with "seize and master" a conviction of the fundamental importance of reason in religion. Ideas structured religious experience,[73] and logic impelled ideas. "Mere" pronouncements were powerful things. In matters lying at the base of a system of belief — and the knowledge of God, intellectually considered, constituted a veritable system, awaiting discovery and application at the hands of redeemed humanity — precision of statement and attention to logical or connotative consequences were indispensable. For the Princeton theologians, emphatic Protestants that they were, the origin and nature of religious authority were fundamental matters deserving of confessional sanction in a religious body.

Thus denominational affairs in the 1890s began to divide Princeton Seminary from the new university over the theological ramifications of human evolution, driving a wedge into an inherent fault line between the two. The seminary, as a theological institution under direct control of the General Assembly, was distinctly more interested in the questions of heresy vexing the Presbyterian church than the officially nonsectarian, broadly theistic college ever was, even under clerical presidents like Patton and his predecessors. It was the seminary's business, after all, to promote and defend fidelity to the system of doctrine contained in the Westminster Confession of Faith.[74] As the Princeton theologians surveyed the field of theological development in the 1890s, it became apparent that the idea of evolution, borrowing prestige from biology, was reinvigorating some of their old doctrinal adversaries. The evolution question became entangled with church-political issues. Besides abetting the secularization of the university by a growing contrast to its sister institution, this mixing of issues had two notable effects at Princeton. Since evolutionism concerned not just naked theories but the worldviews underlying them, it brought into church politics a heightened attention to metaphysical fundamentals — driving a wedge into fault lines

73. See especially Benjamin Breckinridge Warfield, "On Faith in Its Psychological Aspects" (1911), in his *Studies in Theology*, pp. 313-42.

74. Just what constituted fidelity to the system of doctrine was, of course, highly contested. For a partisan yet judicious account of the Princetonian application of confessionalism, see Calhoun, *Princeton Seminary*, 1:217 and 2:124, 136. Calhoun points out both the Princeton theologians' stringency on Calvinistic doctrine and their relative moderation compared to some in the church who wanted a more aggressive approach to the Briggs case (2:136).

inherent *there.* And because church politics concerned such moral matters as loyalty to one's pledge and such spiritual matters as the salvation of eternal souls, it infused the evolution question with a religious potency mere academic discussions could not muster.

CHAPTER EIGHT

Supernaturalism

*Man does not need the immediate action of God only at the begin-
ning of things. Inasmuch as he himself has been evolved as a sinner
under condemnation, he must have God intervene in evolution
and save him from it. Thus it is not so much mere creation for
which we contend, as it is the scheme of divine procedure which
this term denotes; that is, a scheme of supernatural intervention.*

William Brenton Greene Jr., 1896[1]

Human Evolution

Darwinian evolution combined two particularly scandalous ideas: that
matter and chance could do the work of mind, and that man was ultimately nothing more than a particularly well developed animal. In the
first few decades after the appearance of the *Origin of Species,* the Darwinian controversies centered around the former problem, the issue of
design — and the teleologists won. By the 1890s the vast majority of public thinkers had assured themselves and their readers that the reign of
law in creation history only magnified the God who made and upheld
those laws. The writings of McCosh, the Duke of Argyll (George Camp-

---

1. William Brenton Greene Jr., short notice of *The Agnostic Gospel,* by Henry Webster
Parker, and of *Agnosticism and Religion,* by Jacob Gould Schurman, *Presbyterian and Reformed Review* (hereafter *PRR*) 7 (1896): 702.

bell), Henry Calderwood, and other theistic evolutionists enjoyed great success, and if scientists abandoned the old tradition of making explicit theological glosses on their findings, the strength of teleological evolutionisms in the scientific community echoed the explicitly theistic work of the older generation.[2] Meanwhile, however, the second *skandalon* of Darwinism — the denial of human uniqueness by linking all human characteristics to animal precursors via gradual evolution — smoldered and flickered, finally bursting into flame in the fundamentalist controversy of the 1920s.

Already in 1859 Darwin predicted that his theory would spark a revolution in the human sciences. Toward the end of the *Origin* he wrote, "In the distant future, I see open fields for far more important researches. Psychology will be based on a new foundation, that of the necessary acquirement of each mental power and capacity by gradation. Light will be thrown on the origin of man and his history."[3] Beginning in the late 1860s and 1870s, some writers applied the evolutionary idea to the history of human culture.[4] But it was in the 1890s that the revolution began in earnest. Eugene Dubois proclaimed his discovery of the first missing link, *Pithecanthropus erectus* (the "upright ape-man," popularly called "Java man"), in 1892, just as progressive gradualism in sociology and comparative religion were becoming the vogue. At the same time, true to Darwin's prediction, the budding science of psychology turned to both physiological experimentation — seeking by way of hard data to make the science of the mind truly scientific — and broad hypotheses of the natural development of human mind, morals, and religion from lower forms. Human history, like natural history, yielded a tale of gradual progress through definable epochs by a logic of natural development. Even the critical study of the Bible produced an upward story of the history of Hebrew religion, climaxing in Christianity. No matter that these leading ideas in the human sciences all predated Darwin; the name "evolution" energized

2. Peter J. Bowler, *The Eclipse of Darwinism: Anti-Darwinian Evolution Theories in the Decades around 1900* (Baltimore: Johns Hopkins University Press, 1983), chapter 3: "The Decline of Theistic Evolutionism."

3. Charles Darwin, quoted in Charles Hodge, *Systematic Theology* (New York: Scribners, 1872-73; reprint, Grand Rapids: Eerdmans, 1993), 2:19.

4. Jon H. Roberts, "Religious Reactions to Darwin," in *The Cambridge Companion to Science and Religion*, ed. Peter Harrison (New York: Cambridge University Press, 2010), p. 84. Herbert Spencer had already done so in 1857. Michael Ruse, *Monad to Man: The Concept of Progress in Evolutionary Biology* (Cambridge: Harvard University Press, 1996), p. 30.

them and established their scientific status, and though premises and conclusions often got mixed up together, the general impression grew that science in its various fields was converging on a grand world-explanation in evolution. Henry Drummond captured the drama of that moment in the 1890s for the popular reader: "Each worker toiled in his own little place — the geologist in his quarry, the botanist in his garden, the biologist in his laboratory, the astronomer in his observatory, the historian in his library, the archæologist in his museum. Suddenly these workers looked up; they spoke to one another; they had each discovered a law; they whispered its name. It was Evolution. Henceforth their work was one, science was one, the world was one, and mind, which discovered the oneness, was one."[5]

To incorporate human origins and history into the grand sweep of evolution was, on this account, not to denigrate humanity but to crown it as the climax of creation, the supreme goal toward which all nature had been striving for countless aeons. If the idea of simian ancestry was hard to take, finding evolution's goal in the production of humanity quickly made up for it. Human evolution on this non-Darwinian reading became not a chance corollary to a history of life indifferent to man's existence, but the grand finale of the world's story. It elevated humanity; giving man the place of preeminence at the top of the family tree, it set him apart from the brutes even as it tied him genetically to them. A prehuman skeleton in the closet was nothing to be ashamed of. To trace this pedigree was a high calling. In the opening words of Drummond's book, "The last romance of Science, the most daring it has ever tried to pen, is the Story of the Ascent of Man."[6] In this story science found its reason for being and man met his noblest self. His production was the preoccupation of the universe; his future was the fulfillment of the ages. His progress was assured, driven by the momentum of all nature.[7] One

5. Henry Drummond, *The Ascent of Man*, 14th ed., Lowell Lectures, ca. 1892 (New York: James Pott and Co., 1907), pp. 8-9. Drummond was indeed popular: his earlier book, *Natural Law in the Spiritual World* (1883), sold fabulously. So enticing were profits that unscrupulous publishers in America pirated it no less than fifteen times. James R. Moore, *The Post-Darwinian Controversies: A Study of the Protestant Struggle to Come to Terms with Darwin in Great Britain and America, 1870-1900* (Cambridge: Cambridge University Press, 1979), p. 7.

6. Drummond, *The Ascent of Man*, p. 1.

7. Bowler observes that the link between progressionism and human evolution survived even the enormous disorientation of Western culture after World War I. It was that

might even say that evolution, for a time, gave back what heliocentrism had taken away: the cosmic importance of humankind.[8]

This sanguine account of man's blood relations pleased and placated many people, including many ministers of the gospel. Those who disliked Calvinism's dark view of human nature were happy to buttress their theological position with all the strength of status the latest science had to offer. With a bloodhound's nose for the slightest whiff of anti-Calvinism, the theologians of Princeton had no trouble scenting out this tendency. But they agreed with a great deal of what Drummond and others were saying about the place of humankind in the world. They were willing, to a degree perhaps surprising, to entertain seriously the question of human evolution, despite its unfortunate connections to merely natural religion.

It is not difficult to recognize in Drummond's "romance" something of the beatific vision Arnold Guyot had taught at Princeton for thirty years until his death in 1884. James McCosh, in *The Religious Aspect of Evolution* (1888), carried the ameliorative momentum of evolution up to humanity and onward to the very kingdom of Christ. This work, one of his last, consisted of a series of lectures, the Bedell Foundation Lectures, delivered at Kenyon College, an Episcopalian institution in Ohio. To prepare the lectures McCosh consulted the works of a broad spectrum of scientists: Dana, Le Conte, Geikie, Dawson, Conn, and Cope. He also relied heavily on personal consultation with Princeton naturalists Macloskie and Scott, and especially followed Guyot's little book, *Creation*.[9] What McCosh's consulting scientists had in common, despite their differences over transmutation, was a goal-directed, grand vision of progress in natural history culminating in the appearance of humankind. McCosh especially liked Guyot's doctrine of foreshadowings or anticipations in nature of things to come, such as the appearance of mam-

---

strong, that deep. "The scientific study of human origins remained insulated from this loss of faith in progress" into the 1940s, by retaining its explicitly non-Darwinian view of evolution. Peter J. Bowler, *The Non-Darwinian Revolution: Reinterpreting a Historical Myth* (Baltimore: Johns Hopkins University Press, 1988), p. 151.

8. Ruse, *Monad to Man*, pp. 526, 538.

9. James McCosh, *The Religious Aspect of Evolution* (New York and London: Putnam, 1888). His note on p. xxi cites Dawson's *Story of the Earth and Man*, Cope's *Origin of the Fittest*, "and especially . . . Conn's excellent work," *Evolution of To-Day*, in addition to personal consultations with Princeton colleagues. On p. 69 McCosh gives special credit to Guyot.

mals in the age of reptiles. The arrival of man summed up all the foreshadowings of previous earth history. McCosh dwelt on Guyot's view of the "Sabbath Age," the present aeon, human history, in which God rested from his creative labors in the physical realm while human effort carried progress into the moral and spiritual dimension. As each biblical day consisted in evening and morning, so the present epoch began in the darkness of sin, the weary battle between the spirit and the flesh, and a dim knowledge of both earth and heaven — but a day would dawn, in human history, when righteousness and peace would rule the world. This morning of the seventh day, the culmination of mundane history, would bring the millennial kingdom of Christ on earth. As with the Lord a day is a thousand years, so the millennium of Revelation 20 would be nothing less than "a geological epoch."[10] Thereafter, following John's prophecy, the present heavens and earth would pass away in fire, God would judge the quick and the dead, and the full light of day — light too dazzling to permit us to see what lay ahead — would bring in the eternal state of blessedness with God. "I can see no farther into the endless light that stretches out beyond," wrote the aged McCosh in his concluding words. "My hope is to be there and live forever; then I shall know, even as also I am fully known."[11]

As in his previous works, McCosh emphasized evolution's testimony to God: a collocation of second causes implemented the divine plan, leading the mind ineluctably to the great First Cause and intelligent design. Also as before, he stressed the gaps that evolution could never fill: the origin of light, life, consciousness, and spirit, all requiring supernatural activity. The burden of *The Religious Aspect of Evolution,* however, was not to prove God's existence, but to set forth the glory of his providential plan in the world — to point the believer to the great goal of history, and indeed of evolution, in the kingdom of God. It was an exercise in the proper division of labor between science and religion, drawing expressly religious lessons from the truths of the natural world.

As a story of grand continuity, McCosh's Bedell Lectures naturally brought up the question of human evolution. He wrote, "If any one ask me if I believe man's body to have come from a brute, I answer that I know not. I believe in revelation, I believe in science, but neither has revealed this to me; and I restrain the weak curiosity which would tempt

10. McCosh, *Religious Aspect of Evolution,* p. 91.
11. McCosh, *Religious Aspect of Evolution,* p. 95.

me to inquire into what cannot be known. Meanwhile I am sure, and I assert, that man's soul is of a higher origin and of a nobler type."[12] McCosh, an outspoken exponent of the factuality of evolution, drew back at the question of human origins. His zeal for the theory did not carry him beyond what he regarded as the established facts of the case. He allowed the possibility of human bodily evolution, but denied any evolutionary origin of the soul.[13]

In his first year as professor at Princeton Seminary, B. B. Warfield wrote a lengthy review of *The Religious Aspect of Evolution*,[14] his discussion there forming the basis of his lectures on theological anthropology written later that year. He deemed evolution a theory "still on its probation," declaring himself a "pure agnostic" as to its truth as a theory of speciation in general. But when it came to human evolution, the point at which McCosh himself retreated into agnosticism, Warfield felt it his duty as a theologian to address the question at some length. He did so in his lectures on the doctrine of man.

Any hypothesis, Warfield stated, must "run a double gauntlet": it must show it *can* account for the facts, and it must show it *does* account for them better than any other hypothesis that has also met the first test. "Everything is not true that might possibly be true: often two theories are equally able to account for the facts. The race is run between the various theories that have been shown to be able to account for the facts."[15] But

12. McCosh, *Religious Aspect of Evolution*, pp. 79-80.

13. John T. Duffield, Princeton's mathematics professor whose article "Evolutionism Respecting Man, and the Bible" (1878 — see chapter 5, note 25) had argued the impossibility of reconciling the scriptural account of man and woman with an evolutionary one, claimed in 1897 that McCosh was always careful to separate the question of "evolution in general" from that of human evolution, disallowing the latter. It seems, though, that in *The Religious Aspect of Evolution* McCosh tempered that proviso slightly. Duffield's objections remained just as strong as before. Duffield, "Evolutionary and Biblical Anthropology," letter to the editor, *New York Tribune*, 13 January 1897.

14. I refer here to the MS version of the review, Warfield MSS. It was trimmed down considerably (for space considerations?) before publication in the *Presbyterian Review*, jointly edited at that time by Warfield and Briggs.

15. Warfield, MS Notes on Anthropology. Notice here that Warfield was not looking for airtight certainty, but for relative certainty — asking not whether a hypothesis was proved beyond a shadow of a doubt but whether it was, first, possible, and second, the best of the possible theories. Thus his verdict of "not proven" did not represent the naïve quest for certainty, much less some straw man enabling him to dismiss evolutionary theory out of hand, that some interpreters of Baconianism and Common-Sense Realism have been quick to find among nineteenth-century evangelicals. For an extreme allegation of

as of 1888 the crux of evolutionary investigation concerned "whether the facts known can be accounted for on this theory." And "if this is true, evolution is as yet not even entered for the race of theories: what folly to claim for it already the prize!" On this score Warfield chided his revered mentor. McCosh, he said, "has allowed his enthusiasm to run away with his judgment."

But Warfield was not content to declare evolution "not proven" and so to drop the subject. He went on to discuss the Darwinian theory at length, concluding from the geological record, the embryological recapitulation theory, the estimated age of the earth, his extensive personal knowledge of breeding,[16] and the arguments for orthogenesis, that "any form of evolution which rests ultimately on the Darwinian idea, is very improbable. . . . As to whether species have in any way come by descent, I am more of a pure agnostic."[17]

Just at this point Warfield turned to discuss "the religious bearing of evolution," clearly echoing the title of McCosh's book. He affirmed McCosh's theistic discussion of the matter completely. But he hastened to add, "to be a theist & a Xian are different things, and a thoroughgoing evolutionism cannot be held in consistency with some other Xian doc-

---

Protestant insistence on airtight certainty, see Herbert Hovenkamp, *Science and Religion in America, 1800-1860* (Philadelphia: University of Pennsylvania Press, 1978), p. x.

16. Warfield's father was an avid breeder of shorthorn cattle, authoring several books on the subject. After college young Ben worked for a year as the editor of a cattle breeder's journal in his hometown, Lexington, Kentucky. He continued to direct some cattle breeding of his own even when a professor at Western Seminary, by correspondence with his father. In his brother's home in Easton, Pennsylvania, pictures of ancestors and shorthorn cattle alternated on the walls. (Interview with Benjamin B. Warfield II, December 1994, Orange City, Fla.)

17. Warfield, MS Notes on Anthropology. For an example of orthogenetic science Warfield cited Hubrecht's paper at the sesquicentennial of Princeton College, which traced man's separate line of ancestry from a mouse-like insectivorous mammal in the Mesozoic era, or possibly from an amphibian ancestor *before* the age of reptiles. Apes and humans (not to mention monkeys, perhaps all other mammals, and even reptiles) evolved separately from a very ancient common ancestor, in parallel lines according to the combined action of an inner law of development and similar responses to similar environmental conditions. On this reading, humans were not descended from apes at all. The branching tree of Darwinism was in danger of being replaced with a "plantation of canes" — separate, parallel lines of development — "each growing independently from common soil." Warfield pasted into his anthropology notes the unsigned *PRR* review of Hubrecht's book, from which review this quotation is taken. Note the vast difference between this orthogenetic view and what we now think of as the theory of evolution.

trines" — namely, "the *substantiality & immateriality of the soul &* its consequent persistence in life after the death of the body." For the common doctrine of the soul to stand, God must have interfered in evolution at one point at least, when "an immaterial principle of life" appeared.[18] Whether that occurred at the appearance of humankind or at some time earlier — even at the very beginnings of life — Warfield was willing to leave a moot point. In other words, despite his warning against the incompatibility of pure naturalistic gradualism and the Christian doctrine of the soul, Warfield considered it not just philosophically adequate, but biblically adequate, to entertain the idea of an evolutionary history of the soul!

In the next five years or so Warfield augmented this section of the lectures with a discussion of Joseph Le Conte's *Evolution and Its Relation to Religious Thought* and John Romanes's *Mental Evolution in Man*.[19] He disagreed strenuously with their attempt to evolve soul from body, but if a separate, nonmaterial origin and essence of the soul were granted, he was willing to consider the possibility that an immaterial aspect of animal life had served as a precursor to the human soul, forming a second and essentially separate evolution alongside the physical one. Perhaps the best indication of Warfield's openness to this question is a published symposium he organized in the first year of his new theological quarterly, the *Presbyterian and Reformed Review*. Warfield sought contributions from a variety of disciplines, inviting paleontologists William Berryman Scott and John William Dawson, theologians William G. T. Shedd and John DeWitt — all Princetonians or men with close sympathies with Princeton — but also theistic evolutionist Henry Calderwood of Edinburgh and philosophers John Dewey of Michigan and Edward H. Griffin of Johns Hopkins.[20] He asked them to consider the question

---

18. Warfield, MS Notes on Anthropology.

19. In an article for the *Princeton Review,* Le Conte had written that "the anima of animals is spirit in embryo fast asleep in the womb of nature." Joseph Le Conte, "The Psychical Relation of Man to Animals," *Princeton Review* (1884): 260.

20. Henry Calderwood to Warfield, 11 March 1890, and Edward H. Griffin to Warfield, 14 March 1890, both in the Warfield MSS. Calderwood and Griffin declined to contribute, but all the others did participate. Griffin, by the way, had studied at Princeton Seminary in the mid-1860s, and contributed five articles to the *PRR* in 1901 and 1902. Shedd was a renowned conservative Presbyterian theologian at Union Seminary, New York; DeWitt taught apologetics at McCormick Theological School, Chicago, taking the chair of church history at Princeton in 1892.

"What is animal life?" Their contributions all indicated that the main thrust of the inquiry concerned the existence of an immaterial principle in brute creation, and its relation to the human soul. The answers were as diverse as the list of contributors; Warfield wanted a full range of opinion to get the discussion going. Scott's answer, though, suggests that Warfield may have derived his own view from discussions with the Princeton paleontologist. Scott wrote,

> There being this complete continuity between the physical structure of man and that of the brutes, are we justified in assuming a like continuity between their psychical natures? Upon this question the evolutionists are divided, one school following Darwin in believing that human nature in its totality, physical, mental and moral, is a product of evolution, while the other school maintains, with Wallace, that man, or at least the human mind, cannot be so accounted for. . . . [I]f it shall eventually prove that it has pleased the Almighty to create the human soul by a process of gradual evolution, rather than by an immediate fiat, I do not see why the scheme of Christian philosophy may not assimilate that new truth (should it turn out to be one) as readily as the once startling but now familiar doctrines of astronomy and geology.[21]

Scott argued that the one-to-one correspondence in physical parts between humans and animals made the metaphysical issue in animals equally applicable to humans. "If we accept materialism as applied to the lower animals," he wrote, "we cannot escape it as applied to ourselves." He therefore rejected Huxley's (and Shedd's) view that animals were mere automatons.[22] By the same token he welcomed the possibility that the human soul derived from an immaterial principle in animal life. In this way the hypothesis of soul-evolution could actually serve the defense of the faith, for it headed off the bogey of materialism that had always lurked behind the evolution question.[23]

21. William Berryman Scott, "What Is Animal Life?" *PRR* 1 (1890): 452.

22. This was a heated issue, dating back to John Tyndall's scandalous Belfast Address in 1874, where Tyndall agreed with Huxley (see chapter 5, note 42, above). Both British scientists drew McCosh's fire *against* such forms of evolutionism, in defense of dualistic metaphysics and the Christian faith.

23. Scott, "What Is Animal Life?" p. 451. These considerations help explain why Patton's Princeton could not only tolerate but encourage the kind of researches into physiological psychology and mental development that Baldwin undertook in the 1890s. A similar animus against materialism underlay Henri Bergson's theory of the *élan vital* in his

In his anthropology lectures Warfield asked whether evolution — including such ideas as we have been discussing — was "consistent with the Biblical account of the origin of things in general & of man in particular." He answered with a qualified yes. "I am free to say, for myself, that I do not think that there is any general statement in the Bible or any part of the account of creation, either as given in Gen I & II or elsewhere alluded to, that need be opposed to evolution. The sole passage which appears to bar the way is the very detailed account of the creation of Eve." Following A. A. Hodge's letter to him during the Woodrow affair three years earlier, Warfield considered the account of Eve "a very serious bar in the way of a doctrine of creation by evolution." Woodrow construed it as a miracle, superseding the natural course of evolution up to that point, but Warfield found that reading unnatural, probably for the reasons Hodge had shared with him. He allowed the position as a possibility, however, concluding that on this whole question of human evolution "there is no *necessary* antagonism of Xty to evolution, *provided that* we do not hold to too extreme a form of evolution." Christians must acknowledge the constant activity of God in upholding and directing natural law to bring about his purposes, and they must allow his "occasional supernatural interference for the production of *new* beginnings," not to mention outright miracles like the incarnation and resurrection. If they did that, he said, they "may hold to the modified theory of evolution & be Xians in the ordinary orthodox sense" — and this regarding not just evolution in general, but human evolution.[24] Simply stated, Warfield exonerated Woodrow.

Over the next three decades Warfield refined and amplified this initial discussion of the evolution question at the intersection of anthropology and theology. He came to believe that the work of theistic evolutionists like McCosh tended to lump together the modes of supernatural activity in an ultimately destructive way (see below), and on that basis, as well as on biblical and doctrinal grounds, to step back from his early hypothetical allowance for an immaterial evolution of the soul.[25] He re-

Creative Evolution (1911), reviewed favorably for Princeton by S. A. Martin: *Princeton Theological Review* (hereafter *PTR*) 10 (1912): 116-18.

24. Warfield, MS Notes on Anthropology.

25. Warfield's assistant in the department of systematic theology, Caspar Wistar Hodge Jr., stated his position on possible antecedents of the human body and soul more precisely than Warfield ever did, but with an evident sense of perfect conformity to his mentor's views. He required supernatural intervention at least in the production of the soul, but did not deny the possibility that God, intervening at that point to produce something utterly be-

mained highly skeptical of Darwinian evolution, but while he continued to profess his agnosticism on the matter of speciation by descent, he found the idea not only agreeable as a method of divine activity, but also conformable to the orthodoxy of John Calvin himself.

Warfield's frank and proactive approach to the question of human evolution was remarkable. Theologians, especially conservative theologians, were often loath to entertain disorienting scientific truth claims until the prevalence of the new views backed them into a corner. From their own point of view this was entirely appropriate, for their time-honored doctrines had a great deal of accumulated discussion and evidence to commend them. "Beardless" new sciences owed a proper deference to the first and oldest science.[26] Warfield's willingness as a theologian, therefore, to consider the idea of human evolution, even before the greater part of the scientific community had affirmed it, and indeed when the issue had just proved disastrously divisive in a sister denomination, showed an eager confidence in science not often attributed to conservatives. It betokened a continued close communication between the seminary and the college, where evolutionary thinking was strong and thriving. And it reaffirmed Princeton's commitment to its old Battle Plan of offense: to reconnoiter the field and to seize new weaponry in the interests of molding the age. Warfield welcomed science and entertained its speculations as well as its "well-ascertained facts,"[27] reserving words of war for those he considered the actual aggressors: infidel worldviews, attacks on the veracity of Holy Writ, and denials of distinctive Christian doctrine.

---

yond the capabilities of natural law, worked on an animal soul to produce the human one. It was expressly not an evolution, but a creation, whether mediate or immediate (see chapter 9 below). Also relevant was the ancient question of the origin of each human soul since Adam: Was each soul created by God out of nothing (creationism) or derived from the parents (traducianism)? Princeton's historic position, which Warfield perpetuated, was the creationist one (see Charles Hodge, *Systematic Theology,* 2:68-76) — but for some reason the Princetonians almost never argued from this issue to the evolution question.

26. Theodore Dwight Bozeman, *Protestants in an Age of Science: The Baconian Ideal and Antebellum American Religious Thought* (Chapel Hill: University of North Carolina Press, 1977), p. 114.

27. George M. Marsden, in *Fundamentalism and American Culture: The Shaping of Twentieth-Century Evangelicalism, 1870-1925* (New York: Oxford University Press, 1980), pp. 111-12, argues that Baconian and Scottish Common-Sense views of "fact" made evangelicals, including the Princetonians and Warfield in particular (p. 116), denigrate the important role of hypothesis in the legitimate development of science. If this was the case with some evangelicals, it was not the case with Warfield.

Degenerationism

Impressed as the Princetonians were with the orderly, progressive ways of God's working in the world, and zealous as they were for scientific system in theology, they remained convinced that the only religion worth having was the old-time gospel of salvation by grace. Natural theology provided a philosophical footing for their theological enterprise, but revealed religion — redemption in Christ, revealed in the Bible — was its heart. Theism was useless except as a prolegomenon to Christianity. The Princetonians had decided that evolutionism, rightly understood, only strengthened natural theology, and that God's activities in revelation and even in redeeming the world followed a pattern of growth. Princeton found a good deal of truth or possible truth in evolutionism — but there remained plenty to reject. Evolution's "ascent of man" elaborated the creation story of human uniqueness and importance in the universe, but it did scant justice to redemptive religion's cardinal themes of sin and salvation.

The place of sin in Christian theology — its epistemological ramifications as well as its doctrinal centrality — became a topic of heightened concern at Princeton around 1900, largely in response to evolutionary views of religion, Scripture, and doctrine. For four years beginning in 1899-1900 Warfield offered an extracurricular seminar entitled "Evolution in Its Relations to Theology," from which, unfortunately, no notes survive. More revealing are the seminary's Stone Foundation guest lectures from this period, including Abraham Kuyper's famous series on Calvinism (1898-99), which argued a radical disjunction between believing and unbelieving science, grounded in sin; Henry Collin Minton's work *The Cosmos and the Logos* (1901-2), which devoted an entire lecture to sin, "The Empirical Surprise," and another to its outworkings in "man as a factor in the cosmos"; James Orr's *God's Image in Man and Its Defacement in Light of Modern Denials* (1903-4); and Herman Bavinck's *Philosophy of Revelation* (1908-9).[28]

---

28. Abraham Kuyper, *Calvinism* (New York: Fleming H. Revell Co., 1898); Henry Collin Minton, *The Cosmos and the Logos* (Philadelphia: Westminster, 1902); James Orr, *God's Image in Man and Its Defacement, in the Light of Modern Denials,* 2nd ed. (New York: A. C. Armstrong and Son, 1906); Herman Bavinck, *The Philosophy of Revelation* (New York: Longmans, Green, and Co., 1909). Other Stone Lectures of related interest to the evolution question in general, but not the question of sin, are George Frederick Wright's work "The Historical Character of the Old Testament Interpreted and Supported by Recent Scientific Investigation," 1904-5, published as *Scientific Confirmations of Old Testament History,* 2nd ed. (Oberlin, Ohio: Bibliotheca Sacra Co., 1907), and Daniel E. Jenkins's "Function and

Against those evolutionary theorists who construed Christianity as a product of natural development, both as a system of belief and as a personal experience, the Princeton theologians and their allies reasserted the powerful, problematic presence of sin in human nature.

Minton, a former student of Warfield and one of his favorite reviewers of evolutionary philosophies and evolutionary views of religion for the *Presbyterian and Reformed Review,* lamented the widespread lack of discrimination on these topics. Both the public and the leaders of evolutionary thought displayed a zeal for unification that lumped all kinds of processes together willy-nilly, forgetting to look for the distinctive modes of operation of those processes. He wrote in his review of Drummond's *Ascent of Man,*

> At the risk of saying it the ten thousandth time, there is evolution and evolution. Drummond blandly assures us that "after all the blood spilt, evolution is simply history." And who, forsooth, does not believe in history? . . . Alas! how important that men should be loyal to their definitions. Spinoza was called the God-intoxicated man; this age might be called the *evolution-intoxicated* age, and, truly, many of its leading thinkers, otherwise "clothed and in their right mind," seem *evolution-mad.*[29]

Especially when it came to religion, Minton found the mantra of "evolution" extremely misleading. For if evolution meant a natural unfolding of progress, ever upward, the history of religions and the experience of the sinner gave the lie to it. "Evolution made a wandering prodigal," Minton wrote; "it was a *revolution* that brought him back to his father's house." True religion, the religion of redemption in Christ, required a radical

---

Right of Anthropomorphism in Religious Thought," 1905-6 (not published). Warfield also offered an extracurricular course entitled "Beza and the Supra-Lapsarian Theory," a consideration of the timing of God's decree with respect to the Fall, as understood by Calvin's successor. Courses are listed in the seminary catalogues, in PTS Special Collections.

29. Henry Collin Minton, review of *The Ascent of Man,* by Henry Drummond, *PRR* 6 (1895): 139, emphasis in original. Minton was a former student of Warfield at Western Theological Seminary and served from 1892 to 1902 as Stuart Professor of Systematic Theology at the new Presbyterian seminary in San Francisco. He provided dozens of reviews on philosophical subjects to Warfield's journal and its successor, the *Princeton Theological Review.* In 1901 he gave the Stone Lectures at Princeton Seminary, *The Cosmos and the Logos.* The following year he moved to the Princeton area to take the pastorate of First Presbyterian Church in Trenton, serving there till 1918. *Who Was Who in America,* vol. 1 (Chicago: A. N. Marquis Co., 1942), p. 849.

transformation of human nature, a miracle in the heart. "Evolution may assume to be natural; the grace of God is supernatural."[30] Apart from grace, the unfolding of the potentialities of fallen human nature led only to a degeneration of the divine image. In religion the arrow of natural development pointed down, not up.

Dogmaticians had explored and debated the religious capabilities of fallen human nature since the early Christian centuries: Augustine versus Pelagius, Luther versus Erasmus, Calvinists versus Arminians, Princeton versus New Haven. While the Princetonians stressed natural theology's place in the philosophical foundation of systematic theology, they argued strenuously, in line with their Augustinian doctrinal tradition, for the hopeless insufficiency of sin-deflected, man-made religion. Natural theology was true, but apart from grace, human wickedness limited its worth to the entirely negative function of securing the sinner's self-condemnation.[31] Redemptive religion, both in content (God's work in history for the salvation of sinners) and in personal experience (God's work in converting the individual heart), came from above, from outside the natural realm of experience. It did not *arise from* this world, but *intruded into* it. True religion was a matter of grace, not of nature. Left to nature, human religion degenerated into idolatry.

For many decades — long before the blitz of evolutionary sociology and comparative religion in the 1890s — Princeton and its allies had tempered their beatific vision of creation's progress with a very serious consideration of the power of sin in human history. At the close of creation God pronounced his work good, but history began with a cataclysmic defection from original goodness. Natural history proceeded progressively, unfolding the marvelous plan of nature, but the fall of man introduced a new, corrupt development. William G. T. Shedd of Union Seminary, one of Princeton's best friends in the New School branch of the Presbyterian church, expressed these ideas as early as 1863, in a work Princeton apologete William Brenton Greene Jr. still found compelling a full half-century later.[32]

---

30. Minton, review of *The Ascent of Man*, p. 142, emphasis in original.

31. See chapter 7, note 55, above.

32. William Brenton Greene Jr., review of *Christian Faith and the New Psychology: Evolution and Recent Science as Aid to Faith,* by David O. Murray, *PTR* 9 (1912): 113. Similar to Shedd on the two arrows of religious evolution, and closer to home, was Princeton Seminary professor James Clement Moffat's two-volume work, *A Comparative History of Religions* (New York: Dodd and Mead, 1871-73).

In the introduction to his *History of Christian Doctrine,* Shedd defined history by way of the growth analogy: it was "an evolution from a potential basis," the unfolding of germinal potentialities into actuality, "organically connected," and "created to grow." "In brief, whatever has been constitutionally *inlaid* either in matter or in mind, by the Creator of both, is destined by Him, and under His own superintendence, to be evolved." Shedd had no problem with calling history, not just natural history but human history, an evolution.[33] But he was careful to discriminate between development and "improvement." "Whether the movement be upward, or downward; from good to better, or from bad to worse" depended "upon the nature of the potential base from which the expanding process issues." Material nature, as a pure creation of God, could only produce healthy and normal development.[34] But allow free will — as the creation of humans and angels did — and "the original foundation, laid in creation, for a legitimate growth and progress, may be displaced, and a secondary one laid by the abuse of freedom." The Fall did just that. It initiated "a false development, and an awful history, if not supernaturally hindered." God created nature, including human nature, good; but man created sin, a strict act of creation, out of nothing. The product of the Fall was nothing less than "a new historic germ," on the basis of which "development may be synonymous with corruption and decline, as well as with improvement." Human history now consisted in a conflict between two evolutions: an organic growth from the corrupt germ, and an organic growth from the germ restored by grace. Secular history proceeded naturally — it was not wholly a tale of ruination, thanks to the providential restraining hand of God, but essentially a tale of "false development" taking its natural, and yet unnatural, course. Sacred history, on the other hand, proceeded on the basis of a supernatural

---

33. William G. T. Shedd, *A History of Christian Doctrine,* 2 vols. (New York: Charles Scribner's Sons, 1863), 1:7-10. Shedd's terminology underscores the contextual importance of nonbiological developmentalisms contemporary with or predating Darwinism.

34. Shedd, *History of Christian Doctrine,* 1:7-10. Not all evangelicals agreed with Shedd on this point. The reviewer of Hugh Miller's *Footprints of the Creator* for the *Biblical Repertory and Princeton Review,* for example, argued as follows: "The types which succeed each other, in the successive geological eras of the paleozoic world, were, as every one knows, in an ascending series of complexity and completeness; but there was no transition from one type into another; and the history of each type was a *history of degradation,* as if strangely and solemnly symbolizing and foreshadowing the degeneracy of the race which was to crown and complete the whole." *BRPR* 23 (1851): 173, emphasis in original.

intervention that restored the original germ. Taken as a whole, human history was a combination of these two competing tendencies.[35]

Proponents of this sin-driven, downward human development often called it "degeneration" — a fitting term, for it conveyed the notion of sinking below a former normal condition, the consequences exactly of the Fall. It was the opposite of the assumed "ascent of man" by continuous evolution from the brute through necessary stages of savagery and heathenism to civilization and high ethical monotheism. It was not, however, antidevelopmental. The very term came from the language of breeding. To the degenerationist, savagery was just as much a result of development as civilization was, only the savage had unfortunately developed *downward* from an originally better state.[36] Why assume that present-day "savages" represented "primitive man"?[37] According to

35. Shedd, *History of Christian Doctrine,* 1:15-22. For Shedd, "This new and higher history, this new and higher evolution of a regenerated humanity, is the theme of the Church Historian." Note that many of Shedd's themes echo plainly in the work of B. B. Warfield: degeneration in natural religion and savage society, progressionism in revelation and doctrinal history, the crucial distinction between creation and evolution (see below), and a doctrine of providence by virtually unbroken law according to the sovereign decree of God, expressly countering both chance and fate.

36. Champions of degenerationism included John William Dawson and the Duke of Argyll, the one a hearty antitransmutationist, the other an equally hearty theistic evolutionist. Argyll's *Primeval Man* (1872) argued specifically against Sir John Lubbock's theory of primitive savagery. The *Princeton Review,* under Lyman Atwater, reviewed it favorably (*BRPR,* n.s., 2 [1873]: 182). Dawson agreed with Argyll's degenerationism in his *Origin of the World* (1877), a manifesto of his views just at the time McCosh and Hodge were courting him for Princeton. On Hodge's degenerationism, see note 39 below. So too Mark Hopkins, former president of Williams College ("Personality and Law — the Duke of Argyll," *Princeton Review,* n.s., 10 [1882]: 194-95). Degenerationism was especially popular in the United States, according to Jon H. Roberts, who observes that the subject has not received sufficient historical attention (*Darwinism and the Divine in America: Protestant Intellectuals and Organic Evolution, 1859-1900* [Madison: University of Wisconsin Press, 1988], pp. 109, 110, 285 n. 43). More recent scholarship has rectified that neglect somewhat — see Ruse, *Monad to Man,* and David N. Livingstone, *Adam's Ancestors: Race, Religion, and the Politics of Human Origins* (Baltimore: Johns Hopkins University Press, 2008).

37. Warfield, open as he was to prehuman ancestry, asked this question outright. Reviewing James Macdonald's *Religion and Myth* (*PRR* 4 [1893]: 687-88), he chided the mere "assumption that in studying any given savage tribe we are studying 'primitive man.' . . . Mr. Macdonald quite naïvely speaks of 'African and other primitive peoples,' and the like. But the African savages are no more primitive man, in time, than the Parisian *jeunesse dorée.* Who can prove them nearer in custom and thought? . . . Before we deal so freely with 'primitive man' we shall do well to begin by following the famous advice as to the

Scripture, humanity had begun in a condition of natural sinlessness and monotheism, in unbroken fellowship with its Creator. Human nature was essentially, naturally, good.[38] But in consequence of the Fall, sin often sank human society into savagery and barbarism, and all natural religion manifested some degree of degeneration from the original knowledge of God, unless countered by supernatural revelation.[39]

A pre-Darwinian developmentalist idea, degenerationism offered the possibility of an evolutionary history of religion that did not reduce the Bible to a natural product, or Judaism and Christianity to the same status as pagan religions. The Princetonians were quick to seize this opportunity to defend the faith. Using the tools of modern biblical criticism, archeology, and comparative religion, they joined the scientific attempt to trace the developmental history of religion, but they questioned the direction of evolution's arrow. Religions did indeed develop, they argued, but their natural course was often downward, and the facts of comparative religion often supported a tale of degeneration better than a tale of evolutionary progress.[40]

Princeton's church history professor, James Clement Moffat, argued along these lines as early as 1872.[41] John William Dawson did so in

---

preparation of 'broiled hare' — 'First, catch your hare.'" Though it involved a point of religious dogma, Warfield held the theory of primitive savagery up to historical investigation. As evidence against Macdonald's assumption he cited Edward Westermarck's *History of Human Marriage*, reviewed anonymously (by him?) the previous year (*PRR* 3 [1892]: 604-5).

38. Benjamin Breckinridge Warfield, "Calvin's Doctrine of the Creation" (1915), in his *Calvin and Calvinism*, in *The Works of Benjamin B. Warfield*, ed. Ethelbert D. Warfield et al., vol. 5 (New York: Oxford University Press, 1931; Grand Rapids: Baker, 1991), pp. 289, 317-18, citing Calvin's *Institutes* (1.14.3 and 1.14.16); cf. Charles Hodge, *Systematic Theology*, 2:241.

39. Charles Hodge argued thus against Comte. "Not only revelation, but all history and tradition, go to show that the primitive state of our race was its highest state, at least so far as religion is concerned. Monotheism was the earliest form of religion among men. To that succeeded nature-worship and pantheism, and to that polytheism. It is a historical fact that monotheism was not reached by a process of development. Monotheism was first; it gradually perished from among men, except as miraculously preserved among the Hebrews, and from them diffused through the medium of, or rather, in the form of, Christianity. It extends nowhere beyond the influence, direct or indirect, of the supernatural revelation contained in the Bible. This is a fact which scientific men should not overlook in their deductions." Charles Hodge, *Systematic Theology*, 1:259.

40. See, for example, Joseph K. Wight, "Confucianism," *BRPR* 30 (1858): 226-61.

41. Short notice of *A Comparative History of Religions*, by James Clement Moffat, *Presbyterian Quarterly and Princeton Review*, n.s., 1 (1872): 411-12.

1877.[42] When comparative religion became a really hot issue in the 1890s, the Princeton theologians, true to form, hastened to participate actively in the new science, fully confident that here as elsewhere the legitimate tools of scholarship would serve orthodoxy best. They invited Samuel H. Kellogg[43] to give the Stone Lectures for 1891-92; his lectures were titled "Modern Theories of the Origin and Development of Religion." A longtime missionary in India, Kellogg brought firsthand experience to his discussion of comparative religion. After considering how to define religion in a precise and yet inclusive way, Kellogg criticized, in turn, the naturalistic religious developmentalisms of Herbert Spencer and Friedrich Max Müller. He labored to show that the history of religions in India especially contradicted Müller's view. Then he presented his own theory, a degenerationist one, marshaling evidence from the religions of Egypt, India, Persia, Babylon, China, West Africa, and Europe. Francis R. Beattie, Kellogg's reviewer in the *Presbyterian and Reformed Review,* observed Kellogg's stress on "the significance of sin as a dark, sad fact. . . . By reason of sin the development is abnormal, and on this account it is unscientific to ignore the workings of sin, as so many do, in the accounts given of religious development." Kellogg concluded on grounds of historical evidence that primitive man was monotheistic, and that subsequently, in Beattie's words, "the law of development has been degradation." The downward law had held among the Hebrews as well, except where God had mercifully revealed himself to them throughout their history. Beattie summarized: "On account of sin the natural tendency of men has been to fall away from monotheism; and the glory of the Hebrew nation and of Christianity is that supernatural intervention has preserved, perpetuated and expanded original monotheistic belief."[44] All nations alike were subject to a law of religious degeneration due to sin — God's chosen people had no right to boast on that score, for they possessed the oracles of God in spite of, not because of, their behavior. All Old Testament history, with its recurring themes of Israel's apostasy and God's undying faithfulness, told this story.

---

42. John William Dawson, *The Origin of the World according to Revelation and Science* (New York: Harper and Bros, 1877).

43. This was the same man who tried to draw A. A. Hodge into the Woodrow affair seven years earlier. See chapter 6 above.

44. Samuel Henry Kellogg, *The Genesis and Growth of Religion,* Stone Lectures for 1891-92 (New York and London: Macmillan, 1892); Francis R. Beattie, review of Kellogg, *PRR* 5 (1894): 103-6.

William Brenton Greene Jr., successor to Patton's Stuart Chair, also argued the degenerationist case for primitive monotheism. A graduate of Princeton College under McCosh and Atwater, and of Princeton Seminary under A. A. Hodge, Greene was a successful preacher at Philadelphia's Tenth Church for about ten years before his call to Princeton. He lacked the European training Warfield and others had enjoyed, and the seminary considered other candidates before calling him to the post.[45] But he proved a steady, productive reviewer for the theological quarterlies, and by virtue of his chair he was one of the most constant respondents at Princeton to cultural-evolutionary theories. He was responsible for addressing social theory as part of his course on Christian ethics, and for treating the relationship between Christianity and other religions in his apologetics course.[46] His reviews of Edward Caird's and Max Müller's Gifford Lectures helped to sound the alarm against the transformation of natural-theological inquiry into a kind of learned special pleading for a naturalistic view of religion.[47] With Hodge, Shedd, and Kellogg he rejected the old positivist vision of the history of religion — what he called "the naturalistic evolution of belief" from animism upward — but embraced the language of evolution to convey a decidedly downward story. Commenting on Frank Byron Jevons's *Introduction to the History of Religion,* Greene wrote,

> With a single exception, the evolution of religion has been regressive rather than progressive. Neither has it obeyed the same laws as in the case of the animal or plant. We have not had "first the blade, then the ear, then the full corn in the ear." On the contrary, when men, though knowing God, glorified Him not as God, they changed the glory of the uncorruptible God into an image made like to corruptible man, and to birds, and four-footed beasts and creeping things. This, however, is not against the principle of "the survival of the fittest." Such a religion is the fittest for those who "professing themselves to be wise have become fools."[48]

45. Before Greene they looked to Timothy G. Darling of Auburn and John DeWitt of McCormick (who took church history instead). Warfield to Darling, 2 March 1892, and George D. Baker to Warfield, 24 May 1892, both in Warfield MSS.

46. "Outline Syllabi" of Greene's lectures from 1894, 1905-6, and 1921 are preserved in the PTS Special Collections.

47. Greene, reviews of *The Evolution of Religion,* by Edward Caird, *PRR* 6 (1895): 125-33, and of *Natural Religion,* by Friedrich Max Müller, *PRR* 5 (1894): 95-103.

48. Greene, review of *An Introduction to the History of Religion,* by Frank Byron Jevons,

Even in as Bible-thumping a mode as this, Greene did not dismiss evolutionism altogether. Spencer's own principle argued against Spencer's doctrine: for sinful humanity, not wishing to hold the God of the Bible in their knowledge, religious development proceeded fittingly downward.

As an apologist Greene gathered his data from the research of others, perpetuating the old theological style of learned quotation rather than hands-on investigation. But others in the new seminary faculty followed the pattern McCosh had encouraged in his Bright Young Men. Using the latest German methods, John D. Davis, an undergraduate under McCosh and a seminary student of William Henry Green, argued a developmental case for the authority of the Old Testament. As winner of the seminary's Hebrew Fellowship, he enjoyed two years of study at the University of Leipzig (1884-86), where he learned the new science of Assyriology. He then returned to Princeton's Old Testament department to work alongside his mentor. His tightly argued little book *Genesis and Semitic Tradition,* published in 1894, championed a degenerationist alternative to what the Germans later called the "Babel-Bibel" theory, using the very methods they had taught him.[49]

The ancient Greeks and Jews knew of Babylonian traditions concerning primitive times, but modern scholars had questioned the genuineness of their reports, Davis explained in his introduction. Then in 1872 George Smith uncovered several caches of cuneiform tablets containing the Babylonian myths of creation, the flood, and other stories strikingly similar in theme and even in minute particulars to the stories in the Bible. These appeared in print in 1876 as *The Chaldean Account of Genesis.* The findings suggested that "much, perhaps all, of the doctrine taught in Israel concerning primitive times was an inheritance from Babylonia,"

PRR 9 (1898): 139. Note Greene's explicit tying of the degenerationist principle to the words of Rom. 1:21-22, the classic passage on the insufficiency of natural theology.

49. Virtually the only secondary source on Davis is a brief section of Marion Ann Taylor, *The Old Testament in the Old Princeton School (1812-1929)* (San Francisco: Mellen Research University Press, 1992), pp. 253-59. As a compend of information her book is quite useful, though that usefulness is seriously compromised by the fact that her endnotes get hopelessly out of order in at least one place. Also regrettably, she indulges in rather Whiggish interpretation, repeatedly faulting the Princetonians for lacking the good sense to develop in a direction she would approve. She overlooks the promise the Princetonians saw in their scientific use of the degenerationist hypothesis, almost ignoring *Genesis and Semitic Tradition.* On her telling it would appear that Davis was boringly mouthing the old party line in the old forms, just a bit more rationalistically than before.

and inaugurated the science of Assyriology.[50] Instead of avoiding the similarities and their import, Davis embraced them as aids to elucidating the early chapters of Genesis, establishing the antiquity of the Hebrew narratives as traditions, and contributing a variety of historical particulars, of greater or lesser value, that were lacking in the Bible.

It was obvious, Davis wrote, that the Babylonian tradition was related to the Hebrew — the question was *how*, especially how each related to the original (presumably oral) source.[51] Treating each story in turn — the creation of the universe, the sabbath, the creation of man, the creation of woman, the temptation, Cain and Abel, the Deluge, the Tower of Babel, and others — Davis compared the two accounts to see which was more likely the older, purer source. Case by case he concluded in favor of the Hebrew tradition, the Babylonian representing a degradation, the Hebrew a purer transmission, of an original tradition that was monotheistic and highly ethical. For the creation of the universe, for example, he traced the divergence of the two traditions geographically to southern Mesopotamia, and sketched the steps by which the particulars of the Babylonian account displayed a perversion of the original doctrine into polytheistic nature-worship.[52] Davis did not dwell on the supernaturalness of the original revelation; his intention was rather to argue on the strictest scientific terms that the evidence supported the priority of the Hebrew tradition and that it even suggested the path of degeneration the Babylonian account took. Davis consid-

50. John D. Davis, *Genesis and Semitic Tradition* (New York: Charles Scribner's Sons, 1894), p. iii. See also Oswald T. Allis, "Assyriological Research during the Past Decade," *PTR* 12 (1914): 229-64.

51. Davis, *Genesis and Semitic Tradition*, p. 8. He had no compunction about positing oral sources behind the early histories in Genesis. Moses had to get his information from somewhere, and the Princetonians certainly did not believe it was (much less had to be) *dictated* by God. Rather, God so guided the process of writing and redacting as to render the product infallible. See John D. Davis, "Old Testament History: The Earlier Period," MS lecture notes taken by Alexander N. MacLeod (Fall 1924), PTS Special Collections. For Davis's affirmation of literary evolution in the production of the OT, see especially his review of *The Problem of the Old Testament Considered with Reference to Recent Criticism*, by James Orr, *PTR* 5 (1907): 303-9.

52. Davis, *Genesis and Semitic Tradition*, pp. 20-21. Writing some fourteen years earlier, Alexander MacWhorter drew a contemporary lesson from this point — namely, that the basic choice in religion remained one between worship of the Creator (following the Hebrews) and worship of the creation (following the Chaldeans). MacWhorter, "The Edenic Period of Man," *Princeton Review*, n.s., 1880, part 2 (July-December): 62-91.

ered his conclusion a very natural one, provided the inquirer approached the question without first presupposing the upward evolution of religion. In places where the evidence was inconclusive, he frankly said so. Much unlike the vituperative defenses some writers offered, Davis's book was calm, judicious, and precise.

But the Princetonians did not view degenerationism as the whole story. While savagery and paganism represented downward development, there was plenty of upward development in the natural course of human culture, traceable in history and furnishing equally useful weaponry against the "destructive critics." When Davis succeeded old "Rabbi" William Henry Green in the chair of Oriental and Old Testament Literature in 1901, his inaugural address, "Current Old Testament Discussions and Princeton Opinion," took a developmental line quite different from the degenerationism of his Babel-Bibel book. As in his earlier work and Green's work before it, Davis devoted his research to refuting the "development theory" of the so-called higher criticism — not, however, for its developmentalism as such. According to the theory of Wellhausen and Kuenen, analysis of the first five books of the Bible revealed that they were not written by Moses at the dawn of Hebrew national history but assembled by series of redactors toward the end of that history, after the Babylonian captivity, codifying a compound of practices that had evolved gradually over centuries of Hebrew religious life. The objectionable aspect of this theory was not its interest in historical development, but its denigration of the sacred text's own claims to give a faithful history of God's dealings with his chosen people.

Davis argued that the rituals of worship God commanded of Moses were tailored to the conceptions and tastes of Near Eastern peoples at an already high stage of religious development. Rankings of priests, special ceremonial robes, intricate regulations governing ministerial conduct, a multiplicity of sacrificial offerings and occasions, and the minutely ritualized cult as a whole formed the Egyptian religious milieu out of which Moses led the Hebrews. "The formal worship, viewed in each detail and accessory, and the *tout ensemble,* was a finished product of evolution," Davis stated. "Evolution had been going on for centuries, for millenniums. The simple and obvious had become complex and recondite. The ideas lying at the base of primitive institutions had been wrought out in minute detail and given a subtle expression. Public worship had reached a state of high refinement. Can it be thought strange that the Hebrew legislator should start the national worship of his people with an elaborate ritual?"[53] In this view, the giving of the Law did involve natural development. God's commands to Moses appropriated the products of cultural evolution in Egypt, the "conceptions and tastes" that formed the "conscious needs concerning forms of worship when Moses appeared." God gave the Law supernaturally to Moses, but prepared the people for it by the evolution of religious ritual in Egypt. Egyptian religion was certainly idolatrous, and in that sense degenerate, but its sensibilities and cultic apparatus, the product of a great civilization, were the fruit of natural "evolution." The Princetonians were great believers, after all, in civilization, and held no brief for the denial of its development — especially when such evolution stood on the side of orthodox ideas like the divine authority and Mosaic authorship of the Pentateuch. Davis fought one evolutionary idea with another: the "high refinement" of public worship already at the time of the exodus contradicted the assumed history behind the documentary hypothesis.[54]

Joining Davis in 1900, new professors James Oscar Boyd and Robert Dick Wilson continued this kind of historical countercriticism in Princeton's Old Testament department.[55] University librarian Ernest Richardson took part in the effort, contributing a lengthy article on bibliographic data and the practices of record keeping in and around Egypt at the time of the exodus.[56] The Princetonians sought to meet historical

53. John D. Davis, "Current Old Testament Discussions and Princeton Opinion," *PRR* 13 (1902): 196-97. He says William Henry Green's *Hebrew Feasts in Their Relation to Recent Critical Hypotheses concerning the Pentateuch* (New York: Robert Carter and Brothers, 1885) first showed him the evolution of religion in the ancient Near East.

54. Thus when Davis said, "The development theory has been pronounced by this department to be unscriptural and anti-biblical," not "in bitterness or with invective, but simply as the correct description of the fact," he did not mean that the Princetonians refused all developmentalism whatever. The "evolution" of human institutions was a fact as patent and old as the study of history. It was the particular "development theory" of the "destructive critics" that Davis and Green opposed. Davis, "Current Old Testament Discussions," pp. 198-99; cf. William Henry Green, *The Higher Criticism of the Pentateuch* (New York: Charles Scribner's Sons, 1895).

55. Brief examples include Boyd's review of *Die Beziehungen zwischen Israel und Babylonien*, by J. Köberle, *PTR* 8 (1910): 292-95, and Wilson's review of *Avesta Eschatology Compared with the Books of Daniel and Revelations* [sic], by Lawrence H. Mills, *PTR* 9 (1911): 483-85.

56. Ernest Cushing Richardson, "Documents of the Exodus," *PTR* 10 (1912): 581-605. Richardson found known data on literacy and literary culture to contradict the "picture-background" of the "received critical view" — the historical milieu the critics imagined. He offered instead what he considered a more "natural" theory of cumulative transmission, one that upheld the historicity and authority of the books of Exodus through Judges.

critics on the common ground of historical data, in developmental terms, yet without granting their naturalistic assumptions. In Princeton's view, careful scholarship showed religious development to be a two-way street: sometimes upward, by the grace of God, but often downward. When it came to human beings — created in the divine image, but fallen and corrupt — "nature" was an idea fraught with tension, seriously complicating any story of the "natural" course of cultural, and especially religious, evolution. In Princeton's eyes the destructive critics failed to appreciate sin's consequences for evolution, and so abused the true insights of developmentalism.

The Nature of the Supernatural

In the autumn of 1896, following the college's sesquicentennial anniversary and rechristening as Princeton University, Warfield opened the seminary year with an address entitled "Christian Supernaturalism." Taking his lead from John Bascom's recent statement that "the relation of the natural and supernatural is the question of questions which underlies our rational life," Warfield called upon the seminary to position itself between the "two extremes of atheistic naturalism and superstitious supernaturalism."[57] The cure for science's increasingly antisupernaturalistic bias was not a pendulum swing in the other direction, Warfield believed, but a careful investigation of the middle ground, guided both by well-established Christian doctrine and by the newer insights of natural science. The nineteenth century had produced not only a scientific revolution, with its boons and its excesses, but an explosion of what Warfield regarded as more or less hopeless religious quackeries as well: transcendentalism, spiritism, mind-cure, adventism, the "Higher Life," Oberlin perfectionism, John Humphrey Noyes's "Bible communism," and — worst of all, to Warfield and his invalid wife — the empty promises of that bizarrely named religion of Mary Baker Eddy's, Christian Science.[58] Naturalism, or as the Princetonians now be-

---

57. Benjamin Breckinridge Warfield, "Christian Supernaturalism," in his *Studies in Theology,* in *The Works of Benjamin B. Warfield,* ed. Ethelbert D. Warfield et al., vol. 9 (New York: Oxford University Press, 1932; Grand Rapids: Baker, 1991), p. 25.

58. See Benjamin Breckinridge Warfield, *Counterfeit Miracles,* Smyth Lectures for 1917-18 (New York: Charles Scribner's Sons, 1918); also his *Perfectionism,* vols. 1 and 2, in *The Works of Benjamin B. Warfield,* ed. Ethelbert D. Warfield et al., vols. 7 and 8 (New York: Oxford University Press, 1931; Grand Rapids: Baker, 1991).

gan to phrase it, "antisupernaturalism," was the philosophical enemy the Princetonians fought most characteristically; but superstition, too, was alive and flourishing. In their bid to retain a properly Christian supernaturalism in an evolutionary age, the Princetonians strove also to define it against obscurantism and credulity.

"The atheistic naturalism of the eighteenth century has long since taken up its abode with the owls and bats," Warfield intoned, "but the world has not yet learned its lesson." A movement more powerful now drove the modern world to practically the same conclusion, the denial of the supernatural. Under "the magic watchword of 'evolution'" a fundamentally pantheistic worldview "strives to break down and obliterate all the lines of demarcation which separate things that differ," reducing all being to the blind interplay of forces that the monist, in his more religious moments, called God.[59] Willing on the one hand to consider the possibility even of human evolution, Warfield on the other hand minced no words about the pernicious effects of evolutionary monism. "How absolutely determinant the conception of evolution has become in the thinking of our age, there can be no need to remind ourselves," Warfield said, without complaint. "It may not be amiss, however, to recall the anti-supernaturalistic root and the anti-supernaturalistic effect of the dominance of this mode of conceiving things," he added — "and thus to identify in it the cause of the persistent anti-supernaturalism which at present characterizes the world's thought." Evolutionism too often, too freely served monistic rationalism, a revival of the Enlightenment's refusal to bow to the God revealed in Scripture. The path was different, but the end was the same: an impulse, in Bascom's words, "to curb the supernatural."[60]

This is by now a familiar line of argument, but it is noteworthy to find Warfield himself fingering evolution as an accomplice in the shell

---

59. Warfield, "Christian Supernaturalism," p. 28. Warfield was fond of saying that the only real difference between a rationalist and a mystic was one of "temperature." Each located religious authority inside the self, where either unaided reason or mystical experience produced the only acceptable conviction of truth. Collapsing all authority into internal authority, each tended toward pantheistic monism, the identification of self with the all, and the all with God. A warm monist was a mystic; a cool one was a rationalist. This figure first appeared in Warfield's review of *Hours with the Mystics*, by Robert Alfred Vaughan, *PRR* 5 (1894): 358; he continued to use it as late as 1917, in "Mysticism and Christianity," in *Studies in Theology*, p. 656.

60. Warfield, "Christian Supernaturalism," p. 28.

game of modern antisupernaturalism. The Princetonians had for decades preserved an attitude of calm patience as they separated the question of scientific fact from its philosophical uses or misuses. Now even in Warfield, that paragon of Princetonian confidence in science, a dark undertone sometimes shaded the discussion of evolutionism. The old foes of Hodge's and Atwater's day (positivism and materialism) and of Patton's early tenure (antitheism) had merged in a category called antisupernaturalism — and found their expression and justification, Warfield had to admit, in the idea of evolution.[61]

But the answer, as before, was not to raise an outcry against evolutionary thinking, but to recall it to the wider truths of God's world. "How shall we so firmly brace ourselves that, as the flood of the world's thought beats upon us, it may bring us cleansing and refreshment, but may not sweep us away from our grasp on Christian truth?" Warfield asked. "How, but by constantly reminding ourselves of what Christianity is, and of what as Christian men we must needs believe as to the nature and measure of the supernatural in its impact on the life of the world?"

> Christian truth is a rock too securely planted to go down before any storm. Let us attach ourselves to it by such strong cables, and let us know so well its promontories of vantage and secure hiding-places, that though the waters may go over us we shall not be moved. To this end it will not be useless to recall continually the frankness of Christianity's commitment to the absolute supernatural. And it may be that we shall find profit in enumerating at this time a few of the points, at least, at which, as Christian men, we must recognize, with all heartiness, the intrusion of pure supernaturalism into our conception of things.[62]

Warfield set an agenda for himself and his school: to probe the nature of the supernatural, identifying its points of "intrusion" into God's standard operating procedure, natural law. In the next few decades he set about the task. It fell neatly into two parts, a metaphysical and a religious one. Warfield pondered the modes of supernatural activity — the differences between creation, providence, and miracle, and their revealed place

---

61. This point is important because later fundamentalists took up the identification of evolutionism as the root of all evil in modern religious thought. Warfield even names four of the five future "fundamentals" in this piece.

62. Warfield, "Christian Supernaturalism," p. 31.

in Christian doctrine[63] — and he then applied those understandings both to judge the putative supernaturalism of various religious movements and to shed light on such pressing theological issues as the modes of revelation and the nature of Christian regeneration. Beginning within the long-standing metaphysical discourse of Christian theology, he used the issues raised by evolutionism (providentially raised, in his view) to clarify that discourse, and then turned to apply it back in the religious arena.[64]

Warfield's starting point for this inquiry into the metaphysics of evolution was the claim of theistic evolutionists, especially his old mentor McCosh, that evolution represented God's "method of creation." As he considered this claim in the light of his inherited theological categories, he encountered a conundrum, for the workings of natural law, and thus evolution, fit under the category of *providence*, a category carefully distinguished, traditionally, from *creation*. "Who can say," he asked in 1896, "whether creation itself, in the purity and absoluteness of that conception, may not be progressive, and may not correlate itself with and follow the process of the providential development of the world, in the plan of such a God — so that the works of creation and providence may interlace through all time in the production of this completed universe?"[65] This somewhat indistinct possibility played in Warfield's mind until he refined it decisively in an article written for a little periodical called the *Bible Student*[66] in 1901 — probably the fruit of his consideration of these issues in his extracurricular seminar "Evolution in Its Relations to Theology."

63. For Warfield and the other Princetonians an inquiry into the supernatural was not a contradiction in terms. For many naturalists a strong argument for naturalism was the claim that only natural laws were rationally accessible — what might happen outside the realm of law was almost by definition unpredictable, unknowable. "God did it" was just the kind of impenetrable "explanation" they set out to replace. Science asked *how* things occurred, by what means. But for the Princetonians the activities of God were eminently reasonable, whether supernatural or not — witness Greene's view that the kingdom of God grew in this world by a process properly called progressive evolution, parallel to the process of God's working in natural history (see chapter 7 above). Philosophy could penetrate something of the supernatural; theology could go further, having a divine revelation to work from.

64. See especially the polemical articles Warfield wrote at the very end of his life, 1918-20, reprinted in *Perfectionism*.

65. Warfield, "Christian Supernaturalism," p. 37.

66. The *Bible Student* was a venture in popularizing conservative theological views to a lay audience, mainly Sunday school teachers and less academically inclined pastors. It was begun and run jointly in its early years by Warfield and William Marcellus McPheeters, a comrade in the Southern Church. I am indebted to Rev. William O. Harris, former archivist of Princeton Seminary, for this information.

Warfield came to a conclusion somewhat startling for a theologian open to evolution: the contention that "evolution" and "creation" were "mutually exclusive" terms — that "'Evolution' . . . is the precise contradictory of 'creation.'" Citing Charles Darwin as a prime example, Warfield asserted that evolution's attraction for many thinkers lay precisely "in its assumed capacity to explain the origin of things without the assumption of creation" and creation's God.[67] But his point was not at all to abandon the reader to a stark either/or, creation *or* evolution. Thankfully, evolution proved unsuited to Darwin's purpose — at best it could offer only an infinite series in place of the eternal God, landing us back with the ancient Greeks at the dawn of Western philosophy, asking whether a chain of any length could hang from nothing, and answering, as they did, *No*. Evolution was the opposite of creation, but evolution needed creation in the first place.

Some theistic evolutionists[68] called on God to create the original world stuff, and on evolution to account for its subsequent modification. But thus to arrange creation and evolution led, Warfield argued, to confining God's creative activity to the beginning of the world process, ruling out any subsequent acts directly supernatural, any subsequent intrusions into the natural course of things. This was deism, and unacceptable to the Christian, for the whole life and work of Christ involved the intrusion of the supernatural into human history, starting with the incarnation itself. Whatever its good intentions, this brand of theistic evolution, by virtue of its muddled metaphysics, collapsed into deism.

Other theistic evolutionists[69] classed evolution in the theological category of "mediate creation," but to Warfield this was equally problematic. Evolution as modification meant *providence*, God's supernatural direction of natural causes to effect a predetermined end. It was a mode of supernatural activity, but always an indirect mode. Theistic evolutionists

---

67. Warfield, "Editorial Notes," *Bible Student*, n.s., 4, no. 1 (July 1901): 3. "Darwin asserted that he would cease to care for 'evolution' if it did not supersede the necessity for assuming even a directing activity of God."

68. Warfield's example here was Otto Pfleiderer, "Evolution and Theology," in *Evolution and Theology and Other Essays*, ed. Orello Cone (London: Adam and Charles Black, 1900). Warfield, "Editorial Notes," pp. 1-2.

69. Here Warfield cited naturalist Edward Drinker Cope and a Dr. R. S. McArthur, who in turn cited Hartshorne, Asa Gray, McCosh, Baden Powell, and the Duke of Argyll. His prime example of this mistake, though, was the Roman Catholic J. A. Zahm's *Evolution and Dogma*. Warfield, "Editorial Notes," pp. 4-7.

went wrong in allowing the language of evolution as God's "method of creation" to suggest that evolution belonged in the category of mediate creation rather than providence. A mediate creation was an act of God within the web of natural causes, but producing something the natural causes themselves could never produce — it was the intrusion of direct supernatural power into the natural order, as when Jesus turned water into wine. Since the water had no power in itself to become wine, it was not, properly speaking, a means God used to effect the miracle; it was only the object miraculously acted upon by an immediate, supernatural cause. The water was there by God's providence, but it became wine by a miracle, a mediate creation. Unfortunately, the term "mediate creation" suggested *creation* by means, by second causes, *by providence* — something definitionally impossible. All creation proper was direct supernatural activity; it never used means, though it often acted on objects. When creation and providence worked together, "each contributing something to the effect," yielding "mixed products of the immediate and mediate activity of God," that was mediate creation.[70]

The upshot of all these distinctions was this: to define evolution as a mediate creation tended to reduce the category of mediate creation to mere providence, thus throwing us back to deism, to "natural religion." The biblical miracles, the incarnation and resurrection of Christ, the believer's regeneration, the hope of glory — all these were instances of mediate creation, the intertwining of God's distinct modes of activity as Creator and Sustainer. Mediate creation was the supernatural mode that set historic Christianity apart from the natural religion that so many "liberals" smilingly substituted for the real thing. To make providence do the work of mediate creation, as theistic evolutionists tended to attempt, was impossible — and, said Warfield, it was deadly for Christian supernatu-

---

70. Warfield took his definition of mediate creation from the seventeenth-century Calvinist theologian Wollebius (Johannes Wolleb of Basel, 1586-1629), citing his *Compendium Theologiae Christianae* (orig. 1626). "'Creation,' he says, 'is that act by which God, for the manifestation of the glory of His power, wisdom, and goodness, has produced the world and all that is in it,' — we relapse now into his Latin — *'partim ex nihilo, partim ex materia naturaliter inhabili,'* — that is to say, in part, out of nothing, and in part out of pre-existing material indeed, but material not itself capable of producing this effect. Again: 'to create is not only to make something out of nothing but also *ex materia inhabili supra naturae vires aliquid producere,'* — to produce something out of this inapt material, above what the powers intrinsic in it are capable of producing." Warfield, "Editorial Notes," p. 5. Warfield almost certainly taught these distinctions to his students; we know his assistant did by 1906-7 (see chapter 9 below).

ralism. Evolution was providence, not a "method of creation," and providence was no substitute for miracle. Thus evolution presented no threat to Christian supernaturalism, once you got the metaphysics straight — and supernaturalism presented no threat to evolution, the reign of law, once evolution recognized its inability to take the Creator's place.

Warfield even went so far as to call on John Calvin himself to confirm the orthodoxy of this view of things. In the article "Calvin's Doctrine of the Creation" (1915), Warfield explained that the great reformer identified providence, not mediate creation, as the mode of God's activity in the origination of life-forms. Not having benefit of geology's discoveries, Calvin believed God had created everything in the space of six literal days — taking pains, interestingly enough, to explain why it took so *long*, considering that the Almighty could have done it all in a flash.[71] But insofar as he distinguished modification from creation, ascribing to providence the protracted, progressive activity of God over the six creative days, Calvin taught, in Warfield's opinion, "pure evolutionism." The passage is worth quoting at length:

> Calvin's doctrine of creation is, if we have understood it aright, for all except the souls of men, an evolutionary one. The "indigested mass," including the "promise and potency" of all that was yet to be, was called into being by the simple *fiat* of God. But all that has come into being since — except the souls of men alone — has arisen as a modification of this original world-stuff by means of the interaction of its intrinsic forces. Not these forces apart from God, of course: Calvin is a high theist, that is, a supernaturalist. . . . all the modifications of the world-stuff have taken place under the directly upholding and governing hand of God, and find their account ultimately in His will. But they find their account proximately in "second causes"; and this is not only evolutionism but pure evolutionism.[72]

71. The answer: it was "a condescension of God in distributing His work into six days that our finite intelligence might not be overwhelmed with its contemplation" — a manifestation of his paternal care for his creatures, humankind. Warfield, "Calvin's Doctrine of the Creation," pp. 298-99.

72. Warfield, "Calvin's Doctrine of the Creation," pp. 304-5. Warfield cited Bavinck's Stone Lectures to support the claim — Bavinck said that the incorporation of Aristotle into Christian theology had introduced the idea of development to Christian thinkers, arousing "'no objection whatever. . . . On the contrary, it received extension and enrichment by being linked with the principle of theism.'" Warfield added, "Calvin accordingly very naturally thought along the lines of a theistic evolutionism" (p. 306 n. 45).

Warfield hastened to add, "Calvin doubtless had no theory whatever of evolution; but he teaches a doctrine of evolution" in its essential points, hampered only by his ignorance of the geologic timetable. Had he lengthened the six days into aeons of the earth's growth, Warfield ventured to speculate, "Calvin would have been a precursor of the modern evolutionary theorists."[73]

Warfield had noticed, then, that old-style theistic evolutionism tended toward theological naturalism, and he had found a cure that allowed him to retain both his belief in the likelihood of evolution and his belief in supernatural Christianity. His approach followed the old Princeton tack. Abstruse though it was, his metaphysical discussion was precisely the sort of thing a theologian, as opposed to a philosopher or a natural scientist, ought to contribute to the evolution question. Its very difficulty served to highlight the folly of inexpert forays into the theological domain.

Can we properly call Warfield a theistic evolutionist? His article in the *Bible Student* took exception to merely theistic schemes, arguing that theism was not enough. Much of the antisupernaturalism in modern thought proudly wore the theistic label, but shared with the deists of old an antipathy to any intervening divine activity — this was something the Calvinists of Princeton could not abide. No hope for the sinner lay within himself or the world system; only the miracle of spiritual rebirth could make these dead bones live. Warfield was a theist, but more than a theist; an evolutionist, but more than an evolutionist. Theism and evolutionism were to him only partial, natural visions of the work of the living, redeeming, supernatural God.[74]

73. Warfield, "Calvin's Doctrine of the Creation," pp. 305-6.

74. Both historians and theologians have disagreed over whether to call Warfield a theistic evolutionist. For example, Noll and Livingstone are sure the label fits; Fred Zaspel is equally sure that it does not. David N. Livingstone and Mark A. Noll, "B. B. Warfield (1851-1921): A Biblical Inerrantist as Evolutionist," *Isis* 91 (2000): 283-304; Livingstone, *Adam's Ancestors*, pp. 159-61; Fred G. Zaspel, *The Theology of B. B. Warfield: A Systematic Summary* (Wheaton, Ill.: Crossway, 2010), pp. 369-87. For my take on this issue, see the conclusion.

CHAPTER NINE

Fundamentalism

Sooner or later, I am sure, the eyes of men will be opened and they will see — would to God they might see it now! — that the great battle of the twentieth century is in its final issue a struggle between a Dogmatic Christianity on the one hand and an out-and-out naturalistic philosophy on the other.

Francis Landey Patton, 1903[1]

No one will doubt that Christians of to-day must state their Christian belief in terms of modern thought. Every age has a language of its own and can speak no other. Mischief comes only when, instead of stating Christian belief in terms of modern thought, an effort is made, rather, to state modern thought in terms of Christian belief.

Benjamin Breckinridge Warfield, 1913[2]

"It appears to have been early observed," B. B. Warfield wrote in 1918, "that the mills of the gods grind very slowly: and hasty spirits have been only partially reconciled to that fact by the further observation that they

---

1. Francis Landey Patton, "Theological Encyclopaedia," in *Biblical and Theological Studies, by the Members of the Faculty of Princeton Theological Seminary* (New York: Charles Scribner's Sons, 1912), pp. 33-34. This was Patton's inaugural address as seminary president, 1903.

2. Benjamin Breckinridge Warfield, review of *Foundations*, by B. H. Streeter et al., *Princeton Theological Review* (hereafter *PTR*) 10 (1913): 528.

do their work exceedingly well." Warfield was a great believer in process, finding most things of value in this world to come by sustained effort over time. The heavenly mills ground slowly, but well; this, Warfield believed, was God's way, whether in creation or redemption. History — time and development — framed human existence. Growth was the rule of life, both natural and spiritual, and growth came by pain, patience, and effort. It was a mark of narrow vision, even of inferior piety, to seek to bypass time and demand quick fixes from God.

> Men are unable to understand why time should be consumed in divine works. Why should the almighty Maker of the heaven and earth take millions of years to create the world? Why should He bring the human race into being by a method which leaves it ever incomplete? Above all, in His recreation of a lost race, why should He proceed by process? Men are unwilling that either the world or they themselves should be saved by God's secular methods. They demand immediate, tangible results. They ask, Where is the promise of His coming? They ask to be themselves made glorified saints in the twinkling of an eye. God's ways are not their ways, and it is a great trial to them that God will not walk in their ways.

"They love the storm and the earthquake and the fire," Warfield complained. "They cannot see the divine in 'a sound of gentle stillness,' and adjust themselves with difficulty to the lengthening perspective of God's gracious working." God's normal procedure is to work slowly, by process, by growth — but people have trouble seeing God in the effort of everyday. They expect the supernatural to intrude suddenly and strikingly. "They look every day for the cataclysm in which alone they can recognize God's salvation."[3]

To anyone familiar with the young-earth creationism and catastrophic premillennialism we now associate with the fundamentalist movement, Warfield's words here seem a world apart. But change came quickly. Three years after he penned these lines Warfield was dead; a year later the fundamentalist controversies broke out in earnest with two events in New York City. In February 1922 William Jennings Bryan

---

3. Benjamin Breckinridge Warfield, "The Victorious Life" (1918), in his *Perfectionism*, vol. 2, in *The Works of Benjamin B. Warfield*, ed. Ethelbert D. Warfield et al., vol. 8 (New York: Oxford University Press, 1932; Grand Rapids: Baker, 1991), p. 561. In this article Warfield details his view of the Christian life as itself a process or growth.

wrote an article for the *New York Times,* "God and Evolution," sparking a media and legislative battle that in three years' time directed hundreds of reporters and the attention of millions to the celebrated "monkey trial" in Dayton, Tennessee. In May 1922 Harry Emerson Fosdick, a Baptist minister supplying the pulpit of New York's First Presbyterian Church, preached a sermon called "Shall the Fundamentalists Win?" It launched a fifteen-year struggle in the Presbyterian Church (USA), splitting Princeton Seminary, the church's mission work, and the denomination, and culminating in the ironic trial of a conservative, by liberals, for heresy. These two trajectories were partially intertwined; again and again they intersected in Princeton. The heirs of the combined legacy of McCosh and Hodge, the legacy personified in Warfield until 1921, fought out the decade among themselves — but on a national stage.

The *Princeton Theological Review* for 1922 carried four articles portending the issues and battles soon to break out. The inaugural address of Warfield's successor, Caspar Wistar Hodge Jr., opened the year's first number: "The Significance of the Reformed Theology Today." Hodge had assisted Warfield in the department of theology for some twenty years. He presented Calvinism — creedal, Westminster Calvinism — as the crying need of the modern world.[4] His address recalled Princeton's dogmatic particularism, the hearty Calvinism that set it apart from much of nineteenth-century evangelical theological development and made the Princetonians uneasy allies of transdenominational fundamentalism.

"Liberalism or Christianity?" by J. Gresham Machen, also appeared in January. Its blunt title indicated Machen's belief that a moment of truth had come in the church, the time to separate the sheep from the goats, doctrinally speaking. Liberalism only masqueraded as Christianity, he argued; liberals should have the courage and honesty to admit that the religion they taught, whatever its merits, was not the historic faith.[5] It was Machen who led the exodus of students and faculty from Princeton Seminary after the church forced its reorganization in 1929, who formed an Independent Board of Foreign Missions in protest against the liberalism of the church's official board, and who was the only Presbyterian to stand trial for heresy in the twentieth century.

William Brenton Greene Jr.'s article "Yet Another Criticism of the

---

4. Caspar Wistar Hodge Jr., "The Significance of the Reformed Theology Today," *PTR* 20 (1922): 1-14.

5. J. Gresham Machen, "Liberalism or Christianity?" *PTR* 20 (1922): 93-117.

Theory of Evolution" followed in the October number. Citing Princeton University scientists William Berryman Scott and Edwin Grant Conklin, Greene endeavored to show that evolution was a world philosophy, not a set of scientific facts, and that the great metaphysical question facing modern thinkers was a radical choice between evolutionism and supernaturalism. In a reversal of his earlier allowances, Greene declared that evolution could account for species (or, as he now called them, "variations") only "within the type."[6]

The fourth article, also in October, came from the hand of George McCready Price: "The Fossils as Age-Markers in Geology." A Seventh-day Adventist with little formal scientific training, Price taught geology at a tiny Adventist college in Nebraska. His article, like his books before it, proposed nothing short of a revolution in science, repudiating the geologic timescale and the succession of strata, and explaining the entire fossil record as the product of Noah's flood.[7] As Ronald Numbers has shown, Price's "flood geology" eventually played a direct, highly influential role in the development of fundamentalist scientific creationism.[8] Until 1922 Price was a complete stranger to Princeton. His view of geology contradicted every Princetonian since Dod and Hodge; his stance outside the scientific mainstream contradicted Princeton's Battle Plan of three generations to "mold the age." Yet seminary professor Oswald T. Allis, editor of the *Review,* purposely asked Price for an article.

In the next several years Princetonians opposed each other on both sides of both issues, theological liberalism and evolutionism. From the American Museum of Natural History in New York, Henry Fairfield Osborn, one of McCosh's proudest Bright Young Men, led a print war to thwart Bryan's antievolution campaign, then rallied scientific troops and media attention to Dayton for the Scopes trial. In the Presbyterian General Assembly, seminary director Clarence E. Macartney teamed up with Bryan to lead the fundamentalist contingent in the battle over Fosdick's sermon. Biology professor Edwin Grant Conklin headed the American Association for the Advancement of Science's committee on evolution, formed to quell popular suspicion that evolution was a "mere guess." In-

6. William Brenton Greene Jr., "Yet Another Criticism of the Theory of Evolution," *PTR* 20 (1922): 537-61.

7. George McCready Price, "The Fossils as Age-Markers in Geology," *PTR* 20 (1922): 585-615.

8. Ronald L. Numbers, *The Creationists: The Evolution of Scientific Creationism* (Berkeley: University of California Press, 1993), centers around Price's views and influence.

ternal strife over Princeton Seminary's polemical tradition focused the Presbyterian fundamentalist controversy on that institution, where President J. Ross Stevenson and Professor Charles R. Erdman faced off against Professor J. Gresham Machen.[9] At stake were Princeton's long-standing war against naturalistic worldviews, its solidarity within the citadel of faith, and the once-celebrated peace it had struck with evolution.

Pure Supernaturalism

Twenty years after William Berryman Scott became the first trained scientist to teach transmutationism at Princeton, another grandson of Charles Hodge joined the seminary's department of dogmatic theology. Caspar Wistar Hodge Jr. (1870-1937) was the son of Warfield's revered mentor in New Testament, whom Warfield once described as "my divinity on earth."[10] Wistar Sr. had been one of Charles Woodruff Shields's most outspoken critics and had originated the idea of bringing Guyot and Atwater to the seminary to lecture on science and religion in the 1860s.[11] Wistar Jr. (or, as some students called him, "Wee Hodge") earned a Ph.D. in the philosophy department of Patton's College of New Jersey, where he studied under Alexander T. Ormond and James Mark Baldwin. His doctoral dissertation, "The Kantian Epistemology and Theism," was praised by Patton as "capital," and appeared in part in the *Presbyterian and Reformed Review*.[12] He had a taste for physiological psychology as well, publishing a few articles in Baldwin's *Psychological Review*. After advanced study in Heidelberg and Berlin, he returned to the newly renamed Princeton University as an instructor in philosophy, then took an associate professorship in ethics at Lafayette College, where Warfield's

9. See Bradley J. Longfield, *The Presbyterian Controversy: Fundamentalists, Modernists, and Moderates* (New York: Oxford University Press, 1991), and Darryl G. Hart, *Defending the Faith: J. Gresham Machen and the Crisis of Conservative Protestantism in Modern America* (Baltimore: Johns Hopkins University Press, 1994).

10. Warfield to Archibald Alexander Hodge, ca. 1881, Hodge Family MSS, PU Library.

11. Caspar Wistar Hodge to Charles Hodge, 9 March 1860, Hodge Family MSS. Wistar Hodge minced no words on Shields, calling him a "fizzling city preacher" and "green gosling" whose imaginative discourses were "filled in with a wonderful lot of namby-pamby & sing-song."

12. Caspar Wistar Hodge Jr., "The Kantian Epistemology and Theism" (Ph.D. diss., Princeton University, 1894), pamphlet (Philadelphia: McCalla and Co., 1894), PTS Special Collections.

brother Ethelbert served as president. After this first career in philosophy Hodge entered Princeton Seminary, graduating in 1901. He immediately became Warfield's assistant in systematic theology. In 1907 he was inaugurated as assistant professor in that department; on Warfield's death in 1921 he acceded to the foremost chair of the seminary. His very biography made him something of a culmination of old Princeton.[13]

Early in Hodge's seminary teaching career (1906-7) Warfield entrusted him with the portion of second-year theology that treated the origin of species, particularly of man. What Warfield had covered in one longish lecture in 1888, Hodge now treated in five — an indication itself of the increased complexity of the situation at the start of the twentieth century. Hodge articulated his discussion systematically, as might be expected from a trained philosopher, echoing his grandfather's style far more than Warfield's. But in both the identification of root issues and the conclusions he drew, Hodge followed Warfield closely, devoting three of the five lectures to "the mode of man's origin." These hinged on the question of human evolution, a question he considered in light of Warfield's three modes of supernatural activity: evolution, mediate creation, and creation (or, respectively, providence, miracle, and creation proper).

Hodge stressed at the outset the Bible's near indifference to the scientific particulars of the case. Its main concern was with "the nature of man and his primitive or original condition" — Adam's sinless communion with God before the Fall, the starting point of the whole covenant theology. But Hodge refused the Ritschlian device of separating Christianity from historical and scientific fact. The Bible was full of "psychological statements" in the Old Testament and especially in Paul's teachings on *sarx* (body), *psyche* (soul), and *pneuma* (spirit), he said, so that clearly "the Bible is making statements in a sphere which is also open to scientific investigation" — this from a man who had done graduate laboratory research in physiological psychology. By the same token, to the limited degree that the Scripture did give information on the mode and time of human origins, such data must be taken seriously. It would not do to claim that the Bible's teaching "is *so general* that *any* scientific hypothesis will fit with it." "The Bible does teach enough of a definite character upon these questions of anthropology to place it in conflict with a prevalent *speculative* view *supposed* to be based upon assured scientific

---

13. *Biographical Catalogue of Princeton Theological Seminary,* vol. 1, 1815-1932, comp. Edward Howell Roberts (Princeton: Trustees of the Seminary, 1933), p. 504.

discoveries. The modern so-called scientific view upon these points, which after all is a speculative construction, does stand in conflict with that of the Bible."[14] Hodge believed firmly in what his grandfather had called the "twin daughters of heaven" — the ultimate concord of science and religion — but, like his grandfather, he was not afraid to acknowledge a conflict when he saw one. It was clear to him already in 1906-7 that "the modern so-called scientific view" of human evolution demanded the elimination of any intrusive supernaturalism, and that that demand struck at the heart of redemptive Christianity.[15]

In spite of that serious disclaimer, however, Hodge told his students in no uncertain terms that the Bible's teaching on human origins did not exclude the possibility of prehuman ancestry. After a brief exegesis of Genesis 1 and 2 that borrowed from John Laidlaw's *Bible Doctrine of Man*,[16] Hodge concluded that the Bible taught positively "that man was created by God, and apparently God was more directly concerned in man's origin than in that of the rest of creation," and that man's body "was dust from the earth, i.e., it was made out of preexisting material." Humankind originated in a mediate creation — this was the Bible's teaching. As to "whether the immediately preceding link in the genetic series was a clod of earth or an organic form," Hodge said the Bible was indifferent. What mattered was that man "was *made* — i.e., his rise is not due simply to the *unfolding* of the second causes or phenomenal series under Divine guidance or Providential control. There was an *intrusion* of originating or creative activity on the part of God *somewhere* in the origin of man."[17]

14. Caspar Wistar Hodge Jr., MS Notes on Anthropology (Systematic Theology course, middle year), Lecture 1, PTS Special Collections. The quotation is taken from sheet 3 (Hodge did not number the pages), and I have spelled out his abbreviations. Emphasis in original.

15. Here Hodge followed James Orr's Stone Lectures at PTS (1903-4), *God's Image in Man and Its Defacement, in the Light of Modern Denials*, 2nd ed. (New York: A. C. Armstrong and Son, 1906), which, though friendly toward transmutationism, emphasized the irreconcilable conflict between antisupernaturalistic evolution and Christianity on the question of human origins and human nature. Orr's lectures strongly influenced the Princetonians. They were required reading in theology instructor Finley Jenkins's upper-level elective course on "the doctrine of man" (designed entirely with reference to the evolution question) in the late 1920s. Finley DuBois Jenkins, "The Doctrine of Man," MS lecture notes taken by Alexander N. MacLeod (1928), PTS Special Collections.

16. John Laidlaw, *The Bible Doctrine of Man; or, The Anthropology and Psychology of Scripture*, 2nd ed. (Edinburgh: T. & T. Clark, 1895; reprinted 1905).

17. C. W. Hodge, MS Notes on Anthropology, sheets 11-12, abbreviations spelled out, emphasis in original. "As to the *mode* of man's origin all it says is (to use Dr. Warfield's ex-

As to this "somewhere," Hodge said the Scripture "leaves room" for animal precursors of not only the human body but also the soul. Genesis 2 said God breathed into man's nostrils the breath of life, but Hodge pointed out that throughout the Bible the breath of God was "the animating principle of the whole animal creation," so that the passage "does not say in so many words that God made the body and the soul," differentiating, that is, between the two acts. The passage simply did not give particulars. Since the book of Ecclesiastes seemed to assign "a more direct activity of God" to the origin of the soul, Hodge concluded that it was either "immediately created by God (i.e., from nothing)" or it bore "a genetic connection with lower forms of soul life," forms that in themselves lacked "the power or potency to produce it [the human soul] simply under God's guidance." God may have made man from an animal progenitor, but if so he did it by a miracle. Hodge allowed a theory of descent, but expressly not of evolution. Though possibly making use of "a preceding form of life," God used supernatural power to make humanity, "i.e., a mediate creation analogous to the turning of water to wine."[18]

Hodge was arguing from the Bible, seeking to discern what it affirmed positively and what it left open, in view of the prevalence of scientific theories of human evolution. He allowed as fully biblical both the evolution (not just the mediate creation) of the human body and the mediate creation (from animal precursors, but not by mere evolution) of the human soul. He also allowed the creation of the soul ex nihilo.[19] He

---

pression) that God made man of animated dust or stuff, *and* man owes his animation to the will of God" (sheet 10).

18. C. W. Hodge, MS Notes on Anthropology, sheet 13, abbreviations spelled out. Note that this allowance of animal precursors to the soul was expressly *not* a doctrine of soul evolution. Hodge insisted that it was an act of creation, whether mediate or immediate. Thus his position here differed from what we observed Warfield toying with in the early 1890s, where human souls *evolved* from animal souls after the creation of soul life further back in the family tree (see chapter 8 above).

19. C. W. Hodge, MS Notes on Anthropology, sheets 13-14. "Thus to sum up — We must make room for the *Supernatural* in the mode of man's origin. First. This may be in both body and soul. If so it must be a mediate creation of the body and may be a mediate creation or immediate creation of the soul. Or second. The Supernatural may enter only in [the case of] the soul. If so then it must be either a mediate or an immediate creation. We think that the Scripture account of the mode of man's origin leaves room for these alternatives. In general it gives the impression of a more immediate activity of God in the creation of man, but not necessarily without the intervention of second causes" (emphasis in original). Again I have spelled out his abbreviations.

worded his conclusion not in terms of where to allow evolution, but in terms of where to require supernatural intrusion. "Thus to sum up," he stated, "we must make room for the *Supernatural* in the mode of man's origin." His conclusion was not "humans may have evolved," but "we must make room for the Supernatural." Scripturally, it was a matter of indifference what forebears humanity may have had; what counted was the recognition of not just divine activity in nature, but *intrusive* divine activity at this crucial point. Hodge stressed the metaphysical question, as had Warfield before him. He did so not merely to preserve the possibility of miracle for the sake of redemptive religion, but expressly because on his reading the Bible did not permit a purely evolutionary — that is, a purely natural — account of human origins.

Hodge thus made the metaphysical question also a biblical question. It was not, however, the biblical question the fundamentalists asked. Fundamentalists (of the Bryanite antievolutionist variety) said the biblical question was about ancestry; Hodge said it was about supernatural intrusion. Fundamentalists rejected all theories of brute ancestry alike, as theories of "human evolution." Hodge found the Bible indifferent to the question of ancestry, but emphatic on the question of supernatural intrusion to produce man. He allowed the possibility of animal forebears, but not of human evolution (that is, by providence, solely by means of natural causes), at least not for the production of the soul. His position was nearly identical to that of George Frederick Wright, professor of the harmony of science and revelation at Oberlin. As Ronald Numbers has shown, Wright was profoundly influenced by the Princetonians, especially through an evening of earnest discussion with Warfield and Green in the early 1890s.[20] Since to distinguish descent from evolution simply did not fit the categories of creationism-versus-evolutionism, there was a sense in which Hodge and Wright (and Warfield) allowed "human evolution" and a sense in which they denied it. The body *may* have come by providence (evolution); the soul *must* have come by creation (whether ex nihilo or mediate). If evolution meant brute ancestry, they allowed it; if evolution meant no supernatural intrusion, they denied it.[21]

20. Numbers, *The Creationists*, pp. 26, 29.

21. Basing his excellent study on the polarity between creationism and brute ancestry — a polarity that has indeed marked scientific creationism since the 1920s — Numbers has difficulty seeing coherence in Wright's position. He writes, "Wright's true views on evolution, especially on the origin of humans, remain as puzzling today as they did to [fundamentalist leader A. C.] Dixon in 1915. Did he believe, as he wrote in *The Fundamentals*, that

After the world war, when fundamentalist preachers Amzi C. Dixon, William Bell Riley, and John Roach Straton teamed up with William Jennings Bryan in a crusade against human evolutionism — meaning any theory of prehuman ancestry whatsoever — Hodge continued to teach his seminarians from these lecture notes, with very few changes apparent in the manuscript.[22] Bryan's attempt to secure a statement against "human evolution" from the Presbyterian General Assembly of 1923[23] also appears not to have swayed Hodge from his earlier position. He weathered the storm quietly, perhaps feeling the difficulty of the situation more acutely because of his position in Warfield's chair, and certainly sensing that his careful distinctions were incompatible with the broad brush of Bryanism.

---

humans 'came into existence as the Bible represents, by the special creation of a single pair,' or, as he wrote in *Origin and Antiquity of Man,* that 'man is genetically connected with the highest order of the Mammalia'? As a veteran of the Darwinian debates, Wright certainly knew that the term *special creation,* as commonly used, ruled out a genetic connection. How could such a clear-thinking, knowledgeable person make such apparently contradictory statements about the most emotionally laden issue connected with evolution? Was he merely tailoring his language to meet the expectations of different audiences or to camouflage his true views?" (*The Creationists,* p. 35). In answer Numbers suggests that Wright rendered "creation" and "evolution" as synonyms, holding with James Dwight Dana and James Orr to a concept of "emergent evolution." Numbers is correct to point to what Wright considered a false dichotomy in order to solve the apparent contradiction — but if Wright held with Wee Hodge, then Numbers's solution ("emergent evolution") merges two concepts just where they should be distinguished. For them, creation and evolution *were* utterly distinct processes, yet they could operate in tandem, namely, in miracle (mediate creation) — and in their view the Bible's teaching on human origins focused on just that combination of modes. That idea, however, differed fundamentally from "emergent evolution," which located creative power within the evolutionary process, thus conflating the terms. Numbers apparently got the idea from David N. Livingstone, *Darwin's Forgotten Defenders: The Encounter between Evangelical Theology and Evolutionary Thought* (Grand Rapids: Eerdmans; Edinburgh: Scottish Academic Press, 1987), pp. 70, 150.

22. Lecture 3, on the hypothetical status of evolutionism, showed no changes to speak of — not even any updating of the scientific authorities. His bibliography appended to Lecture 1, however, did add Scott's *Theory of Evolution* (1917), Conklin's *Direction of Human Evolution* (1921), Louis T. More's *Dogma of Evolution* (1926, delivered as the Vanuxem Lectures at Princeton University), William Hallock Johnson's *Can the Christian Now Believe in Evolution?* (1926), and Price's *Phantom of Organic Evolution* (1924). That Hodge kept abreast of the issue is clear from his reviews for the *Princeton Theological Review.*

23. Lefferts A. Loetscher, *The Broadening Church: A Study of Theological Issues in the Presbyterian Church since 1869* (Philadelphia: University of Pennsylvania Press, 1954), p. 111; Longfield, *The Presbyterian Controversy,* chapter 3.

Hodge's paleontologist cousin found himself in a similar bind, but within the scientific community. Scott wrote forcefully in support of evolution's factuality, even lending a hand in a treatise by a Presbyterian minister against religious denunciations of evolution within his denomination.[24] But after 1923, when a group of leading scientists responded to Bryan by publishing a pious declaration of religious liberalism (see below), Scott stepped out of the arena,[25] even though the scientists' religious counteroffensive was mounted by Scott's best friend, Osborn, and his close colleague, Princeton University biologist Edwin Grant Conklin. Charles Hodge's grandsons, teaching on evolution at the university and the seminary, found the highly polarized situation of the 1920s uncongenial to their Old Princetonian views of science and religion: the unity of truth and the division of labor.

Hodge's mediating position on human origins in the 1920s was all the more remarkable for his conviction that evolutionary naturalism lay behind the evils of theological modernism. His inaugural address as Warfield's successor made no bones about the intellectual antecedents of the "new theology." "It is claimed by its advocates that it is a theology determined by the modern scientific movement," he observed, "but in reality it is the product of a philosophical dogma rooted in Kant and Darwin." Despite the wide array of competing schools within this new theology, Hodge discerned several common principles uniting them: the eradication of the old distinction between the natural and the supernatural, so that God became only "the immanent law of the world," never intervening in the natural process; a belief in man's natural perfectibility, not seeing sin as a barrier to the sufficiency of natural religion, so that

24. William Berryman Scott, *The Theory of Evolution, with Special Reference to the Evidence upon Which It Is Founded* (New York: Macmillan, 1917), explained that the theory was incapable of absolute demonstration, but showed the wide array of evidence in its favor. Scott was agnostic as to evolution's mechanism, but was a decided evolutionist nonetheless. In 1922, at the request of Rev. Hay Watson Smith, he provided a letter supporting human evolutionism against some of James Orr's old arguments. He also read the manuscript of Smith's book. Smith, *Evolution and Presbyterianism* (Little Rock: Allsopp and Chapple, 1923), pp. 19-20, 92-94.

25. Scott felt impelled to defend the scientific status of evolution, but, true to old Princetonian form, refused to participate in scientific pontifications on religion. With Osborn and Conklin he declared evolution a fact, but the mechanism as yet a mystery (see below). His name was conspicuously absent, however, from their religiously modernist "Joint Statement upon the Relations of Science and Religion," *Science* 57 (1 June 1923): 630-31.

the Bible itself "gives us no revealed truths; it simply nourishes the religious life from which doctrine is supposed to spring"; and a corresponding naturalistic idea of redemption that "needs no divine and supernatural Redeemer." The new theology trusted in natural religion, finding evolution's naturalistic bent perfectly suited to the old infidel doctrines of human sufficiency. "All Christian doctrine is merged in the stream of evolution, the result being that all that is distinctive of supernatural Christianity, *i.e.*, the Christianity of the New Testament, is explained away. For Christian truth is not the product of man's nature, and every attempt to explain Christianity as the culmination of the naturalistic evolution of religious thought, must end in the reduction of the doctrinal content of Christianity to that of bare natural religion."[26]

But though the liberals inflected natural religion in evolutionary terms, Hodge did not propose to answer with an antievolutionary campaign. Despite liberal claims, the root issue was not a scientific theory or law, but an underlying naturalistic metaphysic. "It is only when natural science fails to observe the limitations of its knowledge," Hodge explained, "and attempts to construct a naturalistic view of the world — in a word, when it becomes unscientific, speculative, and dogmatic — that it can be claimed as the cause of the new theology." These words harked back to antebellum Princeton, to Albert Dod, Charles Hodge, and Lyman Atwater. One might even say that Wee Hodge now faced as a present, powerful foe the fulfillment of his forebears' predictions. But if his answer differed from Bryan's, it differed also from Dod's and Atwater's. Hodge found the solution to evolutionary naturalism not in the denial of evolutionary science, nor in an epistemological argument for metaphysical dualism.[27] He found it instead in a reassertion of Calvinism, "the Re-

---

26. C. W. Hodge, "Significance," pp. 4-5, 8.

27. C. W. Hodge, "Significance," p. 9. To meet "the false plea that religion is a matter of life and feeling only" — what Hodge called a "false anti-intellectualism" in religion, springing from Kant's philosophy — he proposed no mere introspective empiricism, no induction of "the facts of consciousness" considered as philosophical data apart from religious definitions, but "a vindication of our natural knowledge of God from the point of view of Augustine and Calvin and the Reformed Theology which recognizes the innate religious sense in all men, or the *semen religionis* as it was called. This alone will give an adequate basis by which to meet the religious agnosticism which underlies the new theology." Hodge affirmed the animus of the old philosophical project, but subsumed it under religious categories. Was this a move away from "evidentialism" toward the "presuppositionalism" of the Dutch Calvinists Kuyper and Bavinck?

formed Faith," which in the purity of its conception, he said, "is really just Christian supernaturalism come to its full rights."[28]

Following Warfield, Hodge defined Calvinism's "formative principle" as "the vision of God in His Majesty." Its exalted view of the sovereign God — the Almighty who chooses his elect, who decrees all that comes to pass, with whom no faultfinder may contend, God of both the process and the gaps — was the precise antidote to the root evil of naturalism: "the denial of the power of God to make bare His arm and intrude in the world for man's salvation." The new theology limited God by his creation; celebrating his immanence in natural law, it denied his prerogative to act outside it. The Reformed theology, by contrast, accorded to God all the power due his holy name. Warfield had found in Westminster Calvinism "the ripest fruit of Reformed creed-making," embodying in its careful confession the fullest development of "theism, religion, evangelicalism" — the hallmarks of supernatural Christianity.[29] Hodge now pointed out the precise suitability of these principles for the present conflict with naturalistic theology. Calvinism interpreted everything in the universe, both the physical and mental spheres, "as the unfolding of the eternal purpose of God." It refused "to limit God either by

28. C. W. Hodge, "Significance," p. 11.

29. Warfield used breeder's language to argue that Calvinism represented Christianity's ideal type. "Calvinism is not a specific variety of theism, religion, evangelicalism, set over against other specific varieties, which along with it constitute these several genera, and which possess equal rights of existence with it and make similar claims to perfection, each after its own kind. It differs from them not as one species differs from other species; but as a perfectly developed representative differs from an imperfectly developed representative of the same species.... Calvinism conceives of itself as simply the more pure theism, religion, evangelicalism, superseding as such the less pure. It has no difficulty, therefore, in recognizing the theistic character of all truly theistic thought, the religious note in all actual religious activity, the evangelical quality of all really evangelical faith." Benjamin Breckinridge Warfield, "Calvinism" (1908), in his *Calvin and Calvinism*, in *The Works of Benjamin B. Warfield*, ed. Ethelbert D. Warfield et al., vol. 5 (New York: Oxford University Press, 1931; Grand Rapids: Baker, 1991), pp. 355-56. Developmentalism also served his argument that the Westminster Confession, coming at the end of the Reformation period, benefiting from more than a century of Protestant polemical work and a wide communication between British and Continental Reformed churches, was "the ripest fruit of Reformed creed-making, the simple transcript of Reformed thought as it was everywhere expounded by its best representatives." Warfield, "The Westminster Assembly and Its Work" (1908), in his *The Westminster Assembly and Its Work*, in *The Works of Benjamin B. Warfield*, ed. Ethelbert D. Warfield et al., vol. 6 (New York: Oxford University Press, 1931; Grand Rapids: Baker, 1991), pp. 58-59.

the world of nature or the human will." Thus Calvinism was pure theism. In its stark predestinarianism it required an attitude of radical dependence on God, trusting for salvation neither in works of righteousness nor in the response of the natural human heart to the gospel. God alone received all the glory — this was pure religion. And finally, this radical dependence on divine grace, not on any natural human merit or power, was the core of the gospel, pure evangelicalism. Hodge urged the importance of consistent Calvinism, pure trust in God's grace without any admixture of trust in man, as the only solid ground of defense against naturalism. This was "the tremendous significance of the Reformed Theology for us today."

> We are being told that the Reformed Faith or Calvinism is dead today or at least about to pass away. Doubtless it has not many representatives among the leaders of religious thought, nor does it court a place alongside of the wisdom of this world. But wherever humble souls catch the vision of God in His glory, and bow in adoration and humility before Him, trusting for salvation only in His grace and power, there you have the essence of the Reformed Faith. Once let this life blood of pure religion flow from the heart to nourish the anaemic brain and work itself out in thought, and it will wash away many a cobweb spun by a dogmatic naturalism claiming to be modern, but in reality as old as Christianity itself.[30]

---

30. C. W. Hodge, "Significance," pp. 12-14. Cf. Benjamin Breckinridge Warfield, review of *Le Problème du Dieu,* by Victor Monod, *PTR* 9 (1911): 151-52: "The real distinction between the Reformed and the Kantian movements in their relation to the idea of God . . . concerns very distinctly the question of His sovereignty. The difficulty with Kantian speculation has been indeed to find any place for God at all in its scheme of things. . . . In a word the sixteenth century conceived man as the creation of God, existing for God and serving His ends; men now are prone to think of God as, if not exactly the creation of man, yet as existing for man and serving man's ends. The center of the universe has shifted; and God has become as has been, perhaps wittily, perhaps bitterly, said, very much a domestic animal which man keeps, as he does his horse or his cow, to meet certain specific needs of his being." Again (p. 156), "The *scandalon* of this [Augustinian-Reformed] body of thinking has ever been, and is, that it thinks of God as God, and will not have his glory diminished by the exaltation of man. . . . The 'problem of God' is to be solved for the twentieth century as for all that have preceded it, not by deifying man and abasing God in his presence, but by recognizing God to be indeed God and man to be the creation of His hands, whose chief end it is to glorify God and to enjoy Him forever. And this is . . . just Calvinism."

The Moment of (Historical) Truth

In its strong commitment to Calvinist orthodoxy Princeton Seminary differed significantly from the larger fundamentalist movement, much of which held a Wesleyan-Arminian doctrine of human ability, and which, as a transdenominational movement whose very name indicated the selection of a small set of basic doctrines, tended toward doctrinal reductionism just where Princeton emphasized full confessional inflection. But insofar as the Princetonians regarded Calvinism as the most consistent form of supernatural Christianity, they greeted other supernaturalist Christians as true kin. Warfield even conceived such fellow believers outside his confessional fold as implicit Calvinists,[31] something Hodge's inaugural clearly echoed. The Princetonians for decades had been coming to an understanding of their battle as less ecclesiastical than intellectual: theologically, a war with natural religion, and philosophically, a war with naturalism. At least since the founding of the *Presbyterian and Reformed Review* they had sought to build alliances across denominations, often against foes within their own church. They came increasingly to see a stark polarity between friends and foes, the dividing line running untidily through existing bodies of organization. What set parties apart, Warfield insisted, was not personal piety or a warm attachment to "evangelicalism," and certainly not degree of scholarship or expertise in "criticism." Rather, the fundamental dividing line followed one's attitude to the supernatural, something the current array of affiliations covered over. Already in 1895 he wrote, "What is needed above everything in these days of confusion is some electric spark to flash through the world of thought and crystallize parties on their lines of real cleavage. Above everything, the world needs to know on which side men are standing, and we need not doubt that there are many who need to have their real position revealed even to themselves."[32]

31. Warfield, "Calvinism," p. 356. "Whoever believes in God; whoever recognizes in the recesses of his soul his utter dependence on God; whoever in all his thought of salvation hears in his heart of hearts the echo of the *soli Deo gloria* of the evangelical profession — by whatever name he may call himself, or by whatever intellectual puzzles his logical understanding may be confused — Calvinism recognizes as implicitly a Calvinist, and as only requiring to permit these fundamental principles — which underlie and give its body to all true religion — to work themselves freely and fully out in thought and feeling and action, to become explicitly a Calvinist."

32. Benjamin Breckinridge Warfield, short notice of *Die Literatur des alten Testaments nach der Zeitfolge ihrer Entstehung,* by G. Wildboer, *PRR* 6 (1895): 537.

It is tempting to see in this statement a plain anticipation of fundamentalism. Certainly the idea of a radical polarity, separating those on the side of the angels from those not, was and is a prominent (we might say fundamental) feature of fundamentalism. But Warfield's idea of "implicit Calvinism" militates against any easy identification. He welcomed as a fellow believer, "by whatever name he may call himself, or by whatever intellectual puzzles his logical understanding may be confused," anyone who shared in thought, feeling, and action the "fundamental principles" of Calvinism — belief in God (theism), utter dependence on him (religion), and a cry of *soli Deo gloria* in response to his divine grace (evangelicalism). Warfield's "fundamental principles" were distinctly *not* the "five fundamentals" of the fundamentalists, nor did he propound them to serve the same purpose they did.[33]

Still, the desire to discern "lines of real cleavage," to define parties according to the logical tendency of their basic beliefs, must rank high among the salient intellectual characteristics of the fundamentalist impulse — and the perennial Princetonian concern for first principles, not to mention a shared enmity against liberalism's evacuation of historic dogmas, did make for common cause between Princeton Seminary and transdenominational fundamentalism. It was a Princeton theologian who in the 1920s became the intellectual champion of a radical antithesis between liberalism and Christianity: a tough-minded libertarian confessionalist named John Gresham Machen.

In November 1921, six months before Fosdick's notorious sermon, Machen addressed an annual convention of church elders in the Chester (Pa.) Presbytery; his talk was entitled "The Present Attack against the Fundamentals of Our Christian Faith, from the Point of View of Colleges and Seminaries."[34] The address appeared in the *Princeton Theological Review* for January 1922 with the stark title "Liberalism or Christianity?" and formed the basis for Machen's most famous book, *Christianity and Liberalism* (1923). As the fundamentalist controversy escalated, Machen's fame spread as an incisive, erudite champion of the old-time religion. Shortly before the Scopes trial, the *New York Times* featured Machen as an exponent of fundamentalism in a full-page article prominently placed at the head of its second section, facing him off against

33. On the "five fundamentals," see Loetscher, *The Broadening Church*, p. 91; cf. several lengthier discussions in Longfield, *The Presbyterian Controversy.*
34. Machen, "Liberalism or Christianity?" p. 93.

Vernon L. Kellogg, its chosen voice of evolutionism. Machen had declined to write an antievolutionary article, offering instead a piece on the nature of Christianity, "What Fundamentalism Stands for Now," but the *Times* ran it against Kellogg's "What Evolution Stands for Now" anyway.[35] This sort of publicity brought Machen's work to national attention; soon his readers included Walter Lippmann and H. L. Mencken, who, rejecting his religious orthodoxy, heartily applauded his precision and forthrightness.[36]

In "Liberalism or Christianity?" Machen contrasted the world of seminaries and universities to "the world at large." People in the academy understood and acknowledged the opposition between liberal and historic Christianity, but in the world at large, liberal ministers, liberal Sunday school materials, and the liberal religious press were "at pains . . . to maintain a pretence of conformity with the past." This Machen regarded as nothing short of deceit.[37] He proposed to unmask the pretender. "With regard to the presuppositions, as with regard to the message itself," he wrote, "modern liberalism is diametrically opposed to Christianity." Its views of God, man, the seat of religious authority, Jesus Christ, and the way of salvation were distinctly at odds with the Christianity of the New Testament. Its pantheizing tendency merged the Creator with his creation; its faith in human goodness denied the dilemma of sin. It located religious authority in personal experience rather than biblical statements. It made Christ's deity just a particularly well developed case of the divinity of all humanity, and the significance of his death a matter of moral example, not atonement for sin. Machen avowed the liberal's perfect right to devise a religion to his liking, but denied him the right to call it Christian.

The argument hinged on what Machen meant by "historic Christianity." He insisted that his argument was not a personal attack, not a

35. Ned B. Stonehouse, *J. Gresham Machen: A Biographical Memoir* (Grand Rapids: Eerdmans, 1954), p. 401. The *Times* articles appeared on 21 June 1925.

36. Hart, *Defending the Faith*, pp. 66-69. See Lippmann's *Preface to Morals* (1929) and Mencken's obituary of Machen, "Dr. Fundamentalis." Cf. also Pearl Buck's "Tribute to Dr. Machen," her inveterate opponent in the battle over Presbyterian missions in the 1930s (*New Republic*, 27 January 1937): "He was a glorious enemy because he was completely open and direct in his angers and hatreds. He stood for something and everyone knew what it was. . . . In a present world of dubious woven grays, his life was a flaming thread of scarlet, regardless and undismayed. He was afraid of nothing and of no one."

37. Machen, "Liberalism or Christianity?" p. 110.

weighing of ideals, but a purely historical question. Averring that only the founders of Christianity, Christ and the apostles, had the right to define its meaning, he appealed to historical criticism to disprove the liberal claim to have recovered the religion of Jesus — a religion that looked suspiciously like the naturalistic one they had devised for themselves.[38] In point of pure historical fact, Machen declared, the critics' "historical Jesus" was one of the strongest arguments *against* liberal Christianity, for Jesus himself was a stark supernaturalist whose message was preeminently a gospel — good news — of the meaning of an *event*.[39]

In one sense Machen's emphasis on the historical content of the gospel simply perpetuated a cardinal Princetonian position harking back to Charles Hodge's polemics against the New England theology. Like Hodge, Machen refused to relegate religion to the domain of feelings and aspirations apart from questions of fact.[40] But Machen gave the historical question a new prominence. History not only gave content to faith, it also provided the chief epistemic route to Christian supernaturalism. Science had nothing to say about the supernatural, for it dealt with natural laws and their effects. The supernatural simply lay beyond its ken. Supernatural intrusions into the natural order were expressly not rules of natural cause and effect; they were particular events, not general laws. A supernatural occurrence was an immediate forthputting of divine power, an act of God not mediated by natural law. It was metaphysically immediate, but as a past event it was epistemically mediate, knowable only on the principle of authority or testimony. Short of personal encounter, the only way to ascertain events as long past as those described

38. Machen, "Liberalism or Christianity?" pp. 95-97, 106-7. "The truth is that the life-purpose of Jesus discovered by modern liberalism is not the life-purpose of the real Jesus, but merely represents those elements in the teaching of Jesus — isolated and misinterpreted — which happen to agree with the modern program" (p. 107). Cf. Willis J. Beecher's witty description of the naturalists' Jesus: "a nice, queer, plucky, lovable man, who came into post mortem psychological relations with Peter and Paul, whereby they were led to become founders of a new religion." Beecher, review of *The New Schaff-Herzog Encyclopædia of Religious Knowledge*, vol. 6, edited by Samuel Macauley Jackson, *PTR* 8 (1910): 463.

39. Machen, "Liberalism or Christianity?" p. 96.

40. See Charles Hodge's series of exchanges with Edwards Amasa Park on the "Theology of the Intellect and of the Feelings" in *Bibliotheca Sacra* and the *Biblical Repertory and Princeton Review*, 1850-51, recounted and partially reprinted in Mark A. Noll, ed., *The Princeton Theology, 1812-1921: Scripture, Science, and Theological Method from Archibald Alexander to Benjamin Breckinridge Warfield* (Grand Rapids: Baker, 1983), pp. 185-207.

in the New Testament lay in the weighing of testimony — in historical inquiry. That held whether the events in question were naturally or supernaturally caused; as event-claims seeking substantiation, they were all subject to the same method of inquiry. Only — and this was a major point — one's philosophical presuppositions would determine the field of believable causes. Thus a common method, the weighing of testimony, united all historical inquirers, and the limits of history's prerogatives only highlighted the importance of metaphysical precommitments. Like science, history could not directly determine the possibility of the supernatural, but unlike science, history could indirectly ascertain a supernatural event. Supernatural occurrences were not scientific, but as alleged events they were knowable via testimony — via history.[41]

Machen was not alone in this view of the religious and apologetical importance of history, though he did become Princeton's chief spokesman on that score by the time of his inauguration as assistant professor of New Testament in 1915. He devoted his inaugural address, "History and Faith," to a vindication of the historicity of Christian belief and an exposé of the failure of modern theological attempts to devise a Christianity that transcended history. Noting that the elimination of the historical in Christianity amounted to its redefinition as universal, natural religion[42] — theism perhaps, but not the good news of salvation in Jesus — Machen argued that careful historical work made modernism's view of Christ impossible. The Jesus of the Bible was a supernatural person: an impossibility for modern naturalism.[43] Here was a stark either/or thrust upon the current theological debate by the facts of history. By the early 1920s Machen began pressing all parties to admit it.[44]

41. See note 49 below.

42. This was a favorite point of Warfield's. See Benjamin Breckinridge Warfield, joint review of *Mysticism in Christianity,* by W. K. Fleming, and *Mysticism and Modern Life,* by John Wright Buckham (1916), in his *Critical Reviews,* in *The Works of Benjamin B. Warfield,* ed. Ethelbert D. Warfield et al., vol. 10 (New York: Oxford University Press, 1932; Grand Rapids: Baker, 1991), p. 366.

43. J. Gresham Machen, "History and Faith," *PTR* 13 (1915): 337, 342, 348-49. "In the wonders of the Gospel story, in the character of Jesus, in His mysterious self-consciousness, in the very origin of the Christian Church, we discover a problem, which defies the best efforts of the naturalistic historian, which pushes us relentlessly off the safe ground of the phenomenal world toward the intellectual abyss of supernaturalism, which forces us, despite the resistance of the modern mind, to recognize a very act of God" (p. 349).

44. In "Liberalism or Christianity?" Machen portrayed the crisis with liberalism as the worst crisis the church had ever faced. "It is a great mistake to suppose that liberalism

Machen believed that history stood on the side of supernatural Christianity. Liberalism — "a common degradation of an originally noble word" — was just naturalism in religion.[45] Modern criticism revealed historic Christianity, the religion of Jesus and the apostles, whether true or not, to be a distinctly supernaturalistic religion. Liberals read their naturalism back into the New Testament, but history itself opposed their claim to the Christian name. Liberals brought a presupposed naturalism to their historical work, confining Jesus to the natural order while defining the "religion of Jesus" as an essential attitude to God that transcended historical particulars. Machen turned the naturalists' guns on themselves, finding their own method of history to yield a Jesus whose religion was not at all the liberals' natural religion, but a message of supernatural salvation from sin.

George Marsden has made quite a point of Machen's view of history, portraying it as the naïve belief, derived from an outmoded Common-Sense Realism, that events were raw "facts" apprehended directly. On his reading Machen failed to recognize the inescapability of a conditioning matrix of interpretation surrounding any so-called fact. Liberals, by contrast, as good post-Kantians, appreciated the force of historical relativism.[46] This turns out, however, not to have been the case. Liberals routinely made appeals to the "facts" of history at least as positivistically as Machen and the Princetonians did. The whole force of Machen's counterthrust was to foil the antisupernaturalists with their own weapons. Even the unorthodox outsider Herbert Croly, editor of the *New Republic,* implicitly supported Machen here, though he drew a different lesson from this bit of history. Croly argued that liberalism (or "modernism") had indeed departed radically from historic Christianity — and bully for modernism. What the church needed were men courageous enough to admit the fact and abandon outworn allegiances, frankly devising a new religion suited to modern realities.[47]

---

is merely a heresy — merely a divergence at isolated points from true Christian teaching. On the contrary it proceeds from a totally different root. . . . Christianity is being attacked from within by a movement which is anti-Christian to the core" (p. 114).

45. Machen, "Liberalism or Christianity?" pp. 93-94.

46. George M. Marsden, "J. Gresham Machen, History, and Truth," *Westminster Theological Journal* 42 (1979): 157-75.

47. Herbert Croly, "Naturalism and Christianity," *New Republic* 34 (28 February 1923): 9-11; cf. his article "The Cure for Fundamentalism," *New Republic* 43 (10 June 1925): 58-60. On this score even the modernists at the University of Chicago Divinity School admitted, "Per-

But Marsden is right to point to history as a crucial concern of the Princetonians in their battle with liberalism. It is an important point, for the liberals routinely dismissed Princetonian counterarguments as somehow lacking in historical appreciation.[48] What the liberals meant to establish, however, was not historical relativism, but the final irrelevancy of historical particulars to faith. The thought worlds of antiquity and modernity were radically different; a religion could remain true across such a conceptual gulf only if it did not at all depend on specific ideas or doctrines. It was not so much that the past *wie es eigentlich gewesen* lay beyond our knowledge,[49] much less that truth changed over

---

haps there is no lesson which liberalism more needs than the plain truth that one cannot eat his cake and have it too." Gerald Birney Smith, Shirley Jackson Case, and D. D. Luckenbill, "Theological Scholarship at Princeton," *American Journal of Theology* (1913): 97.

48. Smith, Case, and Luckenbill, "Theological Scholarship at Princeton," pp. 95-96. "Christianity is to them a system of revealed truth. In its essence it is non-human, and its history is not so much the story of the development of human aspirations under the stress of historical circumstances, as it is a record of movements of conformity and of nonconformity." While true in its observation of Princeton's refusal to regard Christianity as a natural religion, this statement is primarily a dig at Princeton's leading role in the heresy trials of the nineteenth century. It completely misses the strong element of developmentalism in Princeton's view of the Bible and church history. More just is the criticism of Patton's presentation of dogmatic history: it "puts the systems of thought ('isms') foremost as if they were actual entities existing almost independently of the social and psychological ferment of the period under description. There is the recognition of the fact that thinking did take this form or that; but just *why* men should wish to put forth antievangelical ideas is left in the dark. Indeed, one feels that in the analysis of naturalism there is almost no real insight into the vital reasons for the existence of this method of thinking." In Patton's defense, however, it must be said that a historical survey was only incidental to his purpose in the article cited, the delineation of theological encyclopedia. His sermons, for example, often dwelt on the appeal of unbelief.

49. Nineteenth-century German historian Leopold von Ranke famously set as his goal the fully objective recounting of the past "as it actually was." Many liberals held to the Rankean ideal as part of their quest to discover the history behind the Bible. Some did deem historical knowledge epistemically inferior, unable to bear the weight of religious commitment, following "Lessing's ditch." See Warfield's lengthy exposition and answer in "Christless Christianity" (1912), in *Christology and Criticism,* in *The Works of Benjamin B. Warfield,* ed. Ethelbert D. Warfield et al., vol. 3 (New York: Oxford University Press, 1929; Grand Rapids: Baker, 1991), pp. 316-27. As prime examples Warfield cited Rudolf Eucken, *Können wir noch Christen sein?* (1911), and Arthur O. Lovejoy, "The Entangling Alliance of Religion and History" (*Hibbert Journal,* 1907); also Ernst Troeltsch. On p. 321 Warfield recommended Wee Hodge's "admirable general account" of the relations of faith and history, "Fact and Theory," in Hastings's *Dictionary of Christ and the Gospels* (1908). Cf. Edwin H. Kellogg (Princeton Theological Seminary, Class of '06, winner of the apologetics fellow-

time. Rather, liberals sought a transcendent "essence" of Christian attitude to connect them with Jesus, one independent of historical particulars, unchanging and universal to the core. The liberal theological project characteristically portrayed Christianity as the pinnacle of natural
religious evolution, embodying the best in all religions and enabling the
modern Christian to look with charity and brotherly affection on all
alike. Like relativism, it aimed at toleration, but it was thoroughly
essentialistic — the precise opposite of relativism.[50]

Together with the liberals, the Princetonians looked to history to
identify Christianity. But where liberals presupposed a framework of naturalistic religious development, often identifying historical rigor with
the use of that framework, and severed the meaning of Christianity from
the flux of historical particulars, the Princetonians presupposed a
supernaturalistic religious development — based on a God who sover-
eignly decreed historical processes and who occasionally intervened in
them — and brought it to bear on the empirical data of the historical record. Both groups took a profound interest in historical questions; both
used the same empirical tools. Both indulged in some degree of teleological developmentalism concerning religious history. But they operated
under differing conceptions of God. This was just Machen's point, and on
that score, at least, it seems he was right.[51]

Darwin's Nadir

For all his enchantment with an evolutionary view of the natural world,
seeing in evolution God's majestic activity through providence to carry
out his eternal decree, B. B. Warfield had to confess in the first decades of
the twentieth century that the fortunes of Darwinism were, as he said of
the fortunes of Calvinism, "not at present at their flood."[52] Historians

---

ship, son of Samuel Kellogg the Stone Lecturer and champion of James Woodrow), review
of *Modern Thought and the Crisis of Belief*, by R. M. Wenley, *PTR* 8 (1910): 123-24.

50. These observations are based especially on Warfield's assessment of the situation,
forcefully argued in "Christless Christianity," pp. 313-67, and "The Essence of Christianity and
the Cross of Christ" (1914), in *Christology and Criticism*, pp. 393-444. In each case, Warfield argues in distinctly developmental terms to show orthodoxy's superior affirmation of history.
The point about relativism is my own. See also Hart, *Defending the Faith*, pp. 99-100.

51. Here I deliberately allude to the conclusion of H. L. Mencken's obituary of Machen,
"Dr. Fundamentalis," *Baltimore Evening Sun*, 18 January 1937, section 2.

52. Warfield, "Calvinism," p. 365.

easily forget that the strength of the antievolution campaign of the 1920s owed a good deal to the plausibility of its complaint that science teachers were foisting a "mere hypothesis" on an unwilling, taxpaying public, expecting them not only to accept it but also to underwrite it — a hypothesis with allegedly dire implications for religion and public morality, yet for which scientists expected all the deference due an established fact or law. This complaint was a complicated one, involving issues of freedom and democracy as much as science and religion.[53] Each point carried more than a little credibility. Many friends of transmutationism agreed with the fundamentalists that it was outrageous to force people to pay to have their children taught a worldview they deemed inimical to their most cherished convictions. If a large body of religious leaders (including the Princetonians) found evolution in some form compatible with belief in the Bible, a very large body sincerely did not. And as a question of science, evolution in the 1920s, though entrenched in the scientific community, was a theory in crisis.

By the early years of the century many scientists acknowledged a woeful lack of agreement on the mechanism of evolution. Virtually all held that species came by "descent with modification," the higher forms from the lower over vast periods of time, but what drove speciation remained a matter of severe contention. In Britain and America non-Darwinian evolutionisms flourished while scientists paid homage to Darwin's name.[54] On the Continent several prominent evolutionists frankly repudiated Darwin along with his mechanism, natural selection. Vitalistic theories such as Henri Bergson's "creative evolution" joined the older growth-analogy evolutionisms in a new emphasis on the need of an immaterial, directing principle in variation. German scientists began to speak of "the deathbed of Darwinism." Albert Fleischmann even repudiated the theory of descent altogether; others such as August Pauly distinguished between the "fact" of evolution (speciation by descent over vast aeons) and the "theory" devised to explain it (natural selection,

---

53. On the political dimensions of Bryan's crusade, see Edward J. Larson, *Summer for the Gods: The Scopes Trial and America's Continuing Debate over Science and Religion* (New York: BasicBooks, 1997), especially chapter 2.

54. Princetonians Baldwin and Osborn were outstanding non-Darwinian popularizers of the identification of Darwin's name with all evolutionism. James Mark Baldwin, *Darwin and the Humanities* (New York: Macmillan, 1902); Henry Fairfield Osborn, *From the Greeks to Darwin: An Outline of the Development of the Evolution Idea* (New York: Macmillan, 1913; orig. 1894).

orthogenesis, the inheritance of acquired characters, mutation, or the *élan vital*). Already in 1902 Hugh M. Scott reported to the *Bible Student* that the Germans were saying scientists had established "the *fact* of evolution, the fact that plants and animals have a long history and were not created as they are, . . . but the *how* of the history as taught by Darwin has failed to prove itself true. His theory of natural selection has fallen to the ground."[55]

Many Bible believers greeted the news of Darwinism's demise with glee, interpreting scientific concessions of the inadequacy of natural selection to portend the downfall of evolution altogether. The rise of fundamentalist antievolutionism dates from just this time, when Alexander Patterson's tract *The Other Side of Evolution* (1903) persuaded A. C. Dixon to the cause. When in 1904 the *Bible Student* passed from Warfield's hands to the newly formed American Bible League, it began to carry pieces like Luther Townsend's article "The Collapse of Evolution" and George Frederick Wright's article "The Mistakes of Darwin and His Would-Be Followers," developing by the century's second decade into a major fundamentalist organ.[56]

The Princeton theologians, for their part, retained their qualified evolutionism, but they did feel rather vindicated by Darwinism's fall from favor, for they had championed non-Darwinian developmentalism all along, allowing the likelihood of speciation by descent but reserving the importance of teleology and supernatural intervention. William Hallock Johnson, in his Stone Foundation lectures at Princeton Seminary in 1914, contentedly declared that evolutionary theory was moving away from its

55. Hugh M. Scott, "Present Status of Evolution," *Bible Student*, n.s., 5 (1902): 360-61. Scott frequently reviewed German books for Warfield's journals, of which the *Bible Student* was one at this time. Scott cited an article by Pauly, "True and False in Darwin's Teachings," in the Munich *Allgemeine Zeitung:* "half a dozen" German books, including one by Prof. Eimer on butterflies; and recent issues of the *Beweis des Glaubens*. "All show that even science now admits the need of a directing mind in order to produce by evolution a living, thinking creature out of dead matter." Cf. Albert Fleischmann, *Die Descendenztheorie; gemeinverständliche Vorlesungen über den Auf- und Niedergang einer naturwissenschaftlichen Hypothese* (Leipzig: A. Georgi, 1901); August Pauly, *Wahres und Falsches an Darwins Lehre* (Munich: E. Reinhardt, 1910).

56. Numbers, *The Creationists*, pp. 16, 32-33. Warfield and McPheeters ran the *Bible Student* prior to 1904 (see chapter 8, note 66, above). The periodical was renamed the *Bible Student and Teacher* in that year, the *Bible Champion* in 1913, and *Christian Faith and Life* in 1931, all presumably under the American Bible League. All told, this "third series" ran through forty-five volumes, from 1904 to 1939.

unfortunate early associations with materialism.[57] But the most important Princetonian assessment of Darwin's eclipse came from the man who found in Calvin a doctrine of "pure evolutionism" — B. B. Warfield.

Recalling his days as an undergraduate under McCosh for the *Princeton Alumni Weekly,* Warfield wrote in 1916,

> No, he did not make me a Darwinian, as it was his pride to believe he ordinarily made his pupils. But that was doubtless because I was already a Darwinian of the purest water before I came into his hands, and knew my *Origin of Species,* and *Animals and Plants under Domestication,* almost from A to Izard. In later years I fell away from this, his orthodoxy. He was a little nettled about it and used to inform me with some vigor — I am speaking of a time some thirty years agone! — that all biologists under thirty years of age were Darwinians. I was never quite sure that he understood what I was driving at when I replied that I was the last man in the world to wonder at that, since I was about that old myself before I outgrew it.[58]

Warfield penned these words with his *Alumni Weekly* audience in mind — worldly-wise men of means who thought of him chiefly as a stiff ecclesiastic, a champion of Westminster confessionalism in an antisectarian age. With an air of witty assurance he played on this reputation to highlight his "falling away" from Darwinian "orthodoxy." A cattle breeder and the son of a cattle breeder, young Warfield had been fascinated with ge-

---

57. William Hallock Johnson, *The Christian Faith under Modern Searchlights,* Stone Lectures, 1914 (New York: Fleming H. Revell Co., 1916), pp. 69, 86. Johnson (College of New Jersey '88, Princeton Theological Seminary '96) taught Greek and New Testament at Lincoln University, a Negro college in Pennsylvania. On scientific antimaterialism in the 1920s and 1930s, see also Elazar Barkan, *The Retreat of Scientific Racism: Changing Concepts of Race in Britain and the United States between the World Wars* (Cambridge: Cambridge University Press, 1992), p. 119.

58. Benjamin Breckinridge Warfield, "Personal Recollections of Princeton Undergraduate Life: IV. The Coming of Dr. McCosh," *Princeton Alumni Weekly* 16, no. 28 (19 April 1916): 652. Fred Zaspel considers this passage Warfield's only clear and definitive statement of his own views of evolution — and takes it to demonstrate that Warfield expressly disbelieved in evolution by about 1881 and continued in that disbelief at least until 1916. But Warfield was speaking here specifically of Darwinism, not broadly of evolution. Zaspel is on better ground when he says that Warfield "never explicitly endorsed" evolution, though he did continuously allow it "as a possibility both theologically and theoretically." Fred G. Zaspel, *The Theology of B. B. Warfield: A Systematic Summary* (Wheaton, Ill.: Crossway, 2010), pp. 386-87.

netic descent and found Darwin's metaphor of selective breeding extremely compelling. McCosh's equation of natural selection with divine design no doubt helped him reconcile his faith with science, but by the time he replaced A. A. Hodge at Princeton Seminary he had begun to question McCosh's conviction that evolution, particularly evolution by natural selection, was an established fact.[59] By the turn of the century he was convinced that Christian theology required a degree of supernatural intervention in the world process, so that the theistic identification of natural law with divine providence was not enough. Now, when the fortunes of Darwinism proper hit their all-time low, Warfield could speak with exclamation of a long-gone time when all young biologists were Darwinians — and allude with satisfaction to the fact that evolutionists had since come around to his non-Darwinian view.

Warfield spelled out his assessment of Darwinism in a review of Vernon L. Kellogg's *Darwinism To-day* (1907), published in the *Princeton Theological Review.* Kellogg, professor of entomology and lecturer on bionomics at Stanford University, subtitled his book "a discussion of present-day scientific criticism of the Darwinian Selection Theories, together with a brief account of the principal and other proposed auxiliary and alternative theories of Species-forming." Warfield hailed the book as a work long awaited, lucid in its account of "what Evolution means, in general, and what that particular theory of Evolution known as Darwinism really is," and especially helpful for its account of "the widespread revolt of biological investigators during the last few decades against the principle of Natural Selection," the heart of Darwinism. Kellogg conceded that natural selection had been "discredited and cast down" as the all-sufficient or most important factor in evolution, but he proclaimed nonetheless that it remained "the final arbiter in descent control," and stood "unscathed, clear and high above the obscuring cloud of battle." In other words, Kellogg admitted that natural selection did not produce variations, but insisted that its operation as a "final arbiter," selecting among variations, remained untouched.[60]

59. See Benjamin Breckinridge Warfield, MS Notes on Anthropology (Warfield MSS, PTS Special Collections) and "Charles Darwin's Religious Life: A Sketch in Spiritual Biography" (1888), in his *Studies in Theology,* in *The Works of Benjamin B. Warfield,* ed. Ethelbert D. Warfield et al., vol. 9 (New York: Oxford University Press, 1932; Grand Rapids: Baker, 1991), pp. 541-82.

60. Benjamin Breckinridge Warfield, review of *Darwinism To-day,* by Vernon L. Kellogg, *PTR* 6 (1908): 641-42.

Here Warfield took exception. He viewed the Darwinian theory as "*logically complete* in the simple postulates of variation, struggle for existence, the survival of the fittest." To object, as so many did, that Darwinism overlooked the "production of the fittest," was, he said, to miss the point. No internal drive toward improved fitness was necessary; the mere "difference" inherent in the distinction between individuals provided a field for the operation of natural selection.[61] "Wherever two individuals exist it is inevitable that one will be 'fitter' than the other," and if indeed overpopulation causes the majority of individuals to die out, "the survival of the 'fittest' seems certain." If such conditions persist over generations, Warfield said, "the line of descent must follow the line of relative fitness."[62]

But having endorsed Darwinism proper as "logically unassailable," Warfield found it lacking in "actual working power." As he argued in a neighboring article, while Darwinism presupposed a desperate struggle for existence, in point of observation "the average animal is a well-to-do-animal." Balance, rather than struggle, was nature's norm. "What survives from generation to generation is obviously not a few hard-pressed 'fittest,' but the normal somewhat pampered 'average.'"[63] Further, even supposing such a struggle for existence, would the variations be great enough? Would they diverge from type, rather than fluctuating around a center? Genetics and mutation theory seemed to argue otherwise. Meanwhile, physicists' calculations of the age of the earth left Darwinism precious little time to bring about the panorama of life from amoeba to man. "What has really happened, if the palaeontological record has anything at all to tell us," was just such a sweeping process of upward development, moving through the chain of being "with a rapidity which confounds thought." Ubiquitous struggle ran contrary to daily observation, genetic variations stubbornly reverted to type, and physicists' calculations of the age of the earth fell far short of what the fossil record would require on Darwin's theory. Warfield's conclusion: "The formal completeness of the logical theory of Darwinism is fairly matched, therefore, by its almost ludicrous actual

61. Here Warfield took the sting out of Darwinism's apparent reign of chance. Whatever the principle of variation, the operation of natural selection evidenced divine design, just as McCosh had said. Thus, apparently, Warfield felt no need to relocate design in individual strivings (neo-Lamarckism) or embryological development (orthogenesis).

62. Warfield, review of *Darwinism To-day*, p. 643, emphasis mine.

63. Benjamin Breckinridge Warfield, review of *No Struggle for Existence: No Natural Selection*, by George Paulin, *PTR* 6 (1908): 651.

incompetence for the work asked of it." Kellogg had put the matter too gently; Darwinism was not just "'seriously discredited in the biological world,' but practically out of the running."[64]

But none of the alternative evolutionary theories impressed Warfield as nearly so good as Darwin's for completeness and tangibility. The "lay reader" of Kellogg's book "may be excused if, reading over the outlines of these several theories, he is oppressed with a sense of their speculative character; in a word, of their unreality." And this impression Warfield claimed as his own: "For ourselves we confess frankly that the whole body of evolutionary constructions prevalent to-day impresses us simply as a vast mass of speculation, which may or may not prove to have a kernel of truth in it."[65] In a neighboring article he put it even more strongly, practically identifying his view with the author's: "He does not quite know what is true, but he seems to himself to know quite conclusively that Darwinism is not true."[66]

Thus when scientists were claiming to have established the "fact" of evolution while yet working to hone a "theory," Warfield took precisely the opposite view. He stuck to the "double gauntlet" image he had introduced in his anthropology lectures in 1888: any theory must show first its plausibility, then its evidence in fact — this was the proper scientific method of hypothesis and verification. But Kellogg's book revealed the "amazing zeal" with which evolutionists pursued their theories, zeal rather unbecoming in supposedly dispassionate scientists. "It is not merely that every man has his theory and sets great store by it, however speculative it may be. It almost seems at times that facts cannot be accepted unless a 'causo-mechanical' theory be ready to account for them: which looks amazingly like basing facts on theory rather than theory on facts. . . . as if it were 'causo-mechanical' theories rather than facts that

64. Warfield, review of *Darwinism To-day*, p. 644. Livingstone's statement that "Warfield's endorsement of Darwinism was not unqualified" seems not nearly strong enough. Livingstone, *Darwin's Forgotten Defenders*, p. 115. However, Livingstone is here using Darwinism in a general sense, meaning evolutionism.

65. Warfield, review of *Darwinism To-day*, p. 646. "All that seems to us to be able to lay claim to be assured knowledge in the whole mass is that the facts of homology and of the palaeontological record suggest that the relation of animate forms to one another may be a genetic one."

66. To continue the quotation: "It would seem that we must take this as Mr. Paulin's final word to us: and it seems to us far from an unsatisfactory word." Warfield, review of *No Struggle for Existence*, pp. 652-53.

our biological investigators are on the lookout for."[67] Kellogg, for example, dismissed German neo-vitalism out of hand, because it involved "the working in animate nature of forces deeper — or higher — than physico-chemical ones." It was the old truncation of reality Warfield's predecessors had fought a half-century earlier: materialism and "a definitely polemic attitude — of a rather extreme kind — towards teleology." He found this feeling of déjà vu "extremely depressing," for it returned the debate to matters that should have been settled long ago by McCosh and others. "Teleology is in no way inconsistent with — rather is necessarily involved in — a complete system of natural causation." There was no escaping theism, even on completely naturalistic terms; this was the positive lesson of the theistic evolutionists. But now evolutionists tended to reject not only the supernatural interventionism demanded by Christianity, but also the teleology demanded by theism — to return, in other words, to the long-discredited antitheism of Darwin, even while rejecting the selection theory that undergirded it. "This gives the disagreeable appearance to the trend of biological speculation — we do not say of biological investigation — that it is less interested in science for science's sake, that is, in the increase of knowledge, than it is in the validation of a naturalistic world-view: that it is dominated, in a word, by philosophical conceptions, not derived from science but imposed on science from without." What Kellogg called "the scientific spirit," Warfield regretfully concluded, was really "an *a priori* philosophical attitude" — an antiteleological and antitheistic prejudice controlling much scientific thought.[68]

After more than forty years' consideration of Darwinism and evolutionism, Warfield believed science had pretty conclusively destroyed Darwin's theory, but had failed so far to find a rival theory as plausible — let alone to find one to accord with actual facts. In 1916 he reiterated these positions.[69] In light of his career-long theme of appreciation for process in God's works, his openness to human evolution, and especially his reading of Calvin on providence, it would be a serious mistake to class Warfield as any kind of antitransmutationist. His verdict of "not proven" was no attempt to dodge a doctrine of descent, even touch-

67. Warfield, review of *Darwinism To-day*, p. 647.
68. Warfield, review of *Darwinism To-day*, p. 649. Cf. his review of *The Natural Theology of Evolution*, by J. N. Shearman, *PTR* 14 (1916): 325: "Men desire to retain the conclusion which Darwin reached while rejecting the evidence on which Darwin reached this conclusion."
69. Warfield, review of *The Natural Theology of Evolution*, p. 326.

ing man. But his announcement of the failure of the Darwinian hypothesis and the insufficiency of rival theories, together with his opposition to naturalistic metaphysics and the demands for theological adjustment that often accompanied evolutionism, gave the Princetonians who survived him ample opportunity to derive an antievolutionary position from his own.

Antievolutionism

Opposition to evolutionism entered the legal arena only after World War I, when observers linked German aggression and atrocities to the Darwinian struggle for existence and ethics of "might makes right."[70] The emergence of a movement to use state laws to ban the teaching of evolution — a movement that found a powerful leader in former presidential candidate and secretary of state William Jennings Bryan — profoundly altered the terms of discourse about evolution. Prior to the war, antievolutionists had still largely trusted science to work out the question, with occasional goadings from the guardians of religion. Now the battle shifted from persuasion to coercion, from a contest of "experts" (scientists and ministers) to a popular vote, where the stakes were far higher than ever before. Jobs and reputations on both sides were exposed to the popular will; ideas about past ages now carried dire consequences for civilization and morality. When Bryan challenged evolutionist scientists in 1922, he crossed a border between science and religion that religious leaders themselves had largely respected for three-quarters of a century. More importantly, he carried with him a weapon neither side had used in the history of the republic: the coercive power of the law. It is no wonder that scientists retaliated and the war quickly escalated.

Bryan began attacking evolution publicly in the spring of 1920, speaking to church audiences. Soon he took his message to college campuses, where he began to attract media attention. Early in 1922 his speech at the University of Wisconsin–Madison infuriated its president, Edward A. Birge, whose denunciations of Bryan prompted the Great Commoner to call on parents in Wisconsin to replace Birge with some-

---

70. Ferenc Morton Szasz, *The Divided Mind of Protestant America, 1880-1930* (University: University of Alabama Press, 1982), p. 109. Szasz notes that Bryan was persuaded to this view by A. C. Dixon and by Benjamin Kidd's *Science of Power* (1918).

one who would not ridicule their faith. Sensing a good story, the *New York Times* invited Bryan to present his case. He gladly complied, and "God and Evolution" appeared in print on February 26.[71] Bryan took the latest major declaration of the crisis in Darwinism — English geneticist William Bateson's address at the recent meeting of the American Association for the Advancement of Science (AAAS) in Toronto — to argue that evolution in general was only a "guess," not a fact or law of science. Relatively unconcerned about the origin of animals, Bryan aimed to undermine the doctrine of *human* evolution, which he regarded as a dire threat to Christian civilization. Darwin's nadir provided him with an opportunity.[72] Bryan reported that Bateson "tells with real pathos how every effort to discover the origin of species has failed," yet the British geneticist insisted that his faith in evolution was "unshaken" even though he had admitted the absence of explanatory grounds for that belief. "Here is optimism at its maximum," exulted Bryan. "They fall back on faith." In view of evolution's decidedly subfactual status, he argued, to oppose the teaching of human brute ancestry was not at all to "exclude science and return to the dark ages." "We do not ask for the exclusion of any scientific truth, but we do protest against an atheist teacher being allowed to blow his guesses in the face of the student."[73]

The Sunday *Times* article startled Princeton alumnus and former Princeton professor Henry Fairfield Osborn from his "reposeful researches" in New York's American Museum of Natural History, according to his own account. Thoroughly aroused, the aging paleontologist published a swift retort the following week, the beginning of a print war between them that culminated three years later in one of the great media fests of the 1920s, the trial of John Scopes for teaching evolution in violation of a new Tennessee law.[74] Osborn's initial reply to Bryan, "Evolution

71. Szasz, *Divided Mind*, pp. 110-11.

72. For a full account of Bryan's views, see Lawrence W. Levine, *Defender of the Faith: William Jennings Bryan; The Last Decade, 1915-1925* (New York: Oxford University Press, 1965). A more recent study is Michael Kazin's excellent biography, *A Godly Hero: The Life of William Jennings Bryan* (New York: Anchor Books, 2006). See especially his chapter 12 and epilogue.

73. William Jennings Bryan, "God and Evolution," *New York Times*, 26 February 1922, reprinted in part in "William Jennings Bryan on Evolution," *Science* 55 (3 March 1922): 242-43.

74. Osborn, "Crossing Swords with the Fundamentalists," in his *Evolution and Religion in Education: Polemics of the Fundamentalist Controversy of 1922 to 1926* (New York: Charles Scribner's Sons, 1926), pp. 3-7. "I engaged in this struggle for truthfulness in educa-

and Religion," averred in no uncertain terms that evolution was an established fact of thoroughly neutral science, a "natural law" that "should be
taught in our schools simply as Nature speaks to us about it, and entirely
separated from the opinions, materialistic or theistic, which have clus-
tered about it."[75] At the same time, though, he argued that this neutral
fact carried high moral and spiritual force.[76] Princeton University biologist Edwin Grant Conklin, who contributed to the *Times* a reply of his
own alongside Osborn's, accused Bryan of "attempting to establish an in-

---

tion with all my power. For a time I dropped everything else." Osborn had a right to feel an-
tagonized: he had devoted much of his energy as director of the American Museum to
constructing a grand exhibit on human evolution, designed to highlight the tremendous
leap forward he believed to have taken place in the appearance of Cro-Magnon Man. See
Ronald Rainger, *An Agenda for Antiquity: Henry Fairfield Osborn and Vertebrate Paleontology at the American Museum of Natural History, 1890-1935* (Tuscaloosa: University of Alabama Press, 1991). A conscious heir to McCosh, Osborn aimed his evolutionary researches
and theories at disproving "the nightmare of Darwinism" (Bowler's phrase, meaning a
chance universe — see Peter J. Bowler, *The Eclipse of Darwinism: Anti-Darwinian Evolution
Theories in the Decades around 1900* [Baltimore: Johns Hopkins University Press, 1983],
p. 132; cf. Osborn, "Evolution and Daily Living," *Forum* 73 [January-June 1925]: 171-72) and
establishing the independence of mind from matter. He viewed his museum work as a
public trust, taking care to let the facts of nature speak directly to students and especially
children, subverting the allure of hypotheses one learns in books. Osborn, *Creative Education in School, College, University, and Museum* (New York: Charles Scribner's Sons, 1927); cf.
his "How to Teach Evolution in the Schools," *School and Society* 23 (9 January 1926): 28.
Baptist fundamentalist John Roach Straton attacked Osborn where it hurt, posting on the
front of Calvary Baptist Church a placard that read, "Is the American Museum of Natural
History Misspending the Taxpayers' Money and Poisoning the Minds of the School
Children with False and Bestial Theories of Evolution?" Osborn, "Evolution and Daily Living," p. 169. No wonder Osborn took such a public lead in the battle with Bryanism.

75. "Evolution has long since passed out of the domain of hypothesis and theory, to
which Mr. Bryan refers, into the domain of natural law. Evolution takes its place with the
gravitation law of Newton." Osborn, in Osborn and Edwin Grant Conklin, "The Proposed
Suppression of the Teaching of Evolution," *Science* 55 (10 March 1922): 264 (extracted from
"Evolution and Religion," *New York Times*, 5 March 1922). Cf. his "How to Teach Evolution,"
pp. 28-29. Teachers may "strip science of the elements of human error clothing it and present nature face to face"; in this way evolution "may be taught without involving even a
shade of our scientific philosophy."

76. Osborn and Conklin, "Proposed Suppression," p. 264. In a passage he repeated frequently over the next several years, Osborn wrote, "The moral principle inherent in evolution is that nothing can be gained in this world without an effort; the ethical principle inherent in evolution is that the best only has the right to survive; the spiritual principle in
evolution is the evidence of beauty, of order, and of design in the daily myriad of miracles
to which we owe our existence."

quisition for the trial of science at the bar of theology!" — and "medieval theology," at that.[77]

Soon Conklin was heading the AAAS's effort to combat Bryan's crusade.[78] Its council issued a public "Statement on the Present Scientific Status of the Theory of Evolution," affirming that "no scientific generalization is more strongly supported by thoroughly tested evidences than is that of organic evolution," and that the evidence for human evolution was "sufficient to convince every scientist of note in the world."

Had the scientists restricted their maneuvers to assertions of evolution's factuality, perhaps the escalation of hostilities would have ceased. But instead they ventured to define the religious significance of evolution — a move bad enough for its associations with the notorious instances of scientific trespassing into religion in the days of Huxley, Tyndall, Haeckel, and Spencer, but even worse under present circumstances, for Osborn and Conklin proclaimed in the name of science and evolution the very doctrines of theological modernism, plugging their cause directly into an extremely touchy religious issue. Osborn declared that "the naturalist [i.e., scientist] needs a credo . . . very different from that drilled into his youthful mind and memory before the world entered into universal acceptance of the law of Evolution." He perpetuated old Princeton's concern for teleology in nature and the immateriality of the soul, but he banished religion from discussions of "fact" and rendered all religion as natural religion.[79] Conklin's antiorthodoxy was more flagrant; in an article for *Scribner's* called "Science and the Faith of the Modern," he identified "the old philosophy and theology of supernaturalism and tradition" with "the old, naïve faith of childhood and of the childhood age of the race" — a faith that preferred inspiration to truth, that had "no proper conception of nature and of natural law," whose specific commandments were "especially well suited to immature minds," and whose doctrines of retribution and atonement had "no longer any place in civilized society." Science had discredited the old faith; the task at hand was "to adjust religion to science, faith to knowledge, ideality to reality, for adjustment in the reverse direction will never happen." With a pantheizing sleight of hand the Princeton theologians recognized all too easily, Conklin substituted evo-

77. Conklin, quoted in Osborn and Conklin, "Proposed Suppression," p. 266.

78. Numbers, *The Creationists*, p. 364 n. 33.

79. Henry Fairfield Osborn, "Credo of a Naturalist," *Forum* 73 (January-June 1925): 486-94; cf. his "The Earth Speaks to Bryan," *Forum* 73 (January-June 1925): 796-803.

lution for God in familiar Bible passages. Evolution was "the 'power, not ourselves, that makes for righteousness.'" What evolution had in store for future generations, "it hath not entered into the heart of man to conceive."[80] He meant to reassure his readers of the piety of evolutionary religion, but on many his words had the opposite effect.

Evolutionist espousal of religious modernism found its most powerful public expression in "A Joint Statement upon the Relations of Science and Religion," published in *Science* in 1923. Robert A. Millikan, the Nobel prize–winning physicist, penned the declaration in consultation with Osborn and secured an impressive collection of signatures from religious leaders, scientists, and "men of affairs."[81] In a spirit McCosh and Hodge would have heartily approved, the statement deplored the tendency of recent controversies "to present science and religion as irreconcilable and antagonistic domains of thought." But the statement bought peace at the expense of union. Science and religion did not conflict, it said, because they simply did not come into contact with one another. Each dealt with "distinct human needs," supplementing rather than displacing or opposing the other. Science dealt with "facts," religion with "consciences, the ideals and aspirations of mankind."[82] Mollifying as the statement was intended to be, it sought compromise in the isolation of religion from the realm of fact. It continued to emphasize the "importance" of religion, but consigned it to scientific and historical unreality. This was simply to side with Ritschl. To Machen and those who agreed with him, the separation of religion from science was the root issue in the battle with liberalism, for Christianity staked its hope of heaven on earthly events in the life, death, and resurrection of the Savior. To sever

80. Edwin Grant Conklin, "Science and the Faith of the Modern," *Scribner's Magazine* 78 (November 1925): 451-58. On Conklin's religious views, see his autobiographical contribution to Louis Finkelstein, *Thirteen Americans: Their Spiritual Autobiographies* (New York: Harper and Bros., 1953); cf. Jane Maienschein, *Transforming Traditions in American Biology, 1880-1915* (Baltimore: Johns Hopkins University Press, 1991), pp. 208-14.

81. "A Joint Statement upon the Relations of Science and Religion," printed under the title "Science and Religion," in *Science* 57 (1 June 1923): 630-31. Signers included Henry van Dyke, the Princetonian poet who publicly forsook his pew at Princeton's First Presbyterian Church when Machen began to preach against liberalism; Millikan, Osborn, and Conklin, but not Scott; and Herbert Hoover, then secretary of commerce, among other cabinet officials, a governor, a former senator, a rear admiral, and four corporate presidents.

82. "Joint Statement," p. 630. The statement accorded religion the "more important" place by virtue of its spiritual functions, and closed with an affirmation of man's "spiritual nature" and of the "sublime conception of God which is furnished by science."

religion from fact would vitiate the gospel. In the federated republic of science and religion, secession was too great a price for peace.[83] Osborn, Conklin, and the signers of the "Joint Statement" inflamed the issue by taking public sides, as evolutionists, with Ritschlian religious liberalism, which Machen fingered as non-Christian — thus giving added force to Bryan's claim that evolution meant irreligion.

Meanwhile, two of the professors at Princeton Seminary who worked most closely with the fundamentalists on the religious issue — Machen and Old Testament professor Robert Dick Wilson — steered away from Bryan's antievolutionism, refusing to peg the doctrine of descent as the root of all evil. As the Scopes trial approached in the summer of 1925, Osborn shifted his efforts into high gear: he conferred with Clarence Darrow and the rest of the defense counsel; urged "the best biologic thought of America" to Dayton to be available as expert witnesses for evolution; "kept in close touch" with those who went; hastily collected his essays into a single volume, *The Earth Speaks to Bryan,* for presentation to the lawyers at the trial; and flooded Dayton with a thousand pamphlet copies of his initial article for the *New York Times,* "Evolution and Religion."[84] Bryan, who entertained hopes of using the stadium at Vanderbilt University to stage the trial, responded by seeking a panel of experts of his own, among them Machen and Wilson, to testify on behalf of a five-point "Indictment against Evolution" he had drawn up.[85] But the

83. When it came to science and religion, Machen, a southerner with strong sympathies for states' rights, was a decided unionist. Here I am putting a deliberately ironic spin on the heritage Marsden and others have used to help explain Machen's willingness to split from the seminary and the church. See George M. Marsden, "Understanding J. Gresham Machen," *Princeton Seminary Bulletin* 11 (1990): 46-60; also Hart, *Defending the Faith,* and Longfield's chapter on Machen in *The Presbyterian Controversy.*

84. Henry Fairfield Osborn, *The Earth Speaks to Bryan* (New York: Charles Scribner's Sons, 1924); Osborn, *Evolution and Religion in Education,* pp. 6-7. Osborn published a whole series of books, pamphlets, and collected essays on evolution and education, most of them published by Scribner's. Notable are *From the Greeks to Darwin* (1894, 1905, and 1924), "Huxley and Education" (pamphlet, 1910), *The New Order of Sainthood* (1913), "Evolution and Religion" (pamphlet, 1923), *Evolution and Religion in Education* (1926, selling over 11,000 copies in one year), *Creative Education* (1927), *Man Rises to Parnassus* (Vanuxem Lectures at Princeton University, 1927).

85. Bryan to Machen, 23 June 1925 (Machen MSS, Westminster Theological Seminary Library); Bryan to Robert Dick Wilson, 23 June 1925 (Wilson Papers, formerly in private possession of Allan Alexander MacRae, late president of Biblical Theological Seminary); Gordon H. Turner to Bryan, 3 June 1925 (Box 47, Bryan MSS, Library of Congress). Here is Bryan's "Indictment" in full: "First: It disputes the Bible account of man's creation. Second:

Princeton theologians stayed away from the show. In a careful reply, Machen explained that his area of expertise, "a defense of the supernatural in the New Testament," did not make him "competent to render expert testimony" with regard to evolution. He expressed some sympathy with Bryan's cause, but specified "naturalistic" evolution as the foe.[86]

Looking back at the Scopes trial now, it is difficult to reenter the thought world of 1925 and to see Bryan's attempt as anything other than the absurd debacle that H. L. Mencken's editorials, Frederick Allen's popular history, and Jerome Lawrence and Robert E. Lee's drama *Inherit the Wind* have etched into the national consciousness.[87] Antievolutionism seems such a complete renunciation of modernity that a conversion to it

Its logic, by disputing the miraculous and the supernatural, eliminates all that is vital in our revealed religion. Third: By rejecting the doctrine of individual regeneration — the basis of Christianity — evolution discourages all reform and makes improvement depend upon long drawn-out physical and mental changes in man. Fourth: Evolution, when accepted in its entirety, and with all its implications, would carry us back to the brute struggle by which man, according to the evolutionists, has come up from the brute, which means, if logic has any compelling force, that man must turn backward toward the brute if he substitutes the law of love. A fifth indictment can also be sustained, namely, that evolution diverts attention from the great practical problems of life to useless speculation as to the distant past and the distant future. [C]onfidential; not for publication." The attorneys in Dayton first suggested to Bryan that he assemble a panel of experts. Those he invited included fundamentalist leaders J. Frank Norris, John Roach Straton, and William Bell Riley; evangelist Billy Sunday; professors C. B. McMullen (Centre College, Ky.), Herbert C. Noonan, S.J. (St. Ignatius College, former president of Marquette), Howard A. Kelley (Johns Hopkins — he said yes), Louis T. More (University of Cincinnati), Machen, and Wilson; Price and several others. Bryan MSS, box 47.

86. Machen also took exception to point five of Bryan's "Indictment," because it "might possibly be interpreted to indicate hostility to pure science in education, in contrast to directly practical subjects." Machen to Bryan, 2 July 1925, Machen MSS. Wilson's reply has not survived, or perhaps he never sent one. He was in great demand in conservative and fundamentalist circles as a speaker, traveling often, especially in the summer, and notorious for not answering letters. As the editor of *The Life of Faith* (London) informed him, a British inquirer complained "that Her Majesty the Queen, Lord Balfour and the Prime Minister all acknowledged his communications, and he is certainly very anxious to hear from you"! (J. Kennedy Maclean to Wilson, 13 June 1927, Wilson Papers). Wilson did, however, make a contribution to Bryan Memorial University, founded "to carry on, as best it may, his work of combating the teaching of materialism and agnosticism in schools and colleges" (W. C. Haggard, treasurer, to Wilson, 5 March 1930, Wilson MSS).

87. Marion Elizabeth Rodgers, *Mencken: The American Iconoclast* (New York: Oxford University Press, 2005), chapter 25; Frederick Lewis Allen, *Only Yesterday: An Informal History of the Nineteen-Twenties* (New York: Harper and Brothers, 1931), pp. 195-206. *Inherit the Wind* appeared first as a play (1955) and later as a movie (1960, with three further remakes).

would have to be radical, dramatic, and obscurantist. At the time, however, neither evolution nor "creationism" (the term was not yet in use as it is today) had a definite model to explicate it, and in view of the dearth of convincing theory, the line between the two amounted to a metaphysical one — the affirmation or denial of any supernatural intervention in natural law. The Princetonians did not laugh Bryan out of court. In fact, when Bryan delivered a salvo against evolution at Princeton's First Presbyterian Church in 1923, his hosts were seminary president J. Ross Stevenson and Professor Charles Erdman[88] — Machen's inveterate opponents on the ecclesiastical question of liberalism, who refused to withdraw the Christian label from modernist religion.

Aging apologetics professor William Brenton Greene Jr. provides a good example of the fuzzy line between evolutionism and antievolutionism in the 1920s. In his article for the October 1922 issue of the *Princeton Theological Review*, "Yet Another Criticism of the Theory of Evolution," Greene welcomed the "lively interest" in the evolution question aroused by Bryan's crusade, and undertook to pronounce upon the question from his own field of expertise, religious philosophy. Greene had never been a great fan of transmutationism, finding it to provide the common ground where materialism and idealism — the two forms of metaphysical monism — met.[89] As Patton's successor, he believed moderns faced a choice between naturalistic monism (whether idealistic or materialistic) and supernaturalistic dualism, a worldview that affirmed natural law and process but reserved God's prerogative to intervene. Greene believed in science, and like Warfield he withheld judgment on the question of descent while maintaining his metaphysical convictions against all comers. But when scientists admitted their lack of a viable theory of evolution, yet insisted on the fact of evolution, and on that basis insisted also on the unacceptability of supernatural intervention, Greene had had enough. Citing Scott and Conklin, he argued that evolutionist scientists had adopted the Spencerian vision, so that "the characteristic contention of the evolutionist is both that the universe is 'a continuous development' [Scott], and that it is 'a continuous development' only." He contin-

---

88. "Bryan at Princeton Attacks Evolution," *New York Times*, 14 January 1923, p. 15. The article said Bryan was Stevenson's "guest," and "guest of honor at a dinner given by Dr. Charles Erdman."

89. William Brenton Greene Jr., review of *The Evolution of Religion*, by Edward Caird, *PRR* 6 (1895): 128; cf. his "Outline Syllabus on Apologetics and Evidences of Christianity" (pamphlet, n.p.: Hill & Roddy, 1894), PTS Special Collections.

ued, "Logically the hypothesis is a godless one; it enthrones evolution in the room of God, a natural process in place of the Supernatural Being." Against these challenges Greene reasserted "the Supernaturalistic explanation" and simply reverted to what amounted to Arnold Guyot's old view: a world developmentalism that denied transmutation beyond the "type" and explained resemblances between animals on the principle of unfolding design and "conformity to type." He called it "evolution with limits."[90] It was neither evolutionism nor antievolutionism entirely, but it tended in the latter direction.

Oswald T. Allis, professor of Old Testament and editor of the *Princeton Theological Review,* went further. In March 1922 Allis conferred with David S. Kennedy, editor of the militantly conservative weekly *Presbyterian* (Philadelphia), in hopes of finding a scientist who would write on evolution, since it had become such a lively issue. He complained that he did not know whom to approach for such an article — evidently he found Scott either unwilling or undesirable, possibly in view of Greene's belief that continuous evolution led logically to atheism. Kennedy told Allis of George McCready Price, whose article "Outlawed Theories" he had just published in that month's issue of the *Presbyterian.* Allis took up the suggestion, asking Price for an article or series of articles "to defend the teachings of the Scriptures and to show, as far as can be done in the light of present knowledge, that the Bible and Modern Science are not in conflict." He even offered to pay, a departure from normal practice.[91] Price contributed two full-length articles to the *Review,* one challenging fossils as age markers in geology, the other challenging transmutationism outright on the basis of botany.[92]

Price's article on fossils focused on his pet issue, a denial of the fundamental geological belief in a single succession of strata worldwide. A

90. Greene, "Yet Another Criticism," pp. 538, 549-51. Clearly echoing Guyot, under whom he had learned natural history in the first place, Greene stated, "There has been continuous development from the beginning. So far the evolutionist is right. There has not been continuous development *only.* This is the great, the fatal, error of the evolutionist." And a bit later, "The higher takes up all in the lower." It is "not simply the unfolding of the lower. It is all that and *more.* The question is, whence and what this *more?"*

91. Allis to Price, 31 March 1922 (Price MSS, Adventist Heritage Center, Andrews University, Berrien Springs, Mich.). Ron Numbers very kindly informed me of this letter and showed me his copy of it.

92. Price's contributions to the *PTR* are: "The Fossils as Age-Markers in Geology," 20 (1922): 585-615; "Modern Botany and the Theory of Organic Evolution," 23 (1925): 51-65; and a review of *Nomogenesis, or Evolution Determined by Law,* by Leo S. Berg, 25 (1927): 119-22.

Seventh-day Adventist who heartily believed founder Ellen White's interpretation of the Bible — that God created the heavens and the earth in six twenty-four-hour days, and that Noah's flood covered the entire earth — Price formulated a "flood geology" that purported to explain the entire fossil record as a product of the Deluge. He self-published his theory in a little paperback, *Illogical Geology: The Weakest Point in the Evolution Theory* (1906), and expanded and updated it in a whole series of books over the next forty years.[93] His *Review* article compiled a host of geological anomalies to challenge uniformitarianism, but downplayed the flood theory, and concluded with a statement of the limits of inductive science that clearly echoed nineteenth-century Princeton. "True inductive geology will never degenerate into a cosmology. It cannot tell us how life in all of its various forms originated.... The problem of the origin of things belong[s], neither to geology nor to any other of the natural sciences. Inductive geology will never presume to solve this problem; but it points upward."[94]

Price was no expert; despite his college teaching post he had very little training or field experience in geology. At the start of Bryan's crusade in 1922 and again in 1923, when he published his magnum opus, *The New Geology,* proposing to revolutionize the discipline with his flood theory, the scientific community sought to expose him as a mere pretender.[95] Allis, however, stuck by Price, and in 1929 defended his decision to publish him.[96] According to Ronald Numbers, in later years Allis urged John Whitcomb and Henry Morris, authors of the scientific creationist classic *The Genesis Flood* (1961), to acknowledge their debt to Price's work.

Wee Hodge added Price's *Phantom of Organic Evolution* (1924) to the brief bibliography in his anthropology lecture notes, and apparently treated Price's arguments with an open mind, though he never renounced evolution himself.[97] Floyd Hamilton, a Th.M. student at the seminary and

93. For a full discussion of Price's life and views, see Numbers, *The Creationists,* chapter 5.

94. Price, "Fossils as Age-Markers," p. 615.

95. Numbers, *The Creationists,* pp. 91-92.

96. Oswald T. Allis, "Was Jesus a Modernist?" *PTR* 27 (1929): 90 n. 17. He was responding to James H. Snowden, who ridiculed Price's status among fundamentalists as an authority in geology, and who supposed that Allis had not realized what a gaffe he was committing in publishing Price's article. Snowden, *Old Faith and New Knowledge* (New York: Harper and Bros., 1928), pp. 216-17. Ron Numbers told me in conversation that Allis and Price, both of whom lived into their nineties, became lifelong "buddies."

97. C. W. Hodge Jr., MS Notes on Anthropology.

later professor of Bible in Korea, gave credence to Price in a number of book reviews for the *Review* that were frankly antievolutionistic.[98] Price's complaint against the scientific establishment — that they would not give him a hearing because of their prior commitment to a naturalistic worldview[99] — resonated with the Princetonians' own experience, for they felt increasingly marginalized themselves in the theological world on account of their devotion to supernaturalism.

One last event abetted a willingness at Princeton Seminary to turn against the transmutation theory. In June 1925, just a month before the Scopes trial, Louis Trenchard More, a physicist at the University of Cincinnati, delivered the Vanuxem Lectures at Princeton University: "The Dogma of Evolution." The lectures were published immediately in book form. More, like Bateson, affirmed his confidence in the truth of the descent theory, but confessed the lack of a viable mechanism at present. He also took the scientific community to task for promulgating rank dogmatism in the name of science, naming Osborn and Conklin as chief offenders. More deplored "the characteristic blight of Darwinism" — its "unbreathable atmosphere of fatalism" — and even declared that the clergy who had opposed Darwinism on metaphysical grounds "were right" in their predictions of the theory's philosophical abuses. "Step by step with the advance of biological evolution as a scientific hypothesis there grew up the monistic philosophy of naturalism," he stated. Against the scientific assurance that facts supporting a viable evolution theory could not be far to seek, More retorted, "it is not more facts which are needed but some little indication to show that the laws of physics are adequate to include life and its attributes." Though expressing sympathy with Conklin in the battle against Bryan's legal crusade, More rebuked the Princeton biologist for pontificating outside his area of authority. "But, his irritation under fire seems to have confused the clarity of his scientific reasoning to such an extent that he fails to distinguish between evolution as a scientific theory to be investigated in the biological labo-

98. See especially Floyd E. Hamilton, reviews of *The Bankruptcy of Evolution,* by Harold Christopherson Morton, *PTR* 23 (1925): 671, and of *God and Evolution,* by W. R. Matthews, *PTR* 25 (1927): 117. Hamilton is discussed in Numbers, *The Creationists,* pp. 100, 172, and Livingstone, *Darwin's Forgotten Defenders,* pp. 156, 161. Numbers credits Hamilton with purveying Price's theories to the Orthodox Presbyterian Church (the denomination Machen founded after his split from the PCUSA), but notes Hamilton did not follow Price into young-earthism.

99. Numbers, *The Creationists,* pp. 91-93.

ratory, which will stand or fall on the evidence of scientific investigation, and the metaphysical hypothesis of evolution as a guide to social and religious affairs, which is not a problem of biology." Conklin "does not tell us how natural law was instituted nor why, if it was instituted, it cannot be superseded by its institutor," More observed. Further, "We must feel . . . that when he passes from the strictly scientific statement of biological evolution to the evolution of society and religion, he has forsaken scientific methods and is merely expressing an unverifiable opinion as to the future of the race." As for Osborn, the great paleontologist "does not . . . understand that belief in evolution does not make a science unless we can also agree equally on some method of variation."[100]

More had published *The Limitations of Science* in 1914, warning of the great harm that might come of making evolutionary science the fount of all truth, especially in ethics. The Great War only vindicated his views.[101] Here was an evolutionist who called his scientific colleagues to task for their metaphysical dogmatism, just as Princeton had been doing for decades. His critique confirmed the Princeton theologians in their willingness to question evolution's sway, and echoed, in important particulars, the fundamentalist complaint, even as he denounced the legal crusade against the teaching of evolution.

In the charged atmosphere of the 1920s, it is perhaps less surprising that some of the Princeton theologians took up the antievolutionist cause, than that the majority of them, in the face of strong inducements in that direction, retained their former attitude of careful distinction and patient waiting for more light.[102] Some of old Princeton's direst warnings

100. Louis Trenchard More, *The Dogma of Evolution* (Princeton: Princeton University Press, 1925), pp. 24-27.

101. More, *The Dogma of Evolution*, p. 30.

102. Even Walter Lowrie, the Kierkegaard scholar who as a seminarian in the 1880s parted company with Warfield over Calvinism — and who was certainly no fundamentalist — turned his back in disgust on evolutionism. Calling More's book "the first public notice of the demise of Darwinism" (not quite true), he observed, "The death notice ought to have been written, and written long before this, by a biologist as the nearest kin; but because no biologist, zoologist, or paleontologist would announce even in the most euphemistic terms that Darwinism had 'passed,' Professor More, who was a physicist, had to write the obituary — and he did it in very plain words. The news was not welcomed — even by the godly. For in academic circles it is not good form to speak ill of Darwinism. Not for the chivalric consideration that it is mean to hit a man when he is down, but out of consideration for the repute of Science, lest the public should find out that about such an important matter scientists have for several generations been deceived and have been de-

seemed to be coming true — an important reason why fundamentalists flocked to the antievolutionist cause — as scientists used the theory of descent, heedless of questions of epistemic status, to proclaim the intellectual triumph of naturalism, and worse, of theological liberalism. But the Princetonians had other worries on their minds, for by the mid-twenties the seminary itself began to break apart over Machen's assessment of liberalism and its ecclesiastical consequences. The days of old Princeton, and of its Battle Plan, were numbered.

ceivers." Walter Lowrie, introduction to *Religion of a Scientist: Selections from Gustav Th. Fechner,* ed. and trans. Walter Lowrie (New York: Pantheon Books, 1946), pp. 68-69. He treated the Darwinian theory and its implications in distinctly old Princetonian terms (pp. 57, 59). I am grateful to Rev. William O. Harris, former Princeton Seminary archivist, for bringing this piece to my attention.

Conclusion

We also believe in development. All things out of God [i.e., except God] grow. Revelation itself was brought forth gradually through a historic process. And by another process, no less historical, since the close of revelation, its contents have been gradually more and more perfectly apprehended in the thought and life of the Church. Theology, or the human science of the contents of revelation, has been gradually perfected through the last two thousand years, and will doubtless continue to advance until the second coming of the Lord. . . . All true development, while it unfolds and perfects, also preserves the essential identity of the things developed, from the ovum to the accomplished end.

Archibald Alexander Hodge, 1882[1]

But if evolution be true, it becomes a serious matter if it must needs be so violently true as to dislocate the centre of gravity in every system of human thought.

Henry Collin Minton, 1895[2]

1. Archibald Alexander Hodge, "Dean Stanley's Latest Views," *Catholic Presbyterian,* March 1882 — quoted in Charles A. Salmond, *Princetoniana: Charles and A. A. Hodge, with Class and Table Talk of Hodge the Younger* (New York: Scribner and Welford, 1888), pp. 95-96. Contrast this with Mark Massa's claim that Hodge's study of confessional history "uncovered not an evolving, developmental pattern of confessional truth, but an almost mathematically exact identity of creedal witness" across time and place. Mark Stephen Massa, *Charles Augustus Briggs and the Crisis of Historical Criticism* (Minneapolis: Fortress, 1990), p. 73.

2. Henry Collin Minton, review of *The Ascent of Man,* by Henry Drummond, and *So-*

The Unpopularity of Nuance

William Jennings Bryan was not alone in seeking a public declaration from Princeton on the evolution question in the mid-1920s. In view of Princeton Seminary's central place in the Presbyterian controversy, and Machen's position in it at ground zero, the newspapers had already turned to him for commentary and argument as the Scopes trial approached. The church controversy had little directly to do with the question of biological evolution,[3] but inasmuch as it and the "monkey trial" involved fundamentalism, the two were linked in the popular mind. The very week that Bryan sent off his letters to Princeton, the Sunday *New York Times* ran a huge spread on the front page of section 9, entitled "Both Sides: Fundamentalism, Evolution" — pitting Machen against scientist Vernon L. Kellogg, author of *Darwinism To-Day*.

To illustrate the "two sides," the *Times* printed a large drawing of a female figure, "Truth," her arms extended in both directions. To her right stood a minister in his pulpit, dressed in ecclesiastical robes, a large Bible open before him on the lectern. Beneath appeared Machen's article, "What Fundamentalism Stands for Now." To her left, a white-coated chemist conducted his experiments surrounded by the paraphernalia of the laboratory, with Kellogg's article below: "What Evolution Stands for Now." In the center stood the inspiring words, "When Truth Unites Religion and Science." It was a telling illustration. The polarity was so stark, and the female figure of Truth so like an unmasked Justice, that one wonders whether the original concept had been to show Justice with her scales weighing the two sides. After all, the hook for the piece was the upcoming Scopes case, as an insert at the bottom explained: "Because of the approaching trial at Dayton, . . . and because of the apparently widening breach in Protestant churches between Fundamentalists and Modernists, the two articles on this page will attract wide interest." The insert as much as admitted that the plan had been to pit Machen against Kellogg on the origin of species, noting with some

---

cial Evolution, by Benjamin Kidd, *Presbyterian and Reformed Review* (hereafter *PRR*) 6 (1895): 139.

3. Bryan did lead a movement in the 1923 General Assembly against the teaching of evolution, but even the fundamentalist wing of the church did not regard it as the main battleground for their cause. Lefferts A. Loetscher, *The Broadening Church: A Study of Theological Issues in the Presbyterian Church since 1869* (Philadelphia: University of Pennsylvania Press, 1954), pp. 111-12.

disappointment that the Princeton professor had "declined to discuss evolution."[4]

Machen declined similar invitations from *Current History* and other periodicals.[5] Like Bryan, the popular press wanted to connect Princeton's erudite orthodoxy with fundamentalist antievolutionism. But Machen did not want his cause — the exposure and defeat of liberalism in the churches and seminaries — to be sidetracked by the hoopla over Scopes. His article for the *New York Times* stuck to the religious issue. Yet even as he sidestepped the impending trial, Machen suggested that fundamental Christianity could comport quite well with certain aspects of evolutionism.[6]

The article opened with a striking declaration. "The term fundamentalism," Machen wrote, "is distasteful to the present writer." It conjured up images of "some strange new sect," he explained,

> whereas in point of fact we are conscious simply of maintaining the historic Christian faith and of moving in the great central current of Christian life. This does not mean that we desire to be out of touch with our own time, or that we live in a static world without variety and without zest. On the contrary, there is nothing more varied and interesting than the effect of the Christian religion upon different races and different ages; there is no more absorbing story than that of the relations between Christianity and its environment. But what we do mean is that despite changes in the environment, there is some-

4. "Both Sides: Fundamentalism, Evolution," *New York Times*, 21 June 1925, section 9.

5. Ned B. Stonehouse, *J. Gresham Machen: A Biographical Memoir* (Grand Rapids: Eerdmans, 1954), p. 401. Two days after the Scopes trial concluded, *Current History* telegraphed Machen for commentary. He cabled back, "I regret exceedingly that I do not feel competent to contribute an article on the Dayton trial comma since I have never made any special study of the subject of evolution and have not followed closely the details of the trial stop". Machen was something of a libertarian in political outlook, and thus probably unsupportive of the Tennessee antievolution law, whatever his personal beliefs about evolution. He offered the editor instead an article on "the schools and their relation to civil and religious liberty," a topic the papers had all but overlooked. Apparently he was turned down. Machen to Francis Snow, telegram, 23 July 1925 (Machen Papers, Westminster Theological Seminary, Philadelphia).

6. For a fuller discussion of Machen's views on evolution, science, and religion, see Darryl G. Hart, *Defending the Faith: J. Gresham Machen and the Crisis of Conservative Protestantism in Modern America* (Baltimore: Johns Hopkins University Press, 1994), chapter 4: "Science and Salvation."

thing in Christianity which from the very beginning has remained the same.[7]

Here Machen, a fundamentalist pitted against an evolutionist, deliberately employed developmental language to describe his position. He portrayed fundamentalism as "moving" in a "current" rather than inhabiting "a static world." He pointed to the effect of environment upon Christian history, welcoming the study of such influences. Thus his essentialist claim for fundamentalism — that there was "something in Christianity which from the very beginning has remained the same" — made a point of acknowledging with it a process of change. He pictured Christianity as an organism growing in response to its environment, yet retaining, as individual organisms do, an essential identity throughout its history. Machen's very definition of fundamentalism incorporated the growth analogy that underlay much of the evolutionary theory of his day.

At the same time, however, Machen forcefully opposed certain broad philosophical positions often associated with the transmutation of species. He argued that Christianity stood on a distinct metaphysical foundation, one utterly incompatible with the metaphysics of many evolutionists. Beneath the handful of doctrines the fundamentalists employed to identify Christian belief — the famous "five fundamentals" — lay something more basic. Machen called it "simply theism: the belief, namely, that the universe was created, and is now upheld, by a personal Being upon whom it is dependent but who is not dependent upon it." This metaphysical aspect of the doctrine of creation — the distinction between creature and Creator — Machen considered the cornerstone of the Christian belief system. It differed absolutely from "the prevalent pantheism," a view that regarded God as "merely a collective name for the world process itself," or as "related to the world process as the soul of man is related to his body." Machen did not deny "world process" — indeed, he took pains to affirm it — but he refused to identify it with the ultimate Cause of all things.

This was as near as Machen's article came to discussing evolution. It was not transmutation or process that troubled him, but the metaphysics of Evolution with a capital E — the blurring of the distinction

---

7. Machen, "What Fundamentalism Stands for Now," in Hart, *Defending the Faith*, chapter 4. I have omitted the newspaper-style paragraph breaks, which almost certainly were added by an editor.

between Creator and creature, supernatural and natural, thus denying the transcendence of God that marked biblical Christianity. Machen's article showed that this basic philosophical issue, derived from Scripture and indeed implicated in the evolution question, underlay such particular "fundamentals" as Christ's virgin birth, bodily resurrection, and miracles.[8]

While thus refusing to discuss evolution outright, Machen both incorporated and rejected certain aspects of the theory. His article typified the kind of thinking about science that had characterized the Princeton theology since its inception: heartily taking part in and assimilating much of the new scholarship, but always wary of philosophical assumptions and entailments, ever vigilant to defend and establish the reality of supernatural religion. As the fundamentalist controversies came to a head, Princeton Seminary's decades-old assessment of the evolution question remained remarkably intact. It was a position premised on a stark polarity between dualistic supernaturalism and monistic naturalism — recognizing that evolution served the latter category very well, but affirming nonetheless that evolution neither entailed monistic naturalism nor belonged to it as a peculiar possession — but its nuances and careful definitions were not the stuff of which popular press and popular movements are made.

A Legacy of Questions

Our story comes to an abrupt halt in 1929, when the Presbyterian Church in the United States of America forcibly reorganized Princeton Seminary in order to quell denominational strife. Machen, together with a majority of the faculty and of the board of directors, believed the church to be endangered by a new theology that was fundamentally non-Christian. President J. Ross Stevenson and Professor Charles R. Erdman, together with a minority of the faculty and of the board, believed the church to be endangered by a judgmental and schismatic spirit. In the name of Christian brotherhood and representation of the wide spectrum of opinions in the church, the denomination dissolved the seminary's conservative stronghold, its board of directors, and reconstituted oversight of Princeton Seminary under a single, new board of trustees composed of both

8. Machen, "What Fundamentalism Stands for Now."

conservatives and moderates. Machen, a handful of fellow faculty members, and a good number of students left Princeton to found a new, distinctly Old School institution, Westminster Theological Seminary in Chestnut Hill, Philadelphia. While Stevenson assured Presbyterians that Princeton Seminary's doctrinal position remained unchanged, the old battle plan was effectively quashed. The "geography of ideas," to use David Livingstone's phrase, suddenly changed.[9]

Old Princeton's unnatural demise left successors and later interpreters with a number of unresolved questions. Did the Princetonian approach to science and religion — by no means unique to Princeton, but exemplified best by Princeton — deserve to die, even if the seminary's reorganization was unfair? The neoorthodox theologians whom President John Alexander Mackay brought to Princeton Seminary beginning in the 1930s certainly thought so, as did many admirers of the Dutch school of Calvinism led by Abraham Kuyper and Herman Bavinck, for slightly different reasons. In their view the American approach to apologetics had played itself out unsuccessfully, conceding too much by adopting a scientific approach and adapting theology to scientific models. European approaches to science and religion offered a way out of American Presbyterianism's fundamentalist-modernist impasse. Charles Hodge's declaration that theology was a science, comparing its methodology to that of geology, came in for ridicule. As historian James Turner put the point much later, "It was, after all, theologians and ministers who had welcomed this secular visitor into the house of God. It was they who had most loudly insisted that knowledge of God's existence and benevolence could be pinned down as securely as the structure of a frog's anatomy — and by roughly the same method."[10] Followers of Kuyper and Bavinck agreed with Turner's assessment, urging American Calvinists — a great many of whose key leaders in the ethnically Dutch denominations were trained at Princeton Seminary — to forsake Princeton for Amsterdam. In

9. Edwin H. Rian, *The Presbyterian Conflict* (Grand Rapids: Eerdmans, 1940); Loetscher, *The Broadening Church;* Bradley J. Longfield, *The Presbyterian Controversy: Fundamentalists, Modernists, and Moderates* (New York: Oxford University Press, 1991); David N. Livingstone, "Science and Religion: Foreword to the Historical Geography of an Encounter," *Journal of Historical Geography* 20 (1994): 367-83.

10. James Turner, *Without God, without Creed: The Origins of Unbelief in America* (Baltimore: Johns Hopkins University Press, 1985), p. 193. Again, and more pointedly, speaking of the nineteenth-century Reformed approach that Princeton exemplified, Turner writes, "Religion caused unbelief. . . . [T]he defenders of God slowly strangled him" (p. xiii).

evangelical and especially Reformed theological circles, that contest lives on.[11]

Another question is what the Princetonians have to teach us on the evolution question, a matter that depends first on identifying their positions on evolutionism accurately. Here, too, there is disagreement. On the one hand, Andrew Dickson White's *History of the Warfare of Science with Theology in Christendom* ensured James McCosh a place in standard histories of American higher education as a forward-thinking Christian leader who saw the wisdom of making an early peace with evolution — essentially liberal-tending, though not a theological liberal himself, embracing transmutation straightforwardly as God's method of creation. He became a model of wise dealing with the evolution question for insisting that it was a matter for science to settle. Later, as the twentieth century passed its midpoint and antievolutionism was fast coming to function as a sixth "fundamental," thoughtful believers who questioned that new orthodoxy appealed to another Princetonian precedent. "I recall that B. B. Warfield was a theistic evolutionist," wrote J. I. Packer in 1978. "If on this count I am not an evangelical, then neither was he." Warfield in particular became a favorite "Exhibit A" for evolution-friendly believers in the Bible. David Livingstone and Mark Noll brought out a volume of Warfield's collected writings on "evolution, science, and Scripture," while simultaneously touting Warfield to historians of science as "a biblical inerrantist as evolutionist."[12]

On the other hand, believers less friendly to evolution either questioned McCosh's and Warfield's wisdom on that issue, or denied that the Princetonians were the theistic evolutionists they had been made out to

11. See, for example, Paul Kjoss Helseth, *"Right Reason" and the Princeton Mind: An Unorthodox Proposal* (Phillipsburg, N.J.: P&R, 2010); Donald Macleod, "Bavinck's Prolegomena: Fresh Light on Amsterdam, Old Princeton, and Cornelius Van Til," *Westminster Theological Journal* 68 (2006): 261-82; Donald Fuller and Richard Gardiner, "Reformed Theology at Princeton and Amsterdam in the Late Nineteenth Century: A Reappraisal," *Presbyterion* 21 (1995): 89-117; and Hendrik Hart, Johan van der Hoeven, and Nicholas Wolterstorff, eds., *Rationality in the Calvinian Tradition* (Lanham, Md.: University Press of America, 1983).

12. J. I. Packer, *The Evangelical Anglican Identity Problem* (Oxford: Latimer House, 1978), p. 5, quoted in Alister McGrath, *The Foundations of Dialogue in Science and Religion* (Malden, Mass.: Blackwell, 1998), p. 130; Benjamin Breckinridge Warfield, *Evolution, Science, and Scripture: Selected Writings*, ed. Mark A. Noll and David N. Livingstone (Grand Rapids: Baker, 2000); Livingstone and Noll, "B. B. Warfield (1851-1921): A Biblical Inerrantist as Evolutionist," *Isis* 91 (2000): 283-304.

be. Henry M. Morris, head of the Institute for Creation Research, accused Warfield of "pervasive theological apostasy" for his openness to the doctrine of transmutation. More recently Fred G. Zaspel has taken on Livingstone and Noll, asserting that Warfield did not finally embrace evolutionism after all.[13] For some reason, no evangelicals seem interested in reemphasizing the limits and qualifications that McCosh placed on what he called "the development hypothesis," though those limits and qualifications are also significant.

I have purposely striven *not* to bring a preformed set of categories to bear on my subjects in this study, as if we could locate each figure neatly in a taxonomy of belief about evolution that matches positions common today (theistic evolution, progressive creation, etc.). Nor have I conducted an analytic survey of those Princetonians who took up the evolution question, seeking to tease out of the history a new, less anachronistic taxonomy. I have chosen instead to allow the Princetonians both to pose and to answer what *they* took to be the evolution question. I hope I have succeeded in giving them their voice, offering what may be, to us, fresh perspectives on the big questions involved in evolutionary thinking.

Still, readers will want to know in what ways and to what extent the Princetonians "accepted" biological evolution, and this is after all a first step toward learning from their example, whether positively or negatively. In answer to that question I would offer the following summation.

The transmutation of species in brute creation did not much trouble the Princeton theologians, mainly because it lay largely outside the concerns of theology. They believed the Bible could be interpreted, without violence to its integrity, to accommodate geologic time and the slow progress of life-forms. Charles Hodge never embraced the doctrine of transmutation; James McCosh eventually did. But both men allowed the doctrine when properly limited (to brute creation) and explained (as not operating by chance or fatalistic necessity, but carrying out the will of God, who acts both naturally and supernaturally). Their successors at Princeton University embraced transmutation outright; their successors at the seminary allowed it while waiting for more light.

The question of human evolution was the crux of the matter. Here

---

13. Henry M. Morris, *A History of Modern Creationism* (San Diego: Master Book Publishers, 1984), p. 39, quoted in McGrath, *Foundations of Dialogue*, p. 130; Fred G. Zaspel, "B. B. Warfield on Creation and Evolution," *Themelios* 35 (July 2010): 198-211; Zaspel, *The Theology of B. B. Warfield: A Systematic Summary* (Wheaton, Ill.: Crossway, 2010), pp. 369-87.

the Bible tied foundational salvation doctrine to specific historical claims: the fall of humanity from a state of original righteousness by the free choice of Adam and Eve, the solidarity of the human race in Adam, the saving work of Christ as the second Adam. In addition to these biblical doctrines, the Princetonians were deeply concerned to maintain the dualism of mind and body, the reality of a spiritual realm unreachable by empirical science. Thus many of them were willing to entertain the possibility that God made Adam's body by descent with modification from animal ancestors ("from the dust of the ground"), but if so, God had interposed a definite creative act in the elevation of that creature to his full humanity when he breathed into the creature's nostrils the breath of life and man became a living soul. None of the Princeton theologians asserted such a picture of human origins as definite fact; rather they allowed it and at the most held it more or less tentatively.

This last point is borne out by the experience of the second and third decades of the twentieth century, when, as Warfield complained, scientists made increasingly bold claims about the "fact" of evolution just when they were admitting their utter lack of a well-grounded theory to explain it. Worse, under the stress of the antievolution campaign, scientists led by university Princetonians Osborn and Conklin trumpeted liberal theology as the modern faith endorsed by science. In this environment several Princeton theologians were quite willing to reassert their uncertainty about the transmutation of species. Their basic assessment of its theological connections remained the same. What changed was their relative assessment of its likelihood in fact.

Princetonian Developmentalism

Far more interesting than the biological question, both to this author and to the Princetonians themselves, are the many other dimensions of the evolution question. Though it could be used to attack orthodox belief in all sorts of ways, the Princetonians did not reject all evolution as guilty by association with its excesses. We have seen in this study the many ways in which the Princeton theologians expressed their orthodox convictions in developmental terms, finding in the idea of unfolding potentialities not only strong evidence for God as Creator and Governor of the world, but strong arguments for orthodox belief. Development built upon the past, it did not wipe it away. Non-Darwinian evolutionisms heightened the appeal of such developmentalism, and Princeton, as we have seen, recognized an essential kinship with many such ideas. Aside from their apologetical utility, developmental understandings struck the Princetonians in many ways as simply true — revealing God's usual mode of operation in and through the natural order.

B. B. Warfield celebrated the Westminster Confession as "the ripened fruit of Reformed creed-making," making its creation at the end of the Reformation era a plus rather than a minus. Warfield and A. A. Hodge offered their doctrine of biblical inspiration as admittedly somewhat novel in focus, yet argued that it remained in continuity with the older doctrine, in that it developed it further under the new scientific conditions of the nineteenth century. John D. Davis argued from the traces of religious development in the Bible and the Babylonian literature that the Hebrew tradition in Genesis was the more ancient and true. J. Gresham Machen and Stone Lecturer M. W. Jacobus Jr. defended Paul's religion against Harnack and the Ritschlians as the legitimate growth of the perfect seed of Jesus' teachings. James C. Moffat and Princeton's comrade W. G. T. Shedd traced the downward development of religion apart from special revelation, and the upward development of Christian doctrine under God's gracious guidance. Geerhardus Vos furthered the study of biblical theology as a promising way to understand Scripture in its organic, developmental unity, clarifying biblical interpretation while overturning the destructive claims of the so-called higher criticism. Warfield credited the evolution question with providing the stimulus to develop more precise understandings of the modes of divine activity, especially the concept of mediate creation — just as he viewed the development of systematic theology as an evolution from earlier orthodox efforts, not a revolution overturning them.

In all these ways the Princeton theologians found growth-analogy evolutionism helpful both to elucidate traditional Christian belief and to defend it against the challenges of theological liberalism. Their embrace of such evolutionism went far beyond the biological question of transmutation of species and its fit (or not) with the Bible. And it was not just a defensive strategy, useful but otherwise unattractive. They welcomed developmental emphases as positively helpful. A. A. Hodge's statement in the epigraph above captures the affirmative spirit of Princetonian developmentalism.

Still, as Warfield's former student Henry Collin Minton said, "there is evolution and evolution." Not all evolutionisms were created equal.

When religious evolution was construed in wholly naturalistic terms, it made Christianity just another expression of human spiritual aspiration — "the crown and capstone, it may be, of natural religion, but natural religion for all that," to quote Warfield — so that the gospel of liberal Christianity was essentially a warmed-over deism. Here was the link between theological liberalism and naturalistic evolution: both excluded the supernatural as such. If God worked always and only through natural causes, salvation was not a matter of supernatural grace but of natural human achievement, emulating the example of Jesus the great God-conscious man, as indeed the liberals taught. This kind of revolution in theology irked and exasperated the Princeton theologians and their comrades, who at times gave vent to their feelings by lamenting that the world had gone "evolution-mad," or by wisecracking, as did apologetics professor Charles Aiken in a review of a particularly egregious book: "Great is Protoplasm, of which this volume is one of the latest and most typical evolutionary developments. Great is the positivist conception of the universe, and life and history, which is here in a conversational way expounded to us." Evolutionism could be found lurking around just about every objectionable modernist tendency — the Princetonians saw it as the tool, the fundamentalists saw it as the cause, of infidelity.[14]

The key issue, of course, was metaphysical, indeed doctrinal: Did God rule over a universe and human history separate from himself? Was God transcendent and sovereign over, as well as immanent in, the world process? His rule, when mediated through second causes, they called providence, following the careful distinctions in the old Westminster Standards. Providence came within and through process, commonly in the form of development or growth from created potentials. For the Princeton theologians, such goal-directed growth characterized both nature and history, and could be found even in the unfolding of divine revelation and the progress of the church's articulation of doctrine. But God ruled and acted in other, supernatural ways as well — and biblical faith (both the content and the experience) depended on God's supernatural activity. The God of process and providence was also the God of creation and miracle, and it was necessary to keep those distinctions clear.

14. Benjamin Breckinridge Warfield, short notice of *"The Ascent of Man": Its Note of Theology,* by Principal Hutton, *PRR* 6 (1895): 367; Minton, review of *The Ascent of Man,* p. 139; Charles A. Aiken, review of *Personal and Social Evolution with the Key of the Science of History,* by a Historical Scientist, *PRR* 1 (1890): 708.

Bibliography

This bibliography is divided into three sections. The first lists manuscript and archival sources, including pamphlets and memorial books, that are unique to certain collections (or nearly so). Pamphlets of inaugurations and obituaries are listed under the person they treat, since their alphabetization by title would not aid the researcher, and since their authors are often not given. So are lecture notes, whether printed or manuscript, and whether by students or by faculty.

The second section is a straight alphabetical listing, by author where possible, of published primary and secondary sources together. In a work such as this one, a source sometimes serves in both a primary and a secondary capacity.

The third section lists selected articles, reviews, and short notices from the Princeton quarterlies.

1. Manuscript and Archival Sources, Including Pamphlets

PTS Special Collections = Special Collections, Princeton Theological Seminary Library, Princeton, N.J. When an item belongs to a particular MS collection, the name of the collection is given.

PU Archives = Princeton University Archives, Seeley G. Mudd Manuscript Library, Princeton, N.J.

PU Library = Department of Rare Books and Special Collections, Firestone Library, Princeton University, Princeton, N.J.

Bibliography

Aiken, Charles Augustus (1827-92)

"Christian Apologetics: The Lectures Constituting the Course in Ethics and Apologetics, for the Middle and Senior Classes, Princeton Theological Seminary." Princeton: Press Printing Establishment, 1879. PTS Special Collections.

"Exercises Connected with the Inauguration of Rev. Charles A. Aiken, D.D., as President of Union College, Schenectady, New York, Tuesday, June 28, 1870." Albany: Joel Munsell, 1870. PTS Special Collections.

"Inauguration of the Rev. Chas. Augustus Aiken, D.D., as Professor of Christian Ethics and Apologetics in Princeton Theological Seminary, November, 1871." New York: Rogers and Sherwood, 1872. PTS Special Collections.

"Lectures on the Relations of Philosophy and Science to the Christian Religion." Ca. 1888. MS. Charles Augustus Aiken MSS, PTS Special Collections.

"Syllabus of Lectures by Dr. Aiken, on Special Introduction to the Historical Books of the Old Testament." Princeton: Princeton Press, 1889. PTS Special Collections.

Atwater, Lyman Hotchkiss (1813-83)

Faculty file. PU Archives.

MSS. PU Archives.

"Metaphysics." MS notes on his lectures taken by Charles Freeman Richardson, Princeton Theological Seminary, 1864. Bound with notes from Guyot and others. PTS Special Collections.

Bryan, William Jennings (1860-1925)

MS Correspondence. Library of Congress, Washington, D.C.

Davis, John D. (1854-1926)

"Old Testament History: The Earlier Period." Required course, first year. MS student notes, Fall 1924. Alexander Napier MacLeod MSS. PTS Special Collections.

Dawson, John William (1820-99)

MS Correspondence. McGill University Archives, Montreal.

Dod, Albert Baldwin (1805-45)

Hodge, Charles. "A Brief Account of the Last Hours of Albert B. Dod." Princeton: John T. Robinson, 1845. PTS Special Collections.

Duffield, John Thomas (1823-1901)

"Anthropology of Evolutionism and the Bible." Princeton: Princeton Printing Establishment, 1878. PTS Special Collections.

"In Memoriam: John Thomas Duffield." Privately published, n.p., 1901. PTS Special Collections.

Green, William Henry (1825-1900)

"Discourses at the Inauguration of the Rev. William Henry Green, as Professor of Biblical and Oriental Literature in the Theological Seminary at Princeton, N.J., Delivered at Princeton, September 30, 1851, before the Directors of the Seminary." Philadelphia: C. Sherman, 1851. PTS Special Collections.

Greene, William Brenton, Jr. (1854-1928)

"Christian Sociology." Required course, third year. Typescript "syllabus" (full notes), Fall 1926. Alexander Napier MacLeod MSS. PTS Special Collections.

"The New Theology." A paper presented at the request of the Presbyterian Ministerial Association of Philadelphia, June, 1885. PTS Special Collections.

"Official Syllabus for Junior Apologetics." Compiled from Greene's own notes by Clark Alexander and Charles Gurlinger; reedited by Charles T. Leber. Typescript, 1921. William Brenton Greene Jr. MSS. PTS Special Collections.

"Outline Syllabus on Apologetics and Evidences of Christianity." From notes by Frank W. Hill. N.p.: Hill and Roddy, 1894. PTS Special Collections.

"Syllabus of Lectures Delivered in Middle Year on Christian Apologetics." Printed, not published. 1905-6. PTS Special Collections.

Guyot, Arnold Henry (1807-84)

MSS. PU Archives.

"Geology." MS notes from his lectures taken by William R. Barricklo, 1877-78. PU Archives.

"Notes on Geology from Lectures Given by Prof. Guyot." Princeton, 1880. 3 parts. Students' syllabus included. PU Archives.

"Prof. Guyot's Lectures on Geology." MS notes taken by Charles Freeman Richardson, PTS, fall 1863. PU Archives.

"Vol. II of Prof. Guyot's Lectures on Geology." Notes by Samuel R. Comfort. Princeton: Private printing, 1860s. Photocopy. PU Archives.

Cameron, Henry Clay. "Arnold Guyot." N.p., n.d. PTS Special Collections.

Dana, James Dwight. "Biographical Memoir of Prof. Arnold Guyot." From the *Smithsonian Report* for 1886-87. Washington, D.C.: Smithsonian Institution, 1889. Faculty file. PU Archives.

"Exercises at the Unveiling of a Memorial Tablet to Arnold Guyot, Ph.D., LL.D., in Marquand Chapel, Princeton, N.J., Tuesday, June 10th, 1890." Princeton: C. S. Robinson and Co., University Printers, 1890. Faculty file. PU Archives.

Jones, Leonard Chester. "Arnold Henry Guyot." Pamphlet reproduction from Union College faculty papers, vol. 23, 1930. Faculty file. PU Archives.

Libbey, William, Jr. "Life and Scientific Work of Arnold Guyot." New York: American Geographical Society, 1884 (Bulletin no. 3). Faculty file. PU Archives.

Wilson, Philip K. "*Guyot* of Guyot Hall." Leaflet for the Department of Geosciences, PU, 2007.

Hodge, Archibald Alexander (1823-86)

MS Correspondence. Hodge Family MSS. PU Library.

MSS. PTS Special Collections.

"Address of Dr. A. A. Hodge, of Western Theological Seminary, Delivered by Request, before a Synodical Institute Held by Synod of Cleveland, October, 1873." Cleveland: Fairbanks, Benedict and Co., 1873. PTS Special Collections.

"A Discourse in Memory of Archibald Alexander Hodge, D.D., LL.D." Philadelphia: John Wanamaker, 1887. PTS Special Collections.

Paxton, William Miller. "Address Delivered at the Funeral of Archibald Alexander

Hodge, D.D., LL.D., Professor in the Theological Seminary, Princeton, N.J., November 15, 1886." New York: Anson D. F. Randolph and Co., 1886. PTS Special Collections.

Hodge, Caspar Wistar, Jr. (1870-1937)
MSS. PTS Special Collections.

"Addresses Delivered at the Inauguration of Reverend Caspar Wistar Hodge, Ph.D., as Charles Hodge Professor of Didactic and Polemic Theology in Princeton Theological Seminary." N.p., 1921. PTS Special Collections.

"Doctrine of Sin." Elective course, 1 hour. MS student notes, ca. 1927. Alexander Napier MacLeod MSS. PTS Special Collections.

"The Kantian Epistemology and Theism." A dissertation presented to the Faculty of Princeton College for the Degree of Doctor of Philosophy. Philadelphia: McCalla and Co., 1894. PTS Archives.

Systematic Theology lectures. MS, ca. 1907–ca. 1935. Caspar Wistar Hodge Jr. MSS. PTS Special Collections. (These include Notes on Anthropology.)

Hodge, Charles (1797-1878)
MS Correspondence. Hodge Family MSS. PU Library.

MSS. PTS Special Collections.

Memoranda. MS, 11 April 1836–31 March 1878. PTS Special Collections.

Atwater, Lyman Hotchkiss. "A Discourse Commemorative of Dr. Charles Hodge." Princeton: Charles S. Robinson, 1878. PTS Special Collections.

Kennedy, Earl William. "Writings about Charles Hodge and His Works, Principally as Found in Periodicals Contained in the Speer Library, Princeton Theological Seminary, for the Years 1830-1880." Typescript, 1963. Reference. PTS Library.

"In Memoriam: Charles Hodge; Discourses Commemorative of the Life and Work of Charles Hodge." Philadelphia: Henry B. Ashmead, 1879. PTS Special Collections.

Watts, Robert. "The Late Dr. Hodge." Pamphlet, ca. 1880. PTS Special Collections.

Jenkins, Finley DuBois (ca. 1895-1935)
"The Doctrine of Man." Elective course (1 hour) in Systematic Theology. MS student notes, Spring 1928. Alexander Napier MacLeod MSS. PTS Special Collections.

Johnson, George (1872-1961)
"Evidences of Christianity." Required course, second year. Typescript "syllabus" (full notes) for 1925-26. Alexander Napier MacLeod MSS. PTS Special Collections.

Johnson, William Hallock (1865–ca. 1960)
"Reminiscences." Typescript, ca. 1950. William Hallock Johnson MSS. PTS Special Collections.

Lowrie, Samuel Thompson (1835-1924)
Commonplace books. MS ruminations on short subjects. Samuel Thompson Lowrie MSS. PTS Special Collections.

Machen, J. Gresham (1881-1937)
MSS. Westminster Theological Seminary Library, Philadelphia, Pa.

Maclean, John, Jr. (1800-1886)

MSS. PU Archives.

Duffield, John Thomas. "Discourse Delivered at the Funeral of John Maclean, Tenth President of the College of New Jersey." Princeton: Princeton Press, ca. 1887. PTS Special Collections.

Macloskie, George (1834-1920)

"Biology Lecture Notes: Problems of Evolution, Etc." MS notes from his lectures taken by Harry Elmer Bierly, '92, 1891-92. PU Archives.

McCosh, James (1811-94)

MS Correspondence. PU Archives.

"Faith in Christ and Faith in Doctrine Compared and Contrasted." The Baccalaureate Sermon preached before the College of New Jersey, June 23, 1872. Princeton: Stelle and Smith, 1872. PTS Special Collections.

"Unity with Diversity in the Works and Word of God." The Baccalaureate Sermon preached before the College of New Jersey, June 25, 1871. Princeton: Stelle and Smith, 1871. PTS Special Collections.

Dulles, Joseph H. "McCosh Bibliography: A List of the Published Writings of the Rev. James McCosh, D.D., LL.D., Ex-President of Princeton College." *Princeton College Bulletin* 7 (March 1895). PU Archives.

Ormond, Alexander Thomas (1847-1915)

"Notes on Metaphysics Lectures Delivered by Prof. Ormond." MS, taken by A. Tawney, class of 1891. Faculty file. PU Archives.

Osborn, Henry Fairfield (1857-1935)

MSS. American Museum of Natural History, New York City.

MS Correspondence. New York City Historical Society.

"Henry Fairfield Osborn, 1857-1935." Pamphlet of his memorial service at St. Bartholomew's Church, New York. N.p., [1935]. Faculty file. PU Archives.

Patton, Francis Landey (1843-1932)

MS Correspondence. Pressbooks. PU Archives.

MS Correspondence. Francis Landey Patton MSS. PTS Special Collections.

"Addresses at the Inauguration of the Rev. Francis L. Patton, D.D., LL.D., as Stuart Professor of the Relations of Philosophy and Science to the Christian Religion, in the Theological Seminary, at Princeton, N.J., October 27, 1881." Philadelphia: Sherman and Co., 1881. Francis Landey Patton MSS. PTS Special Collections.

"Baccalaureate Sermon Preached before the Class of 1894." Pamphlet apparently excerpted from "A Report of the Exercises at the Opening of Alexander Commencement Hall," ca. 1894. PTS Special Collections.

"Doctrinal Series." Chicago: T. T. Jones, 1879. 1: "Thoughts on the Theistic Controversy." 3: "The Doctrine of Sin." 10: "The Two Adams." PTS Special Collections.

"The Fundamental Doctrines of the Presbyterian Church." In "Addresses Delivered at the Quarter-Century Anniversary of the Reunion of the Old and New School

Presbyterian Churches." Philadelphia: Presbyterian Board of Publication and Sabbath-School Work, 1895. PTS Special Collections.

"The Inauguration of President Patton" (College of New Jersey). New York: Gray Bros., 1888. Francis Landey Patton MSS. PTS Special Collections.

"Speech of Prof. Francis L. Patton, D.D., LL.D., President-Elect of Princeton College, at the Annual Dinner of the Princeton Club of New York, March 15, 1888." New York, 1888. PTS Special Collections.

"Syllabus of Prof. Patton's Lectures on Theism." Princeton: Princeton Press, 1888. PTS Special Collections.

Price, George McCready (1870-1963)
MSS. Adventist Heritage Center, Andrews University, Berrien Springs, Mich.

Princeton Theological Seminary
Catalogues. PTS Special Collections.

Directors Minutes. MS and typescript. PTS Special Collections.

Faculty Minutes. MS and typescript. PTS Special Collections.

Gapp, Kenneth S. "The Princeton Review Series and the Contribution of Princeton Theological Seminary to Presbyterian Quarterly Magazines." Typescript, Princeton Theological Seminary, 1960. PTS Special Collections.

Kennedy, Earl William. "Authors of Articles in the Biblical Repertory and Princeton Review." Typescript, 1963. PTS Special Collections.

"Plan of the Theological Seminary of the Presbyterian Church in the United States of America, Located at Princeton." Elizabethtown, N.J.: Isaac A. Kollock, 1816. PTS Special Collections.

Princeton Theological Society. MS Minute Book, 1879-1885. PTS Special Collections.

"Report of a Committee of the General Assembly of the Presbyterian Church, Exhibiting the Plan of a Theological Seminary." New York: Williams and Whiting, 1810. PTS Special Collections.

Trustees Minutes. MS and typescript. PTS Special Collections.

Princeton University (formerly College of New Jersey)
Catalogues. PU Archives.

Faculty Minutes. MS and typescript. PU Archives.

Memorial Book of the Sesquicentennial Celebration of the Founding of the College of New Jersey and of the Ceremonies Inaugurating Princeton University. New York: Charles Scribner's Sons, 1898. PU Archives.

The Nassau Herald. Yearbook. PU Archives.

"One Hundred Years, 1825-1925: The Philadelphia Society of Princeton University Commemorates the 100th Anniversary of Its Founding, February 4, 1925." N.p., 1925. PU Archives.

The Princeton Book. A series of sketches pertaining to the history, organization and present condition of the College of New Jersey, by Officers and Graduates of the College. Boston: Houghton, Osgood and Co., 1879. PU Archives.

The Princetonian. College newspaper. PU Archives.

Trustees Minutes. MS, later typescript. PU Archives.

Scott, William Berryman (1858-1947)

MS Correspondence. Scott MSS. PU Library.

MS Correspondence (some). Hodge Family MSS. PU Library.

Faculty file. PU Archives.

"Lectures on Geology to the Junior Class, 1882-3." MS. Scott MSS. PU Library.

"Materials for an Autobiography." MS. Scott MSS. PU Library.

"Notes on Mr. Balfour's Lectures on Embryology." MS, taken by Scott, spring 1879. Scott MSS. PU Library.

"Notes on Prof. Huxley's Lectures, Royal School of Mines, 1878-9." MS, taken by Scott. Thomas Henry Huxley MSS. PU Library.

"Syllabus of the Course in Elementary Geology, 1882-83." Princeton: C. S. Robinson and Co., 1883. PU Archives.

Shields, Charles Woodruff (1825-1904)

MS Correspondence. PU Archives.

"History." MS notes from his lectures taken by William R. Barricklo, ca. 1877. PU Archives.

Sloane, William Milligan. "Charles Woodruff Shields: A Biographical Sketch." N.p., n.d. Shields MSS. PU Archives.

Warfield, Benjamin Breckinridge (1851-1921)

MSS. PTS Special Collections.

MS Correspondence. Benjamin Breckinridge Warfield MSS. PTS Special Collections.

"Anthropology." Systematic Theology course, junior year. MS. PTS Special Collections.

Wilson, Robert Dick (1856-1930)

MSS. Historical Center of the Presbyterian Church in America (PCA), St. Louis, Mo.

MSS. PTS Special Collections.

Young, Charles Augustus (1834-1908)

"God's Glory in the Heavens." Lecture delivered at PTS. Cranbury, N.J., 1894. PTS Special Collections.

2. Published Sources and Dissertations

Ahlstrom, Sydney E. "The Scottish Philosophy and American Theology." *Church History* 24 (1955): 257-72.

Aiken, Charles Augustus. "Valiant for the Truth." In *Princeton Sermons,* pp. 50-74. New York: Fleming H. Revell Co., 1893.

Alexander, Archibald. *Evidences of the Authenticity, Inspiration, and Canonical Authority of the Holy Scriptures.* Enlarged ed. Philadelphia: Presbyterian Board of Publication, 1836.

———. *Outlines of Moral Science.* New York: Charles Scribner and Co., 1868; orig. 1852.

Bibliography

Alexander, James Waddell, Jr. *Princeton — Old and New: Recollections of Undergraduate Life*. New York: Charles Scribner's Sons, 1899.

American Association for the Advancement of Science. "A Statement on the Present Scientific Status of the Theory of Evolution." *Science* 57 (26 January 1923): 103-4.

Appleman, Philip, ed. *Darwin*. 3rd ed. Norton Critical Edition. New York: Norton, 2001.

Baldwin, James Mark. *Between Two Wars, 1861-1921: Being Memories, Opinions, and Letters Received by James Mark Baldwin*. Boston: Stratford Co., 1926.

————. *Darwin and the Humanities*. New York: Macmillan, 1902.

————. *History of Psychology: A Sketch and an Interpretation*. Vol. 2, *From John Locke to the Present Time*. New York: Putnam, 1913.

Balmer, Randall H. "The Princetonians, Scripture, and Recent Scholarship." *Journal of Presbyterian History* 60 (1982): 267-70.

Barkan, Elazar. *The Retreat of Scientific Racism: Changing Concepts of Race in Britain and the United States between the World Wars*. Cambridge: Cambridge University Press, 1992.

Bartlett, Samuel Colcord. *Sources of History in the Pentateuch*. Stone Lectures, 1881-82. New York: Anson D. F. Randolph and Co., 1883.

Bavinck, Herman. *The Philosophy of Revelation*. Stone Lectures, 1908-9. New York: Longmans, Green, and Co., 1909.

Biographical Catalogue of Princeton Theological Seminary. Vol. 1: 1815-1932, compiled by Edward Howell Roberts. Vol 2: 1815-1954; biographies, 1865-1954, compiled by Orion Cornelius Hopper. Vol. 3: 1812-1976; biographies, 1900-1976, compiled by Arthur M. Byers Jr. Princeton: Trustees of the Seminary, 1933, 1955, 1977.

"Biographical Sketch of Robert L. and Alexander Stuart." In *Encyclopaedia of Contemporary Biography of New York*, vol. 2. New York: Atlantic Publishing and Engraving Co., 1882.

Bledstein, Burton J. *The Culture of Professionalism: The Middle Class and the Development of Higher Education in America*. New York: Norton, 1976.

Bloom, John A. "On Human Origins: A Survey." *Christian Scholar's Review* 27 (1997): 181-203.

Boller, Paul F., Jr. *American Thought in Transition: The Impact of Evolutionary Naturalism, 1865-1900*. Chicago: Rand McNally, 1969.

Bowler, Peter J. *Charles Darwin: The Man and His Influence*. Oxford: Blackwell, 1990.

————. *The Eclipse of Darwinism: Anti-Darwinian Evolution Theories in the Decades around 1900*. Baltimore: Johns Hopkins University Press, 1983.

————. *Evolution: The History of an Idea*. Berkeley and Los Angeles: University of California Press, 1984.

————. *The Non-Darwinian Revolution: Reinterpreting a Historical Myth*. Baltimore: Johns Hopkins University Press, 1988.

————. *Reconciling Science and Religion: The Debate in Early-Twentieth-Century Britain*. Chicago: University of Chicago Press, 2001.

Bozeman, Theodore Dwight. *Protestants in an Age of Science: The Baconian Ideal and Antebellum American Religious Thought*. Chapel Hill: University of North Carolina Press, 1977.

Brooke, John Hedley. *Science and Religion: Some Historical Perspectives.* Cambridge: Cambridge University Press, 1991.

Brooke, John Hedley, and Geoffrey Cantor. *Reconstructing Nature: The Engagement of Science and Religion.* Oxford and New York: Oxford University Press, 1998.

Brubacher, John S., and Willis Rudy. *Higher Education in Transition: An American History: 1636-1956.* New York: Harper and Bros., 1958.

Bryan, William Jennings. "Mr. Bryan Speaks to Darwin." *Forum* 74 (July-December 1925): 101-7.

————. "William Jennings Bryan on Evolution." *Science* 55 (3 March 1922): 242-43. Partial reprint from *New York Times,* 26 February 1922.

Buck, Pearl. "Tribute to Dr. Machen." *New Republic,* 27 January 1937.

Burr, Nelson R. *A Critical Bibliography of Religion in America.* Princeton: Princeton University Press, 1961.

————. *Education in New Jersey, 1630-1871.* Princeton History of New Jersey, no. 4. Princeton: Princeton University Press, 1942.

Calhoun, David B. *Princeton Seminary.* 2 vols. Edinburgh: Banner of Truth Trust, 1994, 1996. Vol. I: *Faith and Learning, 1812-1868.* Vol. II: *The Majestic Testimony, 1869-1929.*

Cantor, Geoffrey. "What Shall We Do with the Conflict Thesis?" In *Science and Religion: New Historical Perspectives,* edited by Thomas Dixon, Geoffrey Cantor, and Stephen Pumfrey, pp. 283-98. New York: Cambridge University Press, 2010.

Carter, Paul A. "The Fundamentalist Defense of the Faith." In *Change and Continuity in Twentieth-Century America: The 1920's,* edited by John Braeman et al., pp. 179-214. Columbus: Ohio State University Press, 1968.

Cashdollar, Charles D. *The Transformation of Theology, 1830-1890: Positivism and Protestant Thought in Britain and America.* Princeton: Princeton University Press, 1989.

Chambers, Robert. *Vestiges of the Natural History of Creation.* London: J. Churchill, 1844.

"Checklist of Doctoral Dissertations on American Presbyterian and Reformed Subjects, 1912-1982." *Journal of Presbyterian History* 61 (1983).

Clark, Robert E. D. *Darwin: Before and After; An Evangelical Assessment.* Chicago: Moody Press, [1950?].

Collier, Katharine Brownell. *Cosmogonies of Our Fathers: Some Theories of the Seventeenth and the Eighteenth Centuries.* New York: Columbia University Press, 1934.

Collins, Varnum Lansing. *Princeton.* New York: Oxford University Press, 1914.

Conkin, Paul K. *When All the Gods Trembled: Darwinism, Scopes, and American Intellectuals.* Lanham, Md.: Rowman and Littlefield, 1998.

Conklin, Edwin Grant. "Biology at Princeton." *Bios* 19 (October 1948): ca. 151-71.

————. *The Direction of Human Evolution.* New ed. New York: Charles Scribner's Sons, 1923; orig. 1921.

————. "The Future of Evolution." *Yale Review,* n.s., 11 (1922): 748-68.

————. "Science and the Faith of a Modern." *Scribner's Magazine* 78 (1925): 451-58.

Constitution of the Presbyterian Church in the United States, Containing the Confession of Faith, the Larger and Shorter Catechisms . . . , The. Richmond, Va.: Presbyterian Committee of Publication, ca. 1910.

Cook, Calvin Wright. "Drawing Out Leviathan: A Study in Some Interrelations of Political and Theological Thought in America, 1900-1920." Th.D. diss., Princeton Theological Seminary, 1953.

Cooke, Kathy J. "The Gospel of Social Evolution: Religion, Biology, and Education in the Thought of Edwin Grant Conklin." Ph.D. diss., University of Chicago, 1994.

Copleston, Frederick. *A History of Philosophy.* Vol. 5, *Modern Philosophy: The British Philosophers,* Part II: *Berkeley to Hume.* Garden City, N.Y.: Image Books, 1964; orig. 1959.

Croly, Herbert. "The Cure for Fundamentalism." *New Republic* 43 (10 June 1925): 58-60.

————. "Naturalism and Christianity." *New Republic* 34 (28 February 1923): 9-11.

Dana, James Dwight. Review of *Creation; or, the Biblical Cosmogony in the Light of Modern Science,* by Arnold Guyot. *Bibliotheca Sacra* 42 (April 1885): 201-24.

Daniels, George H. "The Process of Professionalization in American Science: The Emergent Period, 1820-1860." In *Science in America since 1820,* edited by Nathan Reingold, pp. 63-78. New York: Science History Publications, 1976. Reprinted from *Isis,* Summer 1967.

Daniels, Winthrop More. "Princeton after One Hundred and Fifty Years." *Review of Reviews* (New York) 14 (1896): 446-50.

Darton, N. H. "Memorial of William Libbey." *Bulletin of the Geological Society of America* 39 (1928): 35-40.

Davis, Dennis Royal. "Presbyterian Attitudes toward Science and the Coming of Darwinism in America, 1859-1929." Ph.D. diss., University of Illinois/Urbana-Champaign, 1980.

Davis, John D. *Genesis and Semitic Tradition.* New York: Charles Scribner's Sons, 1894.

Dawson, John William. *Archaia; or, Studies of the Cosmogony and Natural History of the Hebrew Scriptures.* Montreal: B. Dawson and Son, 1860.

————. *Fifty Years of Work in Canada, Scientific and Educational.* Edited by Rankine Dawson. London and Edinburgh: Ballantyne, Hanson and Co., 1901.

————. "The Historical Deluge in Its Relation to Scientific Discovery and to Present Questions." Present Day Tracts, no. 76. London: Religious Tract Society, ca. 1895.

————. *The Origin of the World according to Revelation and Science.* New York: Harper and Bros., 1877.

Dayton, Donald W. *Discovering an Evangelical Heritage.* New York: Harper and Row, 1976.

Desmond, Adrian J., and James R. Moore. *Darwin: The Life of a Tormented Evolutionist.* New York: Norton, 1991.

Dewey, John. "The American Intellectual Frontier." *New Republic* 30 (22 May 1922): 303-5.

————. *The Influence of Darwinism on Philosophy, and Other Essays in Contemporary Thought.* New York: Henry Holt, 1910.

————. "Science, Belief and the Public." *New Republic* 38 (2 April 1924): 143-45.

Dillenberger, John. *Protestant Thought and Natural Science.* Garden City, N.Y.: Doubleday, 1960.

Dod, Albert Baldwin. "Vestiges of the Natural History of Creation." *Biblical Repertory and Princeton Review* 17 (1845): 505-57.

Draper, John William. *A History of the Conflict between Religion and Science.* New York: D. Appleton, 1874.

Drummond, Henry. *The Ascent of Man.* 14th ed. Lowell Lectures, ca. 1892. New York: James Pott and Co., 1907; orig. 1894.

―――. *Natural Law in the Spiritual World.* 10th ed. London: Hodder and Stoughton, 1884; orig. 1883.

Duffield, John Thomas. "Evolutionary and Biblical Anthropology." Letter to the editor, *New York Tribune,* 13 January 1897.

―――. "Evolutionism Respecting Man, and the Bible." *Princeton Review* 1 (1878): 150-57.

Efron, Noah. "Sciences and Religions: What It Means to Take Historical Perspectives Seriously." In *Science and Religion: New Historical Perspectives,* edited by Thomas Dixon, Geoffrey Cantor, and Stephen Pumfrey, pp. 247-62. New York: Cambridge University Press, 2010.

Elder, Fred Kingsley. *Woodrow: Apostle of Freedom.* Two Harbors, Minn.: Bunchberry Press, 1996.

Finke, Roger, and Rodney Stark. *The Churching of America, 1776-1990: Winners and Losers in Our Religious Economy.* New Brunswick, N.J.: Rutgers University Press, 1992.

Finkelstein, Louis. *Thirteen Americans: Their Spiritual Autobiographies.* New York: Harper and Bros., 1953.

Fortson, S. Donald, III. *The Presbyterian Creed: A Confessional Tradition in America, 1729-1870.* Milton Keynes, U.K.: Paternoster, 2008.

From, Joel L. "Antebellum Evangelicalism and the Diffusion of Providential Functionalism." *Christian Scholar's Review* 32 (2003): 177-201.

Fuller, Donald, and Richard Gardiner. "Reformed Theology at Princeton and Amsterdam in the Late Nineteenth Century: A Reappraisal." *Presbyterion* 21 (1995): 89-117.

Fundamentals, The: A Testimony to the Truth. 12 vols. Chicago: Testimony Publishing Co., 1910-15.

Gasman, Daniel. *The Scientific Origins of National Socialism: Social Darwinism in Ernst Haeckel and the German Monist League.* London: Macdonald and Co.; New York: American Elsevier Publishing Co., 1971.

Gauvreau, Michael. "The Empire of Evangelicalism: Varieties of Common Sense in Scotland, Canada, and the United States." In *Evangelicalism: Comparative Studies of Popular Protestantism in North America, the British Isles, and Beyond, 1700-1900,* edited by Mark A. Noll, David W. Bebbington, and George A. Rawlyk, pp. 219-52. New York and Oxford: Oxford University Press, 1994.

Gerstner, John H., Jr. "Scotch Realism, Kant and Darwin in the Philosophy of James McCosh." Ph.D. diss., Harvard University, 1945.

Giberson, Karl W., and Donald A. Yerxa. "Darwin Comes to America." *Books and Culture* 5, no. 6 (November/December 1999): 30-34.

————. *Species of Origins: America's Search for a Creation Story*. Lanham, Md.: Rowman and Littlefield, 2002.

Gilkey, Langdon. *Creationism on Trial: Evolution and God at Little Rock*. Minneapolis: Winston Press, 1985.

Gillispie, Charles Coulston. *Genesis and Geology: A Study in the Relations of Scientific Thought, Natural Theology, and Social Opinions in Great Britain, 1790-1850*. New York: Harper Torchbooks, 1959; orig. 1951.

Gode von Aesch, A. *Natural Science in German Romanticism*. New York: Columbia University Press, 1941.

Gracia, Jorge J. E. *Philosophy and Its History: Issues in Philosophical Historiography*. Albany: SUNY Press, 1992.

Grave, S. A. *The Scottish Philosophy of Common Sense*. Oxford: Clarendon, 1960.

Green, William Henry. *The Hebrew Feasts in Their Relation to Recent Critical Hypotheses concerning the Pentateuch*. New York: Robert Carter and Brothers, 1885.

————. *The Higher Criticism of the Pentateuch*. New York: Charles Scribner's Sons, 1895.

————. *The Unity of the Book of Genesis*. New York: Charles Scribner's Sons, 1901.

Greene, John C. *Darwin and the Modern World View*. Baton Rouge: Louisiana State University Press, 1961.

————. *Science, Ideology, and World View: Essays in the History of Evolutionary Ideas*. Berkeley: University of California Press, 1981.

Greene, William Brenton, Jr. "The Apologetic Worth of Christian Experience." *Methodist Review* (1901): 756-72.

————. "The Function of the Reason in Christianity." Inaugural address, in *Inauguration of William Brenton Greene, Jr., D.D., as Stuart Professor of the Relations of Philosophy and Science to the Christian Religion*. New York: Anson D. F. Randolph and Co., 1893.

————. "The Supernatural." In *Biblical and Theological Studies, by the Members of the Faculty of Princeton Theological Seminary*, pp. 137-207. New York: Charles Scribner's Sons, 1912.

Gregory, William K. "Biographical Memoir of Henry Fairfield Osborn, 1857-1935." *Biographical Memoirs of the National Academy of Sciences*, 19:53-119. Washington, D.C.: NAS, 1938.

Guralnick, Stanley M. "Sources of Misconception on the Role of Science in the Nineteenth-Century American College." In *Science in America since 1820*, edited by Nathan Reingold, pp. 48-62. New York: Science History Publications, 1976. Reprinted from *Isis*, September 1974.

Gustafson, Robert K. *James Woodrow (1828-1907): Scientist, Theologian, Intellectual Leader*. Lewiston, N.Y.: Edwin Mellen Press, 1995.

Gutjahr, Paul C. *Charles Hodge: Guardian of American Orthodoxy*. New York: Oxford University Press, 2011.

Guyot, Arnold Henry. *Creation; or, the Biblical Cosmogony in the Light of Modern Science*. New York: Charles Scribner's Sons, 1884.

————. *The Earth and Man: Lectures on Comparative Physical Geography, in Its Rela-*

tion to the History of Mankind. Translated by C. C. Felton. Boston: Gould, Kendall, and Lincoln, 1849.

Halsey, LeRoy J. *A History of McCormick Theological Seminary of the Presbyterian Church.* Chicago: by the Seminary, 1893.

Harrison, Peter. "'Science' and 'Religion': Constructing the Boundaries." In *Science and Religion: New Historical Perspectives,* edited by Thomas Dixon, Geoffrey Cantor, and Stephen Pumfrey, pp. 23-49. New York: Cambridge University Press, 2010.

Hart, Darryl G. "Christianity and the University in America: A Bibliographical Essay." In *The Secularization of the Academy,* edited by George M. Marsden and Bradley J. Longfield, pp. 303-9. New York: Oxford University Press, 1992.

————. *Defending the Faith: J. Gresham Machen and the Crisis of Conservative Protestantism in Modern America.* Baltimore: Johns Hopkins University Press, 1994.

————. "'Doctor Fundamentalis': An Intellectual Biography of J. Gresham Machen, 1881-1937." Ph.D. diss., Johns Hopkins University, 1988.

————. "Faith and Learning in the Age of the University: The Academic Ministry of Daniel Coit Gilman." In *The Secularization of the Academy,* edited by George M. Marsden and Bradley J. Longfield, pp. 107-45. New York: Oxford University Press, 1992.

————. "Presbyterians and Fundamentalism." *Westminster Theological Journal* 55 (1993): 331-42.

————. "The Princeton Mind in the Modern World and the Common-Sense Realism of J. Gresham Machen." *Westminster Theological Journal* (1984).

————. "A Reconsideration of Biblical Inerrancy and the Princeton Theology's Alliance with Fundamentalism." *Christian Scholar's Review* 20 (1991): 362-35.

————. "The Troubled Soul of the Academy: American Learning and the Problem of Religious Studies." *Religion and American Culture* 2 (1992): 49-77.

Hart, Hendrick, Johan van der Hoeven, and Nicholas Wolterstorff, eds. *Rationality in the Calvinian Tradition.* Lanham, Md.: University Press of America, 1983.

Hart, John W. "Princeton Theological Seminary: The Reorganization of 1929." *Journal of Presbyterian History* 58 (1980): 124-41.

Helseth, Paul Kjoss. "A 'Rather Bald' Rationalist? The Appeal to Right Reason." In *B. B. Warfield: Essays on His Life and Thought,* edited by Gary L. W. Johnson, pp. 54-75. Phillipsburg, N.J.: P&R, 2007.

————. *"Right Reason" and the Princeton Mind: An Unorthodox Proposal.* Phillipsburg, N.J.: P&R, 2010.

————. "Warfield on the Life of the Mind and the Apologetic Nature of Christian Scholarship." In *B. B. Warfield: Essays on His Life and Thought,* edited by Gary L. W. Johnson, pp. 108-35. Phillipsburg, N.J.: P&R, 2007.

Hicks, Peter. *The Philosophy of Charles Hodge: A 19th Century Evangelical Approach to Reason, Knowledge, and Truth.* Lewiston, N.Y.: Edward Mellen Press, 1997.

Himmelfarb, Gertrude. *Darwin and the Darwinian Revolution.* 1959. Reprint, Chicago: Ivan R. Dee, 1996.

Hodge, Archibald Alexander. Introduction to *Theism and Evolution: An Examination*

Bibliography

of Modern Speculative Theories as Related to Theistic Conceptions of the Universe, by Joseph S. Van Dyke. New York: A. C. Armstrong and Son, 1886.

————. *The Life of Charles Hodge.* New York: Charles Scribner's Sons, 1880.

————. *Outlines of Theology.* 2nd ed. New York: Robert Carter and Bros., 1878.

————. *Popular Lectures on Theological Themes.* Philadelphia: Presbyterian Board of Publication and Sabbath-School Work, 1887.

Hodge, Charles. *Systematic Theology.* New York: Scribners, 1872-73. Reprint, Grand Rapids: Eerdmans, 1993.

————. *The Way of Life.* Philadelphia: American Sunday School Union, 1841.

————. *What Is Darwinism?* New York: Scribner, Armstrong and Co., 1874.

————. *What Is Darwinism? and Other Writings on Science and Religion.* Edited with an introduction by Mark A. Noll and David N. Livingstone. Grand Rapids: Baker, 1994.

Hoeveler, J. David, Jr. *The Evolutionists: American Thinkers Confront Charles Darwin, 1860-1920.* Lanham, Md.: Rowman and Littlefield, 2007.

————. *James McCosh and the Scottish Intellectual Tradition: From Glasgow to Princeton.* Princeton: Princeton University Press, 1981.

Hoffecker, W. Andrew. *Charles Hodge: The Pride of Princeton.* Phillipsburg, N.J.: P&R, 2011.

————. *Piety and the Princeton Theologians: Archibald Alexander, Charles Hodge, and Benjamin Warfield.* Phillipsburg, N.J.: P&R; Grand Rapids: Baker, 1981.

Hofstadter, Richard. *Social Darwinism in American Thought.* Rev. ed. New York: George Braziller, 1959; orig. 1944.

Hovenkamp, Herbert. *Science and Religion in America, 1800-1860.* Philadelphia: University of Pennsylvania Press, 1978.

Hutchinson, William R. *The Modernist Impulse in American Protestantism.* Cambridge: Harvard University Press, 1976.

Huxley, Leonard. "An American Student in Huxley's Laboratory: From the Letters of Professor W. B. Scott." *Cornhill Magazine* 149 (1934): 679-93.

Huxley, Thomas Henry. *American Addresses.* New York: D. Appleton and Co., 1877.

————. *Lay Sermons, Addresses, and Reviews.* New York: D. Appleton and Co., 1870.

————. *Life and Letters of Thomas Henry Huxley.* 2 vols. New York: D. Appleton and Co., 1901.

Illick, Joseph E., III. "The Reception of Darwinism at the Theological Seminary and the College at Princeton, New Jersey." *Journal of the Presbyterian Historical Society* 38 (1960): 152-65, 234-43.

Inauguration of James McCosh, D.D., LL.D., as President of the College of New Jersey, Princeton, October 27, 1868. New York: Robert Carter and Bros., 1868.

Inauguration of William Brenton Greene, Jr., D.D., as Stuart Professor of the Relations of Philosophy and Science to the Christian Religion. New York: Anson D. F. Randolph and Co., 1893. Includes his inaugural address, "The Function of the Reason in Christianity."

Jacobus, Melancthon Williams [Jr.]. *A Problem in New Testament Criticism.* Stone Lectures, 1897-98. New York: Charles Scribner's Sons, 1900.

Jencks, Christopher, and David Riesman. *The Academic Revolution.* New York: Doubleday, 1968.

Johnson, Deryl Freeman. "The Attitudes of the Princeton Theologians toward Darwinism and Evolution from 1859-1929." Ph.D. diss., University of Iowa, 1968.

Johnson, Gary L. W., ed. *B. B. Warfield: Essays on His Life and Thought.* Phillipsburg, N.J.: P&R, 2007.

Johnson, Phillip E. *Darwin on Trial.* Downers Grove, Ill.: InterVarsity, 1991.

Johnson, William Hallock. *The Christian Faith under Modern Searchlights.* Stone Lectures, 1914. New York: Fleming H. Revell Co., 1916.

———. "Pragmatism, Humanism and Religion." *Princeton Theological Review* 6 (1908): 544-64.

Jordan, Philip D. *The Evangelical Alliance for the USA, 1847-1900: Ecumenism, Identity, and the Religion of the Republic.* New York: Edwin Mellen Press, 1982.

Kamen, Michael L. "The Science of the Bible in Nineteenth-Century America: From 'Common Sense' to Controversy, 1820-1900." Ph.D. diss., University of Notre Dame, 2004.

Kazin, Michael. *A Godly Hero: The Life of William Jennings Bryan.* New York: Anchor Books, 2006.

Kellogg, Samuel Henry. *The Genesis and Growth of Religion.* Stone Lectures, 1891-92. New York and London: Macmillan, 1892.

Kemeny, P. C. *Princeton in the Nation's Service: Religious Ideals and Educational Practice, 1868-1928.* New York: Oxford University Press, 1998.

———. "University Cultural Wars: Rival Protestant Pieties in Early Twentieth-Century Princeton." *Journal of Ecclesiastical History* 53 (2002): 735-64.

Kuklick, Bruce. *Churchmen and Philosophers: From Jonathan Edwards to John Dewey.* New Haven: Yale University Press, 1985.

Kuyper, Abraham. *Calvinism.* Stone Lectures, 1898-99. New York: Fleming H. Revell Co., 1898.

Laidlaw, John. *The Bible Doctrine of Man; or, The Anthropology and Psychology of Scripture.* 2nd ed. Edinburgh: T. & T. Clark, 1895; reprinted 1905.

Lamoureux, Denis Oswald. "Between 'The Origin of Species' and 'The Fundamentals': Toward a Historiographical Model of the Evangelical Reaction to Darwinism in the First Fifty Years." Ph.D. diss., Toronto School of Theology, 1991.

Larmer, Robert A. "Intelligent Design as a Theistic Theory of Biological Origins and Development." *Christian Scholar's Review* 36 (2006): 47-61.

Larson, Edward J. *Summer for the Gods: The Scopes Trial and America's Continuing Debate over Science and Religion.* Cambridge: Harvard University Press, 1998.

Le Conte, Joseph. *The Autobiography of Joseph Le Conte.* Edited by William Dallam Armes. New York: D. Appleton and Co., 1903.

Leitch, Alexander. *A Princeton Companion.* Princeton: Princeton University Press, 1978.

Leslie, W. Bruce. *Gentlemen and Scholars: College and Community in the "Age of the University," 1865-1917.* University Park: Pennsylvania State University Press, 1992.

Letis, Theodore P. "B. B. Warfield, Common-Sense Philosophy and Biblical Criticism." *American Presbyterians* 69 (1991): 175-90.

Levine, Lawrence W. *Defender of the Faith: William Jennings Bryan; The Last Decade, 1915-1925.* New York: Oxford University Press, 1965.

Lightfoot, John. *The Whole Works of the Rev. John Lightfoot.* Edited by John Rogers Pitman. 13 vols. London: J. F. Dove, 1822-25.

Lindberg, David C., and Ronald L. Numbers. "Beyond War and Peace: A Reappraisal of the Encounter between Christianity and Science." *Perspectives on Science and Christian Faith* 39 (1987): 140-49.

Lindsell, Harold. "An Historian Looks at Inerrancy." In *Evangelicals and Inerrancy,* edited by Ronald Youngblood, pp. 49-58. Nashville: Nelson, 1984.

Livingstone, David N. *Adam's Ancestors: Race, Religion, and the Politics of Human Origins.* Baltimore: Johns Hopkins University Press, 2008.

————. "Darwinism and Calvinism: The Belfast-Princeton Connection." *Isis* 83 (1992): 408-28.

————. *Darwin's Forgotten Defenders: The Encounter between Evangelical Theology and Evolutionary Thought.* Grand Rapids: Eerdmans; Edinburgh: Scottish Academic Press, 1987.

————. "Evolution, Eschatology and the Privatization of Providence." *Science and Christian Belief* 2 (1990): 117-30.

————. "Farewell to Arms: Reflections on the Encounter between Science and Faith." Paper given at the conference "Christian Theology in a Post-Christian World," the Billy Graham Center, Wheaton College, 22 March 1985.

————. "The Idea of Design: The Vicissitudes of a Key Concept in the Princeton Response to Darwin." *Scottish Journal of Theology* 37 (1984): 329-57.

————. "Science and Religion: Foreword to the Historical Geography of an Encounter." *Journal of Historical Geography* 20 (1994): 367-83.

————. "Science and Religion: Towards a New Cartography." *Christian Scholar's Review* 26 (1997): 270-92.

Livingstone, David N., and Mark A. Noll. "B. B. Warfield (1851-1921): A Biblical Inerrantist as Evolutionist." *Isis* 91 (2000): 283-304.

Livingstone, David N., D. G. Hart, and Mark A. Noll, eds. *Evangelicals and Science in Historical Perspective.* New York: Oxford University Press, 1999.

Loetscher, Lefferts A. *The Broadening Church: A Study of Theological Issues in the Presbyterian Church since 1869.* Philadelphia: University of Pennsylvania Press, 1954.

————. *Facing the Enlightenment and Pietism: Archibald Alexander and the Founding of Princeton Theological Seminary.* Westport, Conn: Greenwood Press, 1983.

Longfield, Bradley J. *The Presbyterian Controversy: Fundamentalists, Modernists, and Moderates.* New York: Oxford University Press, 1991.

Lovejoy, Arthur O. *The Great Chain of Being: A Study in the History of an Idea.* New York: Harper and Row, 1960; orig. 1936.

Lowrie, Walter. Introduction to *Religion of a Scientist,* by Gustav Th. Fechner. Edited and translated by Walter Lowrie. New York: Pantheon Books, 1946.

Lucas, George R., Jr. *The Rehabilitation of Whitehead: An Analytic and Historical Assessment of Process Philosophy.* Albany: SUNY Press, 1989.

Lynch, John M., ed. *"Vestiges" and the Debate before Darwin.* 7 vols. Bristol, U.K.: Thoemmes Press, 2000.

Machen, J. Gresham. *Christianity and Liberalism.* New York: Macmillan, 1923.

———. "Does Fundamentalism Obstruct Social Progress? — the Negative." *Survey* 52 (1 July 1924): 391-92, 426-27.

———. *The Origin of Paul's Religion.* New York: Macmillan, 1921.

———. *What Is Faith?* New York: Macmillan, 1925.

Maclean, John [Jr.]. *History of the College of New Jersey, from Its Origin in 1746 to the Commencement of 1854.* 2 vols. Philadelphia: J. B. Lippincott and Co., 1877.

Macleod, Donald. "Bavinck's Prolegomena: Fresh Light on Amsterdam, Old Princeton, and Cornelius Van Til." *Westminster Theological Journal* 68 (2006): 261-82.

Macloskie, George. "Discussing Prof. Wright's Paper." *Christian Thought* 11 (1893-94): 346-49.

MacPherson, Ryan Cameron. "Natural and Theological Science at Princeton: 1845-1859; *Vestiges of Creation* Meets the Scientific Sovereignty of God." *Princeton University Library Chronicle* 45 (2004): 184-236.

———. "The *Vestiges of Creation* and America's Pre-Darwinian Evolution Debates: Interpreting Theology and the Natural Sciences in Three Academic Communities." Ph.D. diss., University of Notre Dame, 2003.

Maienschein, Jane. *Transforming Traditions in American Biology, 1880-1915.* Baltimore: Johns Hopkins University Press, 1991.

Mandelbaum, Maurice. *History, Man, and Reason: A Study in Nineteenth-Century Thought.* Baltimore: Johns Hopkins University Press, 1971.

Marsden, George M. "Demythologizing Evangelicalism: A Review of Donald Dayton's *Discovering an Evangelical Heritage.*" *Christian Scholar's Review* 7 (1977): 203-11.

———. *The Evangelical Mind and the New School Presbyterian Experience: A Case Study in Nineteenth-Century America.* New Haven and London: Yale University Press, 1970.

———. "Everyone's Own Interpreter? The Bible, Science, and Authority in Mid-Nineteenth Century America." In *The Bible in America: Essays in Cultural History,* edited by Nathan O. Hatch and Mark A. Noll. New York: Oxford University Press, 1982.

———. *Fundamentalism and American Culture: The Shaping of Twentieth-Century Evangelicalism, 1870-1925.* New York: Oxford University Press, 1980.

———. "J. Gresham Machen, History, and Truth." *Westminster Theological Journal* 42 (1979): 157-75.

———. "The New School Heritage and Presbyterian Fundamentalism." *Westminster Theological Journal* 32 (1969-70): 129-47.

———. *Reforming Fundamentalism: Fuller Seminary and the New Evangelicalism.* Grand Rapids: Eerdmans, 1987.

———. *The Soul of the American University: From Protestant Establishment to Established Nonbelief.* New York: Oxford University Press, 1994.

———. *Understanding Fundamentalism and Evangelicalism.* Grand Rapids: Eerdmans, 1991.

———. "Understanding Fundamentalist Views of Science." In *Science and Creationism,* edited by Ashley Montagu, pp. 95-116. New York: Oxford University Press, 1984.

————. "Understanding J. Gresham Machen." *Princeton Seminary Bulletin* 11 (1990): 46-60.

Marsden, George M., and Bradley J. Longfield, eds. *The Secularization of the Academy.* New York: Oxford University Press, 1992.

Martin, Steven. "The Doctrines of Man, Reason and the Holy Spirit in the Epistemology of Charles Hodge." M.A. thesis, Trinity Evangelical Divinity School, 1984.

Mason, Frances, ed. *Creation by Evolution: A Consensus of Present-Day Knowledge as Set Forth by Leading Authorities in Non-Technical Language That All May Understand.* New York: Macmillan, 1928. Includes articles by Osborn, Scott, Conklin, Gregory.

Massa, Mark Stephen. *Charles Augustus Briggs and the Crisis of Historical Criticism.* Minneapolis: Fortress, 1990.

Mathews, Shailer. *The Faith of Modernism.* New York: Macmillan, 1924.

May, Henry F. *The Enlightenment in America.* New York: Oxford University Press, 1976.

Mayr, Ernst. *One Long Argument: Charles Darwin and the Genesis of Modern Evolutionary Thought.* Cambridge: Harvard University Press, 1991.

McClanahan, James Samuel, Jr. "Benjamin B. Warfield: Historian of Doctrine in Defense of Orthodoxy, 1881-1921." Ph.D. diss., Union Theological Seminary, Richmond, Va., 1988.

McCosh, James. *Agnosticism of Hume and Huxley, with a Notice of the Scottish School.* Philosophical Series, no. 6. New York: Charles Scribner's Sons, 1884.

————. *Christianity and Positivism.* New York: Robert Carter and Bros., 1871.

————. *Development: What It Can Do and What It Cannot Do.* New York: Charles Scribner's Sons, 1883.

————. *The Development Hypothesis: Is It Sufficient?* New York: Robert Carter and Bros., 1876.

————. *First and Fundamental Truths.* New York: Charles Scribner's Sons, 1889.

————. "How To Deal with Young Men Trained in Science in This Age of Unsettled Opinion." *Report of the Proceedings of the Second General Council of the Presbyterian Alliance* (Philadelphia, 1880), edited by John B. Dale and R. M. Patterson, pp. 204-13. Philadelphia: Presbyterian Journal Co. and J. C. McCurdy and Co., 1880.

————. *Ideas in Nature Overlooked by Dr. Tyndall: Being an Examination of Dr. Tyndall's Belfast Address.* New York: Robert Carter and Bros., 1875.

————. *The Intuitions of the Mind, Inductively Investigated.* 3rd ed., revised. New York: Robert Carter and Bros., 1872; orig. 1861.

————. "Is the Development Hypothesis Sufficient?" *Popular Science Monthly* 10 (1876): 98.

————. *The Method of the Divine Government, Physical and Moral.* New York: Robert Carter and Bros., 1872; orig. 1850.

————. "Oversight of Students in Princeton College." *New York Evangelist,* 17 April 1884.

————. "The Place of Religion in Colleges." *Minutes of the Proceedings of the Third General Council of the Reformed Churches Holding the Presbyterian System,* pp. 465-80. Belfast, 1884.

————. *The Religious Aspect of Evolution.* New York and London: Putnam, 1888.

————. *The Scottish Philosophy, Biographical, Expository, Critical, from Hutcheson to Hamilton.* New York: Charles Scribner's Sons, 1890; orig. 1874.

————. *The Supernatural in Relation to the Natural.* New York: Robert Carter and Bros., 1862.

————. *The Tests of the Various Kinds of Truth, Being a Treatise of Applied Logic.* New York: Charles Scribner's Sons, 1891; orig. 1889.

————. *Whither? O Whither? Tell Me Where.* New York: Charles Scribner's Sons, 1889.

[McCosh, James]. *The Conflicts of the Age.* New York: Charles Scribner's Sons, 1881.

McCosh, James, and George Dickie. *Typical Forms and Special Ends in Creation.* New York: Robert Carter and Bros., 1856.

McGiffert, Michael. "Christian Darwinism: The Partnership of Asa Gray and George Frederick Wright, 1874-1881." Ph.D. diss., Yale University, 1958.

McGrath, Alister E. *The Foundations of Dialogue in Science and Religion.* Oxford: Blackwell, 1998.

————. *Science and Religion: An Introduction.* Oxford: Blackwell, 1999.

McNeill, John T., and James Hastings Nichols. *Ecumenical Testimony: The Concern for Christian Unity within the Reformed and Presbyterian Churches.* Philadelphia: Westminster, 1974.

Means, John O. "The Narrative of the Creation in Genesis." *Bibliotheca Sacra and American Biblical Repository* 12 (1855): 83-130, 323-38.

Meeter, John E., and Roger Nicole. *A Bibliography of Benjamin Breckinridge Warfield, 1851-1921.* Phillipsburg, N.J.: P&R, 1974.

Mencken, H. L. "Dr. Fundamentalis." *Baltimore Evening Sun,* 18 January 1937.

Metzger, Walter P. *Academic Freedom in the Age of the University.* New York: Columbia University Press, 1964.

Miller, Glenn T. *Piety and Intellect: The Aims and Purposes of Ante-Bellum Theological Education.* Atlanta: Scholars, 1990.

————. *Piety and Profession: American Protestant Theological Education, 1870-1970.* Grand Rapids: Eerdmans, 2007.

Miller, Hugh. *Footprints of the Creator; or, The Asterolepis of Stromness.* With a memoir by Louis Agassiz. 12th ed. Edinburgh: William P. Nimmo, 1870; orig. 1850.

————. *The Testimony of the Rocks; or, Geology in Its Bearings on the Two Theologies, Natural and Revealed.* Edinburgh: William P. Nimmo, 1870; orig. 1857.

Miller, Perry. *The Life of the Mind in America from the Revolution to the Civil War.* New York: Harcourt, Brace and World, 1965.

Millikan, Robert A., et al. "A Joint Statement upon the Relations of Science and Religion." Printed under the title "Science and Religion." *Science* 57 (1 June 1923): 630-31.

Minton, Henry Collin. *The Cosmos and the Logos.* Stone Lectures, 1901-2. Philadelphia: Westminster, 1902.

Minutes of the General Assembly of the Presbyterian Church in the United States of America. New York: Presbyterian Board of Publication. Series.

Moffat, James C. *A Comparative History of Religions.* 2 vols. New York: Dodd and Mead, 1871-73.

Montague, William Pepperell. *The Ways of Knowing; or, The Methods of Philosophy.* 1925. Reprint, New York: Humanities Press, 1978.

Moore, James R. "Evangelicals and Evolution: Henry Drummond, Herbert Spencer, and the Naturalisation of the Spiritual World." *Scottish Journal of Theology* 38 (1985): 383-417.

————. *The Post-Darwinian Controversies: A Study of the Protestant Struggle to Come to Terms with Darwin in Great Britain and America, 1870-1900.* Cambridge: Cambridge University Press, 1979.

————, ed. *History, Humanity, and Evolution: Essays for John C. Greene.* New York: Cambridge University Press, 1989.

More, Louis Trenchard. *The Dogma of Evolution.* Vanuxem Lectures, January 1925. Princeton: Princeton University Press; London: Oxford University Press, 1925.

Moreland, J. P., and John Mark Reynolds, eds. *Three Views on Creation and Evolution.* Grand Rapids: Zondervan, 1999.

Murray, David, ed. *History of Education in New Jersey.* No. 23 of U.S. Bureau of Education, Circular of Information No. 1, 1899: Contributions to American Educational History, edited by Herbert B. Adams. Washington, D.C.: Government Printing Office, 1899.

Nash, Roderick. *The Nervous Generation: American Thought, 1917-1930.* With a new introduction by the author. Chicago: Ivan R. Dee (Elephant Paperbacks), 1990; orig. Macmillan, 1970.

Nelson, John Oliver. "Charles Hodge, Nestor of Orthodoxy." In *The Lives of Eighteen from Princeton,* edited by Willard Thorp, pp. 192-211. Princeton: Princeton University Press, 1946.

Newman, Robert C. "Old-Earth (Progressive) Creationism." In *Three Views of Creation and Evolution,* edited by J. P. Moreland and John Mark Reynolds, pp. 107-8. Grand Rapids: Zondervan, 1999.

Noll, Mark A. *Between Faith and Criticism: Evangelicals, Scholarship, and the Bible in America.* San Francisco: Harper and Row, 1986.

————. "Common-Sense Traditions and American Evangelical Thought." *American Quarterly* 37 (1985): 216-38.

————. "The Founding of Princeton Seminary." *Westminster Theological Journal* 42 (1979): 72-110.

————. *Princeton and the Republic, 1768-1822: The Search for a Christian Enlightenment in the Era of Samuel Stanhope Smith.* Princeton: Princeton University Press, 1989.

————. *The Scandal of the Evangelical Mind.* Grand Rapids: Eerdmans, 1994.

————, ed. *The Princeton Theology, 1812-1921: Scripture, Science, and Theological Method from Archibald Alexander to Benjamin Breckinridge Warfield.* Grand Rapids: Baker, 1983.

Numbers, Ronald L. "Charles Hodge and the Beauties and Deformities of Science." In *Charles Hodge Revisited: A Critical Appraisal of His Life and Work,* edited by John W. Stewart and James H. Moorhead, pp. 77-101. Grand Rapids: Eerdmans, 2002.

―――. "Creation, Evolution, and Holy Ghost Religion: Holiness and Pentecostal Responses to Darwinism." *Religion and American Culture* 2 (1992): 127-58.

―――. *Creation by Natural Law: Laplace's Nebular Hypothesis in American Thought.* Seattle: University of Washington Press, 1977.

―――. *The Creationists: The Evolution of Scientific Creationism.* Berkeley: University of California Press, 1993.

―――. *Darwinism Comes to America.* Cambridge: Harvard University Press, 1998.

―――. "'The Most Important Biblical Discovery of Our Time': William Henry Green and the Demise of Ussher's Chronology." *Church History* 69 (2000): 257-76.

O'Brien, Charles F. *Sir William Dawson: A Life in Science and Religion.* Philadelphia: American Philosophical Society, 1971.

Olson, Richard. *Scottish Philosophy and British Physics, 1750-1880: A Study in the Foundations of the Victorian Scientific Style.* Princeton: Princeton University Press, 1975.

Orr, James. *God's Image in Man and Its Defacement, in the Light of Modern Denials.* 2nd ed. Stone Lectures, 1903. New York: A. C. Armstrong and Son, 1906.

―――. *The Ritschlian Theology and the Evangelical Faith.* London: Hodder and Stoughton, 1897.

Osborn, Henry Fairfield. *Cope: Master Naturalist.* Princeton: Princeton University Press, 1931.

―――. *Creative Education in School, College, University, and Museum.* New York: Charles Scribner's Sons, 1927.

―――. "Credo of a Naturalist." *Forum* 73 (January-June 1925): 486-94.

―――. *The Earth Speaks to Bryan.* New York: Charles Scribner's Sons, 1924.

―――. "Evolution and Daily Living." *Forum* 73 (January-June 1925): 169-77.

―――. *Evolution and Religion in Education: Polemics of the Fundamentalist Controversy of 1922 to 1926.* New York: Charles Scribner's Sons, 1926.

―――. *From the Greeks to Darwin: An Outline of the Development of the Evolution Idea.* New York: Macmillan, 1913; orig. 1894.

―――. "How to Teach Evolution in the Schools." *School and Society* 23 (9 January 1926): 25-31.

―――. "Plain Living and High Thinking at Princeton College Fifty Years Ago." *Princeton Alumni Weekly,* 18 March 1925.

―――. "The Work of Professor William Berryman Scott '77." *Princeton Alumni Weekly,* 5 December 1917.

―――, ed. *Fifty Years of Princeton '77: A Fifty-Four-Year Record of the Class of 1877 of Princeton College and University.* Princeton: Princeton University Press, 1927.

Osborn, Henry Fairfield, and Edwin Grant Conklin. "The Proposed Suppression of the Teaching of Evolution." *Science* 55 (10 March 1922): 264-66. Partial reprint from *New York Times,* 5 March 1922.

Osgood, Charles G. *Lights in Nassau Hall.* Princeton: Princeton University Press, 1951.

Patton, Francis Landey. *Fundamental Christianity.* New York: Macmillan, 1926.

―――. "Theological Encyclopaedia." In *Biblical and Theological Studies, by the Members of the Faculty of Princeton Theological Seminary,* pp. 1-34. New York: Charles Scribner's Sons, 1912.

Bibliography

Persons, Stow. "Evolution and Theology in America." In his *Evolutionary Thought in America*. New Haven: Yale University Press, 1950.

Pfeifer, Edward J. "The Genesis of American Neo-Lamarckism." In *Science in America since 1820*, edited by Nathan Reingold, pp. 221-32. New York: Science History Publications, 1976. Reprinted from *Isis*, Summer 1965.

Pfleiderer, Otto. *Evolution and Theology and Other Essays*. Edited by Orello Cone. London: Adam and Charles Black, 1900.

Polkinghorne, John. *Belief in God in an Age of Science*. New Haven: Yale University Press, 1998.

Presbyterian Ministerial Directory, The. Vol. 1: 1898. Edited by Edgar Sutton Robinson. Cincinnati: Armstrong and Fillmore, 1899.

Princeton Theological Seminary. "The Seminary's Doctrinal Position and Misrepresentation of It." *Princeton Seminary Bulletin* 23 (1929): 5-8.

Rainger, Ronald. *An Agenda for Antiquity: Henry Fairfield Osborn and Vertebrate Paleontology at the American Museum of Natural History, 1890-1935*. Tuscaloosa: University of Alabama Press, 1991.

Rankin, Henry William. "In Behalf of a Philosophia Christiana." (On Charles Woodruff Shields.) *Princeton Alumni Weekly*, 26 April 1929.

————. "Recollections of Professor Ormond." *Princeton Alumni Weekly* 16, no. 15 (19 January 1916): 347-49.

Reingold, Nathan, ed. *Science in Nineteenth-Century America: A Documentary History*. American Century series. New York: Hill and Wang, 1964.

Rian, Edwin H. *The Presbyterian Conflict*. Grand Rapids: Eerdmans, 1940.

Riddlebarger, Kim. "The Lion of Princeton: Benjamin Breckinridge Warfield on Apologetics, Theological Method and Polemics." Ph.D. diss., Fuller Theological Seminary, 1997.

Ritter, William E. "Osborn versus Bateson on Evolution." *Science* 55 (14 April 1922): 398-99.

Roberts, Jon H. *Darwinism and the Divine in America: Protestant Intellectuals and Organic Evolution, 1859-1900*. Madison: University of Wisconsin Press, 1988.

————. "Religious Reactions to Darwin." In *The Cambridge Companion to Science and Religion*, edited by Peter Harrison, pp. 80-102. New York: Cambridge University Press, 2010.

Roberts, Jon H., and James Turner. *The Sacred and the Secular University*. Princeton: Princeton University Press, 2000.

Robinson, William Childs. *Columbia Theological Seminary and the Southern Presbyterian Church, 1831-1931*. Decatur, Ga.: Dennis Lindsey Printing Co., 1931.

Rodgers, Marion Elizabeth. *Mencken: The American Iconoclast*. New York: Oxford University Press, 2005.

Ross, Dorothy. "Historical Consciousness in Nineteenth-Century America." *American Historical Review* 89 (1984): 909-28.

Royce, Josiah. *Herbert Spencer: An Estimate and Review*. New York: Fox, Duffield, and Co., 1904.

Ruse, Michael. *The Evolution Wars: A Guide to the Debates*. New Brunswick, N.J.: Rutgers University Press, 2001.

———. *Monad to Man: The Concept of Progress in Evolutionary Biology.* Cambridge: Harvard University Press, 1996.

Russell, Colin. "The Conflict of Science with Religion." In *The History of Science and Religion in the Western Tradition: An Encyclopedia,* edited by Gary B. Ferguson et al. New York: Garland, 2010.

Russett, Cynthia Eagle. *Darwin in America: The Intellectual Response, 1865-1912.* San Francisco: W. H. Freeman, 1976.

Ruthven, Jon Mark. *On the Cessation of the Charismata: The Protestant Polemic on Post-Biblical Miracles.* Sheffield: Sheffield Academic Press, 1993.

Salmond, Charles A. *Princetoniana: Charles and A. A. Hodge, with Class and Table Talk of Hodge the Younger.* New York: Scribner and Welford, 1888.

Sandeen, Ernest R. "The Princeton Theology: One Source of Biblical Literalism in American Protestantism." *Church History* 31 (1962): 307-21.

———. *The Roots of Fundamentalism: British and American Millenarianism, 1800-1930.* Chicago: University of Chicago Press, 1970.

———. "Toward a Historical Interpretation of the Origins of Fundamentalism." *Church History* 36 (1967): 66-83.

Schaff, Philip, and S. Irenaeus Prime, eds. *History, Essays, Orations, and Other Documents of the Sixth General Council of the Evangelical Alliance.* New York: Harper and Bros., 1874.

Scorgie, Glenn G. *A Call for Continuity: The Theological Contribution of James Orr.* Macon, Ga.: Mercer University Press, 1988.

Scott, Hugh M. "Present Status of Evolution." *Bible Student,* n.s., 5 (1902): 360-61.

Scott, William Berryman. *Some Memories of a Palaeontologist.* Princeton: Princeton University Press, 1939.

———. *The Theory of Evolution, with Special Reference to the Evidence upon Which It Is Founded.* New York: Macmillan, 1917.

Scovel, Raleigh Don. "Orthodoxy in Princeton: A Social and Intellectual History of Princeton Theological Seminary, 1812-1860." Ph.D. diss., University of California, Berkeley, 1970.

Secord, James A. *Victorian Sensation: The Extraordinary Publication, Reception, and Secret Authorship of "Vestiges of the Natural History of Creation."* Chicago: University of Chicago Press, 2001.

Segal, Howard. "The Patton-Wilson Succession." *Princeton Alumni Weekly,* 6 November 1978.

Selden, William K. *Princeton Theological Seminary: A Narrative History, 1812-1992.* Princeton: Princeton University Press, 1992.

Sewny, Vahan D. *The Social Theory of James Mark Baldwin.* New York: King's Crown Press, 1945; reprint, Augustus M. Kelley, Publishers, 1967.

Shedd, William G. T. *A History of Christian Doctrine.* 2 vols. New York: Charles Scribner's Sons, 1863.

Sheets-Pyenson, Susan. *John William Dawson: Faith, Hope, and Science.* Montreal: McGill-Queen's University Press, 1996.

Shields, Charles Woodruff. *The Final Philosophy; or, System of Perfectible Knowledge*

Issuing from the Harmony of Science and Religion. New York: Scribner, Armstrong and Co., 1877.

—————. *The Order of the Sciences, an Essay on the Philosophical Classification and Organization of Human Knowledge*. New York: Charles Scribner's Sons, 1882.

—————. *Philosophia Ultima*. Philadelphia: J. B. Lippincott and Co., 1861.

—————. *Religion and Science in Their Relation to Philosophy: An Essay on the Present State of the Sciences*. New York: Scribner, Armstrong and Co., 1875.

Simpson, S. S. "Biographical Memoir of William Berryman Scott, 1858-1947." *National Academy of Sciences of the United States of America, Biographical Memoirs* 25 (1948): 175-203.

Sloan, Douglas. *The Scottish Enlightenment and the American College Ideal*. New York: Teachers College Press, 1971.

Sloane, William Milligan. *The Life of James McCosh*. With Large Autobiographical Sections. New York: Charles Scribner's Sons, 1896.

Smith, David P. *B. B. Warfield's Scientifically Constructive Theological Scholarship*. Eugene, Ore.: Pickwick, 2011.

Smith, Gary Scott. "Calvinists and Evolution, 1870-1920." *Journal of Presbyterian History* 61 (1983): 335-52.

—————. *The Seeds of Secularization: Calvinism, Culture, and Pluralism in America, 1870-1915*. Grand Rapids: Christian University Press, a subsidiary of Eerdmans, 1985.

Smith, Gerald Birney, Shirley Jackson Case, and D. D. Luckenbill. "Theological Scholarship at Princeton." *American Journal of Theology* (1913): 94-102.

Smith, Hay Watson. *Evolution and Presbyterianism*. Little Rock: Allsopp and Chapple, 1923.

Smout, Kary Doyle. *The Creation/Evolution Controversy: A Battle for Cultural Power*. Westport, Conn.: Praeger, 1998.

Snowden, James H. *Old Faith and New Knowledge*. New York: Harper and Bros., 1928.

Speir, Francis. "Personal Recollections of Princeton Undergraduate Life: V. The College in the Seventies." *Princeton Alumni Weekly* 16, no. 30 (3 May 1916): 700-701, and no. 31 (10 May 1916): 719-21.

Stevenson, Louise L. *Scholarly Means to Evangelical Ends: The New Haven Scholars and the Transformation of Higher Learning in America, 1830-1880*. Baltimore: Johns Hopkins University Press, 1986.

Stewart, John William. "The Tethered Theology: Biblical Criticism, Common-Sense Philosophy, and the Princeton Theologians, 1812-1860." Ph.D. diss., University of Michigan, 1990.

Stonehouse, Ned B. *J. Gresham Machen: A Biographical Memoir*. Grand Rapids: Eerdmans, 1954.

Street, T. Watson. "The Evolution Controversy in the Southern Presbyterian Church with Attention to the Theological and Ecclesiastical Issues Raised." *Journal of the Presbyterian Historical Society* 37 (1959): 232-50.

Szasz, Ferenc Morton. *The Divided Mind of Protestant America, 1880-1930*. University: University of Alabama Press, 1982.

Taylor, Marion Ann. *The Old Testament in the Old Princeton School (1812-1929)*. San Francisco: Mellen Research University Press, 1992.

Thomas, Keith. *Religion and the Decline of Magic*. New York: Scribner, 1971.

Thompson, Robert Ellis. *A History of the Presbyterian Churches in the United States*. American Church History series, no. 6. New York: Christian Literature Company, 1895.

Topham, Jonathan R. "Science, Religion, and the History of the Book." In *Science and Religion: New Historical Perspectives*, edited by Thomas Dixon, Geoffrey Cantor, and Stephen Pumfrey, pp. 221-43. New York: Cambridge University Press, 2010.

Trinterud, Leonard J. "Charles Hodge: Theology — Didactic and Polemical." In *Sons of the Prophets: Leaders in Protestantism from Princeton Seminary*, edited by Hugh T. Kerr. Princeton: Princeton University Press, 1963.

Turner, James. *Without God, without Creed: The Origins of Unbelief in America*. Baltimore: Johns Hopkins University Press, 1985.

Vander Stelt, John C. *Philosophy and Scripture: A Study in Old Princeton and Westminster Theology*. Marlton, N.J.: Mack, 1978.

Van Til, Cornelius. *The Defense of the Faith*. Philadelphia: P&R, 1955.

Van Till, Howard J., Davis A. Young, and Clarence Menninga. *Science Held Hostage: What's Wrong with Creation Science and Evolutionism*. Downers Grove, Ill.: InterVarsity, 1988.

Veysey, Laurence R. *The Emergence of the American University*. Chicago: University of Chicago Press, 1965.

Vos, Arvin. *Aquinas, Calvin, and Contemporary Protestant Thought: A Critique of Protestant Views on the Thought of Thomas Aquinas*. Grand Rapids: Christian University Press, 1985.

Vos, Geerhardus. *The Letters of Geerhardus Vos*. Edited by James T. Dennison Jr. Phillipsburg, N.J.: P&R, 2005.

———. *Redemptive History and Biblical Interpretation: The Shorter Writings of Geerhardus Vos*. Edited by Richard B. Gaffin. Phillipsburg, N.J.: P&R, 1980.

Wacker, Grant. *Augustus H. Strong and the Dilemma of Historical Consciousness*. Macon, Ga.: Mercer University Press, 2005.

———. "The Demise of Biblical Civilization." In *The Bible in America: Essays in Cultural History*, edited by Nathan O. Hatch and Mark A. Noll. New York: Oxford University Press, 1982.

Wallace, Peter J. "The Foundations of Reformed Biblical Theology: The Development of Old Testament Theology at Old Princeton, 1812-1932." *Westminster Theological Journal* 59 (1997): 41-69.

Wallace, Peter J., and Mark A. Noll. "The Students of Princeton Seminary, 1812-1929: A Research Note." *American Presbyterians* 72 (1994): 203-15.

Warfield, Benjamin Breckinridge. *Biblical Doctrines*. In *The Works of Benjamin B. Warfield*, edited by Ethelbert D. Warfield et al., vol. 2. New York: Oxford University Press, 1929; Grand Rapids: Baker, 1991. Among others, this work includes the following articles: "On the Biblical Notion of 'Renewal'" (1911), pp. 439-63; "Predestination" (1909), pp. 3-70; "The Prophecies of St. Paul" (1886), pp. 601-40; "'Redeemer' and 'Redemption'" (1915), pp. 375-98.

Bibliography

————. *Calvin and Calvinism.* In *The Works of Benjamin B. Warfield*, edited by Ethelbert D. Warfield et al., vol. 5. New York: Oxford University Press, 1931; Grand Rapids: Baker, 1991. Among others, this work includes the following articles: "Calvinism" (1908), pp. 353-69; "Calvin's Doctrine of the Creation" (1915), pp. 287-349; "Calvin's Doctrine of the Knowledge of God" (1909), pp. 29-130.

————. *Christology and Criticism.* In *The Works of Benjamin B. Warfield*, edited by Ethelbert D. Warfield et al., vol. 3. New York: Oxford University Press, 1929; Grand Rapids: Baker, 1991. Among others, this work includes the following articles: "Christless Christianity" (1912), pp. 313-67; "The Essence of Christianity and the Cross of Christ" (1914), pp. 393-444; "The Supernatural Birth of Jesus" (1906), pp. 447-58.

————. *Counterfeit Miracles.* Smyth Lectures, 1917-18. New York: Charles Scribner's Sons, 1918.

————. *Critical Reviews.* In *The Works of Benjamin B. Warfield*, edited by Ethelbert D. Warfield et al., vol. 10. New York: Oxford University Press, 1932; Grand Rapids: Baker, 1991. This work includes the review of *Mysticism in Christianity*, by W. K. Fleming, and *Mysticism and Modern Life*, by John Wright Buckham (1916), pp. 366-72.

————. "Editorial Notes." *Bible Student*, n.s., 4, no. 1 (July 1901): 1-8.

————. *Evolution, Science, and Scripture: Selected Writings.* Edited by Mark A. Noll and David N. Livingstone. Grand Rapids: Baker, 2000.

————. "Introductory Note" to *Apologetics; or, the Rational Vindication of Christianity*, by Francis R. Beattie. Richmond: Presbyterian Committee of Publication, 1903.

————. *Perfectionism.* Volume 1. In *The Works of Benjamin B. Warfield*, edited by Ethelbert D. Warfield et al., vol. 7. New York: Oxford University Press, 1931; Grand Rapids: Baker, 1991. Among others, this work includes the following articles: "Albrecht Ritschl and His Doctrine of Christian Perfection. I. Ritschl the Rationalist" (1919), pp. 3-52; "Albrecht Ritschl and His Doctrine of Christian Perfection. II. Ritschl the Perfectionist" (1920), pp. 55-110; "'Miserable-Sinner Christianity' in the Hands of the Rationalists — I. From Ritschl to Wernle" (1920), pp. 113-76.

————. *Perfectionism.* Volume 2. In *The Works of Benjamin B. Warfield*, edited by Ethelbert D. Warfield et al., vol. 8. New York: Oxford University Press, 1932; Grand Rapids: Baker, 1991. Among others, this work includes the following articles: "Oberlin Perfectionism" (1921), pp. 3-215; "The Victorious Life" (1918), pp. 561-611.

————. "Personal Recollections of Princeton Undergraduate Life: IV. The Coming of Dr. McCosh." *Princeton Alumni Weekly* 16, no. 28 (19 April 1916): 650-53.

————. *Revelation and Inspiration.* In *The Works of Benjamin B. Warfield*, edited by Ethelbert D. Warfield et al., vol. 1. New York: Oxford University Press, 1927; Grand Rapids: Baker, 1991. Among others, this work includes the following articles: "The Biblical Idea of Revelation" (1915), pp. 3-34; "The Divine Origin of the Bible" (1882), pp. 429-47; "The Real Problem of Inspiration" (1893), pp. 169-226.

————. *Studies in Tertullian and Augustine.* In *The Works of Benjamin B. Warfield*, edited by Ethelbert D. Warfield et al., vol. 4. New York: Oxford University Press,

1930; Grand Rapids: Baker, 1991. Among others, this work includes the following article: "Augustine's Doctrine of Knowledge and Authority" (1907), pp. 135-225.

————. *Studies in Theology.* In *The Works of Benjamin B. Warfield,* edited by Ethelbert D. Warfield et al., vol. 9. New York: Oxford University Press, 1932; Grand Rapids: Baker, 1991. Among others, this work includes the following articles: "Apologetics" (1908), pp. 3-21; "Charles Darwin's Religious Life: A Sketch in Spiritual Biography" (1888), pp. 541-82; "Christian Supernaturalism" (1897), pp. 25-46; "The Development of the Doctrine of Infant Salvation" (1891), pp. 411-44; "God" (1898), pp. 109-14; "The Idea of Systematic Theology" (1896), pp. 49-87; "The Latest Phase of Historical Rationalism" (1895), pp. 585-645; "Mysticism and Christianity" (1917), pp. 649-66; "On Faith in Its Psychological Aspects" (1911), pp. 313-42; "On the Antiquity and Unity of the Human Race" (1911), pp. 235-58; "The Polemics of Infant Baptism" (1899), pp. 389-408; "The Task and Method of Systematic Theology" (1910), pp. 91-105.

————. *The Westminster Assembly and Its Work.* In *The Works of Benjamin B. Warfield,* edited by Ethelbert D. Warfield et al., vol. 6. New York: Oxford University Press, 1931; Grand Rapids: Baker, 1991. Among others, this work includes the following articles: "The First Question of the Westminster Shorter Catechism" (1908), pp. 379-400; "The Westminster Assembly and Its Work" (1908), pp. 3-72; "The Westminster Doctrine of Holy Scripture" (1893), pp. 155-257.

Warfield, Ethelbert Dudley. "Biographical Sketch of Benjamin Breckinridge Warfield." In *Revelation and Inspiration,* by Benjamin Breckinridge Warfield, pp. v-ix. In *The Works of Benjamin B. Warfield,* edited by Ethelbert D. Warfield et al., vol. 1. New York: Oxford University Press, 1927; Grand Rapids: Baker, 1991.

Wells, David F., ed. *The Princeton Theology.* Grand Rapids: Baker, 1989.

————. *Reformed Theology in America: A History of Its Modern Development.* Grand Rapids: Eerdmans, 1985.

Wells, George A. "Goethe and Evolution." *Journal of the History of Ideas* 28 (1967): 537-50.

Wells, John Corrigan. *Charles Hodge's Critique of Darwinism: An Historical-Critical Analysis of Concepts Basic to the 19th Century Debate.* Lewiston, N.Y.: Edwin Mellen Press, 1988.

Wertenbaker, Thomas Jefferson. *Princeton, 1746-1896.* Princeton: Princeton University Press, 1946.

White, Andrew Dickson. *A History of the Warfare of Science with Theology in Christendom.* 2 vols. New York: D. Appleton and Co., 1896.

White, Edward Arthur. *Science and Religion in American Thought: The Impact of Naturalism.* Stanford: Stanford University Press, 1952.

Wilson, Philip K. "Arnold Guyot (1807-1884) and the Pestalozzian Approach to Geology Education." *Eclogae Geologicae Helvetiae* 92 (1999): 321-25.

————. "Influences of Alexander von Humboldt's *Kosmos* in Arnold Guyot's *Earth and Man* (1849)." *Omega: Indian Journal of Science and Religion* 4 (2005): 33-51.

Wilson, Woodrow. *The Papers of Woodrow Wilson.* Edited by Arthur S. Link. Vol. 6: 1888-1890. Princeton: Princeton University Press, 1969.

Woodbridge, John, Mark A. Noll, and Nathan O. Hatch. *The Gospel in America: Themes in the Story of America's Evangelicals.* Grand Rapids: Zondervan, 1979.

Woodrow, Marion Woodville, ed. *Dr. James Woodrow as Seen by His Friends: Character Sketches by His Former Pupils, Colleagues, and Associates.* Columbia, S.C.: R. L. Bryan Co., 1909.

Wright, George Frederick. *Scientific Confirmations of Old Testament History.* 2nd ed. Stone Lectures, 1904-5. Oberlin, Ohio: Bibliotheca Sacra Co., 1907.

———. "Some Analogies between Calvinism and Darwinism." *Bibliotheca Sacra* 37 (1880).

Young, Davis A. *The Biblical Flood: A Case Study of the Church's Response to Extrabiblical Evidence.* Grand Rapids: Eerdmans, 1995.

———. *Christianity and the Age of the Earth.* Grand Rapids: Zondervan, 1982.

———. "Scripture in the Hands of Geologists (Part One)." *Westminster Theological Journal* 49 (1987): 1-34.

Zaspel, Fred G. "B. B. Warfield on Creation and Evolution." *Themelios* 35 (July 2010): 198-211.

———. *The Theology of B. B. Warfield: A Systematic Summary.* Wheaton, Ill.: Crossway, 2010.

3. Selected Articles, Reviews, and Short Notices from the Princeton Quarterlies

Note: Many of B. B. Warfield's articles are listed in section 2, above, as reprinted in his *Works,* where they are more widely accessible than in the original journals. I have not duplicated their listing here.

Biblical Repertory and Princeton Review (1837-71)

Aiken, Charles Augustus. "Whitney on Language." 40 (1868): 263-92.

Alexander, Stephen. "A Philosophical Confession of Faith." 39 (1867): 416-40.

Atwater, Lyman Hotchkiss. "Herbert Spencer's Philosophy; Atheism, Pantheism, and Materialism." 37 (1865): 243-70.

———. "Knowledge, Faith, and Feeling, in Their Mutual Relations." 33 (1861): 421-43.

———. "McCosh on J. S. Mill and Fundamental Truth." 38 (1866): 416-24.

———. "A Plea for High Education and Presbyterian Colleges." 34 (1862): 635-68.

———. "Rationalism." 38 (1866): 329-61.

———. "Reason and Faith." 32 (1860): 648-85.

———. "Recent Works on Mental Philosophy." 27 (1855): 69-102.

———. "Witherspoon's Theology." 35 (1863): 596-610.

Clark, Joseph. "The Scepticism of Science." 35 (1863): 43-75.

Dewey, Chester. "Man's Place in Nature." 36 (1864): 276-97.

———. "The True Place of Man in Zoölogy." Review of *Contributions to the Natural History of the United States of America,* by Louis Agassiz. 35 (1863): 109-40, 333-47.

Dod, Albert B. "Vestiges of Creation." 17 (1845): 505-57.

Eckard, James R. "The Logical Relations of Religion and Natural Science." 32 (1860): 577-608.

Green, William Henry. "Modern Philology: Its Discoveries, History, and Influence." Review of *Modern Philology*, by Benjamin W. Dwight. 36 (1864): 629-52.

Hodge, Charles. "Diversity of Species in the Human Race: Examination of Some Reasonings against the Unity of Mankind." 34 (1862): 435-64.

————. "The General Assembly." 39 (1867): 440-522.

Lowrie, Walter H. "Man's Mental Instincts." Review of *Francis Bacon of Verulam; Realistic Philosophy, and Its Age*, by Kuno Fischer. 36 (1864): 585-613.

"Materialism — Physiological Psychology." 41 (1869): 615-25.

"Method of Divine Government, The." 23 (1851): 598-624.

Patterson, Robert. "The Antiquity of Man." 40 (1868): 574-608.

Short notice. *Christianity and Positivism*, by James McCosh. 43 (1871): 444-48.

Short notice. *The Course of Creation*, by John Anderson. 24 (1852): 146-51.

Short notice. *Footprints of the Creator*, by Hugh Miller. 23 (1851): 171-73.

Short notice. *Geognosy, or the Facts and Principles of Geology against Theories*, by David N. Lord. 28 (1856): 161-63.

Short notice. *The Great Stone-Book of Nature*, by David Anstead. 36 (1864): 185.

Short notice. *The Indications of the Creator; or, the Natural Evidences of Final Cause*, by George Taylor. 24 (1852): 141-46.

Short notice. *Manual of Geology*, by James Dana. 35 (1863): 170.

Short notice. *Philosophia Ultima*, by Charles Woodruff Shields. 33 (1861): 576.

Short notice. *The Physical and Moral Aspects of Geology*, by William Barbee. 33 (1861): 176-77.

Short notice. *Popular Geology*, by Hugh Miller. 31 (1859): 625.

Short notice. *The Primeval World: A Treatise of the Relations of Geology to Theology*, by Paton J. Gloag. 31 (1859): 376.

Short notice. *The Reign of Law*, by the Duke of Argyll. 39 (1867): 526-28.

Short notice. *The Relations of Christianity and Science*, by N. L. Rice. 35 (1863): 351.

Short notice. *The Supernatural in Relation to the Natural*, by James McCosh. 34 (1862): 361.

Short notice. *Textbook of Geology*, by James Dana. 36 (1864): 379.

"Some Recent Discussions on the Fundamental Principles of Morals." 41 (1869): 176-93.

"Testimony of Modern Science to the Unity of Mankind, The." 31 (1859): 103-49.

Wight, Joseph K. "Confucianism." 30 (1858): 226-61.

Presbyterian Quarterly and Princeton Review (1872-77)

Aiken, Charles Augustus. "The Variable and the Constant in Christian Apology." 1 (1872): 9-28.

Bascom, John. "Evolution, as Advocated by Herbert Spencer." 1 (1872): 496-515.

Cheever, George B. "The Philosophy of Evolution." 4 (1875): 121-57.

————. "Recent Works on Evolutionism and Its Religious Affiliations." 3 (1874): 169-75.

Short notice. *A Comparative History of Religions,* by James Clement Moffat. 1 (1872): 411-12.

Short notice. *The Doctrine of Evolution,* by Alexander Winchell. 3 (1874): 558-59.

Short notice. *Half-Hours with Modern Scientists.* 1 (1872): 614.

Short notice. *Primeval Man,* by the Duke of Argyll. 2 (1873): 182.

Smith, Henry Boynton. "The New Faith of Strauss." 3 (1874): 259-98.

Princeton Review (1878-85)

Atwater, Lyman Hotchkiss. "Proposed Reforms in Collegiate Education." 5 (1882): 100-122.

Boardman, George Dana. "The Genesis of Sin: A Sermonic Study in the Third Chapter of Genesis." 1880, part 2 (July-December): 42-62.

Dawson, John William. "The Antiquity of Man and the Origin of Species." 6 (July-December 1880): 383-98.

————. "Evolution and the Apparition of Animal Forms." 1 (January-June 1878): 662-75.

————. "Haeckel on the Evolution of Man." 5 (January-June 1880): 444-64.

————. "Points of Contact between Science and Revelation." 4 (July-December 1879): 579-606.

————. "Some Desultory Thoughts on Man in Nature." (1884): 219-32.

Hopkins, Mark. "Personality and Law — the Duke of Argyll." N.s., 10 (1882): 194-95.

Le Conte, Joseph. "The Psychical Relation of Man to Animals." (1884): 236-61.

MacWhorter, Alexander. "The Edenic Period of Man." 1880, part 2 (July-December): 62-91.

McCosh, James. "Development and the Growth of Conscience." 1880, part 2 (July-December): 138-44.

Patton, Francis Landey. "The Final Philosophy." 1879, part 1 (January-June): 559-78.

————. "Rationalism in the Free Church of Scotland." (1880): 105-24.

Porter, Noah. "The Newest Atheism." 5 (January-June 1880): 359-92.

Shields, Charles Woodruff. "Philosophy and Apologetics." 1879, part 2 (July-December): 196-207.

Presbyterian Review (1880-89)

Flint, Robert. "Classification of the Sciences" (part 2). 7 (1886): 483-536.

Hodge, Archibald Alexander, and Benjamin Breckinridge Warfield. "Inspiration." 2 (1881): 225-60.

Macloskie, George. "Concessions to Science." 10 (1889): 220-28.

————. "Scientific Speculation." 8 (1887): 617-25.

————. "The Theories of Darwin and Their Relation to Philosophy, Religion, and Morality." 4 (1883): 214-16.

McIlvaine, Joshua Hall. "Evolution in Relation to Species." 1 (1880): 611-30.

Patton, Francis Landey. "Charles Hodge." 2 (1881).

————. "Evolution and Apologetics." 6 (1885): 138-44.

————. Review of *Anti-Theistic Theories: The Baird Lecture for 1877,* by Robert Flint. 1 (1880): 192-93.

Shields, Charles Woodruff. "Reason and Revelation in the Sciences." 6 (1885): 268-88.

Warfield, Benjamin Breckinridge. "The Religious Aspect of Evolution." 9 (1888): 510-13.

Presbyterian and Reformed Review (1890-1902)

Aiken, Charles A. Review of *Personal and Social Evolution with the Key of the Science of History*, by a Historical Scientist. 1 (1890): 708.

Beattie, Francis R. Review of *The Genesis and Growth of Religion*, by Samuel H. Kellogg. 5 (1894): 103-6.

Bryan, W. S. Plumer. Review of *My Life and Times, 1810-1899*, by John B. Adger. 11 (1900): 181-85.

Davis, John D. "Current Old Testament Discussions and Princeton Opinion." 13 (1902): 177-206.

Green, William Henry. Review of *Christ and Criticism*, by Charles M. Mead. 5 (1894): 168-69.

Greene, William Brenton, Jr. Review of *The Evolution of Religion*, by Edward Caird. 6 (1895): 125-33.

———. Review of *An Introduction to the History of Religion*, by Frank Byron Jevons. 9 (1898): 136-39.

———. Review of *Natural Religion*, by Friedrich Max Müller. 5 (1894): 95-103.

———. Short notice. *The Agnostic Gospel*, by Henry Webster Parker, and of *Agnosticism and Religion*, by Jacob Gould Schurman. 7 (1896): 701-3.

Macloskie, George. "Common Errors as to the Relations of Science and Faith." 6 (1895): 98-107.

———. "Theistic Evolution." 9 (1898): 1-22.

Minton, Henry Collin. Review of *The Ascent of Man*, by Henry Drummond, and *Social Evolution*, by Benjamin Kidd. 6 (1895): 136-42.

Patton, Francis Landey. "James McCosh: A Baccalaureate Sermon." 6 (1895): 642-64.

Patton, George S. Review of *Moral Evolution*, by George Harris. 8 (1897): 531-41.

Purves, George Tybout. Review of *Messianic Prophecy*, by Edward Riehm. 3 (1892): 554.

Scott, William Berryman. "What Is Animal Life?" 1 (1890).

Short notice. *The Descent of the Primates*, by A. A. W. Hubrecht. 9 (1898): 780-82.

Short notice. *History of Human Marriage*, by Edward Westermarck. 3 (1892): 604-5.

Short notice. *Pseudo-Philosophy at the End of the Nineteenth Century: I; An Irrationalist Trio; Kidd — Drummond — Balfour*, by Hugh Mortimer Cecil. 8 (1897): 776.

Warfield, Benjamin Breckinridge. Short notice. *"The Ascent of Man": Its Note of Theology*, by Principal Hutton. 6 (1895): 367.

———. Short Notice. *Hours with the Mystics*, by Robert Alfred Vaughan. 5 (1894): 357-58.

———. Short notice. *Die Literatur des alten Testaments nach der Zeitfolge ihrer Entstehung*, by G. Wildboer. 6 (1895): 537.

———. Short notice. *Religion and Myth*, by James Macdonald. 4 (1893): 686-88.

Bibliography

Princeton Theological Review (1903-29)

Allis, Oswald T. "Assyriological Research during the Past Decade." 12 (1914): 229-64.

———. "Was Jesus a Modernist?" 27 (1929): 83-119.

Beecher, Willis J. Review of *The New Schaff-Herzog Encyclopædia of Religious Knowledge*, vol. 6, edited by Samuel Macauley Jackson. 8 (1910): 461-67.

Boyd, James Oscar. Review of *Die Beziehungen zwischen Israel und Babylonien*, by J. Köberle. 8 (1910): 292-95.

Clark, David S. "Theology and Evolution." 23 (1925): 193-212.

Greene, William Brenton, Jr. "The Practical Importance of Apologetics." 1 (1903): 200-226.

———. Review of *Christian Faith and the New Psychology: Evolution and Recent Science as Aids to Faith*, by David O. Murray. 9 (1912): 111-15.

———. "Yet Another Criticism of the Theory of Evolution." 20 (1922): 537-61.

Hamilton, Floyd E. Review of *The Bankruptcy of Evolution*, by Harold Christopherson Morton. 23 (1925): 670-72.

———. Review of *God and Evolution*, by W. R. Matthews. 25 (1927): 115-17.

Hodge, Caspar Wistar, Jr. "The Idea of Dogmatic Theology." 6 (1908): 52-82.

———. "The Significance of the Reformed Theology Today." 20 (1922): 1-14.

Johnson, William Hallock. Review of *The Dogma of Evolution*, by Louis T. More. 23 (1925): 476-80.

Kellogg, Edwin H. Review of *Modern Thought and the Crisis of Belief*, by R. M. Wenley. 8 (1910): 119-24.

Macartney, Clarence E. "The State of the Church." 23 (1925): 177-92.

Machen, J. Gresham. "History and Faith." 13 (1915): 337-51.

———. "Liberalism or Christianity?" 20 (1922): 93-117.

———. "The Relation of Religion to Science and Philosophy." 24 (1926): 38-66.

———. Review of *The Bible for Home and School: Commentary on Galatians*, by Benjamin W. Bacon. 9 (1911): 495-98.

Macloskie, George. "Mosaism and Darwinism." 2 (1904): 425-51.

———. "Outlook of Science and Faith." 1 (1903): 597-615.

Martin, S. A. Review of *Creative Evolution*, by Henri Bergson. 10 (1912): 116-18.

Ormond, Alexander T. "James McCosh as Thinker and Educator." 1 (1903): 337-61.

Patton, Francis Landey. "Benjamin B. Warfield: A Memorial Address." 19 (1921): 369-91.

Price, George McCready. "The Fossils as Age-Markers in Geology." 20 (1922): 585-615.

———. "Modern Botany and the Theory of Organic Evolution." 23 (1925): 51-65.

———. Review of *Nomogenesis, or Evolution Determined by Law*, by Leo S. Berg. 25 (1927): 119-22.

Rankin, Henry William. "Charles Woodruff Shields and the Unity of Science." 13 (1915): 49-91.

Richardson, Ernest Cushing. "Documents of the Exodus." 10 (1912): 581-605.

Warfield, Benjamin Breckinridge. Review of *Darwinism To-day*, by Vernon L. Kellogg. 6 (1908): 640-50.

———. Review of *Foundations*, by B. H. Streeter et al. 10 (1913): 526-38.

————. Review of *The Natural Theology of Evolution,* by J. N. Shearman. 14 (1916): 323-27.

————. Review of *No Struggle for Existence: No Natural Selection,* by George Paulin. 6 (1908): 651-52.

————. Review of *Le Problème du Dieu,* by Victor Monod. 9 (1911): 149-56.

Wilson, Robert Dick. Review of *Avesta Eschatology Compared with the Books of Daniel and Revelations* [sic], by Lawrence H. Mills. 9 (1911): 483-85.

Index

IMPORTANT: Many subject entries include listings of individual thinkers, and often those references are not duplicated under the thinkers' name entries. Readers interested in Aiken's thought, for example, should check not only his main entry (Aiken), but particular subjects as well (e.g., Adam) — see entries below.

Subjects by thinkers are cross-referenced exhaustively in the supplemental index. There, continuing our example, readers will learn that Aiken is also treated under Adam, Fall of humanity, Human evolution, and Human free agency.

Historians are indexed when mentioned in main text or commented upon in footnotes. Their entries are not broken into subentries.

356

lution, 151n56. *See also* Embryology;
Orthogenesis
    Thinkers on: Briggs, 217n46;
Chambers, 30-32; Dawson, 151n56;
Guyot, 36-39; Jacobus, 213-15; S. H.
Kellogg, 249; Machen, 308; McCosh,
151n56; Shedd, 246-47; Vos, 209-13;
Warfield, 215-17, 264
Guyot, Arnold: antitransmutationist,
38, 76, 123, 141, 142, 158, 300; career,
33-34; catastrophist, 38; compared to
Chambers, 36-39; compared to
Drummond, 225-26, 235; *Creation,*
39-46, 235; and Dawson call, 147, 149;
The Earth and Man, 34-37, 159n77;
harmonizes Genesis and geology, 37-
46, 57, 61, 64, 76, 115, 185; lectures at
PTS, 37, 39, 107-8, 180, 184-85, 267;
and museum, 134; and *Naturphilosophie,* 16, 35, 49, 84n21, 158, 176,
217, 219, 225; progressionist, 35-37, 43,
76, 81n15, 113, 121, 142n31, 163, 176,
226, 235-36; on sabbath age, 236; and
W. B. Scott, 104, 154, 157-58, 159n77;
shapes Princeton scientists and
theologians, 217, 219, 220n52; students laud, 135, 137; supernaturalist,
38, 40, 43, 46, 111, 128n78, 158; wants
relief from geology, 143, 146, 152
    Thinkers on: Dana, 142; Charles
Hodge, 80n13, 123; McCosh, 149, 235-
36; Shields, 185

Haeckel, Ernst, 31, 139, 157n71, 217, 295
Hamilton, Floyd, 301-2
Hamilton, William, 195n81
Harnack, Adolf von, 214, 217n46, 314
Harrison, Peter, 52n9
Hartt, Charles Frederick, 144-45
Harvard College, 34, 99, 132, 133, 136,
137n18, 141n27, 200n2. *See also*
Agassiz; Gray
Hegel, G. W. F., 36n41, 39n47, 79
Henry, Joseph, 143
Higher criticism of Bible: characteris-
tics, 213-14, 222, 223, 233, 251-53;
Princetonian defense against, 15-16,
212-13, 214-15, 227, 253-55, 314

Historical events and Christian faith:
liberal view, 281-82, 283-84, 296-97;
Princeton view, 178, 210, 221, 228,
245, 259, 279-84, 296-97. *See also* Inerrancy of Bible; Jesus Christ
    Thinkers on: A. A. Hodge, 163n4;
C. W. Hodge Jr., 283n49; Charles
Hodge, 280; Lessing, 283n49;
Machen, 279-84, 296-97; Ritschl,
296-97; Schleiermacher, 79, 82; Vos,
210-11; Warfield, 283n49
Historicism: as fixed pattern of process, 76, 79-80; as relativism, 5, 282-
84
Hodge, Archibald Alexander: calls for
a "new Paley," 176n35; classmate of
Shields, 175; on development of Bible, 305; on development of doctrine, 217n46, 305, 314; on evolution,
2, 9, 162-63, 165-67; "imprimatur" on
theistic evolution, 9, 162-63; on inerrancy, 10, 17, 161, 314; on mediate creation, 163n6; open to science, 57; on
Patton, 187n63; and W. B. Scott, 153,
154; trains future Princeton theologians, 206, 250; Warfield succeeds
him, 288; on Woodrow affair, 165-67,
170, 241, 243n43
Hodge, Caspar Wistar, Jr.: anthropology lectures, 267-72, 301; Calvinism
the answer to evolutionary naturalism, 265, 274; career, 267-68; on faith
and history, 283n49; follows
Warfield, 241n25, 269n17, 275, 277; on
human evolution, 241n25, 267-72; on
naturalism of theological modernism, 273-74; and Price, 301
Hodge, Caspar Wistar, Sr., 154, 206, 267
Hodge, Charles: aversion to change,
121n61; and battle plan, 93, 96; *BRPR*
editor, 8, 19, 72, 107, 257; and Civil
War, 53; compared with C. W. Hodge
Jr., 269, 274; on confessional subscription, 78, 119; and Dawson, 147,
247n36; doctrine of creation, 77-78,
120-21; evidentialist apologetics, 172,
174; friendships, 20, 112, 118n57; and
Guyot, 37, 111, 147; heads college

27-29; Charles Hodge, 121; McCosh, 112; Patton, 191, 193, 197; Shedd, 246

Humankind, doctrine of: antiquity of the race, 80; liberal view, 245, 248, 255, 279; original monotheism, 247-51; original righteousness, 226, 246, 248, 268, 313; Orr on, 269n15; primitive condition, 80, 245-48; unity of the race, 80, 168. *See also* Adam; Fall of humanity; Human evolution; *Imago Dei*

Hume, David, 83-84, 171n24, 187n60, 220, 221

Huxley, Thomas Henry: agnostic, 110, 155; anti-Christian, 54, 117n52, 146n41; champions evolution, 15, 16, 82n18, 135, 146; on Darwin killing teleology, 171n24; on human evolution, 79, 82, 87-88, 167n14; Macloskie and, 145; *Man's Place in Nature*, 78n10, 80, 82-83; materialist/positivist, 51, 85, 139; military metaphor in, 54, 57; on Hugh Miller, 65n32; non-/pseudo-Darwinian, 79, 82n18, 139, 217; W. B. Scott and, 154-57, 159n76, 165, 240; student quip on, 38n21; trespasser into philosophy and religion, 117n52, 145, 147, 155, 184, 295; turns opponents' guns, 97n42

Thinkers on: C. Dewey, 82-83; Charles Hodge, 78, 117n52; McCosh, 139, 146, 184, 240n22; McCrady, 141n27

Idealism, German: and cultural stages theory, 79-80; dangers, 27-29, 72, 197, 299; and Guyot's developmentalism, 16, 24n14, 35-36, 38, 49, 61, 142n31, 176. *See also* Design argument; Goethe; *Naturphilosophie*

Imago Dei: doctrinal importance, 79; in fallen humanity, 78, 245, 255; Horrible Vision and, 24n16; natural in humans, 78, 81-82

Thinkers on: Dewey, 81-82; Guyot, 43, 46; Charles Hodge, 78, 82n17; McCosh, 112; Orr, 243, 269n15; Spencer, 85

Inductive method: appropriate skepticism of, 91; contrast to *Naturphilosophie*, 35; democratizes science, 59-60; limitations, 25-26, 83-86, 138, 301; Hugh Miller personifies, 64-65; and Protestantism, 25; and sovereignty of each science, 59, 69, 95; tension in Princeton view, 68, 93, 95, 97; in theology, 58-59, 66-69; universally applicable, 52, 59, 66, 69, 83, 86, 93, 95, 97; and *Vestiges*, 25-26, 50; yields facts, 95, 178; yields only probability, 196n85

Thinkers on: Atwater, 85-86, 87-88; Clark, 90-94; Dod, 25-29; Charles Hodge, 66-69; McCosh, 84n21, 88; Patton, 196n85; Price, 301; Warfield, 69

Inerrancy of Bible: and the Dare, 174; and evolution, 17, 61, 161-62, 227, 229; and historical process, 3, 211-12; PCUSA battles, 228-31; Princeton admired and criticized for, 11

Thinkers on: J. D. Davis, 252n51; Green, 227n67; Guyot, 40; A. A. Hodge, 10, 17, 161, 314; Charles Hodge, 92, 103, 119; Vos, 211-12; Warfield, 10, 17, 161, 207n22, 314; Woodrow, 164

Inheritance of acquired characters: "American school" of neo-Lamarckism, 4-5, 49, 159, 217-19; during eclipse of Darwinism, 286; preserves teleology in nature, 143-44, 218

Thinkers on: Cope, 142, 143, 159; Le Conte, 142; Osborn, 159, 217-19; W. B. Scott, 159, 217-19; Spencer, 84-85

Jacobus, Melancthon W., Jr., 213-15, 216, 219, 314

Java man *(Pithecanthropus erectus)*, 167, 233

Jefferson, Thomas, 7, 220

Jenkins, Finley DuBois, 269n15

Jesus Christ: apex of natural religious development, 223, 279, 284, 315; apex of progressive revelation, 210-11; be-

147n44; evolutionism fruitful for, 141; and growth analogy, 217-19; and human evolution, 110, 167; Hugh Miller on, 64-65; Price on fossil record, 266, 300-301; at Princeton, 134-36, 147, 154, 157-59, 161, 204; seeks orderly relationships, 217-19; Warfield on fossil record, 289. *See also* Cope; Marsh; Osborn; Scott, W. B.

Paley, William, 24, 128n78, 176, 177, 180, 184

Pantheism: vs. Calvinism, 228; and evolution, 170, 228, 256, 308; and providence, 121; of Spencer, 85; tendency of *Vestiges,* 27, 38, 40, 46
   Thinkers on: Atwater, 85; Charles Hodge, 76n5, 78, 121, 248n39; Machen, 308; McCosh, 106n25; Patton, 170, 189, 191, 197; Warfield, 256

Patterson, Alexander, 286

Patterson, Robert, 78, 80

Patton, Francis Landey: and academic freedom, 201-4, 230, 240n23; on apologetics, 93n36, 170-71, 175, 180, 182-94, 196-97; career, 14-15, 17, 78n11, 173, 182, 200-201, 206; as college president, 199-205, 230; on epistemology of theism, 194-96; and essentialist categories, 14-15, 283n48; on evolution, 166n12, 167-71, 197-98, 204-5, 228; on Guyot, 33n34; on C. W. Hodge Jr., 267; Marsden on, 204; on McCosh's presidency, 104n20; on presuppositions, 189-90; as seminary president, 201; and Shields, 182-89; Stuart professor, 17, 161, 180, 182, 250, 299; theism lectures, 126n73, 194-98, 257; on theistic foundations, 17, 161, 172, 186-89, 202-5, 207, 208-9, 230, 257; on theological encyclopedia, 207-8, 215-16; trains future Princeton theologians, 206; and Woodrow affair, 167-71

Patton, George S., 226n65

Paul, Saint, 63n29, 99, 168, 213-15, 219, 268, 280n38, 314

Pauly, August, 285-86

Perspicuity: of science, 95, 123, 185; of Scripture, 62, 185

Polygenism, 66n34, 69-70, 79, 80, 114n45. *See also* Adam

Positivism: agnosticism of, 185; college students on, 137-38; enemy behind evolution, 105, 108-12, 146n43, 150, 197-98, 315; of Huxley, 139, 146; and materialism, 76n5; and natural history of religion, 222, 223-24, 250; science of sciences, 181, 185-86, 189n67; and Shields, 181, 186n58; of Spencer, 84-85, 223-24. *See also* Antisupernaturalism; Materialism
   Thinkers on: Atwater, 72-73, 84-87; Greene, 250; Charles Hodge, 76n5, 126; McCosh, 9, 102, 106-12, 126, 139, 146; Patton, 185, 186n58, 197; Warfield, 129, 257

Postmillennialism, 212, 236

Predestination, 2, 275-76. *See also* Decree

Premillennialism, 140n25, 212n37, 264

Presbyterian (Philadelphia newspaper), 300

Presbyterian and Reformed Review: described, 15, 207, 208n25, 277; vs. religious-evolutionary theories, 222-23, 244; symposium "What is animal life?" 239-40

Presbyterian Church, Northern (PCUSA): and confession revision, 228-31; and evolution question, 162, 165, 228-29, 272; fundamentalist controversy in, 11, 265, 266-67, 306, 309-10; and heresy trials, 228-31, 265; and inerrancy, 228-31; New School branch, 132, 245; Old School branch, 20n3, 132, 165, 182; Old School–New School reunion, 77-78, 113, 118n55, 207n22; and Princeton theology, 208, 228-31, 309-10

Presbyterian Church, Southern (PCUS): Warfield's coworkers in, 207n22, 258n66; Woodrow affair, 17, 164-65, 166n12, 168n16

Presbyterian Quarterly and Princeton Review, 118n55

Index

65n32; conflict thesis, 9, 53n10, 54, 57-58, 72n46, 76; contextualist approach, 12, 58n19, 146n42, 310. *See also* Military metaphor
Science and religion, relations of: complaints against scientific trespassing, 66, 69, 79, 111, 146-47, 151, 155, 184, 274, 295-97, 302-3; the Dare, 173-74, 189; distinct epistemologies, 90-91; patience enjoined, 63, 64n31, 65, 66, 79, 185, 188, 257, 303; science aids interpretation of Bible, 61-62, 79, 90, 91, 119, 120, 122, 243n28; scientific freedom, 63, 65, 79, 93-97, 143, 155, 173, 180, 201-3; twin daughters of heaven, 51-52, 60-61, 68, 94, 100, 155, 269; unity of truth, 15, 16, 52-53, 58-61, 90, 92, 93, 95, 174, 175, 183, 186, 273. *See also* Apologetics; Bible; Inductive method; Neutrality; Revealed religion; Shields affair
Science of man, 68, 82, 87-88, 114
Science of the sciences, 69, 181, 186-87, 189n67
Scopes trial, 144, 266, 278, 293, 297-98, 302, 306, 307
Scott, Hugh M., 286
Scott, William Berryman: anti-Darwinian evolutionist, 147n44, 159-60, 169, 217-19, 235, 273n24; conversion to transmutationism, 156; European study, 154-57, 217; on evolution of soul, 239-40; exemplar of Bright Young Men policy, 160; Greene criticizes, 266, 299-300; on Haeckel, 157n71; C. W. Hodge Jr. and, 267, 272n22; Charles Hodge's grandson, 153, 155, 160; Huxley's student, 155-57; on McCosh, 104, 105n22; on Patton, 200; popular geology textbook, 204; and Princeton Scientific Expeditions, 135, 153; refuses scientists' theological liberalism, 273, 296n81; teaches evolution "under God" at Princeton, 17, 154, 157-60, 161, 267; *Theory of Evolution*, 272n22, 273
Scottish Common-Sense philosophy. *See* Common-Sense Realism

Second causes: and evolution, 111, 127, 228, 260, 269; in Westminster Confession, 2, 5, 315
   Thinkers on: Calvin, 261; Guyot, 38; C. W. Hodge Jr., 269-70; Charles Hodge, 118n56, 120-22, 127-28; McCosh, 106, 111, 127-28, 236; Warfield, 127-28, 260
Secord, James A., 22
Secularization of academe, 133, 150n55, 200-201, 230
Shedd, W. G. T., 239, 240, 245-47, 314
Shields, Charles Woodruff: career, 175-76, 180-82; criticizes Charles Hodge, McCosh, and Dawson, 182; C. W. Hodge Sr. criticizes, 267; parallels positivists, 181, 186n58
Shields affair: extreme Princetonian position, 173-75, 183-84; harmony chair at CNJ, 175-82; moment of definition, 15, 17, 182-83; neutral pose, 177-78, 184, 189; Patton answers, 182-90
Sin: Calvinist doctrine, 2, 55n13, 70n41, 202n7; evolutionary doctrine, 144, 223; heightened theological attention ca. 1900, 243; and human history, 236, 245-51, 255; needs cure above nature, 226-28, 232, 244-45, 262, 273, 279; noetic effects, 90, 196, 243; and providence, 121. *See also* Degeneration; Fall of humanity
Smith, Gary Scott, 105n21
Social Darwinism, 107, 224, 292
Soul, origin of: animal precursors, 239-41, 268-71; creationism vs. traducianism, 242n25; evolution denied, 14, 129n79, 313
   Thinkers on: Calvin, 261; C. W. Hodge Jr., 268-71; McCosh, 237; Osborn, 295; Warfield, 129n79, 238-41; Wright, 271
Spencer, Herbert: agnostic, 84-85, 110; compared to *Vestiges*, 85; Cope and, 142; definition of evolution, 84-85; Drummond and, 224-25, 226; evolution is everything, 85n24, 223, 299-300; evolution of religion, 222-23,

233n4, 249, 251; key evolutionist foe, 15, 16, 49, 51, 85, 141n27; science of man, 87-88; science of the sciences, 181, 186n58; social Darwinism, 79, 107; trespasser into religion, 111, 295; truncated inductivism, 51, 84-87. *See also* Positivism

    Thinkers on: Atwater, 47, 72-73, 80, 84-87; Dawson, 117; Greene, 250-51, 299; McCosh, 106, 107, 110, 111, 139, 146n43; Patton, 186n58

Spinoza, Baruch, 21, 26-27, 85, 244

Stevenson, J. Ross, 267, 299, 309

Stevenson, Louise, 10n14

Stone Foundation lectures (PTS): Bartlett, 167n13; Bavinck, 243, 261n72; Flint, 187n62; Jacobus, 213-15; D. E. Jenkins, 243n28; W. H. Johnson, 286-87; S. H. Kellogg, 249; Kuyper, 243; Minton, 59n21, 243, 244n29; Orr, 243, 269n15; Wright, 188n66, 243n28

Straton, John Roach, 272, 294n74

Struggle for life: Calvinism and, 55n13

    Thinkers on: Bryan, 292, 298n85; Cope, 143; Darwin, 32, 47-48; Drummond, 224, 226; Spencer, 84; Warfield, 289

Stuart Chair of the Relations of Science and Philosophy to the Christian Religion. *See* Princeton Theological Seminary

Sun, creation of, 40-42

Supernatural intervention: in gospel history, 117, 163, 228, 245, 246-47, 249, 259, 275, 309; historical discernment of, 280-81; in human origins, 141-42, 163, 166-67, 241, 268-71; modes of, 257-62, 315; in natural history, 17, 38, 42, 46, 77, 129n79, 163, 259, 262, 286, 288, 291. *See also* Revealed religion; Supernaturalism

    Thinkers on: S. Alexander, 77; Atwater, 90; Dana, 141-42; Darwin, 125-26; Dod, 20-21, 24-25; Greene, 232, 299-300; Guyot, 38, 42, 46, 163; A. A. Hodge, 163, 166-67; C. W. Hodge Jr., 241n25, 268-71, 273-74; Charles Hodge, 117, 118n55; Machen, 279-81,

284, 309; McCosh, 110-11, 128n78, 163; Patton, 197; Shedd, 246-47; Spencer, 84; Warfield, 129n79, 241, 257-62, 264, 288, 291; Woodrow, 167n13, 241

Supernaturalism: basic issue in evolution question, 16, 118n55, 197-98, 228, 266, 269, 284, 309; Calvinism its purest form, 274-77; Conklin dismisses as primitive, 295; essential to gospel, 158, 221, 226-28, 229, 245, 257, 269, 274, 281; and historical inquiry, 280-81; of the historical Jesus, 280, 282; McCosh and Hodge contrasted on, 128n78; and process, 263-64; proper ground for defense of faith, 96-97. *See also* Antisupernaturalism; Supernatural intervention

    Thinkers on: Greene, 266; Guyot, 158; C. W. Hodge Jr., 271, 273, 274-76; Machen, 280-81, 282, 298; McCosh, 106, 108-9; Minton, 245; Patton, 187, 191, 196-97, 203n10; Warfield, 241, 255-62, 263-64, 277

Systematic theology: development and, 5, 194, 214, 215-17, 219, 314; distinct from religion, 67, 283n48; and evolution question, 119, 170-71; queen of sciences, 60-61, 66, 68-69, 171, 187, 208; structure, 17, 193, 207-8; Turretin, 61n25. *See also* Foundations; Hodge, Charles; Princeton theology

    Thinkers on: Harnack, 214; Patton, 193, 194, 208n25; Vos, 210; Warfield, 207-8, 215-17, 219, 314

Taylor, Marion Ann, 251n49

Teleological argument. *See* Design argument

Teleology: in archeology and anthropology, 80n12; Darwin denies, 110, 125; deathblow to, 171; in evolution of religion, 225; in liberal theology, 284; Mendelism and, 50; scientists' bias against, 291; victory over Darwinism, 232-33, 286. *See also* Darwinism; Design argument; Growth

Supplemental Index: Subjects by Thinkers

This cross-reference index lists subjects under which a particular thinker appears in the main index (usually in the "Thinkers on" section of the entry). Many of these subjects are *not* duplicated in the main index name entry.

In order to look up a particular thinker exhaustively, use both indexes in combination.